Democratizing
Global Media

Recent Titles in the Series
Changing Concepts of Time
    Harold A. Innis
Mass Communication and American Social Thought: Key Texts, 1919–1968
    Edited by John Durham Peters and Peter Simonson
Entertaining the Citizen: When Politics and Popular Culture Converge
    Liesbet van Zoonen
A Fatal Attraction: Public Television and Politics in Italy
    Cinzia Padovani
The Medium and the Magician: The Radio Legacy of Orson Welles, 1934–1952
    Paul Heyer

Forthcoming
Contracting Out Hollywood: Runaway Productions and Foreign Location Shooting
    Edited by Mike Gasher and Greg Elmer
Global Electioneering: Campaign Consulting, Communications, and Corporate Financing
    Gerald Sussman
Raymond Williams
    Alan O'Connor

Democratizing Global Media

One World, Many Struggles

Edited by
Robert A. Hackett and Yuezhi Zhao

ROWMAN & LITTLEFIELD PUBLISHERS, INC.
Lanham • *Boulder* • *New York* • *Toronto* • *Oxford*

ROWMAN & LITTLEFIELD PUBLISHERS, INC.

Published in the United States of America
by Rowman & Littlefield Publishers, Inc.
A wholly owned subsidiary of The Rowman & Littlefield Publishing Group, Inc.
4501 Forbes Boulevard, Suite 200, Lanham, MD 20706
www.rowmanlittlefield.com

P.O. Box 317, Oxford OX2 9RU, UK

British Library Cataloguing in Publication Information Available

Library of Congress Cataloging-in-Publication Data

Democratizing global media : one world, many struggles / edited by Robert A.
Hackett and Yuezhi Zhao.
   p. cm. — (Critical media studies : institutions, politics, and culture)
  Includes bibliographical references and index
  ISBN 0-7425-3642-4 (cloth : alk. paper) — ISBN 0-7425-3643-2 (pbk. : alk. paper)
  1. Communication in politics. 2. Mass media—Political aspects.
3. Democratization. 4. Democracy. I. Hackett, Robert A. II. Zhao,
Yuezhi, 1965– III. Title. IV. Series: Critical media series.

JA85.D43 2005
306.2—dc22
                                      2004022271

Printed in the United States of America

∞™ The paper used in this publication meets the minimum requirements of
American National Standard for Information Sciences—Permanence of Paper for
Printed Library Materials, ANSI/NISO Z39.48-1992.

Contents

Foreword

Majid Tehranian

This volume has emerged out of the Toda Institute's Globalization, Regionalization and Democratization (GRAD) project, a three-year research program on democratization in the context of regional and global conflicts. The project's ten research teams and nearly one hundred participants met at Oxford, Vancouver, and Budapest (2002–2004) to conceptualize the problems, undertake field research, and prepare chapters for this and other volumes. Consisting of distinguished journalists and communication scholars, the research team represented in this volume focused on media democratization at the national, regional, and global levels.

Three dominant trends are singled out in this volume: globalization, democratization, and media pluralization. The volume ably takes up the interactions among these trends. Globalization is perhaps the most visible of the three. However, it also is the most easily misunderstood trend. We need to unpack the concept to better understand it. Four different types of globalization seem to be simultaneously at work. From top-down, globalization has come to mean a neoliberal hegemonic project to extend the costs and benefits of capitalism worldwide. This particular perspective is best represented by the World Economic Forum, annually meeting since 1970 at Davos, Switzerland. Its views may be therefore called "globalization according to Davos." It represents the interests and perspectives of some thousand global corporations and their political allies.

In December 1999, a second view of globalization emerged out of Seattle when a coalition of labor unions, human rights advocates, and environmentalist activists demonstrated against the World Trade Organization (WTO). The Seattle protests were subsequently replicated at a number of other world cities at which intergovernmental organizations such as the

World Bank, International Monetary Fund, and WTO met. The global perspective that has emerged out of these protests may be considered as "globalization according to Seattle." Its perspective represents the interests and views of those layers of population in the previous industrial countries (PICs) that are losing industries and jobs to the new industrial countries (NICs) in Asia and Latin America.

A third view of globalization is prevalent in the NICs such as China, India, Mexico, and the Association of South East Asian Nations (ASEAN) states. From 1970 to 2000, benefiting from foreign investment and access to overseas consumer markets as well as technological and managerial know-how, the NICs have tried to maximize the benefits and minimize the costs of globalization. The views on globalization in this camp may be collectively labeled as "globalization according to Beijing." Having experienced one of the highest rates of economic growth during the same period, China stands out as the greatest beneficiary of its global linkages with the PICs' consumer markets and some fifty million diasporic Chinese.

A fourth view is represented by those states and nations that have been left off the globalization bandwagon or have chosen to avoid it. Iran, North Korea, Cuba, and much of Africa south of the Sahara fit this model. Their relatively stagnant or negative economic performance may be attributed to a complex variety of factors, including forced or voluntary delinkage from the global economy. The views in this camp are too heterogeneous to pigeonhole, but as a shorthand, let's call them "globalization according to Tehran."

The links between globalization and democratization in this fourfold classification are complex. Davos primarily calls for liberal democracy with an emphasis on the rights of corporate properties, free trade, and unencumbered foreign investment. Seattle, by contrast, calls for a revival of social democracy with an emphasis on equality, the rights of working people, and environmental protection. Beijing and the other NICs are primarily concerned with making a successful transition to industrial economies. Where democracy presents an obstacle to this transition, their ruling regimes happily dispense with it. Where, however, social pressures for democracy are mounting, directed democracy can provide an antidote. China represents the former group. Malaysia, Thailand, the Philippines, and post-Suharto Indonesia provide examples of the latter. This leaves Russia out as an anomaly. Russia had achieved industrialization under the Communist regime. But in its attempts to join the global economy, like some other NICs, it presents a complex pastiche of mafia capitalism camouflaged by directed democracy.

Tehran and its mélange of other disenchanted states reveal a profound ambivalence about the trappings of democracy. Disengagement with the global economy has placed them in a disadvantageous economic position. Democratic development, however, has been hostage to a variety of factors, including revolutions, civil wars, foreign interference, and weak civil societies. In some of the states in this group, communitarian democracy has a strong hold, leading at times to authoritarian or totalitarian methods and at other times to genocide. By communitarian democracy, I mean the dominance of a particular epistemic community based on common religion, ethnicity, or tribal loyalty. In Islamic Iran, it is Shi'ism; in Saddam Hussein's Iraq, it was Sunni Islam; in apartheid South Africa, it was racial domination; in some other African countries, it is often tribal hegemony, sometimes causing genocide (Rwanda) or civil wars (Congo).

What about media democratization? The scholars in this volume present us with a very complex and multifaceted picture. However, we can discern several contradictory trends from their deep narratives. First, the pluralization of media channels has increasingly broken through media national boundaries. Access to global news networks, direct broadcast satellite (DBS), Internet networks, fax machines, and wireless telephony have reduced the power of national media monopolies. Second, however, the convergence of telecommunication and computer technologies, combined with deregulation policies, have led to the emergence of a global media oligopoly market that is commercial, entertainment oriented, and Western biased. Third, development of regional communication networks such as those in the Arab (Al-Jazeera TV) and Hispanic worlds has added a new dimension to media pluralism.

As a consequence, the traditional public sphere of discourse, primarily based on print technology and elite public-opinion formation, is being supplemented with a new electronic version. In the twentieth century, mass media (newspapers and broadcasting) facilitated the emergence of mass societies, mass consumption, and mass movements. Totalitarian regimes often depended on the mass media for their hegemonic projects. Media pluralization and interactivity have created new channels for the expression of democratic sentiments and views. During the past three decades (1970–2000), the democratic movements in Iran, the Philippines, Russia, Eastern Europe, and China have employed cassettes, underground radio, computers, videotapes, and faxes to disseminate their messages. At the global level, the Anti-Landmine Treaty of 1997 was achieved through an alliance of some one thousand nongovernmental organizations employing the Internet as their main channel of communication. In 2003, U.S. presidential candidate Howard Dean demonstrated the potential of the Internet as a mobilizing channel by collecting the largest funds among the Democratic Party presidential aspirants.

But the new media are double-edged swords. The Internet has already been co-opted as a most powerful channel for commercial advertising. Other media channels also are primarily developed as commercial enterprises with an emphasis on sales and entertainment. The media are not the message. The message is the message. And the message often depends on the media structures of ownership and control. State media often provide government messages. Commercial media are frequently aimed at selling audiences to advertisers to maximize revenues; they focus therefore on entertaining programs. Public media, such as the British Broadcasting Corporation and Japan's Nippon Hoso Kyokai (NHK), focus on elite programming with increasing concessions to entertainment in order to compete with the commercial media. Community media reflect the views and tastes of their sponsors. Such media tend to cater to their benefactors, including the organized religions or highbrow elites. The *Christian Science Monitor* and Christian Broadcasting Corporation provide examples of the former. The *New York Times* and Public Broadcasting System in the United States supply examples of the latter.

Under most circumstances, the media have to mediate in several different and complex ways: between the state, market, and civil society forces; between media owners, regulators, professionals, critics, and audiences; and between parties to domestic and international conflicts. In the modern world, the media play the role of the nervous system in an organism. Their dual function is to transmit and interpret signals to the global brain. Traditional media professionals have primarily focused on the transmission function. Journalism courses often emphasize efficiency, accuracy, and veracity in media reporting. As the authors of this volume abundantly demonstrate, the problem with that perspective is that facts do not speak for themselves; the storyteller speaks for them. Transmission and interpretation are inextricably tied together. But the media are also instruments of governance. Their function is to produce legitimacy for those in power. In liberal-democratic societies under commercial media systems, production of legitimation takes on complex mediating forms among the state, market, and civil society. Dominated as they are by commercial interests, but also controlled by state interests under authoritarian regimes, global media present an even more complex picture. The appearance of transborder media channels has opened up new opportunities for democratic challenges to the dominant media.

This volume underscores a vital point in understanding the role of the media in democratic formations. Mediation, the authors argue, must be understood as an instrument of governance and hegemonic formation. How can we then construct media democracy? The authors of this volume raise and respond to that vital question. First, it all depends on what kind of democracy we wish to have: liberal, social, directed, or communitarian? These four rather well-known types of democracy have produced different media systems. Liberal democracies have put their faith primarily in the market (classical liberal) and government regulation (Keynesian neoclassical). The neoliberal trends of the last few decades have returned to the classical-liberal impulses by focusing on privatization and deregulation. The Reagan and Thatcher policies have led to greater global media oligopolies in which nine transnational media corporations (TMCs) now control most of the global print, broadcasting, cable, film, sports, music, Internet, and other cultural industries. The social democracies in Western Europe and elsewhere have continued with government regulation to create a greater balance in the media representation of state, market, and civil society perspectives. Multiethnic societies, prevailing in much of the world, have had to face the realities of multicultural populations. If accepted, multiculturalism fosters communitarian democracy and media cultural pluralism. In the transitional societies of Asia, Africa, and Latin America, however, directed democracy is the norm. To gain respectability, most states have adopted democratic constitutions, but to paraphrase Benjamin Disraeli, there are three kinds of lies: lies, damned lies, and constitutions.

Those regimes that have allowed a multiple media system, comprising state, commercial, public, and community media ownership and control, have often created greater checks and balances. However, few regimes are willing to expose themselves to such diversity with its potential for criticism. After all, the central function of any media system is to manufacture consent. Homogenization of ideas and tastes is often assumed to be the most efficient road to easy governance. Unless civil society forces are alive and well enough to create their own autonomous media systems, state and commercial systems will continue to predominate. Media democracy, like democracy itself, is thus a continuing social struggle. The good news is that expanding channels and media abundance are creating new opportunities for media democracies. Similarly, porous international borders also have allowed "foreign" media to penetrate the domestic domain and question state hegemonic projects. However, without rising democratic social consciousness and movements, such opportunities cannot be seized.

This volume serves a dual purpose. On the one hand, it provides fresh scholarship on media democratization from a variety of national, regional, global, and gender perspectives. On the other hand, it raises the level of democratic consciousness for a general public that often feeds on its own biased national media systems. The editors and authors of this volume have provided us with an enlightening account of the world at this critical historical moment.

Acknowledgments

This book would not have been possible without the generosity and support of the Toda Institute for Global Peace and Policy Research. We especially acknowledge the inspiration of its director Majid Tehranian, the quiet encouragement of deputy director Tomosaburto Hirano, and the administrative skills of program manager Satoko Takahashi. The institute's research program on globalization, regionalization, and democratization (GRAD) initiated the project, supported it financially, and brought together some of the book's contributors at its conferences in Oxford in 2002, Vancouver in 2003, and for a related project in Budapest in 2004.

We also thank the contributors, especially those who responded promptly to our persistent queries! While we could not possibly share all their perspectives, we hope readers will agree that together we have produced a reasonably coherent and useful collection.

We also acknowledge the patient support and advice of Brenda Hadenfeldt, Erica Fast, Kärstin Painter, and Andrew Calabrese at Rowman & Littlefield, as well as the anonymous reviewers commissioned respectively by Toda and Rowman. We have incorporated some, and wish we could have adopted more, of their extremely insightful suggestions. At Simon Fraser University (SFU), student assistants Alexandra Guemili, Karina Hackett, Nawal Musleh, and Amy Wong provided many hours of much-appreciated research, clerical, bibliographic, and word-processing labor. Mark Coté's editorial assistance was timely, sharp, and invaluable, as was the stalwart administrative support of the School of Communication's executive assistant Lucie Menkveld. Financial support from SFU's University Publications Fund, crucial for the final stages of manuscript preparation, is gratefully acknowledged.

Finally, once again we thank our respective spouses and children—Angelika Hackett, Karina Hackett, Melanie Hackett, Jianxing Qian, and Linda Qian—for their continued forbearance and for helping us, in more ways than we have space to articulate, to complete another extended project.

1

Media Globalization, Media Democratization: Challenges, Issues, and Paradoxes

Yuezhi Zhao and Robert A. Hackett

Both hope and critique are at work in this book, which explores some of the complex interactions between globalizing media and processes of democratization. Hope comes not in the naive belief that, unchecked, emerging transnational mass media and communication networks will automatically flatten hierarchies, redistribute power, promote dialog, diffuse awareness, contribute to a pacified world, and build bridges of understanding between peoples, classes, and cultures. Rather, it is faith in people, that collectively they have the capacity to refashion communication as well as political systems to increase the odds of these outcomes.

Critique comes in the recognition that global media are not necessarily enhancing the prospects of peace and democracy. (By global media, we mean not only organizations that operate transnationally but also the articulation of nationally based media systems with global markets and processes.) Some contributors here are disappointed that globalized media do not have the transformative power often attributed to them; others suspect that they are embedded not in peace or democracy but in systems of domination and structural violence.

This book carves out a distinct niche, at the intersections of established and emerging fields of scholarship and political practice. In political science, books on the globalization-democracy relationship abound, but few focus on the role of media. In communication studies, there is much on media globalization and on media and democracy, but few combine these two problematics. Moreover, there is little dialog between cultural and political communication dimensions of the debate about media globalization. And as Cees Hamelink (1995) has noted, the relationship of media to societal democratization is too often treated as a question separate from the democratization of media institutions. Our book attempts to address both democratization through the media—the use of communications by civil society or states to promote democratic processes elsewhere in society—and democratization of the media themselves. Thus, the title has a double meaning. Taken as an adjective, "democratizing" implies a focus on the ways in which public communication can contribute to democratic processes and transformations in broader society, as well as emphasizes democracy as a process, rather than a fixed and finalized state of affairs. Taken as a verb, "democratizing" suggests an imperative to render media institutions themselves more representative, accessible, accountable, and/or participatory.

The book not only joins infrequently connected dots but includes essays from contending theoreticopolitical perspectives, as well as from different disciplinary and professional backgrounds. Both democratization and globalization are essentially contested concepts.

MEDIA GLOBALIZATION

As Majid Tehranian's foreword suggests, few ideas have been more politically (and academically) contentious in the past decade than globalization, partly because "the very idea . . . appears to disrupt established paradigms and political orthodoxies" (Held and McGrew 2002, 2). What is at issue is multidimensional. Is globalization a genuine phenomenon or ideological rhetoric masking more fundamental interests and processes? If it is a "real" process, is it historically novel? Are national cultures and states still the prime locus of personal identities and political life, or are they being displaced, decentered, and hybridized by global processes? Is a new global economy in the making, and does it comprise a new phase or form of capitalism? Who dominates global governance, in whose interests, to what ends, and by what means? Is global poverty increasing, and if so, is globalization the main cause (Held, McGrew, Goldblatt, and Perraton 1999; Held and McGrew 2002)? Is globalization an outgrowth of modernity, denoting the compression of time and space and the growing interdependency of actors, locales, and processes across the planet (Giddens 1990; Appadurai 1996), or is it more specifically the universalization of capitalist social relations and, thus, almost indistinguishable from imperialism (Petras and Veltmeyer 2001)? Finally, do the cultural dimensions of globalization (such as globalization/deglobalization through the Jewish Diaspora formation/deformation, discussed by Dov Shinar in chapter 8) have a significance equal to the globalization/deglobalization of capitalistic economic relations (Bello 2002)?

The complexity and contentiousness of such questions produces responses that cut across the traditional cleavages of Left and Right. Political positions on globalization range from the celebration of a global village and a new era of technological innovation, personal freedom, political democ-

racy, and economic prosperity (e.g., Friedman 2000) to fears that it is leading to "a war of all against all, world domination by a single superpower, a
tyrannical alliance of global elites, global ecological catastrophe, or some
combination thereof" (Brecher, Costello, and Smith 2000, xiv). David Held
and Anthony McGrew (2002, 98–117) identify no fewer than six major paradigms of the politics of globalization: neoliberals, liberal internationalists, institutional reformers, global transformers, statist/protectionists, and radicals
(Marxists, communitarians, anarchists).

Not surprisingly, such disparate perspectives generate quite different views
on the role of public communication media in globalizing processes. Very
schematically, those informed by a liberal-modernization paradigm tend to
focus on media contributions to the transition from authoritarian to liberal-
democratic governance, particularly in countries of the global East and South.
Transnational media, especially those originating in Western liberal democracies, are assumed by and large to be agents of social liberalization and political democratization. This view is characteristic of "media moguls, Western officials, neoconservative thinkers, and technology enthusiasts":

> From a perspective that sees the state as the bogeyman of information democ-
> racy, the globalization of media technologies makes it possible to bypass . . . the
> attempts of authoritarian states to control information flows and to curb the en-
> trance of ideas that autocrats might deem inappropriate. As catalysts of the
> breakdown of government communications monopolies, market reforms cou-
> pled with wider access to media technologies usher in information democracy.
> (Waisbord and Morris 2001, vii–ix)

By contrast, critical political economists and antiglobalization activists
identify Western-based transnational media and "the organization of global
information flows along free-market lines" as agents of domination, eroding
the ability of states to protect "autonomous information spaces" (Waisbord
and Morris 2001, ix).

Both views, particularly the latter, are evident to varying degrees in this
book, but more common is an exploration of the nuanced and sometimes
contradictory relations between political and social democratization and
media globalization. We begin with the shared premises that globalization
usefully delineates a significant, if not necessarily new, phenomenon, and
that mass-mediated communication processes, institutions, and technologies
have both contributed to, and been affected by, the broader wave of globalization. Drawing from Annabelle Sreberny (2000), we discuss below several
dimensions of media globalization: transformations in media firms and markets, forms, flows, effects, and governance, as well as media "globalization
from below"—the transformative use of media within civil society.

These interrelated and highly uneven transformations, accelerating since
the early 1980s, have constituted a major shift in the organizational logics
and governance of communication at national and global levels. For more

than three decades after World War II, the world's communication systems were nationally organized (or reorganized, as in postfascist Germany and Japan), albeit in a context of cold war superpower rivalry between the United States and the Soviet Union. Whereas in the state-socialist nations, nationally organized media were subject to varying degrees of overt censorship and political control, in the West, communications policy was linked to nation-building projects of a liberal-democratic variety. Two key elements of communication policy were national control—the organization of economic, social, political, and cultural life around the nation-state axis—and public service, "the idea that principles of citizenship, equality and democratic participation count as much as or more than the market and private property in decision making" (Schiller and Mosco 2002, 6).

Historically, these two elements constituted major political buffers to the full expression of capital logic in communication sectors. Public broadcasting held monopolies in many Western European countries. In Canada, while the debate between "the state or the United States" served to marginalize more radical democratic alternatives in communication and culture (Mazepa 2003), national control was a prerequisite for a public broadcasting system, which was celebrated as embodying the best of the Habermasian public sphere, providing a more democratic alternative to private broadcasting. Even the United States, the citadel of capitalism, developed a nationally controlled system, prohibiting foreign ownership in telecommunication and broadcasting, notwithstanding the aggressive expansion of American media abroad. A conception of public interest, while vaguely defined, played an important historical role in U.S. communication regulation, signifying objectives other than capital accumulation.

Public service principles were defined, negotiated, and practiced under this particular form of postwar "liberal corporatism" (Curran and Leys 2000, 221), in which "nationally embedded public service principles obstructed the secular deepening and widening of market relationships and commercial advertising in and around network industries" (Schiller and Mosco 2002, 9). This context provided the conditions for American journalism's period of "high modernism," characterized by relatively high professional autonomy and a "regime of objectivity" (Hallin 2000a, 221; Hackett and Zhao 1998).

In the newly independent and decolonized countries of what was then known as the Third World, media systems were not only nominally organized on national lines but also mandated to promote projects of nation building and modernization. In practice, however, these systems were considerably influenced by former colonial powers and transnational capitalists. Associated with their call for better terms of global trade through a New World Economic Order, and with the backing of the anti-Western Communist states, the movement of nonaligned countries (NAM) began in the 1970s to agitate for a New World Information and Communication Order (NWICO, discussed below), partly in order to assert national sovereignty for postcolonial states over communication policies and priorities.

Notwithstanding formal but largely unenforced commitments to transnational norms (such as the Universal Declaration of Human Rights, which includes in Article 19 freedom of opinion and expression), communication policy in the postwar era was conceived and conducted in and through the nation-state framework. As many have noted, one of the reasons globalization is so problematic to existing theory and practice is that it potentially calls into profound question the state's role as a "container" of political rights and democratic accountability. That relation is as important in communication rights and structures (the "public sphere") as in more directly political institutions. Whether reports of the state's demise are "much exaggerated" remains hotly debated by social theorists (Held, McGrew, Goldblatt, and Perraton 1999; Aronowitz and Bratsis 2002) and communication scholars (Curran and Park 2000; Waisbord and Morris 2001). What is clear is that many of the current logics in international communication can be traced to three interrelated transformations during the 1980s.

The first was the implosion of the state-socialist regimes as a result of the democratic aspirations and struggles of their peoples, as well as economic pressures on the regimes from the intensified cold war waged by the U.S. Reagan administration.

Second, the NWICO movement and the nationalist aspirations of Third World states in general were subjugated. This was due both to the internal contradictions of the postcolonial nation-state and to the systematic political, economic, and ideological attacks from the West. Such attacks were of two interlocking types: state-based from the United States and United Kingdom within and beyond the UN system; and corporate-based from Western-based media transnationals, which had much to lose from NWICO's proposed reorganization of international communication (see, e.g., Preston, Herman, and Schiller 1989; Vincent, Nordenstreng, and Traber 1999). Within the UN framework, NWICO's potentially radical media-democratization project was replaced by a narrowly defined developmentalist project emphasizing the provision of Western-based technologies and professional training for Third World journalists. Simultaneously, Third World political elites have retreated from challenging Western corporate domination of communication technology and transnational flows "in favor of negotiating national and regional relationships with the global media powers" (Mosco 1996, 209).

The third development, of course, was the rise of market liberalism as an almost evangelical ideology (one might call it Market-Leninism) and increasingly as a governing logic in economic and social policy, first in the most powerful North Atlantic capitalist states—the United Kingdom and United States—and then elsewhere.

Together, these developments, combined with exponential advances in digital networks and technology, unleashed the force of capital and paved the way for the formation of a market-driven communication system on a global scale. The past two decades have witnessed privatization, commercialization, trade liberalization, and overall deregulation (or rather, market-based reregulation), including the removal of national- and public-interest constraints, in national media systems. As the leading capitalist state, the United States has been in the forefront of this movement (Herman and McChesney 1997; Schiller 2000). The state's role was diminished, both as a provider of media services and as a regulator of media ownership and public interest obligations in broadcasting and telecommunication. The multifaceted process of media globalization can be broadly described in the following six dimensions.

First, the most prominent dimension of media globalization has been the predominance of transnational media firms and markets (as discussed in chapters 3, 4, and 11). Waves of media mergers have yielded massive, large-scale communication conglomerates such as AOL/Time-Warner, Disney, News Corporation, Viacom, Bertelsmann, and a few others. These corporations, with the assistance of suprastate and nation-state powers, in turn, have expanded to the rest of the world through a wide range of technological and organizational forms. To be sure, the extent and scope of commercialization and foreign penetration have been highly uneven in various parts of the world, as well as across different media sectors in these regions. Kai Hafez (chapter 7) points to important limits to the penetration of transnational media within authoritarian regimes. But on the whole, the emerging system is increasingly global in ownership structure, production, distribution, and consumption. Although U.S. information and entertainment corporations still enjoy a prominent position globally, ownership has become more nationally diverse. Through joint ventures and other organizational and financial alliances, media outlets in previously distinct national media systems are structurally linked with major transnational media corporations. Similarly, media production and consumption, of films and advertisings for example, have also been globalized. While some would see this as evidence of a multipolar and pluralized global system, others argue that U.S. cultural domination has been transformed into transnational corporate cultural domination (Schiller 1993).

Second, media globalization entails the rise of not only about ten companies that arguably now dominate transnational media production and flows (chapter 11), but also the spread of commercialized media as the general organizational form for media (notwithstanding a secondary diffusion of the European public service broadcasting model) and the establishment of market-oriented media industries in the South as part of the neoliberal restructuring of global and national communication spaces. More broadly, the diffusion of Western-based media forms has included radio, television, and the Internet as technologies for distribution and reception, as well as program genres and formats and professional ideologies and practices (chapters 2, 13).

Third, transnational media flows—the distribution and diffusion of messages, images, and products through mass and digital communication networks—are dominated by Western-based transnational corporations, and, increasingly, regional production centers such as Mexico and Brazil in Latin America and Japan in Asia (Sinclair 1992; Sinclair, Jacka, and Cunningham 1996; Iwabuchi 2002). At the same time, there is some limited reverse flow and selective incorporation of content, styles, and investment from the global margins within globally dominant media, through coproduction of films, for instance. Selected (and commodified) versions of cultures from the global South, or more accurately, versions with cultural elements from the global South but often with financial and distribution support from transnational corporations, are finding their way to audiences in the North; one thinks of "world music" or of movies such as the Chinese martial arts film *Crouching Tiger, Hidden Dragon* or Rupert Murdoch's News Corporation's *Bend It Like Beckham*, a film on the South Asian immigrant/female experience in Britain. As Western, mostly U.S.-based media corporations expand into foreign countries, foreign corporations also expand into the United States and other Western markets—from Sony, which owned Columbia Pictures, to Televisa, the Mexico media conglomerate, which exports broadcast programming, magazines, and music recordings to the United States (Zhao and Schiller 2001; Paxman and Saragoza 2002, 64–85). But arguably, media audiences outside the global centers of media production are increasingly consuming imported media products, from prime-time entertainment on Canadian television to lifestyle magazines in China (chapter 3).

Fourth, and more ambiguously, the globalization of media flows implies the globalization of media effects, as millions simultaneously experience the same media forms, products, channels, and spectacles (e.g., the death of Princess Diana, the invasion of Iraq). This dimension is more ambiguous in that no homogeneous "effects" can automatically be inferred; much research suggests that audiences interpret media texts differently, and media forms are differentially integrated within different social-class and cultural contexts. However, if one moves beyond media centrism and an empiricist notion of "effects" and considers the media as part of a broad "infrastructure of socialization" that is nonreducible to individual interpretation of specific media texts (Schiller 1977, 1989), it is hard to ignore the correlation between the spread of Western-based media forms, content, and structures to the global South and what Richard Maxwell, in an elaboration of the specific concept of "cultural imperialism" as proposed by Herbert Schiller (1977), has identified as "the replication throughout the periphery of the class structure of the core countries" (2003, 69).

Fifth, media governance is assuming global dimensions. Western-style media regulatory frameworks are being adopted, at least in principle if not practice, in other countries, notably the post-Communist "transition societies" (e.g., chapter 2; see Price, Rozumilowicz, and Verhulst 2002). Within the dominant capitalist countries, the role of communication laws and regulations has also been fundamentally redefined (chapter 11). The promarket and probusiness thrust of the 1996 U.S. Telecommunications Act, which has profound global ramifications, is self-evident. The U.S. Federal Communications Commission, for its part, now sees its role changing from that of "an industry regulator to a market facilitator," promoting competition in domestic and international communications (Thussu 2000, 93). The market principle, although to a lesser degree and in more complicated and contested ways, has also shaped European Union communication policies (McChesney 1999; Mattelart 2000; Schlesinger 2001). Moreover, this shift is occurring at the most fundamental constitutional-judicial level. For instance, in the United States, judicial interpretation has increasingly transformed the U.S. Constitution's First Amendment into a shield, not to promote the democratic communication rights of its citizens, but to "keep the government's laws and regulations off the private media and off advertising as well" (McChesney 1999, 257).

As Seán Ó Siochrú shows (chapter 10), at the global level as well, media governance has undergone a dual shift. First, supranational organizations like the World Trade Organization (WTO) and regional trade agreements (North American Free Trade Agreement, European Union) have assumed a greater role relative to nation-states in setting policy frameworks. Second, notions of public service and universal access are giving way to the market principle and the interests of transnational corporations. The provision of communication has been redefined primarily as a matter of trade to be operated precisely on the commercial logic that the NWICO movement had critiqued; the WTO and other trade bodies have replaced the United Nations as the prime mechanisms for regulating international communication services. Significantly, under the pressure of the United States and a few other developed countries, the governance and organizational structure of the International Telecommunications Union (ITU), a UN agency, was fundamentally reshaped, giving private-sector corporations equal rights alongside nation-state members. Today, the ITU "advises countries to dismantle structural regulations preventing cross-ownership among broadcasters, cable operators, and telecom companies . . . and [is] following the communication agenda set by the world's most powerful nations and the telecommunications corporations based in them" (Thussu 2000, 91–93; see also Hill 1998, 99–121). In this context, it is noteworthy that the ITU, which is more technically oriented, rather than the United Nations, is in charge of organizing the World Summit on Information Society (WSIS) (chapters 12, 14).

The transformations described above have generated a global communication system in the age of pancapitalism—a new order still in search of a proper name. Celebrants call it the "information society" or the "global village." More critical nominations range from the conventional notion of imperialism to Michael Hardt and Antonio Negri's provocative concept of empire. Together with military and financial powers, this communication system, Hardt and Negri (2000, 346) argue, serves as a "fundamental medium of imperial control" through the power of defining reality. Through an increasingly interconnected web of communication outlets, the dominant logic of this system is to facilitate capital accumulation, committing to "creating consumers worldwide" (Schiller 1993), and, more generally, to constitute the world's population into global subjectivities conducive to the interests of transnational capital (Dyer-Witheford 1999, 137).

Within the critical political-economy tradition, many writers regard the above trends as evidence of both the ideological and economic integration of media and communication networks with global capitalism (Herman and McChesney 1997, chapter 1; Schiller 2000). Such corporate- and state-driven "globalization from above," however, has its counterpart in a "worldwide movement of resistance: globalization from below" (Brecher, Costello, and Smith 2000, 10; Dyer-Witheford 1999). This is a sixth feature of media globalization: the very transnational communication networks developed in response to corporate and military needs are being used by civil society activists, including women's groups around the world (chapter 12), to assert their own social, cultural, political, and economic priorities. The power of dominant media is being challenged and contested by alternative media institutions and communicative practices in an increasingly networked world (Couldry and Curran 2003). More recently, an emerging focus of transnational civil society advocacy networks is the governance of transnational media themselves (chapter 10, 14). These developments raise the question of the media as both a source and a target of democratization processes.

MEDIA DEMOCRATIZATION?

Like globalization, democracy is an essentially contested concept. In Western societies, it is nearly universally celebrated; no politician wants to be considered undemocratic, and significantly, while some theorists declare themselves postfeminist, post-Marxist, or postmodernist, few yet wish to be labeled postdemocratic. In countries of the global South and East, acceptance of the concept is more problematic, equated as it sometimes is with alien and unwelcome Western ways of secularism and/or capitalism. The "end of history" euphoria, the democratic capitalist triumphalism, that greeted the collapse of communism in the 1990s has faded in the wake of periodic global economic crises, corruption and economic stagnation in the post-Soviet countries, and resurgent ethnonationalism and religious fundamentalism, particularly in countries where rapid market reforms and political democratization have ignited latent tensions between economically dominant ethnic minorities and a less privileged majority (Chua 2004). And yet, although millions of people in the world may regard the label "democracy" with suspicion, they nevertheless increasingly insist that governments reflect their values and interests. Popular struggles for individual and collective freedom from political, economic, and cultural domination forge ahead all over the world.

This book's contributors, it is safe to say, all support democracy, as an end in itself and/or as a means to just and humane governance. Yet, their answers to the main questions the book poses—what are the roles of globalizing media in democratizing processes? and do media themselves need democratizing?—are rather divergent. One reason is the rich diversity of the multiple and contending concepts of democracy, each offering distinct normative criteria for evaluating the media's performance. During the cold war era, C. B. Macpherson (1965) challenged Western orthodoxy, arguing that even one-party and nonliberal political systems—communism and the newly independent nation-building states of the Third World—could in principle have some claim to democratic legitimacy. Such a claim could be sustained to the (admittedly dubious) extent that those regimes were building democracy, conceived not only as a form of government but as a type of society free of class domination, one able to nourish developmental power—everyone's equal right to the full development and use of his or her capabilities (Macpherson 1965, 58; see also Macpherson 1977, 114; Downing et al. 2001, 43–44). Less problematically, Arthur-Martins Aginam (chapter 6) reminds us that the West has no monopoly on democratic traditions: deliberative processes and a communitarian ethos characterized many precolonial African societies. Such communitarianism entailed a rejection of the Western notion of the abstract individual possessed of "natural rights" and instead prioritized the integrity of kinship relations and tribal collectivities that give individual lives meaning. To be sure, that tradition has a dark side: its limitations on personal freedom, its entrenchment of patriarchal relations, and its potential for conflict with rival communities.

Even liberal democracy, with its roots in the middle-class revolutions and intellectual enlightenment of early modern Europe, is hardly a monolithic political tradition. Schematically, we can identify three broad perspectives on democracy and the media in the economically developed liberal democracies (Hackett forthcoming).

First, a market-liberal vision sees democracy not as an end in itself but as normally the best institutional arrangement to maintain political stability and individual rights, particularly economic rights of ownership, contract, and exchange. Although market liberals often adopt a populist stance, their emphasis on private consumption rather than public virtue meshes with an elitist version of democracy, classically articulated by Joseph Schumpeter (1942; cited in Baker 2002, 130). In this view, democracy is a procedure for selecting leaders, with citizen participation confined mainly to voting every few years—essentially, the role of consumers in a political marketplace. Media in this model are regarded basically like any other industries, best left unregulated by government so as to respond to consumer preferences in the marketplace. If journalism has a civic role, it is mainly to act as a watchdog on government, which is considered the main threat to individual freedom. If market liberals, especially in the United States or United Kingdom, see a democratic deficit in Western media, they attribute it mainly to state intervention in the media sector (particularly public service broadcasting) and/or to the perceived leftist biases of journalists.

The market-liberal/elitist version of democracy has been criticized on many grounds, including its unduly pessimistic view of citizens' participation and its inattention to the excessive power of concentrated wealth in media and government. A second liberal-democratic perspective places a higher value on citizen participation in public deliberation and calls on the media to help constitute a public sphere—"that realm of social life where the exchange of information and views on questions of common concern can take place so that public opinion can be formed" (Dahlgren 1995, 7). As theorized by Jürgen Habermas, the public sphere is characterized ideally by discussion free of domination, equality of participation, and rationality in the sense of an appeal to general principles rather than sheer self-interest. Media's democratic roles include providing each significant group with a forum to articulate and develop its interests, facilitating the search for societywide political consensus by being universally accessible and inclusive, and reconstituting private citizens as a public body in the form of public opinion (Curran 1996, 82–83; Baker 2002, 129–53).

Many public-sphere liberals perceive a malaise in contemporary European and American democracy: declining voter participation, public mistrust and cynicism toward government, disconnection between political and public agendas, trivialization of political discourse, and the like. Malaise theorists find some of the causes in the political environment, such as divisive new issues, the image orientation of political campaigns, and voters' declining allegiance to political parties (Blumler and Gurevitch 1995, 206), but fingers are also pointed at journalistic practices and, to a lesser extent, at media structures. Economic pressures and market reregulation since the 1980s have pushed journalism toward tabloidization and infotainment, it is claimed. The fragmentation of media audiences as channels proliferate has undermined the cohesion of the public sphere and facilitated a politics of division (Turow 1997). Journalists' struggle for autonomy from politicians' spin doctors has driven them to a semiadversarial stance, focusing on politicians' strategies and scandals, rather than on substantive policies. While some scholars critique these "narratives of decline" (McNair 2000, 197; Norris 2000), they have led to modest efforts at reforming journalism practices, if not structures. One example is the public-journalism movement in the United States, involving experiments by newspapers to facilitate community discussion of public issues, rather than simply to report on official sources (Baker 2002, 158–63). As chapters 9 and 13 in this book attest, neither the significance of reforming journalistic ethos and practices, nor the ability of working journalists to effect change, should be underestimated.

While public-sphere liberals often favor such reform of media practices, they tend not to raise fundamental questions about media's market-oriented corporate structures and still less about the social and political order of capitalist liberal democracies. By contrast, radical democrats offer more robust benchmarks for evaluating media performance. If market liberals emphasize individual liberties and restrictions on government power and public-sphere liberals highlight public deliberation about policy, radical democrats add a third dimension—a thoroughgoing view of democracy not just as a set of procedural rules but as a societal environment that nourishes developmental power, as in Macpherson's vision noted above. Such a standpoint seeks not just to reinvigorate representative democracy but to promote more direct participation in decision making, in politics, and in the economy and civil society as well. Radical democrats favor not only political equality but also the more equitable distribution of cultural, social, and economic resources. They regard power relations as antagonistic in societies with structured inequalities; even in prosperous capitalist democracies, political and economic elites may have interests that conflict with those of the subordinate population. Moreover, power is analyzed holistically: a democratic public sphere cannot be insulated from power hierarchies embedded in state, economy, gender, and race. Indeed, there will be an inequality of voices in the public sphere so long as such hierarchies exist—a point made in this book with particular force by Sreberny (chapter 12).

Radical democrats endorse the watchdog and public-sphere models celebrated in the other models, respectively, but they also expect a democratic media system to counteract power inequalities within the social order (McChesney 1999, 288) and to enable horizontal communication between subordinate groups, including progressive social movements as agents of democratic renewal (Angus 2001).

From the viewpoint of radical democrats, many aspects of the political economy of commercialized, corporate-dominated media systems in the West, particularly in the United States, contradict democratic equality and informed participatory citizenship. Myriad structural and other factors—the political interests of media owners and their links with the rest of the business elite, high-entry costs, ownership concentration, the dependence of commercial media on revenue from large-scale advertisers who seek to reach affluent consumers, ownership by conglomerates and convergence between once-separate media industries, the close relationship between media corporations and the governments that are supposed to regulate them in the public interest—are seen as profoundly depoliticizing, inegalitarian, and/or having conservative implications for access to media and for media content, and thus, potentially, for culture and politics as well (Hackett and Zhao 1998; McChesney 1999). As corporate power and commercial logic exert increasing influence over the governance of communication at the global level, Ó Siochrú (chapter 10; see also Ó Siochrú and Girard 2002) summarizes key related areas of concern: the distortion and diminution of the public sphere, the monolithic propagation of consumerism, the enclosure of the "information commons" as knowledge is privatized and commercialized, and the erosion of civil rights in electronic media.

Four Waves of Media Democratization

Given such divergence in conceptualizations of democracy, not to mention uneven developments in the global political economy, it is not surprising that there is no single media democratization project or movement. Indeed, during the past four decades, there have been several waves, each distinct in historical origin and ideological inspiration.

One such wave, the NWICO debate of the 1970s and 1980s noted above, was arguably both a by-product and an integral component of Third World postcolonial struggles for independence and development. It expressed two potentially contradictory aspects of democratization: cultural and communicative sovereignty for postcolonial countries (a state-centered concept, akin to Macpherson's Third World development-oriented model of democracy) and participatory communication to empower citizens within states, a tradition more akin to radical democracy, or democratization from below. The main forum for advancing NWICO was the United Nations, particularly UNESCO, where the domination of the major powers was mitigated by the one-state, one-vote principle. Its culminating document was the 1980 MacBride Report, entitled *One World, Many Voices.* (The continuing relevance of the issues MacBride raised inspired the subtitle of this book.) Carlos Valle (1995, 205–10) argues that MacBride sought a response to five problems of global proportions:

1. The huge gap in the worldwide distribution of the means of communication and the related technological dependence of nonindustrialized countries on the industrialized.
2. The commodification of information, with its negative implications for universal access, the ability of media to meet educational and development needs, popular participation in communication, and the

preservation of cultures in the face of the consumerist lifestyles promoted by advertising.

3. Major imbalances in the flow of information and media content between North and South, compounded by perceived omissions or mis-
representation of the South in transnational North-based media [The international news agencies were a particular focus of attention, but the
debate came to include imbalances in other media forms, such as transborder data flow and advertising (MacBride and Roach 1993, 6)].

4. The threat posed to the information/communications sovereignty of
different countries by such foreign interference as transnational corporate control over data.

5. The development of grassroots or alternative communication forms, intended as tools for popular education, expression, and mobilization.

While the NWICO movement had many limitations, such as the hypocrisy
of Third World leaders who used NWICO's rhetoric of decolonization to intensify repression within their own states, they do not necessarily invalidate
the importance of NWICO's dual critique of international communication in
the 1970s and 1980s: its domination by Western powers and by the logic of
capital accumulation. Indeed, NWICO highlighted a connection that is often
overlooked or taken for granted in debates about press freedom and democratic communication: previously, models and aspirations for democratic
communication, and democracy more broadly, have been articulated, contested, and (incompletely) constructed within the framework of specific
nation-states. In the Third World, the pursuit of national sovereignty in communication was linked to anti-imperialist and other popular movements, not
all of them pursuing violent or Leninist methods, not all of them establishing
internally repressive dictatorships to the same degree—for instance, contrast
China and India. While they do not fit today's liberal definition of democracy, these earlier struggles for national independence against facets of
capitalist globalization can also be understood as struggles for one of the
prerequisites for democratic communication—collective autonomy from external domination.

Moreover, while the official NWICO debate was conducted at the level of
state and interstate institutions, it was arguably also "a people's movement"
that inspired and was inspired by a wide range of actors and communicative
forms in addition to governmental policy makers (White 1988, 20–21). In
Latin America, labor unions and civil society bodies like churches developed
popular radio, traditions noted in chapter 5; and Paulo Freire's educational
philosophy emphasized small-group communication in which the poor articulated their own values and their analyses of the causes of poverty. In India and Africa, popular theater and other traditional folk media have long traditions and have enjoyed success (chapters 4, 6), while small printing

presses and video became tools of trade unions and neighborhood groups in urban settings (White 1988, 22).

A parallel and intellectually overlapping drive for a public voice and participatory communication on the part of oppositional movements has fueled a second wave of media democratization, comprising challenges to concentrated corporate control, hegemonic representations, and/or commercial logic in mass media in the heartland of global capitalism—Western Europe and North America. These challenges grew out of the youth counterculture and the new social movements of the 1960s and 1970s—the antiwar, anti-imperialist, and student-based New Left, the (liberal) civil rights and (radical) Black Power movements in the United States, other ethnic minorities struggling for equality, women's liberation, the Quebec independence movement, environmentalism, antinuclear protest, and so forth. Some theorists (e.g., Melucci 1980) have drawn distinctions between the allegedly identity-oriented "new" social movements and older, more state- and economically oriented movements, notably labor. However, this distinction is overdrawn (Carroll and Hackett 2004). In Western Europe, especially Italy and Britain, the social ferment of the "new" movements was cross-fertilized by militancy on the part of supposedly old labor and socialist movements.

Some of these movements received initially respectful treatment in the dominant media; some, most spectacularly Greenpeace, even found media openings to help launch international campaigns (Dale 1996). But more often, media frames ignored, trivialized, or denigrated oppositional movements (Gitlin 1980; Hackett 1991), encouraging them to create "alternative" or "radical" media (Downing et al. 2001), constituting parallel networks of communication beyond and against corporate and state control—democratization from below. In the decades since, as dominant media have fallen under increasingly concentrated corporate control, efforts to make them more diverse and democratically accountable have expanded to other forms—efforts to transform the relationship between media and audiences through media education and "culture jamming," training and campaigns to promote progressive messages in dominant media, and coalitions aiming at democratic reform of state communication policies and the very structure of media institutions (chapter 11; Hackett 2000). Britain's Campaign for Press and Broadcasting Freedom, founded in 1979, and Free Press, founded in 2003 in the United States, are leading examples of such coalition building.

The democratic deficits of Western media highlighted by radical democratic movements and by public-sphere liberal intellectuals have stimulated the occasional government inquiry and limited reforms, such as ownership ceilings in the United Kingdom, the Fairness Doctrine and other public service obligations in American broadcasting, a right to reply in France, and press subsidies in Scandinavia. Such reforms were enacted before the current era of globalization, and in many countries they have been, and are being, rolled back by neoliberal governments. In the West, media reform remains largely a democratization-from-below initiative.

By contrast, Western states, foundations, and (perhaps ambivalently) media corporations have been much more supportive of a third wave of media democratization—viz., media reform, in conjunction with political and legal reform, in societies in transition from authoritarian to more liberal and/or nominally democratic forms (Price, Rozumilowicz, and Verhulst 2002). Particular effort has been directed toward reform in the former Soviet countries, especially Eastern Europe (chapter 2), since the collapse of communism. This wave thus combines democratization from below (popular movements like the Polish labor union Solidarity, which wanted to overthrow the yoke of one-party Communist rule), from above (liberal elements within the previous regime, most famously Mikhail Gorbachev), and from outside.

Whether such reform has been effective and whether it is a springboard toward a vibrant civil society, rather than incorporation into a globalized, depoliticized consumer culture, are matters up for debate. Different perspectives are evident in chapters 2, 7, and 11. On the whole, the post-Communist media-reform project is arguably less about democratization, in the sense of popular sovereignty and participation in shaping societal decisions on the basis of equal entitlement to the conditions of self-empowerment (Hamelink 1995), and more about liberalization, the regularization of media laws and individual (and corporate) rights of expression vis-à-vis state repression. Indeed, transnational media conglomerates are probably more concerned with protection of intellectual rights and other bottom-line issues than with diversity and freedom of public expression; certainly, they have been able to accommodate to market-friendly military dictatorships, such as in Latin America before the 1980s (chapter 5) and more recently China's emerging market-authoritarian regime (chapter 3; Zhao 2001; 2003). But generalizations are difficult, and nuances abound. For instance, there is no monolithic thrust behind Western efforts to promote reform in the "transition societies," with some competition between American-style commercial (market-liberal) and European-style public-sphere models (chapter 2).

A fourth wave of media democratization arises in the era of the Internet, which has facilitated transnational civil society networks of and for democratic communication. As the most recent development, it deserves extended comment. The very communication networks and information technologies that have been at the center of neoliberal globalization have also been appropriated by antiglobalization—or more accurately, "globalization from below"—movements in many parts of the world. Civil society and nongovernmental organizations (NGOs) have become increasingly important players in global communications in recent decades. As Colin Sparks (chapter 2) demonstrates, the concept of civil society has a complicated intellectual history, and its resurgence was closely linked to struggles for political democratization in Eastern Europe. NGOs began to appear in the international scene in the 1960s and 1970s. An effective communication strategy, including the use of mainstream media, has always been an important component of influential NGOs like Amnesty International and Greenpeace. One especially impressive demonstration of the power of NGOs and their networks was their intervention in the negotiation process, within the framework of the Organization for Economic Development and Cooperation (OEDC), for the Multilateral Agreement on Investment between 1995 and 1998. More than six hundred organizations in seventy countries were involved in the campaign, which successfully derailed a treaty that would have granted unprecedented freedom to capital. Such an intervention could be considered an example of democratization through the media (mainly the Internet, rather than mass-audience outlets). A more dispersed, though no less impressive, development is the emergence of women's networks in the global South (chapter 12).

Not until recently, however, have NGOs devoted to communications politics—democratization of the media—begun to flourish. As can be seen from Ó Siochrú's summary, they are impressively diverse, including NGOs devoted to media education, media monitoring and analysis, the promotion of free speech and the rights of journalists, and advocacy on policies related to global communication (chapters 10, 14).

Here, the NWICO debate, now anathema to UNESCO (Nordenstreng 1999), manifests a positive legacy in civil society mobilization to articulate a democratic alternative vision at the WSIS (chapters 12, 14). The People's Communication Charter and other internationally circulated documents express aspirations for media diversity, accountability, and popular empowerment for social change. And the alternative media, which emerged in national contexts in previous waves of media democratization noted above, now have an expanded and transnational presence through the Internet. Jan Oberg's Internet-based reportage from Iraq (chapter 9) stands as an example of such a medium. Ideologically diverse and organizationally distinctive, NGO media outlets provide a cacophony of voices that complement, mediate, and challenge the dominant global communication system.

Any celebration of transnational civil society, however, must be tempered by sobering realities. First, not all forms of civil society organization are progressive to the extent that they are committed to flattening, rather than sustaining, existing forms of inequalities and relations of domination. Second, even progressive civil society activism has not always achieved its goals. For instance, in Eastern Europe, Sparks (chapter 2) argues that the early promise of a participatory self-governing "civil society" has not come to fruition; instead, it has come to mean simply capitalism, with a press operating on commercial lines and broadcasting subject to influence by governing cliques. China still prohibits nearly a fifth of the world's population from self-organizing or achieving independent representation (apart from the outlawed Falun Gong, which did not receive WSIS-sanctioned civil society organization status and was thus banned from the formal WSIS process) at international conferences like the WSIS (Zhao 2004). The Chinese communication system is now dominated by a hegemonic bloc of transnational media corporations, a bureaucratic capitalist state, and the urban middle class favored by commercial media as consumers (chapter 3; Zhao 2003). A similar systemic bias toward the urban middle class and against the rural poor is evident in India's increasingly commercialized and globalizing media system (chapter 4). And notwithstanding achievements in South Africa, where media democratization was anchored in a broader political and social struggle against apartheid, civil society–driven public broadcasting has become an orphan model in Africa (chapter 6). By contrast, there have been some celebrated cases of success in civil society networking and mobilization in resisting neoliberal globalization in Latin America, most notably the Zapatista rebellion in Mexico in the mid-1990s (chapter 7). More recently, Naomi Klein (2003) reported how, in the struggle against transnational mining, the citizens in Esquel, a small city in southern Argentina, networked with groups such as Greenpeace Argentina and started "digging . . . for information" crucial to local decision making, resulting in a referendum that rejected a Canada-U.S. mining venture.

Still, as Sparks implies (chapter 2), the very concept of civil society as a force independent from, and potentially oppositional to, the state and transnational capital needs to be problematized. The concept is even more problematic when NGOs are taken as surrogates for civil society. To be sure, there are NGO media, like the IndyMedia Centers, that try to give voice to those otherwise marginalized in the global order, but many NGOs have agendas that "are compatible with and serve the neoliberal project of global capital" (Hardt and Negri 2000, 312–13), acting as its "moral arm." Imperial power, some critics argue, has increasingly projected itself into the domain of NGOs, creating, cultivating, and/or transforming them into flexible outsourcing outfits to carry out its objectives—turning them into "co-opted NGOs," or CONGOs (Brecher, Costello, and Smith 2000, 88). Thus, the nation-state transfers some of its power to suprastate bodies such as the WTO from above, on the one hand, while transferring some other functions to NGOs from below, making them part of a "shadow state" (Mitchell 2001).

So, caution is required in assessing the political implications of civil society and of NGOs. Yet, the emergence of transnational networks of women's organizations (chapter 12) and of a potentially mass-based media-reform movement in the United States, the heartland of global capitalism (chapter

11), both indicate something of the positive meaning of civil society and media democratization.

MEDIA GLOBALIZATION AND DEMOCRATIZATION: CONTRADICTORY IMPLICATIONS

The intersections of these complex trends raise issues far more intricate and numerous than can adequately be addressed by any single book or author. We would simply like to flag questions raised by the chapters in this book as areas for future research, debate, and action.

1. *What are the relationships of global media organizations (and the processes of media globalization) to political democratization?* We noted above two contending perspectives, a celebratory and a critical view. But the actual implications of media globalization are of course more complex, contingent upon many internal and external factors and upon medium, content, and context. Many of our authors do not fit easily into either camp. For instance, Hafez (chapter 7) offers a skeptical view of the democratizing impact of global media. But whereas Robert McChesney (chapter 11) sees the democratic limitation of global media as a product of their very logics and their success in dominating new markets, Hafez sees this is as a consequence of their lack of penetration within authoritarian regimes.

Much the same could be said of China. Interpersonal and group communication among university students and intellectuals and the small media form of wall posters were pivotal in the 1989 Tiananmen-era protests. To be sure, Chinese students and intellectuals were making use of foreign shortwave radio broadcasts, especially Voice of America, and extensive global television coverage played a role in the evolving dynamics of the 1989 prodemocracy movement. Sympathetic domestic media coverage, in the context of a divided leadership and a temporary breakdown of the party state's propaganda command structure, also played a role in legitimating and spreading the movement (Zhao 1998; 2001). However, today the relationship between international and domestic media and protest movements in China is quite different from what it was in 1989, due to the changing nature and social constitution of the movements, reconstituted power relations in Chinese society, and a transformed domestic-media political economy, as well as the changed structure of transnational media and their stakes in China (chapter 3; Zhao, 2003). In addition, the Chinese case also underscores the complicated interplay between the internal and external "effects" of media globalization and democratization. For example, although domestic media democratization efforts and extensive foreign media coverage of, and indeed, direct participation in, the Chinese uprising in 1989 did not lead to the democratization of that country, as political scientist Elizabeth Perry has noted, the media spectacle in Tiananmen Square served as an inspiration for other more consequential protests elsewhere in the world: "The demise of Communist regimes across Eastern Europe later that year was undoubtedly accelerated by the Chinese uprising, which had attracted unprecedented media coverage throughout the European continent" (2002, 153).

In Latin America, Javier Protzel argues (chapter 5), broadcasting has developed according to a mainly commercial model that guarantees neither media autonomy from political and economic interests nor good-quality public information. In this respect, there is an overlap with McChesney's argument, but Protzel's tone is one of disappointed liberalism rather than radical democracy. His underlying problematic is a liberal-modernist vision of the public sphere, and what is ultimately at stake for him is the construction of a "modern social subject" based on rights and citizenship. He sees such "secularization" of Latin American politics as an "unfinished project," one in which mass media, whether foreign or domestic, have no monolithic or unilinear role.

Protzel's sentiment toward the unfulfilled liberal-modernist project is certainly widely shared by many analysts on other continents, especially by those who espouse Western-style liberal democracy within a nation-state framework as a political project in the global South. Such analysts often endorse the "media malaise" thesis discussed above—a concern that the decay of traditional party politics, the rise of political marketing, and the central role of television as a medium of the lower classes have led to an unwelcome form of "Americanized" politics. Such analysis, however, arguably manifests the elitism and rationalist bias of the Habermasian public-sphere model, a line of critique well developed by a number of Western scholars and noted by Aginam (chapter 6; see also Schlesinger 1999). The electoral success of Lula da Silva's left-leaning coalitions in Brazil on the basis of a reinvigorated civil society, the autonomous organizing and networking efforts of the disenfranchised and dispossessed in Argentina in the aftermath of an economic collapse, and the return to power of India's more secular Congress Party, among other recent developments, however, demonstrate that there is more to popular politics than cynicism, personality worship, television marketing, and passive spectatorship. Even in China, persistent protests by disenfranchised workers, farmers, and other dispossessed social groups in the face of a repressive state and a highly censored media system have forced issues such as rural poverty onto the national political agenda. Here, as is the case everywhere, concrete social realities defy any preconceived notion about which medium, what information, and what forms of communication are relevant and empowering in localized struggles. In certain areas of rural China, for example, the most subversive communicative activity of farmers struggling against illegal and arbitrary fees by local officials has been organized around the voluntary dissemination of central party policies prohibiting these fees through loudspeakers in public markets and other communal spaces (Zhao 2004, 279–80).

What may be lost in the dichotomy between the alarmist and celebratory views of media globalization are its uneven nature and the apparent class-based structure of transnational media provision and consumption. Indeed, direct access to global media is limited to a relatively small, rich, educated, English-speaking, and probably disproportionately male elite. So, rather than problematically celebrating an emergent "global public sphere," Sparks (1998, 122) calls the resultant communication space an "imperialist, private sphere." Even if this contestable assumption is accepted, however, it may be that such a sphere, hierarchically structured though it be, is compatible with dominant notions of democracy as a market economy with periodic elections. Evaluations of the democratic consequences of media globalization are related not only to different assessments of its impact but also to the normative criteria associated with the respective models of democracy discussed above.

Such evaluations are also linked to broader assumptions about the relationship of public communications media to other social and political institutions and processes. The scholarly and journalistic literature on this topic is vast. Schematically, as implied by our discussion of models of democracy above, Western media have been variously interpreted as the independent watchdog of government, as a lapdog subservient to power, or conversely as a mad dog unduly hostile to authority. In Eastern Europe and other transition societies, the media might be considered lost dogs in search of a stable home. The chapters in this book, however, have largely avoided such one-dimensional characterizations, treating media as sites of transformation and struggle. In situations of political ferment in previously authoritarian regimes, "small" media may be more influential than either official/state media or transnational corporate media (chapter 7); that may be especially the case when small media are linked to the transformative power of social movements (Downing et al. 2001).

By contrast with the political science literature, which has tended to regard media as epiphenomena of other forces or institutions, this book's contributors generally recognize the media's relative autonomy and distinct contributions to social and political change. On the other hand, they have also avoided a tendency, evident in media studies, to overemphasize media organizations "while leaving in shadow the wider processes of society" (Curran and Leys 2000, 221).

2. *What are the political and theoretical implications of the apparent diversification of media ownership and the multidirectional nature of global media flows?* Hafez argues that regional media are a decisive link between globalization and democratization. Are regional media like Al-Jazeera or Brazil's Globo contributing to a more pluralistic or multipolar world order?

We suggest that the question needs to be rethought. At stake here is a contrast between nationalistic/cultural and class-based frameworks of analysis. The former may suggest that interregional and reverse media flows refute "media imperialism," conceived as the one-way flow of U.S. media products to the rest of the world. But such diversification in media flows should not be confused with the arrival of a new operating logic and a new era of democratic choice and expression (Zhao and Schiller 2001). Instead, the logic of capital accumulation is becoming a unifying principle for the global communication system. The formation of the global media system across space is also a process of the "intensification of commodification" (Mosco 1996, 140–211) in media production and the development of "hypercommercialism" (McChesney 1999) both in the United States and elsewhere. In the global media system, it is as if anything can be said, in any language, at any location, as long as it can be said profitably. Within this context, channel proliferation and niche programming signify "merely that the transnational audiovisual industry is willing to 'parasitize,' rather than flatten, cultural differences—where such variations give hope of profitability" (Zhao and Schiller 2001, 140). The imperial "solution" to the reemergence of ethnic and national differences is not to assimilate or negate them but rather to celebrate and manage them in an effective apparatus of command (Hardt and Negri 2000, 200–1). Compared to old-style colonialism, globalization has made it easier for globalizing corporations to integrate local enterprises and to transform local elites into junior partners, as an alternative to politically or economically eliminating them (Sklair 2001, 256).

Thus, it may be a misconception to see globalization and localization as mutually exclusive, and attacking the "cultural imperialism" thesis on the basis of reverse flows misses the point (Schiller 1991). Protzel is surely correct (chapter 5) that while North American media models and corporations have influenced Latin America, it is not a case of mere dependency or imitation; indigenous political cultures have helped shape Latin American politics and media. Our point is that it is not simply a question of cultural geography but of the governing logics of social organization. The production of commercially and transnationally successful *telenovas* by the Mexican media corporation Televisa, for example, can be seen as a sign of the triumph of capital and the commercial logic of cultural production over alternative ways of organizing public communication (Sussman 2001). As Armand Mattelart has also noted (2000, 43), *radionovelas* and *telenovelas* made their debut "under the auspices of foreign agencies and advertisers . . . well before producers in various Latin American countries appropriated them and gave them an autonomous form."

3. *How adequate or relevant are Western models and concepts in understanding and assisting processes of political and media democratization throughout the world?* An ironic dual process appears to be occurring. On

the one hand, Western media discourse and practices are diffusing through both export-push and import-pull. Originating in the European Enlightenment, concepts of liberal democracy and the public sphere are informing media reform in the post-Soviet transition societies (chapter 2). While Aginam (chapter 6) finds little purchase for the concept of public service broadcasting in Africa, no democratic alternative, either within Western or indigenous traditions, appears to be on offer. Elsewhere though, not only Western media corporations and their products but also their models of organization and professionalism are spreading and finding varying degrees of fertile soil, through, for instance, state- and NGO-backed journalism-training programs for journalists.

On the other hand, as arguably the most democratic aspects of the Western media system—professional ethos of objectivity, public service broadcasting—are being exported, they are being undermined in the heartland of global capitalism. Hypercommercialism is seriously eroding the public service ethos in U.S. media (chapter 11). As reformers in the East and South embrace North American journalism's "regime of objectivity" (Hackett and Zhao 1998), radical democratic critics in the West point to its limitations: it tends to skew public discourse toward those with the most cultural, economic, and political capital to preempt structural reform of media, to inhibit a positive relationship between civil society movements and the media, and/or to intensify the level of polarization and potential violence in conflict-laden issues (e.g., chapters 2, 11, 13). Although the power of watchdog journalism, working in tandem with a strong civil society, should not be underestimated, in the context of authoritarian government, systemic social inequalities, and the absence of a broad reformist impulse among urban middle classes, journalistic professionalism has serious limits. In China, journalists' adoption of a watchdog role may expose local scandals, but they are typically "watchdogs on Party leashes" (chapter 3). Even in India, investigative journalism could be muffled by political power, and as is often the case in many other parts of the world, it often fails to articulate the suppressed voices of protest among impoverished rural masses (chapter 4).

These questions raise a more fundamental issue: can contemporary Western capitalist liberal democracy be taken as an adequate benchmark for evaluating media and democracy in the era of planetary capitalism? Typically, theories of democratic communication presume a nation-state framework, focusing on internal political social relations, while, in fact, democratic struggles have always been linked to global political economy and external relations—be it America's anticolonialist war of independence, its civil rights and antiwar movements two centuries later, or the national liberation and anti-imperialist movements in the twentieth-century Third World.

The emerging global order reminds us that democracy is contingent upon relations of hegemony and subordination within the nation-state system and upon the nature of class and ethnic compromise within nation-states. Shinar (chapter 8) provocatively brings to the fore the complicated intersections between imperial politics, class politics, and national politics with the case of Israel; it is a limitation of this book that we were unable to obtain a counterpart analysis from an Arab perspective.

While this is not the place to discuss the historical origins of the Arab-Israeli conflict or to get into the long-standing Marxist debates on class politics and nationalistic politics, the latter issue is certainly central to any critical analysis of the problematic of democratic governance in a capitalist social formation, and chapters 3, 4, and 6 address this issue to various extents. Indeed, one need not accept a radical position that capitalism and democracy are inherently in tension to recognize that at particular historical junctures, they sometimes are. Advanced capitalist market economies (Italy, Germany, Greece) have sometimes reverted to dictatorial rule; and the introduction of market reforms in Asia (Indonesia) and Latin America (Brazil, Chile, Argentina, and other countries) was sometimes preceded and sustained by harsh military dictatorships (Petras and Veltmeyer 2001, 108).

With the planetary expansion of capitalistic social relations under the current wave of globalization, the tension between capitalism and democracy may intensify, even in the heartlands of liberal democracy. In the post–cold war era, a linear, Western-centric, liberal framework appears to underpin the labeling of ex-Communist states as "transitional," implying that the West has reached the end of history. Instead, perhaps we should consider how the end of the cold war, then the 9/11 attacks and the "war on terrorism," have brought "transitional" changes to the West as well: the undoing of the welfare state and social rights, the reconstitution of the warfare/"homeland security" state in the United States, and antiterrorism bills that mandate a variety of infringements on civic rights, including communication rights (chapter 10). We do not need to embrace alarmist invocations of fascism to appreciate that such recent developments point to dedemocratization (Curran and Leys 2000, 225), a movement to a more authoritarian social formation in the core Western liberal democracies. This perspective underscores a sense of democracy and progress without guarantees, in which no country has moral privilege and no linear logic should be taken for granted in the process of democratization. The growing discontent of millions of Americans with the democratic deficit of their own country's media (chapter 11) should remind us that while much existing scholarship tends to analyze the spread of Western media to other parts of the world, globalization has consequences for globalization's political engine, the United States itself. As the U.S. media system globalizes, has it become domestically more democratic, or less?

4. *What are the conditions of democratic communication?*

Assuming the need for the institutional empowerment of citizens' communication rights and capacities and for limits to economic as well as political concentrations of power, an "enabling environment" of a democratic political and legal system seems indispensable (Price, Rozumilowicz, and Verhulst 2002). There is thus the paradox of the state as both a prerequisite for, and a potential threat to, democratic communication. Contrary to liberal assumptions about the inherent democratic inclinations of media institutions and about the state as the obstacle to media democratization, as Daniel Hallin (2000b) argues, the state might play a positive role in the democratization of media. In the case of Mexico, for example, Televisa, the commercial broadcaster, "had to be dragged kicking and screaming by the state" in the direction of greater political openness as Mexico ended the long monopoly of power by the Partido Revolucionario Institucional (PRI; Institutional Revolutionary Party) in 1997. The Mexican example, as Hallin (2000b, 103) further points out, illustrates Michael Schudson's (1994) argument that the state and the democratic public sphere are by no means entirely separate or antagonistic.

Yet, the state, too, has internal and external conditions of existence, and each state has unique political, economic, and cultural trajectories of formation and reformation. Theorizing on communication and democracy has been not only nation-state-centered but has also corresponded to the historical experience of just two countries—Britain and the United States—which have

> remarkably similar leitmotifs in their cultural, economic and political history that mark them out from most other nations on the planet. They have both (since 1865) been stable capitalist democracies, deeply involved in global affairs as imperial powers, not invaded by other nations, strongly marked by a diffuse Protestant Christian tradition, and highly affluent by planetary standards. (Downing 1996, x)

Apart from the enormous question of how to organize political and communication governance democratically on an international and intercultural basis, one of the blind spots of democratic theorizing based on "imperial" nation-states is to overlook the extent to which such nation-states, as "containers" for democratic political life, have often been built upon violence, the subordination of other peoples, and national identities forged against the "other." The case of nationalism and democracy in Israel is illustrative. Shinar (chapter 8) shows that there can be different levels of democratization within a society, related to dominant and subordinate identities, with accordingly different priorities for media democratization.

5. *To what extent is democratization not simply a political process but also a cultural one, involving the media in processes of identity formation much broader than the provision of political information?* At one level, this raises the question of the role of entertainment media, not just journalism, in forging popular culture and as a key aspect of globalization. More broadly, the question of the media's cultural role has become increasingly salient at

the current historical juncture. We have noted above the irruption of ethnic, religious, and other identity-based conflict since the 1980s, both within and beyond nation-state borders. Some see such conflict as a long-anticipated "clash of civilizations," anchored on polarities of modernity/premodernity (Huntington 1996). For others, imperialism, the uneven spread of Western secular models of development, and the globalization and intensification of market relations are at least partly responsible for the "clash of fundamentalisms" (Ali 2003) and for brutally violent backlashes, like the 9/11 attacks on the United States. Media, whether in the form of journalism or entertainment, are key sites for such struggles. In Rwanda and the former Yugoslavia, the media were deeply implicated in the mobilization of particularistic identities and, indeed, specific incitement to horrific violence. In India, television, especially soap operas based on communal myths, played an important role in the rise of Hindu nationalism, even as middle-class consumers tuned in to Western or "glocalized" media (chapter 4). In China, state-engineered modernization and elite-driven global integration, symbolized by the arrival of Hollywood blockbusters, mobile phones, and computer networks, have given rise to two cultural phenomena: first, a massive, nativist, quasireligious Falun Gong movement organized through underground media-distribution channels and the Internet; and second, a transnationally integrated urban elite embedded in the secular religion of consumerism, with CNN, transnational business papers, and consumer magazines as their bibles (chapter 3).

There is an urgent need to bridge the gap between cultural and political analysis to achieve a fuller picture of media democratization in global context. Chapters 5, 6, and 8 in particular point to political culture as a site where the potential for democratic governance is shaped, but it is important to avoid essentialist notions of political culture, which imply that certain cultures are inherently antithetical to democracy. Moreover, at stake are even broader cultural issues—of meaning, subjectivity, and community—beyond the scope of this book.

6. *Would the democratization of public communication reduce the likelihood of war within and between states?* In chapters 9 and 13, the peace/communication relationship, rather than democratization as such, is the primary concern. The links between the democratization of public communication, political democracy, and the prospects for peace are complex, a vast field beyond the scope of this chapter. For Jake Lynch and Annabel McGoldrick, the public expression of diverse opinions is necessary for an informed and self-governing public and for accountable, responsive government, especially on the most fundamental decision a state can make: to wage war. They argue for peace journalism, a reform of professional ethos and practices, to enhance news media's democratic capacity and to mitigate their tendency to escalate conflict.

Peace journalism aims to (re)introduce a sense of agency for journalists, a sense that they can contribute to positive change, thereby calling into question the determinism or fatalism that might be implicit in grand theorizing about the links between war/peace and democratization. On the one hand, a neoliberal position argues that international peace would be best enhanced by replacing dictatorships and fundamentalist regimes with Western-style "open" societies, characterized by capitalism and the formal trappings of representative democracy, and by promoting economic interdependence. This idea has been popularized as the "golden arches" theory by Thomas Friedman (2000), a leading advocate of corporate globalization, who famously observed that no countries with a McDonald's fast-food franchise have gone to war with each other.

On the other hand, a radical critique suggests that, to the contrary, the very logic of the existing world order, characterized by growing inequality, massive refugee flows, collapsing states, and environmental depletion, embodies structural violence (Held and McGrew 2002). Such a system sows the seeds of civil breakdown, insurgent terrorism, and escalating imperial military intervention. In this view, the demilitarization and humanization of culture and the sweeping democratization of social, economic, and political systems would be preconditions of peaceful human governance.

At the risk of caricaturing them, neither position leaves much room for independent agency by journalists within media institutions or by media institutions within the broader social order.

7. *Do grand narratives of democratization, even progressive ones, too often bypass or marginalize the question of hierarchies of race and gender?* While much of the media and globalization literature focuses on the flow of Western, and particularly American, media to the rest of the world, Protzel (chapter 5) calls attention to the significant Latino commercial media in the United States as a challenging reality of globalization. Among other things, this reminds us of the need to pay attention to the implications of the growing importance of ethnic media for citizenship formation within immigrant nations such as the United States and Canada. Sreberny (chapter 12) argues for the need to make gender equality an integral part of the "meaningful democratization" of communications technology and institutions, as well as of social relations generally. Her intervention reminds us that still, too often, analysts pay insufficient heed to the differential impact of globalization processes on men and women, as well as whites and nonwhites. It also forcefully points to the importance of democratization from below, the building of popular networks and nodes of activism outside, and sometimes against, formal political institutions. While we suspect that this book has been more successful in relation to the latter concern, we hope it is a contribution to both.

BOOK ORGANIZATION

The book's chapters are presented in three sections. Part I offers analysis and evaluations of significant aspects of the processes of media globalization in the world's two most populous countries—China and India—and three major regions—Eastern and Central Europe, Africa, and Latin America. While their normative and political standpoints are hardly uniform, the authors' analyses are oriented toward the implications of processes of globalization for media and democratization in their particular regions and countries.

While topically more wide-ranging, Part II concerns conflict and issues of governance that are more politicized on a global level. There are multiple examples of processes and sites of interaction between media, civil society, and state: the role of media in transitions from authoritarian to liberal-democratic rule (with particular examples from Al-Jazeera, the Zapatista rebellion in Mexico, and Palestine), the dilemmas of democracy and collective identity in Israel, the role of transnational media in the 2003 invasion of Iraq, and the emergence of suprastate instruments for regulating (and marketizing) media policies and structures.

The placement of Shinar's chapter on Israeli media and collective identity in this section deserves a word of explanation. While each country and region is now an integral part of the global system, the case of Israel is especially illustrative of some of the national/global and political/cultural processes and dimensions this book aims to address. It is at the heart of a long-standing conflict with global implications, from the era of the cold war to the current supposed "clash of civilizations." It is a place where the nation-state framework is still very much contested, most obviously by Palestinians, foregrounding the relationship between the nation-state, democracy, and media systems. Moreover, the connections between the nation-state and the diaspora, an increasingly important postmodern condition, are especially deep-rooted, and liberal notions of citizenship are still inextricably intertwined with long-standing cultural identities, including those of religion—a situation that still constitutes a core problem of democracy. To the West, the best-known example is Iran's Islamic theocracy, but one should not ignore the manifestation of politicized religion in the West itself, particularly in the United States. The liberal principle of the separation of church and state has never been absolute; nor should it be taken for granted.

Finally, Part III considers emerging civil society practices and movements that aim in various ways to democratize public communication globally—an emerging media-reform movement against the perceived democratic deficit of corporate media in the U.S. heartland of globalization, transnational networks for women's communication, the reform of journalistic practices in the direction of "peace journalism," and a nascent transnational civil society campaign to challenge market-oriented, suprastate institutions that are constituting a new regime of global media governance.

REFERENCES

Ali, Tariq. 2003. *The Clash of Fundamentalisms: Crusades, Jihads and Modernity*. London: Verso.

Angus, Ian. 2001. *Emergent Publics: An Essay on Social Movements and Democracy*. Winnipeg: Arbeiter Ring.

Appadurai, Arjun. 1990. *Modernity at Large: Cultural Dimensions of Globalization*. Minneapolis: University of Minnesota Press.

———. 1996. *Modernity at Large: Cultural Dimensions of Globalization*. Minneapolis: University of Minnesota Press.

Aronowitz, Stanley, and Peter Bratsis, eds. 2002. *Paradigm Lost: State Theory Reconsidered*. Minneapolis: University of Minnesota Press.

Baker, C. Edwin. 2002. *Media, Markets and Democracy*. Cambridge: Cambridge University Press.

Bello, W. 2002. *Deglobalization: Ideas for a New World Economy*. Black Point, NS: Fernwood.

Blumler, Jay G., and Michael Gurevitch. 1995. *The Crisis of Public Communication*. London: Routledge.

Brecher, Jeremy, Tim Costello, and Brendan Smith. 2000. *Globalization from Below: The Power of Solidarity*. Cambridge, MA: South End Press.

Carroll, William K., and Robert A. Hackett. 2004. "Democratic Media Activism through the Lens of Social Movement Theory." Paper presented to International Association for Media and Communication Research (July), Porto Alegre, Brazil.

Chua, Amy. 2004. *World on Fire: How Exporting Free Market Democracy Breeds Ethnic Hatred and Global Instability*. New York: Anchor Books.

Couldry, Nick, and James Curran. 2003. *Contesting Media Power: Alternative Media in a Networked World*. Lanham, MD: Rowman & Littlefield.

Curran, James. 1996. "Mass Media and Democracy Revisited." In *Mass Media and Society*, eds. J. Curran and M. Gurevitch, 3rd ed., 81–119. London: Edward Arnold.

Curran, James, and Colin Leys. 2000. "Media and the Decline of Liberal Corporatism in Britain." In *De-Westernizing Media Studies*, eds. J. Curran and M. Park, 221–36. London: Routledge.

Dahlgren, Peter. 1995. *Television and the Public Sphere: Citizenship, Democracy and the Media*. London: Sage.

Dale, Stephen. 1996. *McLuhan's Children: The Greenpeace Message and the Media*. Toronto: Between the Lines.

Downing, John. 1996. *Internationalizing Media Theory: Transition, Power, Culture: Reflections on Media in Russia, Poland and Hungary, 1980–95*. Thousand Oaks, CA: Sage.

Downing, John D. H., with Tamara Villareal Ford, Geneve Gil, and Laura Stein. 2001. *Radical Media: Rebellious Communication and Social Movements*. Thousand Oaks, CA: Sage.

Dyer-Witheford, Nick. 1999. *Cyber-Marx: Cycles and Circuits of Struggle in High-Technology Capitalism*. Urbana: University of Illinois Press.

Friedman, Thomas L. 2000. *The Lexus and the Olive Tree*. New York: Anchor Books.

Giddens, Anthony. 1990. *The Consequences of Modernity*. Cambridge: Polity Press.

Gitlin, Todd. 1980. *The Whole World Is Watching: Mass Media in the Making and Unmaking of the New Left*. Berkeley: University of California Press.

Hackett, Robert A. 1991. *News and Dissent: The Press and the Politics of Peace in Canada*. Norwood, NJ: Ablex.

———. 2000. "Taking Back the Media: Notes on the Potential for a Communicative Democracy Movement." *Studies in Political Economy* 63: 61–86. Also at www.sfu .ca/~hackett.

———. Forthcoming. "Is There a Democratic Deficit in Anglo-American Journalism?" In *Journalism: Critical Issues*, ed. Stuart Allan. Maidenhead, UK: Open University.

Hackett, Robert A., and Yuezhi Zhao. 1998. *Sustaining Democracy? Journalism and the Politics of Objectivity*. Toronto: Garamond.

Hallin, Daniel C. 2000a. "Commercialism and Professionalism in the American News Media." In *Mass Media and Society*, eds. J. Curran and M. Gurevitch, 3rd ed., 218–37. London: Arnold.

———. 2000b. "Media, Political Power, and Democratization in Mexico." In *De-Westernizing Media Studies*, eds. J. Curran and M. Park, 97–110. London: Routledge.

Hamelink, Cees J. 1995. "The Democratic Ideal and Its Enemies." In *The Democratization of Communication*, ed. P. Lee, 15–37. Cardiff: University of Wales Press.

Hardt, Michael, and Antonio Negri. 2000. *Empire*. Cambridge, MA: Harvard University Press.

Held, David, and Anthony McGrew. 2002. *Globalization/Anti-Globalization*. Cambridge: Polity Press.

Held, David, Anthony McGrew, David Goldblatt, and Jonathan Perraton. 1999. *Global Transformations: Politics, Economics and Culture*. Cambridge: Polity Press.

Herman, Edward, and Robert W. McChesney. 1997. *The Global Media: The New Missionaries of Corporate Capitalism*. London: Cassell.

Hill, Jill. 1998. "US Rules OK? Telecommunications since the 1940s." In *Capitalism and the Information Age: The Political Economy of the Global Communication Revolution*, eds. R. McChesney, E. M. Wood, and J. B. Foster, 99–121. New York: Monthly Review Press.

Huntington, Samuel P. 1996. *Clash of Civilizations and the Remaking of World Order*. New York: Simon & Schuster.

Iwabuchi, Koichi. 2002. *Recentering Globalization: Popular Culture and Japanese Transnationalism*. Durham, NC: Duke University Press.

Klein, Naomi. 2003. "Once Strip-mined, Twice Shy." *The Globe and Mail*, September 29, 2003, A11.

MacBride, Sean, and Colleen Roach. 1993. "The New International Information Order." In *The Global Media Debate: Its Rise, Fall, and Renewal*, eds. G. Gerbner, H. Mowlana, and K. Nordenstreng, 3–11. Norwood, NJ: Ablex.

Macpherson, C. B. 1965. *The Real World of Democracy*. Toronto: Canadian Broadcasting Corporation.

———. 1977. *The Life and Times of Liberal Democracy*. Oxford: Oxford University Press.

Mattelart, Armand. 2000. *Networking the World, 1794–2000*, trans. Liz Carey-Libbrecht and James A. Cohen. Minneapolis: University of Minnesota Press.

Maxwell, Richard. 2003. *Herbert Schiller*. Lanham, MD: Rowman & Littlefield.

Mazepa, Patricia A. 2003. *Battles on the Cultural Front: The (De)Labouring of Culture in Canada 1914–1944*. PhD diss., Carleton University.

McChesney, Robert W. 1999. *Rich Media, Poor Democracy: Communication Politics in Dubious Times*. Urbana: University of Illinois Press.

McNair, Brian. 2000. "Journalism and Democracy: A Millennial Audit." *Journalism Studies* 1, no. 2: 197–211.

Melucci, Alberto. 1980. "The New Social Movements: A Theoretical Approach." *Social Science Information* 19: 199–226.

Mitchell, Katharyne. 2001. "Transnationalism, Neo-liberalism, and the Rise of the Shadow State." *Economy and Society* 30, no. 2: 165–89.

Mosco, Vincent. 1996. *The Political Economy of Communication*. London: Sage.

Nordenstreng, Kaarle. 1999. "The Context: Great Media Debate." In *Towards Equity in Global Communication: MacBride Update*, eds. R. C. Vincent, K. Nordenstreng, and M. Traber, 235–68. Cresskill, NJ: Hampton Press.

Norris, Pippa. 2000. *A Virtuous Circle: Political Communications in Postindustrial Societies*. Cambridge: Cambridge University Press.

Ó Siochrú, Sean, and W. Bruce Girard, with Amy Mahan. 2002. *Global Media Governance: A Beginner's Guide*. Lanham, MD: Rowman & Littlefield.

Paxman, Andrew, and Alex M. Saragoza. 2002. "Globalization and Latin Media Powers: The Case of Mexico's Televisa." In *Continental Order? Integrating North America for Cybercapitalism*, eds. V. Mosco and D. Schiller, 64–85. Lanham, MD: Rowman & Littlefield.

Perry, Elizabeth J. 2002. "From Paris to the Paris of the East—And Back: Workers as Citizens in Modern Shanghai." In *Changing Meanings of Citizenship in Modern China*, eds. M. Goldman and E. J. Perry, 133–56, Cambridge, MA: Harvard University Press.

Petras, James, and Henry Veltmeyer. 2001. *Globalization Unmasked: Imperialism in the 21st Century*. London: Zed Books.

Preston, William, Jr., Edward S. Herman, and Herbert I. Schiller. 1989. *Hope and Folly: The United States and Unesco, 1945–1985*. Minneapolis: University of Minnesota Press.

Price, Monroe E., Beata Rozumilowicz, and Stefaan G. Verhulst. 2002. *Media Reform: Democratizing the Media, Democratizing the State*. London: Routledge.

Schiller, Dan. 2000. *Digital Capitalism*. Cambridge, MA: MIT Press.

Schiller, Dan, and Vincent Mosco. 2002. "Introduction: Integrating a Continent for a Transnational World." In *Continental Order? Integrating North America for Cybercapitalism*, eds. V. Mosco and D. Schiller, 1–34. Lanham, MD: Rowman & Littlefield.

Schiller, Herbert I. 1977. *Communication and Cultural Domination*. New York: M. E. Sharpe, 1977.

———. 1989. *Culture Inc: The Corporate Takeover of Public Expression*. New York: Oxford University Press.

———. 1991. "Not Yet the Post-Imperialist Era." *Critical Studies in Mass Communication* 8: 13–28.

———. 1993. "Transnational Media: Creating Consumers Worldwide." *Journal of International Affairs* 47, no. 1: 48–58.

Schlesinger, Philip. 1999. "Changing Spaces of Political Communication: The Case of the European Union." *Political Communication* 16, no. 3: 263–79.

———. 2001. "Tensions in the Construction of European Media Policies." In *Media and Globalization: Why the State Matters*, eds. N. Morris and S. Waisbord, 95–115. Lanham, MD: Rowman & Littlefield.

Schudson, Michael. 1994. "The 'Public Sphere' and Its Problems: Bringing the State (Back) In." *Notre Dame Journal of Law, Ethics, and Public Policy* 8, no. 2: 529–46.

Schumpeter, Joseph. 1942. *Capitalism, Socialism and Democracy*. New York: Harper & Row, 1976.

Sinclair, John. 1992. "The De-centering of Cultural Imperialism: Televisa-tion and Globo-ization in the Latin World." In *Continental Shift: Globalization and Culture*, ed. E. Jacka, 99-116. Double Bay, New South Wales: Local Consumption Publications.

Sinclair, John, Elizabeth Jacka, and Stuart Cunningham, eds. 1996. *New Patterns in Global Television: Peripheral Vision*. Oxford: Oxford University Press.

Sklair, Leslie. 2001. *The Transnational Capitalist Class*. Malden, MA: Blackwell.

Sparks, Colin. 1998. "Is There a Global Public Sphere?" In *Electronic Empires: Global Media and Local Resistance*, ed. D. K. Thussu, 108–24. London: Arnold.

Sreberny, Annabelle. 2000. "The Global and the Local in International Communications." In *Mass Media and Society*, eds. J. Curran and M. Gurevitch, 3rd ed., 93–119. London: Arnold.

Sussman, Gerald. 2002. "Telecommunications After NAFTA: Mexico's Integration Strategy." In *Continental Order? Integrating North America for Cybercapitalism*, eds. V. Mosco and D. Schiller, 136–62. Lanham, MD: Rowman & Littlefield.

Thussu, Daya Kishan. 2000. *International Communication: Continuity and Change*. London: Arnold.

Turow, Joseph. 1997. *Breaking Up America: Advertising and the New Media World*. Chicago: University of Chicago Press.

Valle, Carlos A. 1995. "Communication: International Debate and Community-Based Initiatives." In *The Democratization of Communication*, ed. P. Lee, 197–216. Cardiff: University of Wales Press.

Vincent, Richard, Kaarle Nordenstreng, and Michael Traber, eds. 1999. *Towards Equity in Global Communication: MacBride Update*. Cresskill, NJ: Hampton Press.

Waisbord, Silvio, and Nancy Morris. 2001. "Introduction: Rethinking Media Globalization and State Power." In *Media and Globalization: Why the State Matters*, eds. N. Morris and S. Waisbord, vii–xvi. Lanham, MD: Rowman & Littlefield.

White, Robert A. 1988. "NIWCO Has Become a People's Movement." *Media Development* 34, no. 1: 20–25.

Zhao, Yuezhi. 1998. *Media, Market, and Democracy in China: Between the Party Line and the Bottom Line*. Urbana: University of Illinois Press.

———. 2001. "Media and Elusive Democracy in China." *The Public/Javnost* 8, no. 2: 21–44.

———. 2003. "Transnational Capital, the Chinese State, and China's Communication Industries in a Fractured Society." *The Public/Javnost* 10, no. 4: 53–73.

———. 2004. "Between a World Summit and a Chinese Movie: Visions of Information Society." *Gazette* 66, nos. 3–4: 275–80.

Zhao, Yuezhi, and Dan Schiller. 2001. "Dances with Wolves: China's Integration with Digital Capitalism." *Info* 3, no. 2: 137–51.

I

MEDIA GLOBALIZATION AND
DEMOCRATIC DEFICITS:
NATIONAL AND
REGIONAL AUDITS

2

Civil Society as Contested Concept: Media and Political Transformation in Eastern and Central Europe

Colin Sparks

In 1989, the tyrannies that had crushed the peoples of Central and Eastern Europe were swept away on a wave of discontent.[1] In country after country, crowds poured into the streets waving banners and shouting slogans that would have guaranteed an unpleasant interview with the secret police just days before. In turn, the secret policemen who had reveled in their role as the instruments of tyranny were filled with apprehension: after all, some of them, in Hungary at least, could remember 1956 and what a genuine popular rising had done with jailors and torturers. It was one of those glorious moments in history when the world was turned upside down, and it seemed possible to remake everything in a new mold better suited to fulfill human aspirations.

High on the list of institutions to be remade were the mass media. For half a century, the press, radio, television, and cinema had been under the minute control of the Communist Party. Censorship was the least of the problems. No open publication could appear that was not authorized by the Communist Party. Except in periods of mass popular discontent, like 1981 in Poland, producing oppositional publications was a secretive and dangerous business. In the worst periods, even listening to foreign broadcasts was risky. No editor or director of the official media could be appointed who was not authorized by the appropriate committee of the Communist Party. For the most important posts in the press and broadcasting, the people with responsible positions were actually very often members of the Central Committee of the party.

A condition for a glittering career as a journalist was to be a loyal member of the party. The system even crushed and perverted the enthusiasm of those who believed its claim to represent the interests of the workers and peasants.

A very distinguished media scholar from one of the least repressive Communist countries tells the story of how he decided against a journalistic career. As a naive young Communist, he investigated and wrote a story about how some local party bosses were exploiting their position for personal gain, in open breach of the law, not to mention the official ideology of the party they claimed to lead. To his astonishment, he was summoned before the party committee, not to be congratulated on exposing corruption, but to be told to stop causing trouble. At that point, he realized, journalism was not for him. That story could be repeated a thousand times in every Communist country. The people who knuckled down and learned to obey the rules produced nothing that contradicted the party line.

But, if in 1989 everybody agreed on the need to change the mass media from mouthpieces of the party leaders into the organs of free information and democratic debate, there was far less agreement on what should be done. It was clear to absolutely everyone that the main reason for the problems of the Communist epoch was that the state had controlled all areas of social life, including the mass media. The road to freedom seemed clear and obvious: roll back the state and allow other institutions to take its place.

Throughout the region, the slogan that everyone used was that the way to free the population from the dead hand of the state was to "empower civil society." A lively and vibrant civil society would act as the guarantor of freedom in general, and of free media in particular. Unfortunately, like many slogans, the concept of civil society was, and is, deeply ambiguous. Agreeing on the slogan was not the same thing at all as agreeing on what to do. To add to the confusion, there were plenty of Western academics and consultants who had ideas about what should and should not be done to the media.

The sudden and apparently total collapse of the old ruling group and its political apparatus, a widespread desire for radical change, and a plethora of schemes for change made the 1990s in Central and Eastern Europe a valuable laboratory in which the merits of different ideas were tested in practical situations. This chapter is concerned with explaining what the different perspectives on change were and how they influenced the outcomes for the media in Central and Eastern Europe. The various meanings of the concept of "civil society" are first examined. Some of the leading issues in media freedom are then explored, and their outcomes are considered from the point of view of democratic media.

WHAT IS CIVIL SOCIETY?

The concept of civil society has a currency very much wider than Central and Eastern Europe, but there is seldom any agreement anywhere as to its precise meaning. The concept has its origins in the eighteenth century and came to its clearest expression in the work of German philosopher Georg Wilhelm Friedrich Hegel ([1820] 1967). He meant by it a realm devoted to the pursuit of private interest, in contrast to the family (the realm of immediate private affection) and the state (the realm of universal interest). This "classical" interpretation of civil society saw it as more or less identical with nascent capitalism, and it was this sense that Karl Marx adopted. The concept then entered the intellectual netherworld, surfacing notably in Antonio Gramsci, where the meaning is not entirely clear. In his best-known formulations—for example, "state = political society + civil society"—he seems to mean that civil society is the sum of all organizations other than those integrated into the state machine (Gramsci 1971, 263). In its more contemporary manifestation, however, the concept is usually traced to the leading Polish oppositionist Adam Michnik. Writing in the mid-1970s, he proposed a political strategy based on building a network of institutions—voluntary schools, publishing houses, social organizations, and so on—independently of the decaying Communist state (Michnik 1985).

Michnik's ideas were taken up in two different ways. The first was largely practical. In 1981, working-class discontent in Poland flared up into a mass strike movement that gave birth to Solidarity and drew in millions from all sectors of society. In the radicalization caused by the constant social action and the intense debates, the idea of civil society came to mean something much more extreme than Michnik and other intellectuals had intended (Pelczynski 1988, 376). The proposal put forward by Solidarity for the mass media was very radical:

> Solidarity demands the abolition of the state administration's monopoly in running radio and television because it is contrary to the constitution of the Polish People's Republic. . . . Solidarity will take action to institute genuine public control over radio and television by appointing a managing and executive body representing government, political parties, trade unions, religious associations, social organizations, professional artists' unions, and self-management groups of the employees who produce and beam the programs. (Goban-Klas 1994, 176)

The intention in broadcasting was the same as in many other areas of social life. In order to democratize the media radically, organizations that could directly claim to represent the people were to be given a real stake in power. The exclusive monopoly of public information and debate held by the state was to be destroyed by giving the decisive say to the citizens and to the people who worked in the media. In the light of what later transpired, it is notable that there is no mention whatsoever of entrepreneurs or the market as vehicles to achieve freedom and democracy. This we may call the "radical" version of civil society.

Solidarity, however, was defeated, and Poland sank into the nightmare of martial law. The opposition was driven underground, and in the new conditions, the meanings of concepts changed and evolved. The majority of the leaders of the opposition in Eastern Europe, and in particular those who had led Solidarity, drew from the experience a deep distrust of popular mobilization. When, in the mid-1980s, the evidence of crisis was so pervasive that the more intelligent representatives of the Communist regime extended an invitation to the opposition, the dominant response in Poland and Hungary was to enter negotiations with their erstwhile oppressors. By the time they entered these negotiations, one commentator noted that "for the Polish opposition [civil society] meant that the struggle for civil society had to take the form of a struggle for bourgeois society" (Ost 1989, 78). Under the horrified gaze of the Western Left, men and women who had led mass strikes, established workers' councils, defied the full might of the Stalinist state, and endured prison and exile in defense of their principles were now proudly proclaiming the need urgently to construct private capitalism (Meiskens Wood 1990). We may call this the "classical" view of civil society since it corresponds more or less exactly with the formulations of Hegel and others in identifying civil society with the market and the pursuit of private interest.

This interpretation of civil society as capitalism was not the only view available. There were, particularly in the West, intellectuals who wished to use the concept as an alternative both to state socialism and the free market. For example, two influential political theorists wrote that the concept of civil society means "a sphere between economy and state" (Cohen and Arato 1992, ix). This view of civil society as essentially the product of voluntary associations like the family and social movements, as opposed to political and economic power, can be seen as an attempt to root an alternative mechanism of social organization firmly in the life world, in opposition to the failure of projects based on economics or political action. What this meant was charmingly exemplified by a leading Czechoslovak dissident, who wrote that civil society meant "writing books, publishing periodicals, putting on plays, holding seminars, exhibitions, concerts, etc." (Dienstbier in Benda et al. 1988, 231). Perhaps unconsciously, this concept of civil society, which we may term the "naive" variant, locates itself squarely in the defining characteristics of the intellectuals. It is a strategy a world away from the strikes and mass meetings that had given the concept its popular currency among the Polish opposition.

The shift in the meaning and social context of the concept of civil society had implications for the kinds of policies proposed for the mass media. The original content of the concept had led, as we saw above, to extremely radical proposals. In this view, the old control of the media "from above" was to be replaced by a new control "from below": the population would cease to be the passive objects of the mass media and become the directors and controllers of public communication. The majority of the opposition abandoned this radical perspective.

For those who now held to the classical interpretation of civil society as equivalent to private capitalism, the strategy was clear: state media needed to be turned into private media as quickly as possible. Private ownership of the press and television would be an important element of civil society and would in turn guarantee democracy.

The followers of the naive interpretation faced a real problem. Both they and their Western cothinkers could see the shortcomings of the state and the market as bases for democratic media, but they were keen to distance themselves from the more radical views that some of them had held in the past (Keane 1991). As one of the most brilliant and influential commentators on the media in the region, Karol Jakubowicz wrote in 1989 that the old aim was to establish control of the media through the institution of what might be termed "direct democracy." That concept might have been valid for periods of heightened tension and social awareness, but in "normal times" most people were not concerned enough about the direction of the media to wish to play any role in their day-to-day control. The solution was to establish what might be termed "representative democracy." Instead of the people themselves being empowered to control the media, there would be mechanisms that allowed a range of different opinions to be put forward, in proportion to the size and influence of the social groups that held such views. This would ensure both a plurality of voices and an opportunity for democratic exchanges:

> Under ordinary circumstances most people would seem to be content to accept representative communicative democracy in the sphere of mass communication, as long as it is a diversified system corresponding to the differentiation of society, including broad participation in the formulation of communication policies, in the organization and management of the media and direct accountability of the media to society and the groups they represent. In representative democracy, decision-making processes should take place in conditions of equality, autonomy and adequate representation. If these conditions are met in the way media are organized and run, and in social communication itself, then representative communicative democracy has a chance of satisfying most of the expectations of a democratic-minded society (Jakubowicz 1993, 44–45).[2]

This model of democratic communication was clearly quite a long way from the views articulated at the high point of Solidarity and was indeed intended as a specific critique of them. Clearly, also, the concept is some distance from the simple identification of civil society with private capitalism that motivated the majority of oppositionists in the region. The proponents of this naive version of the theory of civil society looked to these kinds of institutional changes as the way to establish free and democratic media.

THE MISSIONARIES

Almost as soon as the Communist ministers had cleared their desks to make way for the new order, the issue of what to do about the mass media became a central political problem. As we shall see below, the question of the printed press was settled very quickly, but broadcasting posed much greater problems. An intense debate, which lasted several years, took place over what kind of broadcasting system should replace the old Communist mono-lith. The various currents of opinion about the nature of civil society, whose representatives were now the leaders of political parties, members of parlia-ment, and ministers, naturally had views about what should be done, as did many others. The most opinionated of these came across the newly disman-tled iron curtain from the victorious West. They brought with them a detailed knowledge of how Western media systems worked, of their strengths and weaknesses, and of the different ways in which they related to political de-mocracy. Unfortunately, they also brought with them normative positions that led them to place an emphasis upon different aspects of the Western me-dia. Since these groups all came with the prestige of representing the tri-umphant social system, and they entered a culture in which intellectuals are accorded far more respect than is common in the Anglo-Saxon world, they all found a hearing, even when what they had to say was totally inappropri-ate to the circumstances.

The least important and influential group comprised the critical scholars, who brought to the debate a thoroughgoing and entirely accurate account of the shortcomings of the Western media. Since much of what they had to say about the tendency toward monopoly and the consequences of the com-mercialization of public speech was so incontrovertible, few were prepared to argue seriously against it. It is so obviously and manifestly the case that the famed "impartiality" and "objectivity" and "balance" to which the BBC and the *New York Times* lay claim are valid only within the very narrow limits of official politics; the domination of public life and culture by the personnel, tastes, and discourses of the elites is so overwhelming that it is difficult in good faith the claim the opposite. Rather than a direct challenge, responses to the Western critical scholars took two forms. Those who were already per-suaded of the advantages of capitalist media simply smiled politely and ig-nored what was being said. Those who were ready to hear what the critical scholars had to say also smiled politely, but then asked, "So what should we do?" For complex reasons, most of the critical scholars did not have a very convincing answer to this question. Some stressed the need for radical mea-sures, but these were dismissed as irrelevant to current practice (Downing 1996). Others, perhaps formed in the dominant tradition of Western leftism, which had long been less than sufficiently critical of the Stalinist regimes, found that they had little positive to say. Most found themselves proposing various measures designed to moderate the influence of the free market upon the media.

In this, they found themselves allied with what turned out to be the most influential group of all: the representatives of the Council of Europe, the European Union, the European Broadcasting Union, and the various public broadcasters of Western Europe. These people, too, were concerned about limiting the influence of the market, at least upon broadcasting. Very far from wanting to let loose private capitalism in the media, the consensual view of the official representatives of Western broadcasting was to ensure the establishment of public service in television and, when private broadcasting was permitted, to ensure that it was adequately regulated in order to oblige it to discharge public functions.

The third group was made up of the representatives of various U.S. governmental agencies, foundations, and universities. While these tended to be ideologically committed to the free market as understood in the United States, in practice they were most concerned about the nature of journalistic practices. From fairly early on, it was clear that broadcasting was not to be handed over to the free market, but the kind of reporting that took place there and in the newspaper press was another matter. The main emphasis of these experts was on the provision of training programs aimed at producing a new type of journalist in the region: one who separated fact from opinion, was obsessed with accuracy, and religiously ensured that a range of opinion was quoted with proper attribution.[3]

THE TEST OF PRACTICE

The outcome of the vigorous debates between these different currents of opinion was not resolved by reason and evidence. On the contrary, the developing social situation was at least as important as the merits of argument in deciding the outcome.

The central reality of the transition in Central Europe was that it was marked by what have been called "negotiated revolutions." Despite the fact that the historical tradition in the region had been one of mass opposition to communism (Berlin 1953, Hungary and Poland 1956, Czechoslovakia 1968–1969, Poland 1981, to name only the most dramatic of events), the fall of the regimes was markedly peaceful. In Poland and Hungary, there were negotiations between reform Communists and the more moderate wing of the opposition that led to free elections and a change in political power. In what was then Czechoslovakia and East Germany, there were no reform Communists to negotiate with, and there was a degree of popular mobilization before the regimes collapsed. In what was then Yugoslavia, sections of the bureaucracy mobilized national discontents in the constituent republics and used that to legitimize their continued rule. In Romania, there was what looked like a full-blooded revolution, with shooting, tanks in the streets, and the summary execution of the fallen dictator, but in reality, a section of the old bureaucracy used popular discontent to oust Nicolae Andruta Ceaucescu and his close associates and to place themselves at the head of the new democratic republic.

In all of these cases, there was a striking degree of social continuity. Some of the individuals most closely associated with the old regime vanished from public view, but the structures continued with surprisingly little disturbance. What did change, and it changed fundamentally, was the political order. The old system of complete Communist Party domination over politics was swept away, and there was everywhere intense competition between different political parties. The balance of power between different political forces was, normally, settled by more or less democratic elections. In short: while there was a considerable degree of social continuity, there was a complete political revolution.

The outcomes for the media were different for the press and broadcasting. In the printed press, there were two different developments. The journalists of the existing party press quickly seized control of their titles, often without any clear legal justification. This process was memorably described in the Czech case as "a period of spontaneous transformation with regards to patterns of ownership occurring within a void in respect to legal regulation" (Giorgi and Pohoryles 1994, 154). Very often, these journalists established relations with foreign media corporations, most notably in the case of the local newspapers that been run by the Communist Party in Hungary, where the titles were sold off to the German group Springer, while the journalists of the semiofficial paper *Magyar Hírlap* made the mistake of making a deal with Robert Maxwell (Jakab and Gálik 1991, 21–28). These transformed papers were immediately joined by hundreds of titles, some of which had enjoyed a previous underground existence, while others were entirely new ventures, mostly reflecting the extremely diverse political situation. Some of the former "alternative press," like *Gazeta Wyborcza* in Poland, went from being illegal underground publications to big-selling daily papers. In due course, a number of Western media corporations, usually second tier in scale, established new titles whose main purpose was commercial, rather than political, and introduced journalistic techniques like tabloidization to the region; some of the foreign investors in the existing national press withdrew (Gulyás 1999).

Television was less easily changed. While some Western companies made bids for the former state broadcasters, none of them were accepted, and in all of the countries, a mixed system was established. There remained a state-owned broadcaster, and later commercial systems were licensed. In all cases, the legal framework stated that the state broadcasters accorded with European norms in that they were supposed to be "public service" broadcasters, modeled variously on the BBC, ARD, and other Western examples. In practice, control of these broadcasters was vested in the political elite through broadcasting councils appointed by the self-same political elite. As a result, broadcasting remained highly politicized, with purges of senior officials following regularly on changes in government; substantial political arguments over who should sit on powerful committees have continued into the new century (Minárik 2003).

When the legal basis for private broadcasting was eventually established, many commentators who had become disillusioned with attempts to establish public service broadcasting hoped that this development would lead to politically impartial news and commentary, since it was believed that audience maximization would lead automatically to neutrality. In the event, the granting of broadcasting licenses turned out to be a highly political activity. The most successful broadcaster in the region, the U.S.-owned Central European Media Enterprises (CME), established a model of how to get a license. The initial version involved capital and expertise from the United States allying with local businessmen and former dissidents in order to get a license, then broadcasting largely imported programming (Sparks 1999). This model worked in country after country, and the stations established to exploit the licenses attracted large audiences. TV Nova in the Czech Republic was the first and most successful of these operations, quickly winning 70 percent of the total audience and taking the lion's share of the available advertising revenue away from the state broadcaster.

Far from being confined to the initial period of licensing, the politicization of private television proved to be an endemic feature of the new systems. Nova found itself in continual conflict with the broadcasting authority over issues like illegal advertising, for example of tobacco, but was able to establish sufficient political influence to defy the law, more or less with impunity. This influence was to prove crucial in the conflict within the station that developed in 1999 and continues unabated up to the time of this writing. Private broadcasting followed the Italian model of partisan engagement rather than the U.S. model of impartiality between the established major parties.

As might be imagined from the nature of the media system, the kind of journalism that has evolved has proved to be very partisan in character, which is itself another mark of continuity. Despite the countless training projects, courses, scholarships, and seminars, the practices of Western journalism do not appear to have taken root in the region. Journalists are regularly accused of taking bribes from interested parties, of being subject to pressure from advertisers, of sensationalizing events, of being in the pockets of particular political groupings, and of pursuing private vendettas. In the bitter ethnic conflicts that have marked some of the post-Communist countries, journalists have often been accused of stirring up hatred by their biased and inflammatory reporting. Of course, the journalists would challenge all or some of these charges, but there is no doubt that the majority of reporting and commentary has been much more in the engaged "European" tradition than the preferred objective "Anglo-Saxon" model.

THEORETICAL IMPLICATIONS

There were three clearly distinct interpretations of the meaning of "civil society" at the start of the process of transformation, and the outcomes provide a measure of their efficacy. We may use the evidence of the real historical development to judge the value of the different interpretations as guides to social action.

The radical interpretation, which stressed the direct participation of the mass of the population in the control of the mass media, clearly did not provide a very useful guide to developments. This is hardly surprising given that it was the aim of most of the parties involved in the negotiated revolutions to prevent the emergence of the kind of unruly, unbounded popular movement that had given rise to the radical interpretation and which alone could transform it from an attractive democratic slogan into a concrete program of social action. Nowhere was the rule of the people established in the mass media. Control of the newspaper press fell, variously, to senior journalists or domestic and foreign businesses. There were no attempts to develop forms of ownership in which the readers had the ultimate control of the press. There were no attempts to ensure that weaker titles serving less commercially attractive sectors of the population were supported. There were no mechanisms even for involving readers in the overall content and direction of the newspaper press. Control of broadcasting fell, variously, to the political elite or to commercial enterprises. There were no mechanisms established for giving ordinary people any substantial say in the ways that broadcasters behave. In both the press and broadcasting, the market has been the controlling principle, and a professional hierarchy has been the main organizational form.

The middle position, termed the naive version of civil society above, which saw it as best served by the representation of different social groups in the media, fared hardly any better. None of the press systems that have emerged has made any gestures toward incorporating the interests of voluntary organizations. They are, it is true, now free to establish their own publications at will, and this is an extremely important step forward compared to the old regime, but without guaranteed access to the main media in society, other than through the purchase of advertising space, or any form of support for their own productions, the more poorly funded of these groups face the prospect of marginalization.

In broadcasting, the story was much more complex. Many of the experts who drafted the new broadcasting legislation were themselves persuaded of the value of representative institutions. They looked to the German system of the proportional representation of political and civil groups as being a possible mechanism for establishing at least a measure of institutional participation for their idea of civil society. Given that they occupied a privileged position of technical expertise and that without their active participation, no new broadcasting bills could be adequately formulated, they at least had the opportunity to put forward their ideas. In general, they were extremely unsuccessful in gaining acceptance for plans to institutionalize the organs of civil society. In Poland, where the idea had first come to contemporary prominence, the first draft of a new broadcasting bill proposed that one of the members of the broadcasting council should be a representative of the employees of the main state broadcaster, but even this token representation disappeared from the later bills. The version that finally passed into law made all of the seats on the broadcasting council dependent upon official political actors. Great care was taken to achieve balance, but a balance between the president and the upper and the lower houses of parliament. Elsewhere, there were more determined efforts to put theory into practice, notably in Hungary. The early drafts of the broadcasting bill did indeed explicitly propose that the dominant force on the broadcasting council should lie with groups that would unquestionably be regarded by everyone as representative of civil society: at least half of the membership had to come from groups like science, education, ethnic minorities, women, youth, sports, environmentalists, and religious bodies. This version could not command majority support, and subsequent drafts progressively eroded the position of civil society. In the end, the version that passed gave effective power over the regulation of broadcasting to representatives of the political parties in parliament.

The overall outcomes were everywhere the same: despite the early attempts by experts to give power to organizations held to represent civil society, the eventual result was that power lay with the major political forces in parliament and the presidential palace. It was not civil society but the political elite that was empowered in the reorganization of broadcasting.[4]

The account of the meaning of civil society that came closest to an accurate description of the nature of the transition was the classical one that held it to be identical with private capitalism. In the press, this version has been unmistakably triumphant. The press is overwhelming privately owned and run as a business. Just like in the West, although in a rather less-developed fashion, newspapers and magazines are dependent upon advertising revenues and, therefore, either seek to attract wealthier readers and the advertisers who wish to address them or attempt to reach the widest possible audience in order to win mass advertising. They try, so far as they are able, to tailor their content to particular market segments and to develop those kinds of journalism that will produce the kind of audience they are interested in selling to the advertisers. The clearest example of this is the development of a tabloid press market, which "offered a new type of newspaper content with international and domestic 'gossip,' celebrity news, fashion news, and human interest stories from both Hungary and from different parts of the world" (Gulyás 2000, 121). This is a new kind of journalism for Hungary, as for many of the former Communist countries, although of course it is very well established in the West. This is a kind of journalism that is produced directly by competition in the market. It constitutes the rule of civil society in the shape of uncompromising capitalism.

The case of broadcasting, and in particular of television, forces us to modify the picture somewhat. In both public and private television, there has been a complex interplay between political and economic factors that resist a simple reduction to the logic of the market. Certainly, the financing of the new broadcasting systems, both publicly and privately owned, has been accomplished increasingly through advertising; thus, broadcasting has been marked by intense competition for audiences. To that extent, the new broadcasting systems have embodied the logic of civil society understood as capitalism. On the other hand, the condition for economic activity has always been political favor.

The story of the CME operation in the Czech Republic, TV Nova, is a good illustration of this point. The award of the license was made to an alliance of U.S. and local businesses, on the one hand, and local political figures on the other. Immediately after the license was awarded, there was a change of government, and the new rulers attempted to withdraw the license in order to give it to "their" businessmen. They failed, but in the course of the struggle, they forced out the chair of the broadcasting council. When TV Nova was launched, it was a substantial ratings success and attracted a large share of the (very limited) local advertising. CME attempted, successfully, to export this model to a number of other Central and Eastern European markets, but it was unsuccessful in Poland and Hungary, where its political clout proved insufficient. Failure in these markets, particularly Poland, which is the largest country in the region, meant that it was extremely unlikely that even in the longer term, the overall CME operation would turn a profit. The Czech operation alone, on the other hand, was already by 1999 showing an operating profit. CME tried to sell its whole operation to another company, Scandinavian Broadcasting System (actually owned by U.S. investors), with a better record of running broadcasting on the cheap. The local ally of CME, Vladimir Zelezny, saw an opportunity and seized control of the franchise. One day, he simply switched off the existing program feed from CME and started broadcasting his own alternative, carrying his own advertising. This action, of course, infuriated CME, who attempted to take legal action to get "their" franchise back. Despite intense pressure from the United States (the then secretary of state Madeleine Albright raised the matter personally with the

Czech president), Zelezny had enough political power to pull the Czech broadcasting council and the Czech courts behind him, and he remains in control of the station.[5]

The picture in broadcasting suggests that in practice, the classical notion of civil society as the realm of competing capitals is correct but inadequate. As the classical theorists argued, certain overarching political factors are essential to the functioning of civil society as capitalism. The state is a necessary complement to the market. This is generally the case even in established market economies, but in the case under discussion, the overall process was one that involved transforming state property into private property and replacing the plan with the market as the main mechanism for allocating resources. This was, and still is, a process that could be accomplished either by theft (as was the case with much of the press and many other state properties in the early period) or by political action (as was the case with most of broadcasting and the bulk of the state properties once the initial phase of transition was over). Either way, effective private ownership of productive property, the right to participate in civil society as capitalism, depended very obviously upon political sanction.

HOW DID THE WESTERN ADVISORS FARE?

The outcomes in both broadcasting and the press were very far from the goals that the various groups of experts from the West had envisaged. The critical scholars from the West quite clearly had no influence whatsoever on these developments, at least in the short term, and a discussion of them need not detain us long. They offered a critique of capitalism in a region in which capitalism was rudely triumphant. Perhaps in the longer term, they, or their former students, will find an audience, but in the short term, the force of circumstances was against them.

The U.S. experts could regard the structural position of the press with some satisfaction since the market model was quickly dominant. Broadcasting, on the other hand, evolved into a distinctly European model, with state/public broadcasters everywhere having a central role in the system. Press freedoms and the nature of journalism, similarly, were very distant from the best practices of the United States.

On the face of it, the European experts could claim substantial success. Like the Americans, they could see the evolution of the press market as a success for their model of the media. Formally, too, broadcasting was reconstructed upon recognizably European lines. Indeed, by 2002, the European Commission (EC) was satisfied that the eight former Communist countries that were closest to entry had fulfilled all of the conditions with regard to the structure of their media systems.

The picture is substantially more complex than a simple triumph for the views of Western officials, however. Reviewing the first years of transition, Slavko Splichal memorably has argued that the evolving media systems are "Italian" in character (1994, 143–8), meaning that the evolving structures, although formally meeting the conditions of a capitalist democracy, are in practice very closely linked to competing sections of the political elite. Partisanship in journalism and the politicization of broadcasting are characteristic of such systems. As he points out, this is a condition rather common in southern Europe and is not a feature specific to "postcommunism." Subsequent developments, notably in Italy itself, have given a new emphasis to these similarities.

The EC's acceptance of the "European adequacy" of the media systems in post-Communist countries suggests the limitations of that institution's view of democratic media. Provided the formal criteria are met (e.g., legal provision for a certain proportion of European programming on general television channels), then the EC does not concern itself with issues of substance. There is a good reason for this: to denounce the continuing politicization of Polish broadcasting would be to draw attention to the similar continuing politicization of Italian broadcasting. The media systems of the former Communist countries of Central and Eastern Europe can be seen quite clearly as one variant of the standard "European" model—warts and all.

THREE IMPORTANT RESERVATIONS

This general picture captures the main developments in the region, but it ignores important issues. The outcomes for the media were largely the result of the social forces at play in the transition and, in particular, the absence of any autonomous mass movement interested in a program of genuine democratization. This is not the whole picture.

One exception was very brief. In what was then Czechoslovakia, there was a large opposition but no reform Communists for them to negotiate with: the Russians had jailed, exiled, or demoted to obscurity all of the reformers of 1968. The thoroughly Stalinized Communist Party attempted to resist change when the first demonstrations took place in Wenceslas Square, and naturally their loyal allies in television ignored the unprecedented events. So deep was popular discontent that the ordinary workers of the television system walked out in protest at this censorship, set up a strike committee, and briefly took over the running of the station. The new managers, of course, gave a central place to the evolving popular movement. This outbreak of "radical" civil society, so reminiscent of the high period of Solidarity in Poland eight years before, did not last long. The workers quickly handed control of broadcasting back to managers approved by the new government, and the transition returned to "normal," with the consequences sketched above.

Much longer lasting was the popular movement in what was then the German Democratic Republic. Again, a rigidly conservative party attempted to stand firm against a growing tide of popular mobilizations, and again media workers were in the forefront of publicizing the new conditions. Committees of media workers and citizens effectively took control of the media and the *Volkskammer* (parliament) passed a resolution that entitled civic groups to strong representation in the media (Boyle 1994). The price of unification, however, was that West German institutions were imposed in East Germany, including in media. The citizens committee was dismantled, and the Eastern media were restructured and restaffed with West Germans to fit the standard model of the Federal Republic.

The interest in both of these developments is that while they were short-lived and underdeveloped, they both point to the possibility of the changes in Central and Eastern Europe going very much further than simply replacing party bosses with corporate bosses. When there was a substantial mobilization, the population very clearly started to think about ways of running the media that were much closer to the models proposed in the radical period of Solidarity than to those preferred by the elites meeting at round tables to decide the future of society.

The eventual resolution in East Germany was extremely unusual in the region. Almost alone among the media systems of the transition countries, the media in the new *Länder* not only adopted the form, but also the substance, of the Western media. The reason is that this was the only case where transition terminated in rapid and complete absorption into a large, stable, and successful capitalist state. Elsewhere, the process of change was dependent upon internal social and political forces, in broadcasting as much as anywhere else. In the case of Germany, West German politics determined the outcomes, and West Germany provided the leading personnel (many from Bavaria) who shaped the form and content of the new media.

The dependence of Western outcomes on Western power and Western personnel is vividly illustrated by the third exceptional case, that of Kosovo a decade later. Kosovo had been an integral part of the old Yugoslavia and continued in that status when the new, rump Yugoslavia was formed after the breakup of the federation. The Albanian majority of the Kosovo population (the Kosovars) had long suffered national persecution at the hands of the Serbian majority in Yugoslavia, and this intensified in the new rump, which was led by the notorious former Communist bureaucrat Slobodan Milošević and his gangster friends. In July 1990, Serbian police entered the headquarters of Prishtina Radio and Television (RTP) and expelled the Albanian Kosovar staff. Broadcasting in Kosovo was thoroughly "Serbianized" in personnel and content and continued in this state until the NATO invasion and occupation in 1999. Political authority passed into the hands of UN Mission in Kosovo (UNMIK), which became the effective government.

Among the tasks it faced was the rebuilding of RTP. The "rebuilding" was more or less literal, since the retreating Serbs had taken with them everything they could carry, and the broadcasting headquarters were an empty shell. The task of rebuilding broadcasting was given to the European Broadcasting Union (EBU), and while the Japanese provided the equipment, Europeans provided the strategy and key personnel. They established Radio and Television Kosovo (RTK), a new body whose initial general director was Richard Lucas, who had thirty years in the BBC behind him. Although he yielded this post to a Kosovar in 2001, he remained as the advisor to the general director. He and other EBU people tried to establish a BBC-style public broadcaster that would remain impartial with respect to political parties, cater to the needs of minorities (even the Serbian minority), and adopt the norms of professional production. The Americans had different ideas, and International Research and Exchanges Board (IREX) funded two commercial channels to act as competitors, in which role they have not proved terribly successful. All three channels, however, seem to have adopted "Western" editorial substance to go with their Western organizational forms.

The story is a fascinating one, but the point for us to note is that the task of constructing a "Western" broadcaster was made very much easier by the fact that there was no preexisting organization to take over and modify. The international experts started from scratch and did not have to make any compromises with existing staff. They were able to define the organization's mission, hire and train staff, determine programming and priorities, and ensure the representation of different opinions precisely because they were plenipotentiaries of an occupying power. They simply imposed Western standards on broadcasting. Kosovars did not make the decisions, and when they differed with their Western "advisors," as did the first Albanian Kosovar director, it was they who were forced out. It is one of the great paradoxes of postcommunism that the most developed example of democratic broadcasting, as understood in the West, has been the one constructed by the least democratic of means—the fiat of a foreign government resting on a victorious invasion force.[6]

CONCLUSION

Some of the conclusions from the experiences of Central and Eastern Europe are gloomy ones. The media systems that have been established there fall a long way short even of the limited democratic content of those in the West. They are a huge improvement on the shabby old totalitarian system they replaced, but judged by the aspirations of most of the participants in these momentous events, the media today are very imperfect embodiments of democratic aspirations. Three main lessons can be taken from what has occurred:

1. The attempt to construct Western media in non-Western circumstances proved a hopeless failure. From the point of view of democracy, there is a great deal wrong with the BBC model of broadcasting and the *New York Times* model of print media, but even if one accepts the idealized account of their various virtues that was often presented in the transition countries, the plain fact is that the conditions that allow them to flourish simply do not exist there. There is no socially homogenous elite prepared to delegate control of broadcasting to some of its specialist members. There is no huge and rich advertising market in which one title enjoys an effective monopoly. The BBC model of governance failed in Eastern Europe because there is not that degree of elite consensus that obliges politicians to keep their distance. The *New York Times* model failed because the press market everywhere is divided and competitive, and instead of attempting to satisfy the partisans of all persuasions, the press is forced to align itself with one or another opinion.

2. The version of civil society that came closest to providing an accurate picture of the transitional period was the classical one that identifies it more or less completely with private capitalism. The naive version that sees it as third force, independent of economy and politics, may have its intellectual charms, but it proved inadequate as a guide to social action. The harsh fact is that voluntary associations of the kind privileged in the naive account of civil society lack the social power to impose their will upon the economy and politics. The businessmen and carpetbaggers who had a clearer and more effective notion of what needed to be done with the media elbowed them out of the way in Central and Eastern Europe.

3. There was, and is, a far more radical version of civil society that sees it as enshrined in the participation of the mass of the population in the direct control of major social institutions, including the mass media. It starts to recognize that democracy is fundamentally about the extension of political power to the entire population in the whole of their lives. Perhaps this deeply subversive thought is not most clearly articulated by the phrase "civil society"; certainly, the people who advanced it in Central and Eastern Europe would have been very surprised to learn just exactly who had most strenuously argued that every cook could govern. This version of civil society is anathema to the political and economic elites of both the West and East. It is anathema to many of the intellectuals who want to utilize a less explosive concept of civil society that

privileges their own practices as the highest measure of human good. It was this radical version, however, that emerged out of the great mass movement in Poland in 1981, and it was this version that flickered all to briefly in Czechoslovakia and East Germany.

If we want to hold on to a concept of civil society and to develop it in ways that will provide a robust guide to democratizing our own societies, then it is from this final lesson that we must start. The concept is of value insofar as it articulates the desire of the mass of the population to exercise real control over all areas of their lives. So long as it just an idea, something that we pick to pieces in seminars and conferences, then it is more or less interesting depending upon our personal views. Once it escapes and finds its true home in a mass movement, it is an explosive device that threatens the foundations of the world we live in.

NOTES

1. This chapter deals only with the changes in the Communist countries outside of the old Soviet Union. Change started later and followed a distinctive trajectory, which I do not have space to consider seriously here. An excellent introduction to the complexities of Russia, at least, is provided by Terhi Rantanen (2002). This chapter rests very heavily on my own work. Where I have not given a direct reference, the interested reader can find more details in my book on the transition (Sparks 1998).

2. The date of publication is so late because of the sloth of the publisher. The essay was formulated in 1988 and written in 1989.

3. Of course, these national attributions are a gross simplification, but it is worth persisting with what verges on caricature because, very broadly, the push for public broadcasting came from Europe and the push for "objective" reporting came from the United States.

4. I have discussed these legal changes in much greater detail in my book (Sparks 1998, 120–25).

5. An international tribunal eventually awarded CME some of the money it has lost in the region in a judgment against the Czech state (CME 2003). Zelezny keeps his profitable local franchise. The Czech public will pay for the whole party through taxation.

6. I am indebted for all of my information on Kosovo (or as she properly calls it, Kosova) to Vjosa Berisha's fascinating work, which contains much greater detail about this little-known chapter in recent history. She ends by recording the worries that many in Kosovo had at the time she wrote her work that the return of political power to the hands of Kosovars would mean that the carefully constructed public service broadcaster would be transformed into a politicized state broadcaster just like the others in region (Berisha 2002). Developments since she wrote have certainly made such a negative outcome much more likely. It would be the final paradox if the establishment of parliamentary democracy meant the end of democratic broadcasting.

REFERENCES

Benda, Vlaclav, et al. 1988. "Parallel Polis, or an Independent Civil Society in Central and Eastern Europe: An Enquiry." *Social Research* 55, nos. 1–2: 211–46.

Berisha, Vjosa. 2002. *Media in Kosova: Struggles with Building a Public Service Broadcaster from Scratch*. MA thesis, University of Westminster.

Boyle, Mary-Ellen. 1994. "Building a Communicative Democracy: The Birth and Death of Citizen Politics in East Germany." *Media, Culture and Society* 16, no. 2: 183–215.

Central European Media Enterprises (CME). 2003. *Central European Media Enterprises Annual Report (Form 10-K) 2002*, available at www.sec.gov (accessed September 29, 2004).

Cohen, Jean, and Andrew Arato. 1992. *Civil Society and Media Theory*. Cambridge, MA: MIT Press.

Downing, John. 1996. *Internationalizing Media Theory: Transition, Power, Culture: Reflections on Media in Russia, Poland and Hungary, 1980–95*. Thousand Oaks, CA: Sage.

Giorgi, Liana, and Roland Pohoryles. 1994. *The Media in Transition: The Cases of Hungary, Poland and Czechia*. Vienna, Austria: Interdisciplinary Center for Comparative Research.

Goban-Klas, Thomas. 1994. *The Orchestration of the Media: The Politics of Mass Communication in Communist Poland and the Aftermath*. Boulder, CO: Westview.

Gramsci, Antonio. 1971. *Selections from the Prison Notebooks*, eds. and trans. Quentin Hoare and Geoffrey Nowell Smith. London: Lawrence and Wishart.

Gulyás, Ágnes. 1999. "Structural Changes and Organizations in the Print Media Markets of Post-Communist East Central Europe." *Javnost/The Public* 6, no. 2: 61–74.

———. 2000. "The Development of the Tabloid Press in Hungary." In *Tabloid Tales: Global Debates over Media Standards,* eds. C. Sparks and J. Tulloch, 111–27. Lanham, MD: Rowman & Littlefield.

Hegel, George. [1820] 1967. *Hegel's Philosophy of Right*, trans. T. M. Knox. Oxford: Oxford University Press.

Jakab, Zoltan, and Mihaly Gálik. 1991. *Survival, Efficiency and Independence: The Presence of Foreign Capital in the Hungarian Media Market*. Manchester, U.K.: European Institute for the Media.

Jakuobwicz, Karol. 1993. "Stuck in a Groove: Why the 1960s Approach to Communication Democratization Will No Longer Do." In *Communication and Democracy*, eds. S. Splichal and J. Wasko, 33–54. Norwood, NJ: Ablex.

Keane, John. 1991. *The Media and Democracy*. Cambridge, MA: Polity Press.

Meiskens Wood, Ellen. 1990. "The Uses and Abuses of 'Civil Society.'" In *The Retreat of the Intellectuals: Socialist Register 1990*, eds. R. Miliband and L. Panitch, 60–84. London: Merlin.

Michnik, Adam. 1985. *Letters from Prison and Other Essays*. Berkeley: University of California Press.

Minárik, Matú?. 2003. *Private Television in Poland and Slovakia*. International Policy Fellowships policy paper, March 2003, available at www.policy.hu/minarik (accessed June 23, 2003).

Ost, David. 1989. "The Transformation of Solidarity and the Future of Central Europe." *Telos* 79: 69–94.

Pelczynski, Zibigniew. 1988. "Solidarity and 'The Rebirth of Civil Society' in Poland, 1976–81." In *Civil Society and the State: New European Perspectives*, ed. J. Keane, 361–80. London: Verso.

Rantanen, Terhi. 2002. *The Global and the National: Media and Communications in Post-Communist Russia*. Lanham, MD: Rowman & Littlefield.

Sparks, Colin. 1999. "CME in the Former Communist Countries." *Javnost/The Public* 6, no. 2: 25–44.

Sparks, Colin, with Anna Reading. 1998. *Communism, Capitalism and the Mass Media*. London: Sage.

Splichal, Slavko. 1994. *Media beyond Socialism: Theory and Practice in East-Central Europe*. Boulder, CO: Westview.

3

Who Wants Democracy and Does It Deliver Food? Communication and Power in a Globally Integrated China

Yuezhi Zhao

Media democratization was at the forefront of the struggle for political reform in China in the 1980s as it began pursuing the processes of market reforms and integration with the global market system. Journalists and liberal intellectuals were the heroic figures in this struggle. Disillusioned with traditional party journalism and inspired by liberal concepts of press freedom, they allied themselves with the reformist faction of the party and attempted to redefine their role as mouthpieces of the people instead of the party. This struggle culminated in the prodemocracy movement in 1989, when journalists reported student protests in Tiananmen Square sympathetically and marched in the streets to demand press freedom and increased autonomy from the party state (Zhao 1998). The international media, from shortwave radio to foreign network television, played a significant role in this struggle. Casting aside the veneer of objectivity and impartiality that normally characterizes their reporting of electoral politics, they provided alternative communication for students and intellectuals, and by televising protests from Tiananmen Square—as well as by positively framing them in a typical liberal-democratic narrative of freedom-loving individuals fighting an authoritarian Communist regime—they helped legitimate the movement globally and mobilized international opinion in its favor. Iconic images from the movement, from the goddess of democracy to dramatic man-versus-tank television footage, remain part of the collective, global media memory of a bygone era.

Since 1989, however, the substance and dynamics of domestic and global media politics in China have changed significantly. While individual journalists and domestic media outlets continue to resist political control in their own ways, there has not been any major systemic confrontation between the Chinese state and media since 1989. Instead, the domestic media have emerged as one of the most lucrative sectors of Chinese state capitalism (Zhao 2000a). The majority of Chinese journalists have secured a privileged socioeconomic status, enjoying levels of job satisfaction comparable to those of their American counterparts (Chan, Pan, and Lee 2004). At the same time, however, one witnesses intensified struggles over media access and representation by disenfranchised social groups, from grievance-stricken individuals lining up at China Central Television's reception area in an attempt to get an investigative-reporting television crew to expose a case of social injustice, to desperate workers trying to publish their own newsletters and Falun Gong practitioners repeatedly hacking into state-controlled media to promote their own messages.

Transnational media corporations, for their part, have been busy negotiating with the Chinese state over terms of market entry since the mid-1990s. If the 1980s ended with the Chinese state abruptly cutting off live satellite television coverage from Tiananmen Square immediately after the June 4 suppression, the new century started with triumphant announcements from Time-Warner and News Corporation about their successful entry into the cable television market in China's affluent Pearl River delta. By October 2003, Rupert Murdoch, who once pronounced that satellite television would bring an end to authoritarian regimes everywhere, was coaching top Chinese leaders at the Central Party School in Beijing on how to calculatedly liberalize the Chinese media market for domestic and global capital, ensuring them that "the potential of the open market doesn't represent any loss of power" ("Murdoch's Appeal" 2003). There has been a shift in priority in mainstream Chinese media policy and academic discourses from the democratization of the party-controlled media system to the capitalization and structural consolidation of the Chinese media industry, due to the pressure of increased foreign competition brought on by media globalization. This has become especially acute in the aftermath of China's World Trade Organization (WTO) accession in 2001, which secures expanded access to the Chinese media market for transnational media corporations in the areas of print media distribution, Internet investment, and audiovisual importation, distribution, and exhibition (Zhao and Schiller 2001; Hu 2003; C. C. Lee 2003).

This chapter addresses the changing dynamics of media democratization and globalization within the broad context of transformed Chinese state-society relations and the evolving domestic and international political economy of media amid China's accelerated integration with global capitalism. Just as the establishment of capitalist social relations in China has not yet brought to the country a democratic political order, expanded media globalization through increased penetration of transnational media has not led to the democratization of the Chinese media system. On the contrary, the globally integrated Chinese media system is emerging as an important pole of an increasingly authoritarian communication order in the post-9/11 global politics of security and surveillance.

STATE AND SOCIETY IN POST-1989 CHINA: A CONTEXTUAL OVERVIEW

Capitalism and Press Freedom Revisited

Although the aforementioned quest for press freedom by journalists and their urban middle-class allies and the Chinese state's suppression of this liberal aspiration has been turned into another forbidden topic in domestic media discourses, 1989 remains an important reference point for any discussion of media democratization in China. After all, this is a classic episode of a "heroic struggle for press freedom." It fits in perfectly with a liberal narrative about the evolution of a free press, that is, a press that is freed from direct state control. While, from the perspective of China's democratic transition, it is understandable that such suppression should be generally perceived as a setback, it can be viewed creatively from the viewpoint of China's capitalistic socioeconomic transition. In other words, it is important to make an analytical distinction between two transitions in China: a capitalistic transition (i.e., from a planned to market economy and capitalistic economic and social relations) and a democratic transition (i.e., from an authoritarian political system to a democratic one). Although a market economy is often considered to be a necessary precondition for a liberal-democratic political order, in China, the state's sustained suppression of popular demands for political participation in the reform process, dramatized by the military crackdown in 1989, created the repressive political conditions for the implementation of drastic economic reforms and a whole decade of authoritarian capitalist developments in the 1990s. In other words, the ruling elite's resistance to a democratic transition and the state's military intervention—in the form of a violent crackdown—preceded the further installation of capitalistic social relations in China and the country's relatively successful transition to a market economy.

In retrospect, if Maoists are utopian in believing that they can build an egalitarian socialist society in China, liberals both inside and outside China are naive in believing that a capitalist economy can be a free and spontaneous order without state intervention, including the suppression of press freedom (see Wang 2003). Such a historical trajectory is by no means unique to China. As Barrington Moore has demonstrated, even the rise of the liberal-democratic system in England was not as benign as is often assumed. "That the violence and coercion which produced these results took place over a long space of time, that it took place mainly within a framework of law and order and helped ultimately to establish democracy on a firmer footing, must not blind us to the fact that it was massive violence exercised by the upper classes against the lower" (1993, 29). The suppression of radical ideas (which had flourished during the brief years of complete liberty of the press in England between 1641 and 1660) through either state censorship or economic marginalization was part and parcel of this process (Hill 1972). As James Curran argues, the apparently independent and advertising-supported capitalist press was not the outcome of a simple unfolding of some libertarian principle, but the product of calculated liberalization on the part of British reformers. For example, the principle objective of repealing the stamp duty, initially a key instrument used by the state to curtail the press, was to unleash market forces in the newspaper industry "to destroy radical working class journalism" that had posed a threat to the capitalist order (1978, 55).

In China, the suppression of liberal-democratic forces in 1989 and the marginalization of party establishment leftists in 1992 through Deng Xiaoping's suppression of political debate over the direction of reform, preceded the state's all-out embrace of the market and the extensive economic reforms implemented throughout the 1990s. These reforms have included price reforms, the introduction of the stock market, the massive inflow of foreign capital, the commodification of labor and social services, the partial withdrawal of the state in welfare provisions ranging from medical care to free housing and education to the urban workforce, and the privatization of state-owned enterprises. If reform in the 1980s lead to change without losers, the deepening of market reforms in the 1990s created clear classes of winners and losers (Naughton 2000). In particular, the deepening of the market reforms has meant the ruthless extraction of agricultural surplus and the uprooting of the Chinese peasantry. In urban areas, this has meant the subjection of labor to market forces and massive layoffs in state enterprises. None of this could have been accomplished without state repression of the freedom of press, association, and assembly, and especially the public voices of those economically, socially, and culturally disenfranchised during these processes.

In short, the military crackdown on a popular uprising in 1989 and Deng's imposition of an end to elite ideological debates in the media about the political nature of the reforms in 1992, which effectively marginalized elite opposition to the further implementation of capitalist social relations in China, served as preconditions for the massive layoffs in the state sector and the deeply corrupt process of primitive capital accumulation in the 1990s (Zhao 2001). This is not to suggest that the Chinese party state played a capitalist vanguard role according to some predetermined historical logic. On the contrary, at every historical conjuncture, this process was full of struggles, compromises, contingencies, and the hegemonic articulation of various political and social forces at both the elite and popular levels. After all, as Deng stated

clearly at the onset of the economic reforms, this was to be a process of trying to "cross the river by feeling the stones." The indeterminate nature of this
process is evidenced both by the elite divisions before and during 1989—
leading to the demise of two party general secretaries between 1986 and
1989—and the intensive struggles between competing discourses of reform
in the early 1990s (both inside and outside the party) and between regional
and national media (Fewsmith 2001; Zhao 2002a).

A Party State Transformed

As the party state continues to lead China's transition to capitalism, most
recently by joining the WTO and thus further integrating the Chinese economy with the global capitalist system, it has also substantively transformed
itself and redefined its political nature. While Deng sanctioned capitalist-
style economic reforms by adopting pragmatism and prohibiting ideological
debates, his successor Jiang Zemin supervised a series of major political and
ideological changes between the late 1990s and the Sixteenth Party Congress
in November 2002. These ranged from recognizing private business as an
important component of the socialist market economy in the Chinese constitution, to repositioning capitalists and the newly enriched managerial and
professional strata as the de facto advanced productive and cultural forces
that the party represents. The party's constitution was revised to redefine the
party as not only a vanguard of the working class but also of the Chinese
people and nation. Instead of being overthrown by new social forces in a
middle-class-led democratic revolution, the party is proactively incorporating and co-opting these new social strata. After all, China's contemporary
business and middle classes were incubated through the process of market
reform that the party initiated. Indeed, China observer Bruce Gilley has
noted that the party's politics now look "more and more like the right-wing
authoritarianism of a Suharto of Indonesia or a Franco of Spain than anything
Marx might have dreamt up" (2001, 18). As the Chinese Communist Party officially redefines itself as a nationalistic, all-people party, the nominal socialist state has evolved into a market-authoritarian developmental state.

The recognition of the capitalistic nature of the party state does not necessarily require the projection of an image of the prereformed Chinese state as
a workers' and farmers' paradise. Despite its socialist rhetoric, the party has
never truly acted in the interests of the main constituents it claims to represent, that is, the majority of the Chinese population. While urban workers in
the state sector did enjoy considerable economic and social benefits under
state socialism, the Chinese peasantry lived in a state of class apartheid, confined to the land through the household-registration system. With an estimated thirty million starving to death during the Great Leap Forward–induced
famine, the Chinese peasantry suffered the most devastating consequences of

the Maoist industrialization and development strategies. But the shifts in the Chinese state's developmental priorities and power basis in the reform period have been drastic. To be sure, the party has not been completely free to shed its socialist and anti-imperialist pretensions at will, and there has been considerable resistance toward the development of capitalist social relations both at the elite and popular levels. There is, however, no doubt that the Chinese state has been proactively transforming itself from a "dictatorship of the proletariat" into an authoritarian regime representative and protective of the interests of domestic and transnational capital, the rising urban consumer strata, and, above all, its own bureaucratic interests.

A Society Reconstituted

The installation of the market and the transformation of the Chinese state have gone hand in hand with the reconstitution of social relations. The 1990s witnessed a rapid process of social stratification, economic polarization, class recomposition, and transformation of other social relations, most notably gender relations. Today, China is one of the most economically polarized societies in the world. Popular writer He Qinglian (2000) describes a pyramid social structure with a tiny and highly interlocking political and economic elite on the top, accounting for 1 percent of the workforce; an underdeveloped middle class of business owners, managers, professionals, and technical experts, accounting for 15.8 percent; and the rest of the population, composing more than 80 percent of the workforce, which survives either at the bottom or margins of Chinese society. He earned her fame by publishing a book that exposed official corruption and was initially tolerated by the authorities. However, He's analysis of accentuated social divisions engendered by the reform process threatened to bring back a long-suppressed discourse on social class, and she was forced into exile in the United States in 2001. However, a 2001 study by the Chinese Academy of Social Sciences validated her basic description of the new social structure in China, while softening her language by foregrounding the rise of a middle class as a positive social development and using an onion rather than a pyramid as the metaphor to describe the hierarchical Chinese social structure formed on the basis of differentiated access to political, economic, and cultural capital (Lu 2001).

As the conventional liberal narrative goes, a market economy creates a middle class, which will be the social force that leads democratic transition. The reality, however, is that China's "middle" classes are a minority at the top of the Chinese social hierarchy. As sociologist David Goodman has observed, rather than being politically alienated from the party state or seeking their own political voice, this new middle class "appear[s] to be operating in close proximity and through close cooperation" with the party state (1999, 261). Rather than playing the role of democrats willing to share the fruits of economic development with the majority of the Chinese population, many seem to behave more like aristocrats, willingly or unwittingly relying on state repression to secure their economic and social privileges vis-à-vis demands for economic and social justice by disenfranchised social groups. Many, meanwhile, have transferred their assets abroad, acquired foreign passports, and moved members of their families abroad, enjoying flexible citizenships (Ong 1999) in the postmodern transnational ethnoscape. Attempting to enjoy the best of both worlds, these individuals have little commitment to the development of a democratic polity within the Chinese nation-state. Although there have been well-known cases in which lawyers, professors, and other urban professionals have advocated legal rights on behalf of dispossessed social groups such as migrant workers and farmers, overall, members of the Chinese middle class have not been in the forefront of promoting the rule of law, a basic feature of any democratic polity. As Ching Kwan Lee writes, "[T]he irony [in China] is that rather than entrepreneurs or the rising middle classes, whose interests reside in evading the law rather than promoting it, it is the popular classes, viz., workers and peasants, who champion the cause of 'bourgeois' legal rights!" (2002, 220).

Recast Protagonists of Social Contestation and Competing Notions of Democracy

As part and parcel of the transformation of the Chinese party state and the reconstitution of the Chinese social structure, the protagonists of social contestation in Chinese politics have also been recast. With the (re)constitution of the urban educated elite into the middle-class strata, struggles for subsistence and social justice by groups at the bottom of Chinese society—specifically, laid-off workers in state enterprises, overtaxed farmers in economically depressed rural areas, ethnic minority groups in remote regions, and more recently, ordinary urban residents deprived of their housing entitlements by real estate developers—have become the main forms of social contestation since the early 1990s (Perry and Selden 2003). The quasi-religious Falun Gong movement, which cuts across various social groups and other underground religious movements (Thornton 2003; Madsen 2003), meanwhile, has demonstrated the cultural bankruptcy of both the party's social-engineering project and the post-Mao political and cultural elite's top-down modernization mission.

Together with this change in the composition of social contestation is a transformation in the discourse on democracy. On the one hand, market liberalism, political authoritarianism, and state nationalism, as discourses that serve the interests of the ruling elite, have become dominant ideological forces in China. To be sure, Western-style liberal democracy continues to enchant China's small liberal elite. They have called for constitutional governance as a more desirable and sustainable form of elite bargaining and management of social conflicts. There is also the possibility that village-level elections, implemented by the party as a means of popular containment, may creep up to the township level. Many of today's regime protesters, unlike the protesters in 1989, however, do not speak the language of liberal democracy. Although some make liberal rights–based appeals and there has been a broad trend of increasing rights consciousness among regime protesters (Pei 2003), many protesting workers and farmers articulate subsistence-based moral-economy claims (Perry 1999). The resistant and insurgent identities of Chinese farmers continue to draw upon discursive resources rooted in peasant rebellions in the imperial era and "longstanding village and lineage loyalties" (Perry and Selden 2003, 9). Meanwhile, some Chinese workers, disillusioned with a party that still claims to rule in their name, have reembraced a radical class discourse on their own, with slogans such as "down with political and economic exploitation and oppression," "yes to socialism, no to capitalism," and "protecting workers' class interest" (Perry 1999; C. K. Lee 2003). Dai Qing, a prominent Chinese journalist, related to me in a personal conversation that protesting workers in northeast China even put up the sign "we don't want democracy, we want food."

At stake here are different notions of democracy and the interests of different social groups in the evolving Chinese political structure. Although neoauthoritarians and the liberal elite may regard this purported slogan as proof that workers are not ready for democracy, it is also likely that the workers feared that the kind of elitist democracy imagined by China's liberal elites might not pay back wages and deliver food and jobs. Indeed, their agenda differs from that of the students and intellectuals in 1989. Similarly, the popularity of Falun Gong underscores a popular yearning for spirituality, identity, and community, even pure physical fitness (in contrast to state- and commercially sponsored spectator sports—highlighted by the Chinese state's Olympic ambitions) that goes beyond a narrow definition of electoral political democracy. In addition to political and economic rights, broader issues of culture, meaning, and identity are at stake.

THE POLITICAL ECONOMY OF A CHANGED MEDIA SYSTEM AND THE NEW POLITICS OF MEDIA DEMOCRATIZATION

The new politics of media democratization is inextricably linked with the above-described political, economic, social, and cultural transformation and accelerated global integration on the one hand, and with the changed domestic and global media political economy and media culture on the other.

Political Control: An Old Trade with New Tricks

To be sure, the party state continues to exercise tight political control of the media. The tens of thousands of worker and farmer protests, many of them large in scale and involving violent confrontations with state authorities, for example, simply do not happen as far as the Chinese media are concerned. Ordinary Chinese who provided details of these protests to the Chinese National People's Congress and the international media have received jail sentences as long as ten years (Zhang 1999). The Chinese state's persistent attempt at establishing one of the world's most repressive regimes of Internet control has been extensively documented in Western journalistic and scholarly literature (McCormick 2002/2003).

As the party state tries to control new technologies of communication, it has also adopted new technologies of control. For example, "passive censorship," or "cold treatment" in official terminology, which aims at limiting the impact of oppositional ideas to a small circle through media neglect, has been practiced and accepted as more practical than complete censorship in maintaining ideological domination amid media proliferation. Previously, the party's self-righteous impulse of maintaining ideological purity and its self-proclaimed status as the monopoly holder of truth would typically lead it to organize a public critique of ideas deemed "incorrect." As part of a "no debate" decree installed by Deng and the party leadership's own increasing cynicism over the truthfulness of its messages and the effectiveness of its propaganda endeavors, the party realized that public criticism of oppositional and "deviant" ideas often inadvertently amplified them. Nowadays, if a problematic publication were to evade the censorship system and appear in the market, authorities would quickly and quietly try to stop its distribution but would not use the mass media for public criticism. Consequently, as Geremie Barmé (1998) has observed, although controversial books have been published over the past few years, their reception is often limited to a small urban intellectual elite. In fact, the Chinese state is consciously pursuing a policy of differentiated control. Mass-media outlets, for example, are not supposed to transmit information from the Internet freely, even from major government-sponsored websites. In this sense, the fate of critical ideas in the partially liberalized and fragmented Chinese media system is increasingly similar to that of critical ideas in Western media systems.

At the same time, as the party drifts to the Right politically and "is moving to reposition itself as a de facto right-wing dictatorship" (Gilley 2001), leftist ideas have become the targets of party censorship. Indeed, the leadership was so afraid of critiques of "capitalist restoration" and charges that it betrayed its avowed core constituency of Chinese farmers and workers that it directly and indirectly resulted in the shutdown of two Marxist theoretical journals after they spoke out against the rightward drift of the party in the summer of 2001. For the same reason, Chinese critics of globalization—covering a wide ideological spectrum from unreconstructed Maoists to anti-American nationalists, old-fashioned bureaucrats and protectionists, neo-Marxist academics, and admirers of globalization protesters in the West—have been marginalized in the channels of public communication. A detailed analysis of mainstream Chinese media discourse on China's WTO accession agreement with the United States in 1999 reveals a pattern of press coverage that conceals crucial information about the agreement and disallows any domestic criticisms of the party state's policies (Zhao 2003b). This marks a consistent pattern. After all, the primary objective of Deng's closure of ideological debates on the political nature of the economic reforms was not simply to block liberal-democratic ideas from abroad but to shut down indigenous leftist voices in the media. As Michael Robinson, an American computer engineer who helped build the Chinese Internet, recalls, "In the Chinese Internet's infancy, the first three sites that the government blocked were two antigovernment sites—and one Maoist site. What threatens them? . . . The heartland" (Gutmann 2002). Although the party still prohibits private ownership of the media as a matter of principle and bans Internet access to selected foreign media outlets and other politically sensitive sites, its most feared media outlets are from within, including the indigenously grown and now globalized Falun Gong movement, leftist pamphlets, and especially newsletters put out by labor activists.

Market Constraints and the Promises and Limits of Professionalism

Accelerated commercialization and state-engineered market consolidation have transformed state-subsidized and single-minded propaganda organs into state-controlled, advertising-supported, and self-interested economic entities. Although the news media are still treated as the party's political propaganda organs, commercialization is a state-mandated policy (Zhao 1998; 2000a). Moreover, the Chinese state has actively merged existing media operations in various sectors to form media conglomerates in an attempt to achieve political control, economic efficiency, and international competitiveness. Rather than putting pressures on domestic media to democratize their operations by providing more diverse perspectives, the pressures of international competition have provided the perfect excuse for the party to consolidate its media power by merging existing media outlets and establishing various media conglomerates. State-engineered media conglomeration has strengthened the power of existing party-controlled core-media organizations and further marginalized smaller and local media outlets, including those in the economically depressed hinterland. China's party-controlled media conglomerates are now deeply entrenched in the dominant political economic order as a lucrative sector of state capitalism. They have little reason or incentive to offend the party since they can negotiate profitable market conditions, including joint ventures with transnational media corporations, as long as they follow the party line (Zhao 2001; Lee 2002). In this context, the promotion of an authoritarian-market social order serves the interests of both the state and the media, domestic and foreign owned alike. Mass entertainment, including Chinese versions of *Who Wants to Be a Millionaire* and other reality shows, business reporting, consumer advice, and sensational crime stories framed in a law-and-order narrative, are politically safe and financially rewarding.

Similarly, the occupation of journalism has solidified its middle-class status. A nascent and localized form of Western-style professionalism has emerged as a competing journalistic paradigm to traditional party journalism (Pan and Lu 2003). Some have channeled their reformist sensibilities by producing *60 Minutes*–inspired investigative journalism within permissible political limits, becoming "watchdogs on Party leashes" (Zhao 2000b). To be sure, their reformist ethos is sincere, their commitment to some notion of social justice and equality genuine, and the political and social implications of their work significant. They also have to overcome tremendous micropolitical obstacles to produce each investigative story (Zhao 2000b; 2003a; McCormick 2002/2003). Some have risked their lives in the pursuit of investigative reports. Others have even suffered state prosecutions and received jail terms on dubious and politically motivated corruption charges—a well-known case in early 2004 involves two Guangdong journalists for their exposure of police brutality and the SARS epidemic. But overall, journalists' economic and social isolation from the lower social strata is turning them into a silent partner of the party in sustaining a marketized and party-dominated media system. While political censorship matters, it is by no means clear that even if left alone, journalists would not suppress news about social unrest out of concern for political stability. Indeed, given the changes in the Chinese social structure and the nature of social movements, it is no longer realistic to expect mainstream journalists to identify with, let alone to become participants in, new forms of social contestation—be it the culturally based Falun Gong movement or the economically and socially based workers' and farmers' protests.

Although aspirations for a Western-inspired notion of professionalism, defined as being independent from political and economic power, remain strong among Chinese journalists (Pan and Chan 2003), the pursuit of success, defined as moving ahead in the career hierarchy and becoming a star journalist (or more bluntly, to become the hottest-selling journalistic labor commodity in an increasingly competitive media market) have also emerged as a strong value orientation. In 2001, the best-paid and most sought-after journalist in China was a female reporter who developed an "unusual" personal rapport with the foreign coach of the Chinese national soccer team and was thus capable of securing exclusive access to a crucial news source in an extremely competitive sports-news market. Many of her colleagues in the Chinese media, instead of questioning her ethics and professionalism, turned her into a celebrity and a symbol of the rising market value of journalists.

The notion of journalistic professionalism, despite its universal appeal (especially for journalists working under tight state control in authoritarian countries), has particular historical conditions of existence. In addition to relative autonomy from the state, it presupposes relative autonomy from market imperatives. Aside from its various limitations, not the least being its own elitism and scope of operation within narrow elite interests (Hallin 2000; McChesney 1999), the high modernism of American professional journalism, as Daniel Hallin (2000) demonstrates, was closely linked to the relatively stable capital-accumulation environment of a bygone era, when newspapers were under the management of private families and not yet subjected to the dictates of stock markets, and when television networks, under a stable state-regulated oligopoly, could afford to invest in news production and run news divisions as money-losing operations. In the intensively competitive media environment in China today, where "news creates value" has become an operating slogan for many market-driven media outlets, journalistic professionalism has become the double victim of the state and the market. Chinese journalists gained little ground against state control when excessive commercialism and the pressures of domestic and foreign competition turned them into agents of capital accumulation.

Instead of catching up with Western journalism in its high-modernist phase of political independence and professional autonomy, postreform Chinese journalism converges with global waves of media conglomeration, the rise of hypercommercialism (McChesney 1999), "market-driven journalism" (McManus 1994), and trends toward tabloidization in global journalism (Sparks and Tulloch 2000). However, this is not to deny that there are liberalizing and, indeed, democratizing aspects of market-oriented journalism in China (Zhao 1998). As Manjunath Pendakur and Jyotsna Japur (1996) have demonstrated in the context of media liberalization in India, it would be too simplistic to conflate genuine middle-class dissatisfaction with state control and state media with a one-dimensional embrace of consumerism. Indeed, as García Canclini ([1995] 2001) has argued, the consumer-versus-citizen dichotomy is too simplistic as a framework of media critique. Still, it is important to emphasize the structural constraints in the transplanting of Western-style professionalism into the Chinese media.

Nor have foreign joint ventures provided attractive role models for media professionalism in China. In fact, although Chinese journalists are envious of the relative political autonomy of Phoenix TV (a Hong Kong–based satellite television station with partial investment from Rupert Murdoch's Star TV and accessible to selected Chinese cable audiences), as far as professionalism is concerned, Sally Wu, the station's best-known and most heavily promoted star reporter/news anchor, was the laughingstock of Chinese and Hong Kong reporters. Rather than being known for her tough questions, Wu is known for prefacing her question to former Chinese premier Zhu Rongji with the statement, "You are my idol." China Entertainment Television, a privately owned Hong Kong–based satellite channel initially aimed at the mainland Chinese market, famously advertised itself as a channel that contains "No Sex, No Violence, No News." The channel, once wholly owned by Time-Warner and more recently jointly owned by Time-Warner and Hong Kong media tycoon Richard Li, is now officially available to cable audiences in the Pearl River delta. Whatever programming innovations it has undertaken to attract a mainland Chinese audience, aggressive local news reporting has not been part of the business strategy. Foreign investors, in fact, are willing to yield to Chinese pressures to eliminate journalism altogether to enter the Chinese media market.

The impact of American journalism on the development of professionalism in China is also complicated. On the one hand, ideals of Western professional journalism continue to enchant a significant number of Chinese journalists. On the other hand, the perception of mainstream American journalism's lack of professionalism and objectivity in its reporting of major international events in the past few years has further undermined Chinese journalists' confidence in transcendent professional values, while reinforcing their acceptance of hypercommercialism and allegiance to the party's nationalistic agenda. Examples of unprofessional reporting in American journalism that have appeared in Chinese media and academic literature have included the U.S. media's sensationalized reporting of the Clinton sex scandal and what is perceived by many Chinese journalists to be highly biased and nationalistic American reporting of major international events—from former Russian president Boris Yeltsin's storming of the Russian parliament, to NATO's bombing of the Chinese Embassy in Belgrade in 1999, to the invasion of Iraq in 2003.

Finally, any analysis of the potentials and limits of professionalism must be contextualized within China's broader media and social structure. The structural transformation of the state-controlled and advertising-based Chinese media industry has meant that a minority of the population, namely the political and economic elite and the mostly urban-based middle class, has been constituted as the most favored and most influential media audiences. Although domestic television has a wide reach, print media, still a more important means of political communication in China, remains elite oriented. Even the most successful mass-appeal papers reach only a small percentage of the urban population. Small-circulation business and consumer-oriented media outlets, many of them increasingly professional both in their formats and substance, and sometimes even under various forms of cooperation with foreign companies, have proliferated and competed with each other for the same affluent middle-class consumers in core urban centers. More and more media outlets are dedicating themselves to the informational and entertainment needs of affluent urban consumers. There are few publications for industrial workers, farmers, and other disenfranchised social groups. Those that do exist, such as the *Workers' Daily*, *China Women's News*, and *China Farmers' News*, have limited editorial independence and have declined both in circulation and institutional power in the 1990s as they do not constitute premier advertising vehicles (Zhao 2000a). Although the Internet, much celebrated for its democratizing potential, had reached some eighty million users by the end of 2003, access remains limited to mostly affluent city dwellers whose primary concerns are far removed from those of the majority of the population. When journalists and media outlets act in accordance with the dictates of the market, the inherent biases of the market, including its tendency to marginalize radical perspectives and issues of concern to groups that do not constitute advertisers' "most needed audience," may actually fit with the party's censorship objectives (Zhao and Schiller 2001) and help it forge new hegemonic alliances with the business and affluent urban strata. In short, far from being inherently antithetical to party propaganda, market forces may have actually helped to neutralize dissent at a time when the bottom line is the party line.

TRANSNATIONAL MEDIA: FOSTERING A TRANSNATIONAL CONSUMER STRATA IN CHINA?

As the party consolidates its media power in the context of intensified pressures of international competition in the post-WTO world, the Chinese media market is increasingly the playing field of domestic and transnational media conglomerates. Although there is much expectation about the democratizing implications of foreign media, it is important to remember that foreign media capital enters China to make a profit, not to challenge the Chinese state or serve as a voice for the politically and economically marginalized groups. The words and deeds of Rupert Murdoch and other global media barons have demonstrated eloquently the priorities and political commitments of transnational media operating in China (McChesney 1999; Klein 2000). A "globalization equals democratization" framework is problematic for a number of reasons. First, it underestimates the ability of the Chinese state to negotiate with transnational capital over the terms of market entry. Second, it contradicts the well-documented double standards of the U.S. media, which still dominate transnational communication, in the coverage of global affairs and their complicity in sustaining authoritarian regimes throughout the world. Third, it is predicated upon a cold war–informed assumption about a preordained ideological conflict between China and the United States that is no longer self-evident in the post–cold war, and especially post-9/11, world. Finally, such a perspective is oblivious to profound social tensions in China and the complicated power relations between the semi-integrated Chinese media industries, the Chinese state, and an increasingly polarized and conflict-laden Chinese society (Zhao 2003c; 2004).

In fact, in addition to imported and "glocalized" content, which has helped to liberalize, but not necessarily democratize, Chinese society, foreign capital has long circulated in Chinese media markets through strategic joint ventures and venture-capital investments in business, information technology, and consumer magazines; upscale and specialty satellite television markets; and Internet portals and websites. In the print media, areas of operation have included specialized publications for China's rising technological-information elite and consumer and lifestyle magazines for affluent urban consumers. Typically sold at 20 yuan (U.S. $2.50) per issue, the equivalent of one day's income for an ordinary worker in China, these publications help the rising urban Chinese consumer strata to globalize their lifestyles and serve as indispensable symbols of social distinction and identity formation.

In the broadcasting sector, the Rupert Murdoch–invested Phoenix TV claimed to reach 44.98 million households in China, or 15.9 percent of total Chinese television households in the late 1990s (China Mainland Marketing Research Co. 1998). Similar to readership of foreign-invested joint-venture publications, the Phoenix audience in China is no ordinary audience. Rather, it is an audience constituted by political, economic, and cultural privileges (Zhao 2003c). Compared with the average Chinese television audience, the Phoenix viewers are characterized by "three highs and one low": high official rank, high income, high education level, and low age. As the *Wall Street Journal* wrote, "Phoenix's stylish shows are a must-see for a growing middle class fed on, and fed up with, a diet of state-run television" (Chang 1999). On the one hand, Phoenix TV refrains from critical reporting on domestic Chinese politics and social issues and has been politically highly opportunistic on several occasions—for example, by broadcasting a highly charged nationalistic concert immediately after NATO's bombing of the Chinese Embassy in Belgrade in early 2001 and by launching a propaganda campaign against Falun Gong immediately after the Chinese state banned the movement. On the other hand, unlike stated-controlled media outlets, Phoenix TV can report breaking global news with more immediacy and more freedom. For example, while Chinese state television restricted reporting of the 9/11 terrorist attacks, Phoenix TV, with its privileged access to U.S. sources, especially footage from News Corporation's Fox TV, provided extensive coverage of the event. It was such an attractive alternative source of news on the event that some affluent Chinese booked rooms in luxury hotels in order to watch Phoenix TV. Similarly, while the state-owned China Central Television at least has some obligation to appeal to a broad domestic audience by producing the kind of investigative journalism that exposes social problems, particularly regarding corrupt rural officials and the plights of Chinese farmers in the country's hinterlands, Phoenix TV has no such commitment. Instead, it provides exactly what its upwardly mobile and outward-looking audience is interested in—the latest global news; the latest business, travel, and consumer information; and above all, uplifting, light entertainment to match the spirit of China's rising middle class and the other "winners" of globalization. That is, unlike Chinese state television—which not only has to fulfill the party's propaganda orders but also has to cater to the needs of different social constituents, from children to retirees to rural residents to soldiers and ethnic minorities—Phoenix TV, with neither a state-socialist legacy nor public service duties, can tailor its programming to the group with the highest consuming power.

With the recent official entry of foreign-invested general-interest and specialty satellite channels in selected Chinese regional and national markets, competition for premier media markets is intensifying. Instead of promoting democratic citizenship and serving as means of communication across different social groups inside China, these media outlets establish horizontal communication links among and between China's affluent urban consuming strata with its counterparts in New York, Paris, Tokyo, and other global cities. These cream-skimming media outlets, in turn, are putting further upward market pressures on a domestic communication system that is already skewed toward the affluent social strata.

FOREIGN NEWS, TRANSNATIONAL COMMUNICATION NETWORKS, AND SOCIAL MOVEMENTS

What about the role of foreign media operating outside China in democratizing Chinese communication and society? In 1989, foreign-based media were at the forefront of covering the student-led democracy movements. Their saturated coverage helped to ingrain the movement's images, heroes, and messages into global popular consciousness. The main protagonists of this movement, the students and intellectuals, spoke English to journalists, put up their signs in English, and had the material and cultural resources to construct a goddess of democracy in Tiananmen Square, thus consciously incorporating foreign media as part of their communication strategy. Their protests occurred in central Beijing and other major urban centers, allowing foreign media easy access. Their messages fit in well with liberal-democratic ideology. Moreover, in 1989, none of the major U.S. television networks had any financial interests in China, and other than the lives of their own journalists, these networks had little to lose in China.

Today, with the exception of Falun Gong, whose members are dispersed both inside and outside China, the primary protagonists of social contestations in China have shifted from Beijing-based students and intellectuals to farmers and laid-off workers in remote areas inaccessible to foreign journalists. Even with the best efforts of foreign television crews, the Chinese state's tightened control has made it impossible for the foreign media to cover similar protest-spectacles as they once did in Tiananmen Square. Today, such critical coverage does not come from major media sources; rather, a lone dissident based in Hong Kong, who fled mainland China in 1993, and who maintains access to mainland Chinese sources via a cell phone and pager and is supported by a small annual grant from the U.S. Congress, acts as the sole source of an estimated two-thirds of all news reports on human rights violations in China. With the tightening of the legal regime in Hong Kong, even the viability of this source is reportedly under threat (York 2002). Although human rights discourse continues to serve as a broad ideological framework for international media reporting on China, the protagonists of Chinese social movements—be they farmers, workers, or Falun Gong activists—do not chant easily translatable slogans of freedom and democracy. Instead, they are protesting the economic, social, and cultural consequences of China's market reforms and global integration. Thus, if these protests are physically less accessible to the transnational media, they are also ideologically less compelling to the transnational media, themselves the "new missionaries of global capitalism" (Herman and McChesney 1997). Moreover, unlike the situation in 1989, all the major U.S. television networks, still the most powerful global media outlets, are now part of transnational entertainment conglomerates with vested business interests in China. Even with the best intentions of individual journalists, none of them can afford to offend the Chinese state with sustained reports of social conflicts in China.

Chinese state censorship and declining critical Western media reporting aside, the overwhelming majority of China's disenfranchised workers and farmers do not have easy access to the Internet, nor do they listen to foreign shortwave radio as part of their daily cultural routine. Thus, on the one hand, the members of the middle-class strata are well connected to their transnational counterparts through mobile phones, the Internet, and special-interest niche-market satellite channels and magazines. They are well furnished with the latest global news flashes, the most up-to-date stock market quotes from New York, the latest entertainment reports from Hollywood, and the latest fashion trends from Paris. On the other hand, China's disenfranchised and protesting social groups have been largely cut off from parallel social struggles in the rest of the world. Their movements remain sporadic, localized, disconnected, and single issue–driven (Perry and Selden 2003). In exile, Chinese political activists are effectively isolated from domestic social movements. Although there have been persistent attempts by overseas political activists to send information through the Internet, those who have access to the Internet are not necessarily the ones with the political interest to act on this critical information. So far, the only protest movement that has been able to make effective use of international media, especially the Internet, has been the Falun Gong. However, this movement's quasireligious, fundamentalist orientations and its ideological closure, especially its insistence on uniformly positive media endorsement of its messages and activities, are in the end fundamentally incompatible with any notion of a democratic discourse. That China's accelerated integration with the West, the rise of the Internet, and the intensified flow of population in and out of China in the processes of globalization should have nurtured not a democratic revolution of the 1989 type, but rather a nativist, conservative, and antimodernist discourse such as Falun Gong, testifies to the profound ideological contradictions of globalization and raises disturbing questions about the supposed inherently emancipatory nature of globalized and networked communication (Zhao 2003d).

In short, political control, the inherent biases of a market-driven media system, the limits of journalistic professionalism, and changed dynamics of intersection between domestic- and international-media political economy and culture have prevented both domestic and transnational media from serving as effective vehicles of popular expression and communication across different social groups in post-1989 China. If democracy is to come from interactions among social movements and public discussions (Wang 2003), this is precisely the role that the party-controlled, market-dominated, and increasingly globally integrated media in China are not playing. As a vanguard party that originally came to power in 1949 through a conscious strategy of forging a counterhegemonic bloc with oppositional political and social elements, the party is making every effort to prevent the formation of alliances among various forces in opposition to its rule today, and especially to prevent the circulation of news about social unrest in the mass media, and the formation of linkages between politically active intellectuals and protesting social groups (Goldman, 1999). The party, given its own political history, particularly its own successful communicative strategies in forging a hegemonic bloc for the Communist revolution, knows all too well the importance of communication in the mobilization of social movements.

With increased social polarization and mounting social pressures from below, it is perhaps fair to say that the most urgent task for the majority of China's urban middle class, including journalists, has become popular containment through the suppression of radical social consciousness and ideological pacification in general, rather than opposition to authoritarian state power (Zhao 2003a). The urban middle class may dislike the party and harbor more liberal views, but its members are allying themselves with the promarket faction of the party in marginalizing the voices of both the radical Left and Right, while mediating the voices of other social groups in the name of building a strong and powerful China. The issue of media democratization continues to be linked with the politics of containment—namely of the voices of China's disenfranchised, like unemployed workers, the rural poor, and other politically, economically, and culturally marginalized groups. While stories about Chinese media censorship and the plight of China's underclasses will continue to appear sporadically in the elite Western media, transnational media capital, just like transnational capital in other sectors, has everything to gain from a stable political environment and low labor cost secured by an authoritarian Chinese state (C. C. Lee 2003, 10). Politically, although there will be continuing conflicts between the Chinese state and the globally hegemonic U.S. state, for the time being, a common stake in maintaining the stability of the global market system and the antiterrorist agenda are increasingly unifying the interests of the ruling elites both in China and in the United States. Murdoch earned the honor to coach the Chinese leadership on how to build "an exemplary media industry" in China by October 2003, and in that month U.S. President Bush praised "a China that is stable and prosperous . . . and works to secure the freedom of its own people" (*Bush Calls* 2003).

CONCLUSION

The democratization of Chinese communication remains an elusive goal in this era of accelerated marketization and globalization. The media inside China, foreign-invested or not, continue to serve as agents of social control and channels of communication of, by, and for the hegemonic bloc of the reformed party state, a rising middle class, and transnational capitalist interests. But just as the battle for market shares among different media firms is intensifying in the post-WTO Chinese media market, struggles for communicative power and individual and collective autonomy among various social forces are also intensifying. Highly organized Falun Gong practitioners have successfully hacked into state-controlled cable television networks and satellite systems and waged a protracted propaganda war with the Chinese state and dominant media institutions. Meanwhile, isolated and desperate individuals from other disenfranchised social groups, above all, rural women, have resorted to death as the only and final means of social communication and resistance (Lee and Kleinman 2003). The suicide rate among rural Chinese women is the highest of all population groups in the world (Rosenthal 1999). How to connect the macropolitics of media democratization and globalization with the "militant particularism" (Williams 1989) of these communicative social subjects and the micropolitics of the everyday production of meaning remains a formidable challenge.

REFERENCES

Associated Press. 2003. "Murdoch's Appeal to Chinese Leaders." October 9, 2003, available at www.afr.com/articles/2003/10/09/1065601040384.html (accessed October 12, 2003).

Barmé, Geremie. 1998. "Spring Clamor and Autumnal Silence: Cultural Control in China." *Current History* 97, no. 620: 257–62.

Bush Calls U.S., Australia Partners in Terrorism Fight. 2003. White House transcript of U.S. President George W. Bush's speech to the Australia Parliament, October 23, 2003, available at http://usembassy.state.gov/tokyo/wwwh20031024a3.html (accessed October 27, 2003).

Chan, Joseph Man, Zhongdang Pan, and Francis L. F. Lee. 2004. "Professional Aspirations and Job Satisfaction: Chinese Journalists at a Time of Change in the Media." *Journalism & Mass Communication Quarterly* 81, no. 2: 254–73.

Chang, Leslie. 1999. "A Phoenix Rises in China: Rupert Murdoch's Satellite TV Thrives, Legalities Notwithstanding." *The Wall Street Journal*, March 26, 2002, B4.

China Mainland Marketing Research Co. 1998. *An Overview of Phoenix TV's Audience Rating in Mainland China.* Beijing: China Mainland Marketing Research Co.

Chipman, Kim. 2002. "Playboy's Interest in China Rises." *The Vancouver Sun*, October 22, 2002, D11.

Curran, James. 1978. "The Press as an Agency of Social Control: A Historical Perspective." In *Newspaper History: From the 17th Century to the Present Day*, eds. G. Boyce, J. Curran, and P. Wingate, 51–75. London: Constable.

Fewsmith, Joseph. 2001. *China since Tiananmen: The Politics of Transition.* Cambridge: Cambridge University Press.

García Canclini, Néstor. [1995] 2001. *Consumers and Citizens: Globalization and Multicultural Conflicts*, trans. George Yúdice. Minneapolis: University of Minnesota Press.

Gilley, Bruce. 2001. "Jiang's Turn Tempts Fate." *Far Eastern Economic Review* (August 3, 2000): 18–20.

Goldman, Merle. 1999. "Politically-Engaged Intellectuals in the 1990s." *The China Quarterly* 159: 700-711.

Goodman, David. 1999. "China's New Middle Class." In *The Paradox of China's Post-Mao Reforms*, eds. M. Goldman and R. MacFarquhar, 241–61. Cambridge, MA: Harvard University Press.

Gutmann, Ethan. 2002. "Who Lost China's Internet?" *Weekly Standard,* February 15, 2002, available at www.weeklystandard.com/Utilities/printer_preview.asp?idArticle =922 (accessed July 1, 2004).

Hallin, Daniel C. 2000. "Commercialism and Professionalism in the American News Media." In *Mass Media and Society*, eds. J. Curran and M. Gurevitch, 3rd ed., 218–37. London: Arnold.

He, Qinglian. 2000. "China's Listing Social Structure." *New Left Review* 5: 69–99.

Herman, Edward, and Robert W. McChesney. 1997. *The Global Media: The New Missionaries of Corporate Capitalism.* London: Cassell.

Hill, Christopher. 1972. *The World Turned Upside Down: Radical Ideas during the English Revolution.* London: Temple Smith.

Hu, Zhengrong. 2003. "The Post-WTO Restructuring of the Chinese Media Industries and the Consequences of Capitalisation." *The Public/Javnost* 10, no. 4: 19–36.

Klein, Naomi. 2000. *No Logo.* Toronto: Knopf Canada.

Lee, Chin-Chuan. 2002. "Chinese Communication: Prisms, Trajectories, and Modes of Understanding." In *Power, Money, and Media: Communication Patterns and Bureaucratic Control in Cultural China,* ed. Chin-Chuan Lee, 3–44. Evanston, IL: Northwestern University Press.

———. 2003. "The Global and the National of the Chinese Media: Discourses, Market, Technology, and Ideology." In *Chinese Media, Global Contexts,* ed. Chin-Chuan Lee, 1–31. New York: RoutledgeCurzon.

Lee, Ching Kwan. 2002. "From the Specter of Mao to the Spirit of Law: Labor Insurgency in China." *Theory and Society* 31, no. 2: 189–228.

———. 2003. "Pathways of Labour Insurgency." In *Chinese Society: Change, Conflict and Resistance,* 2nd ed., eds. Elizabeth J. Perry and Mark Selden, 71–92. New York: RoutledgeCurzon.

Lee, Sing, and Arthur Kleinman. 2003. "Suicide as Resistance in Chinese Society." In *Chinese Society: Change, Conflict and Resistance,* eds. E. J. Perry and M. Selden, 2nd ed., 289–311. New York: RoutledgeCurzon.

Lu, Xueyi. 2001. *A Report on Research into China's Social Strata.* Beijing: Shekewenxian chubanshe.

Madsen, Richard. 2003. "Chinese Christianity: Indigenization and Conflict." In *Chinese Society: Change, Conflict and Resistance,* eds. E. J. Perry and M. Selden, 2nd ed., 271–88. New York: RoutledgeCurzon.

McChesney, Robert. 1999. *Rich Media, Poor Democracy: Communication Politics in Dubious Times.* Urbana: University of Illinois Press.

McCormick, Barrett L. 2002/2003. "Recent Trends in Mainland China's Media: Political Implications of Commercialization." *Issues and Studies* 38, no. 4/39, no. 1 (December/March): 175–215.

McManus, John H. 1994. *Market-Driven Journalism: Let Citizens Beware?* Thousand Oaks, CA: Sage.

Moore, Barrington, Jr. 1993. *Social Origins of Dictatorship and Democracy: Lord and Peasants in the Making of the Modern World.* 2nd ed. New York: Beacon Press.

Naughton, Barry. 2000. "The Chinese Economy: Fifty Years into Transformation." In *China Briefing 2000,* ed. T. White, 49–70. Armonk, NY: M. E. Sharpe.

Ong, Aihwa. 1999. *Flexible Citizenship: The Cultural Logics of Transnationality.* Durham, NC: Duke University Press.

Pan, Zhongdang, and Lu Ye. 2003. "Localizing Professionalism: Discursive Practices in China's Media Reform." In *Chinese Media, Global Contexts,* ed. Chin-Chuan Lee, 215–36. New York: RoutledgeCurzon.

Pan, Zhongdang, and Joseph Man Chan. 2003. "Shifting Journalistic Paradigms: How China's Journalists Assess 'Media Exemplars.'" *Communication Research* 30, no. 6: 649–82.

Pei, Minxin. 2003. "Rights and Resistance: The Changing Contexts of the Dissident Movement." In *Chinese Society: Change, Conflict and Resistance,* eds. E. J. Perry and M. Selden, 2nd ed., 23–46. New York: RoutledgeCurzon.

Pendakur, Manjunath, and Jyotsna Japur. 1996. "Thinking Globally, Program Locally: Privatization of Indian National Television." In *Democratizing Communication? Comparative Perspectives on Information and Power,* eds. M. Bailie and D. Winseck, 195–217. Cresskill, NJ: Hampton Press.

Perry, Elizabeth J. 1999. "Crime, Corruption, and Contention." In *The Paradox of China's Post-Mao Reforms*, eds. Merle Goldman and Roderick MacFarquhar, 308–29. Cambridge, MA: Harvard University Press.

Perry, Elizabeth J., and Mark Selden. 2003. "Introduction: Reform and Resistance in Contemporary China." In *Chinese Society: Change, Conflict and Resistance*, eds. E. J. Perry and M. Selden, 2nd ed., 1–22. New York: RoutledgeCurzon.

Rosenthal, Elisabeth. 1999. "Women's Suicides Reveal Rural China's Bitter Roots." *The New York Times*, January 24, 1999, A12.

Sparks, Colin, and John Tulloch. 2000. *Tabloid Tales: Global Debates over Media Studies*. Lanham, MD: Rowman & Littlefield.

Thornton, Patricia M. 2003. "The New Cybersects: Resistance and Repression in the Reform Era." In *Chinese Society: Change, Conflict and Resistance*, eds. E. J. Perry and M. Selden, 2nd ed., 247–70. New York: RoutledgeCurzon.

Wang, Hui. 2003. *China's New Order: Society, Politics, and Economy in Transition*, ed. Theodore Huters. Cambridge, MA: Harvard University Press.

Williams, Raymond. 1989. *Resources of Hope: Culture, Democracy, and Socialism*. London: Verso.

York, Geoffrey. 2002. "Gusty Critic of China Fears for His Safety." *The Globe and Mail*, June 25, 2002, A3.

Zhang, Weiguo. 1999. "10 Years in Jail for Providing Information to Radio Free Asia on Labor Protests inside China." *The Christian Science Monitor*, February 24, 1999, 6.

Zhao, Yuezhi. 1998. *Media, Market, and Democracy in China: Between the Party Line and the Bottom Line*. Urbana: University of Illinois Press.

———. 2000a. "From Commercialization to Conglomeration: The Transformation of the Chinese Press within the Orbit of the Party State." *Journal of Communication* 50, no. 2: 3–26.

———. 2000b. "Watchdogs on Party Leashes? Contexts and Limitations of Investigative Journalism in Post-Deng China." *Journalism Studies* 1, no. 2: 577–97.

———. 2001. "Media and Elusive Democracy in China." *The Public/Javnost* 8, no. 2: 21–44.

———. 2002a. *Media and Ideology in China: The Left, the Right, and the Poverty of Political Imaginations*. Paper presented at the Fifty-second Annual Convention of the International Communication Association, Seoul, Korea.

———. 2002b. "The Rich, the Laid-Off, and the Criminal in Tabloid Tales: Read All About It!" In *Popular China: Unofficial Culture in a Globalizing Society*, eds. P. Link, R. Madsen, and P. Pickowicz, 111–35. Lanham, MD: Rowman & Littlefield.

———. 2003a. "Underdogs, Lapdogs, and Watchdogs: Journalists and the Public Sphere Problematic in China." In *Chinese Intellectuals between the State and the Market*, eds. G. Xin and M. Goldman, 43–74. New York: RoutledgeCurzon.

———. 2003b. "'Enter the World': Neo-Liberal Globalization, the Dream for a Strong Nation, and Chinese Press Discourses on the WTO." In *Chinese Media, Global Context*, ed. Chin-Chuan Lee, 32–56. New York: RouteledgeCurzon.

———. 2003c. "Transnational Capital, the Chinese State, and China's Communication Industries in a Fractured Society." *The Public/Javnost* 10, no. 4: 53–74.

———. 2003d. "Falun Gong, Identity, and the Struggle over Meaning inside and outside China." In *Contesting Media Power: Alternative Media in a Networked Society*, eds. N. Couldry and J. Curran, 209–24. Lanham, MD: Rowman & Littlefield.

———. 2004. "When the Tide Goes Out, the Rocks Are Revealed." *New Internationalist* 371 (September): 20–21.

Zhao, Yuezhi, and Dan Schiller. 2001. "Dances with Wolves? China's Integration with Digital Capitalism." *Info* 3, no. 2: 137–51.

4

Contested Futures: Indian Media at the Crossroads

Pradip Thomas

The media in India, inclusive of its institutions, policies, ownership patterns, technologies, and priorities, underwent substantive change during the period between 1985 and 2003. In an era characterized by convergence and continuing political and economic instabilities, change remains a haphazard process and prospect. This haphazardness is evident in the many accountability problems related to the privatization of telecommunications and the granting of cellular and FM radio licenses, as well as the innumerable delays in legislating the bill on convergence (Carp 1995). What are the key impulses generating change in the media in India? Where do these impulses come from? Who benefits from these new media arrangements and priorities? Are the media in India merely a reflection of global media, or can the concept of "relative autonomy" be used to describe the media in India? What roles does the state play in media globalization and/or media democratization? Which title best characterizes the media in India—media globalization or media democratization?

It would be limiting to characterize these changes using an either/or framework. In spite of the massive forays by the market into every conceivable area of the Indian economy, the country has a history of democracy and, despite the turn to an exclusive politics in recent years, continues to remain the site for what the writer V. S. Naipaul once described as "a million mutinies." But what has resulted from these million mutinies? Do they represent localized traditions of protest and struggle? Or are there instances of protest coalescing to form viable alternatives to the norm at local, regional, and national levels? And what role do the media, both old and new, play in generating, sustaining, and legitimizing such initiatives? Finally, what do these mutinies mean in the context of a rapidly globalizing India?

THE STATE AND THE MEDIA

One of the failed premises of postmodernity is the decline of grand narratives, such as that of the modern state in networked societies, in the wake of multinational corporations (MNCs) and in the context of the information economy. While new technologies do pose significant challenges to the modern state, for instance, its ability to control information flows (entertainment, capital, ideas), current evidence seems to suggest that the state is responding to this challenge and, as has been the case with surveillance, is attempting to extend its embrace over new information flows. While MNCs and multilateral trade negotiations have compromised the "independence" of any given state, the obverse is also true in the sense that some of the larger states in the south and the north do have the leveraging power to maintain some of their independence. China is by no means a cakewalk for foreign MNCs. In the case of India, the much-heralded economic liberalization that the country is experiencing today is being calibrated by the state on behalf of its domestic and international constituencies. In other words, while economic globalization is, on one level, an imposition, it is, on another level, also the consequence of an active engagement and deliberate commitment by domestic actors with the many processes associated with economic globalization. In the light of the energies devoted to this mediation, the deficit with regards to the state's "public" commitments and responsibilities is becoming a visible reality. Given these real deficits and externally and domestically inspired economic priorities, the state and civil society often find themselves at loggerheads with each other—and India is no exception to this rule.

This chapter explores some of the public deficits of the state that result from these external and domestic economic pressures, their consequences for the media in India, and the role of democratic media in creating the spaces and opportunities for another development. The Indian state remains a powerful force in the shaping of India's economic future. It is also, in the wake of the turn to *Hindutva* (literally, the Hindu nation), implicated in defining identity in India and legitimizing the quality of Indianness. The state has also been a primary actor in the shaping of communications in India today. This shaping occurs in direct and indirect ways:

- Direct: This is demonstrated by its primary role as the shaper of communication policies in India, whether in the area of old or new media, and regulatory environments related to old and new media, including the press, broadcasting, telecommunications, and the Internet, providing largesse to sympathetic media and, in its monopoly, punitive sanctions against media that are deemed to transgress official limits. Until the early 1990s, media ownership in India was a shared enterprise, with the state controlling broadcasting and the infrastructures related to satellites and telecommunications and with the private sector controlling ownership of the press, advertising, and the film industry. However, privately owned media were regulated by the state, and legislations were invoked from time to time to bring them into line. During the infamous Emergency (1975–1977), the press was actively repressed. The advent of satellite and cable television has led to changes in broadcasting. A number of domestic and transnational players are involved in commercial satellite broadcasting today, and the state channel, Doordarshan, has responded by commercializing some of its services and attempting to compete with the new players. The presence of the state continues to be a defining feature of the mediascape in India. It has recently been involved in regulating the cable industry and creating "must carry" rules that make it mandatory for cable channels to include Doordarshan in their bouquet of channels, in the streamlining of film finances, and, more recently, in placing limits on foreign ownership of the press and broadcasting.

- Indirect: This is demonstrated by the tacit support that it continues to grant certain media institutions and practices over others, for instance the production of content that is supportive of the cause of Hindutva, such as mythological soap operas, as opposed to contentious serials that expose the chinks in the interpretation of Indian history from within narrow Hindu nationalist perspectives or turning a blind eye to the carving up of cable turf in Mumbai by groups belonging to the Hindu nationalist regional party, the Shiv Sena.

The consequences of this shaping are manifold. The shift from a dirigiste (state-directed) economy to one based on the market has resulted in a shift in communication priorities from a prodevelopment to a promarket focus. The accent today is on state support for the infrastructures of globalization—the software economy, information-technology (IT) development, the media-export industries—and harmonizing the Indian communication-policy environment with externally generated, global requirements. Consequently, there is little support for media practices or media institutions that are not promarket oriented. It is too early to predict whether the recently elected Congress government's prorural outlook will lead to a balance in media representations of Indian realities, or whether there will be another approach to the exercise of state power after the openly antidemocratic stance adopted by the previous Hindu nationalist government led by the Bharitya Janata Party (BJP). The BJP had intentionally "saffronized" politics and society and co-opted a number of federal institutions involved in the maintenance of checks and balances, with the exception of the supreme court. The belligerence over Kashmir, support for the Narmada valley development project, and continuing support for tainted, BJP-based state governments, such as that in Gujarat, which has been implicated in pogroms against minorities, are examples of the previous government's openly nationalistic stance. However, the unexpected defeat of the BJP in the 2004 parliamentary elections at the hands of the rural and urban poor, a defeat that was totally at odds with media predictions, has placed the breaks on the pursuit of hard nationalism and free-market economics. Ordinary people who did not benefit from "India Shining," an electoral slogan adopted by the BJP and its allies, decided to opt for other alternatives—most spectacularly in the southern Indian state of Andhra Pradesh, a state that had become a favorite for global media coverage because of its protechnology head of state Chandrababu Naidu and his ambitions to turn his state into an IT/biotechnology hub.

There are those who believe that governance has become pluralized in contemporary India, given the many nonstate actors, domestic and international, who are, in addition to the state, involved in mediating citizen rights (Chandhoke 2003). However, the exercise of substantive power, in spite of high-caste hand-wringing over the assertive politics of Dalits and other backward classes (OBCs), continues to be in the hands of a largely Brahmin elite, who, despite their relative size, exert a disproportionate influence through their occupying positions of power in government, the civil service, central-government run institutions, and the private sector, including the cultural industry, as well as through their control of the top rungs of Hindu nationalism, for instance, the *Sangh Parivar* (name given to the collective "family" of the Hindu Right). The reality of Brahminization remains a theoretical blind spot for social scientists, especially for those who have adopted new narratives of emancipation related to theories such as postmodernism and postcolonialism. While one can argue that there has been a democratization of rights in India and cite any number of examples to prove one's case, the color of substantive power remains saffron, upper caste, and immutable. The vast majority of Indians remain subjects of, and not citizens in, the "world's largest democracy."

The world's largest democracy is currently poised to become one of the world's largest markets. Planned development is being carried out in conjunction with market forces. The BJP and the Congress are deeply committed to economic liberalization in spite of the fact that some members of the *Sangh Parivar* and allies of Congress (notably the Communists) are not in favor of unrestricted economic liberalization. This is to be expected, given that the hard core of their support comes from business interests.

While there are many real, local success stories (e.g., software, outsourcing, satellite program, call centers, animation industry) that have global consequences (e.g., the controversy over business-process outsourcing [BPO] and its impact on First World labor), the global media accent on India's software industry needs to be tempered by other less palatable stories that are equally real for the people of India, from the feudal constancy of India's political elite and its consequences for democratization, to the rising levels of poverty even in the heartlands of India's software states, notably Karnataka and Andhra Pradesh. Economic globalization continues to be contested as the distance between the increasingly disengaged and disconnected enclaves of prosperity and the real India becomes ever sharper. While a potent source of conflict in contemporary India is Hindu nationalism and the many and varied attempts to reinvent and mediate India solely on the basis of a renascent, recidivist Hinduism, the assault on democracy can by no means be attributable to a single cause. The layering of this discourse with other equally problematic discourses, such as corruption, restricts the potential for social change and the democratization of structures. While these stories and doubtless many others need to be drawn upon to create the big picture, I would like to, for the purposes of this chapter, focus on the following two lesser-known stories that nevertheless reflect the real tensions that remain at the very core of democratization and globalization processes in India.

THE LESSONS OF TEHELKA

Tehelka was a dot-com investigative news service founded by journalists in 2000. It had uncovered a major cricket-match-fixing scandal, then conducted a covert sting operation that netted a swathe of establishment figures, including politicians, such as the present defense minister, and military personnel in a procurement-procurement corruption scandal. The transcripts of the covert video recording were placed on the Tehelka website, and the scandal threatened to bring down the government. But that did not happen. In fact, today, it is Tehelka that is on the run. A number of its journalists have been imprisoned and investors have been scared off; it is on the verge of bankruptcy, its offices have been raided a number of times by the police and the income tax department, and its staff had been reduced from 120 to 4 by 2003. A good number of the senior politicians implicated in the scandal continue to hold senior positions. The exposure of systemic corruption, it would seem, is an issue that affects all politicians irrespective of their party affiliations; hence, the tardy, lukewarm, inconsistent response from coalitional members belonging to the ruling party and the opposition. Even more depressing is the lack of a consistent follow-up by the mainstream media on an issue that could easily have led to the fall of the government. Why was this not done? And what does this reveal about the media in India?

In some ways, this episode is a classic example of the pulls and pressures in contemporary India. It reveals the enormous power of the state apparatus, the many vested interests involved in protecting the status quo, and the lack of transparency and accountability at the highest levels of public office in India. It also points to deficits in civil society, to the inability of civil society and democratic media to create a common front on an issue that was arguably one of the most serious examples of the breakdown of trust and governance in modern India. This scenario stands in stark contrast to the aftermath of the Emergency in the late 1970s, when a number of journalists created new standards in investigative journalism. Today, many of these same journalists have opted to remain silent or, worse, to blame Tehelka for its demise. But this example also reveals the real limits to reporting in "democratic" India today and the existence of a variety of pressures—economic, political, legal—used by the state to rein in dissenting media. "Power," as the Indian writer Arundhati Roy (1999, 61) observes, "is fortified not just by what it destroys, but also by what it creates. Not just by what it takes, but also by what it gives. And Powerlessness reaffirmed not just by the helplessness of those who have lost, but also by the gratitude of those who have (or think they have) gained."

POVERTY: A MISSING DIMENSION IN THE MEDIA IN INDIA

If the above example illustrates the persistence of a control state, the lack of accountability, and the role played by domestic politics in the policing of the media, the second example relates to the reporting of poverty in India, and illustrates the commercial pressures on and the profit orientation and standardization of media content that have become the conspicuous by-products of economic liberalization and media globalization.

In April 2000, the government acknowledged that large parts of India were in the grip of a severe drought. Twelve states in India were affected, including in Rajasthan, twenty-six out of thirty-two districts, and in Gujarat, seventeen districts covering 9,421 villages. There were reports of starvation-related deaths of human beings and cattle. After more than a decade during which issues related to poverty had largely been bypassed by the mainstream Indian media, media audiences were presented with poverty in all its starkness. It was, as Khare (2000, 1) has pointed out, a rude awakening to an India that had been mesmerized by its growth rates and little else. "We have been rudely jolted out of our collective reverie about economic abundance, booming stock markets, cyber revolution and venture capitalism. Just when we had thought that we had entered the New Economy's fast lane, we are suddenly being forced to come to terms with evidence of starvation, destitution and deprivation so familiar in the Old Economy."

The mainstream media had, rather conspicuously, embraced the new economic policy popularized by the Rajiv Gandhi government in the late 1980s with its accent on economic liberalization, privatization, and consumerism. Content priorities had also undergone change, and satellite broadcasting and the new media were responsible for a new global emphasis on lifestyle, fashion, business, sports, entertainment, and personalities at the expense of other concerns, many of which are glaringly visible from the doorsteps and windows of corporate media houses. The rural beat that lacked glamour and has always be seen as a burden by state broadcasters and journalists underwent further downgrading in the context of these new priorities and the accent on targeted viewer and readership. While there has been a quantitative increase in news readership and more pages per issue, including special consumer sections, as well as a variety of entertainment programs on national television, not to mention cable channels, little or no space is devoted to issues related to how the other half lives and dies in rural and urban India. In fact, one could read the national press and be lulled by the global feel to those papers. In a context characterized by such indifference, the vacuum for poverty news has been filled by statistics churned out by the government's publicity machine. The central and state governments, which had been caught off guard by the drought, responded with classic media-management, damage-limitation exercises. The cyber- and media-savvy chief minister of Andhra Pradesh, Chandrababu Naidu, predictably went on the offensive and, as one commentator has remarked,

> The media [we]re inundated with a flood of statistics at regular press conferences and Chandra Babu Naidu himself held weekly video conference sessions with his District Collectors that [were] open to the public and the press to watch. Government hand outs list[ed] the many "action plans" that [were] in the pipeline and endless lists of the quantum of money spent under different heads of expenditure and drought relief. (Menon 2000, 132)

Not surprisingly media reports tend to regurgitate official statistics: the number of tube wells that have been sunk, the people who have benefited from drought relief, the number who are employed in Work for Food campaigns, the amount of money that has been disbursed for drought relief, the amount of fodder that has been procured, and so forth and so on. Few journalists have bothered to verify official statistics or to confirm that out of the 280,000 bore wells in Andhra Pradesh, close to 100,000 are defunct or that most of the 25,000 protected water-supply schemes are nonfunctional. But then, issues related to poverty are typically dealt with in an episodic manner—fleeting, occasional, event-centered. The Indian journalist P. Sainath (2000, 22), who ranks among a handful of journalists covering poverty, is critical of the priorities of post-economic-liberalization journalists in India: "We have full-time fashion correspondents, glamour correspondents and design correspondents . . . 11 correspondents covering business in a non-financial daily in a society where less than 2 per cent of the population have investments of any kind. But in all of these beats, you do not have a single full-time correspondent covering poverty."

Very few of these reports provide information on the reasons for drought—environmental degradation, poor life-support systems, the destruction of common property resources, and the political economy of globalization as it affects the hinterlands. It is only the occasional journalist who opts to investigate the larger, long-term reasons for events such as a drought or is inclined to frame poverty as a process rather than as an event. The few who do, paint a grim picture. Parvati Menon (2000, 130), reporting in one of India's few socially conscious news magazines, *Frontline,* on the effects of the drought on a little hamlet, Gairangadda, in Andhra Pradesh, has this to say on the cumulative reasons for the drought: "The drying up of water sources, both for drinking and agriculture, has led to crop losses, loss of jobs, increasing levels of indebtedness, distress sale of cattle and other assets, increase in out-migration, a sharp drop in purchasing power, which the recent hike in administered prices has added to and a growing population of the undernourished and the hungry." The world fed on a diet of India on the move—Bangalore's Silicon valley, software exports, the number-one destination for IT outsourcing projects, and Cyberabad—is probably not going to hear of the many reports of the suicides of cotton farmers in Andhra Pradesh, the increased activities of the Marxist-Leninist (ML) Naxalite movement, or the recent stories of farmers in this state selling their kidneys as a way of getting out of their indebtedness and poverty (Sekhar 2000). These stories point to the fact that the real India simply cannot be wished away or changed with the right infusions of new technologies.[1]

MEDIA CONSOLIDATIONS IN INDIA TODAY

The media in India today is characterized, on the one hand, by consolidation and, on the other, by state regulation of the media, often from within narrow party political, rather than public, interest. The promarket focus of the present government is reflected in the raft of changes that have been made to previous legislations, for instance, to the Monopolies and Restrictive Trade Practices Act (MRTP) that once curbed excessive concentration of ownership in key economic industries. Deregulation, privatization, and the easing of restrictions on monopolies and cross-sectoral media ownership have led to the emergence of a breed of local entrepreneurs but also to business convergences between old business families and new economic opportunities. The Tatas, the Ambanis, the Thapars, the Modis, and the Birlas are among the venerable business families in India, who between them have substantive interests in the telecoms and media sectors. In fact, these groups have cornered large sectors of the media market. Consolidation is the name of the game today. The Tatas had by the mid-1980s diversified media interests; they were involved in the business of producing both software and hardware for the computer industry (Tata Unisys and Tata Consultancy Services), in telecommunication (Tata Telecom), in advertising and public relations (PR) (Good Relations PR), and in the music industry (Tata-CBS).

After a brief flurry of players in the cellular phone market, there have been consolidations and/or planned mergers between the few remaining players. The biggest of the mergers between BPL, AT&T, Tata Cellular, and Birla has led to the formation of BPL-BATATA, the largest cellular-service provider in the country with 24 percent of the country's cellular-subscriber base.

Consolidation of ownership is also evident in other media-related areas, for example, in cable television, the Internet, and FM radio.

The government has attempted to regulate the rather chaotic cable television industry, with its more than eighty thousand independent cable operators, by way of legislations such as the amended Cable Television Networks (Regulation) Act (2002) and, more recently, by way of a Conditional Access System (CAS) ostensibly meant to make this industry consumer friendly. However, it is clear that the government is veering toward support for the big players. The losers in this game, rather unfortunately, are the local cable outfits that were responsible for ushering in the cable revolution in India in the first place (Kumar 2003). The winners are a small group, including the Hindujas-owned cable TV distribution company, INCableTV, Zee's Siticable, and a few others. This very same pattern of consolidation has affected the Internet service provider (ISP) market. Out of the 437 firms that applied for an ISP license in the late 1990s, only 75 were active in December 2000. Consolidation has also affected local radio. The government attempted to auction 108 FM frequencies in August 2000. Initially, there were bids from twenty-three groups, but the high license fees led to many dropouts and to consolidation in this industry. Today ten leading players operate the twenty-one stations that have so far been licensed. Key players in FM radio include media conglomerates like the Bennet Coleman (*Times of India*)–owned Entertainment Network India Limited that currently operates FM radio stations in thirteen cities in India and Music Broadcast Private Limited, owned by Murdoch's Star Group, that operates six FM stations ("Radio Report" 2002).

GLOBAL MEDIA IN THE INDIAN MARKET

While the state can and does regulate the presence of foreign media players in broadcasting and the news media, it is unclear whether it will indefinitely be allowed to maintain its protectionist policies and its writ over ownership in the domestic media market. Two examples—the government's succumbing to trade-related pressures on the issue of Hollywood imports and its accommodation to global intellectual property rights (IPR) policies—are illustrative of the current dilemmas facing the Indian government.

SECTION 301 AND INDIA

In the 1990s, the United States Trade Representative (USTR) used Section 301 against India, ostensibly in retaliation against India's inability to curb video piracy. There were, however, larger trade- and security-related motives, including the lowering of perceived high tariffs in industrial imports and the opening up of the banking and insurance sectors to foreign investment, along with the immediate motive of positioning Hollywood in the Indian film market. While piracy is a reality in India—the International Intellectual Property Association (IIPA) has estimated 2002 trade losses to the U.S. copyright industry incurred in India to be in the neighborhood of U.S. $468.1 million, covering book, cable, video, music, business software, Internet, retail, and entertainment software piracies (IIPA 2003)—the infinitely larger prospect of earnings from a potential audience for Hollywood in the region of U.S. $200 million led to a larger game plan to carve out 10 percent of the Indian film market by 2000 and to open up the Indian film market. An immediate goal was to pressure the Indian government to lift the restrictive annual import quota of one hundred Hollywood films. While the schedule of commitments agreed to by the Indian government on trade in services dated April 15, 1994, under 2D Audiovisual Services rather blandly states that "ii) Import of titles restricted to 100 per year" (Government of India 1994), the government did, in less than a year, in 1995, decide to increase this quota from one hundred to two hundred films a year, to the delight of the Motion Picture Association of America (MPAA), which represented the interests of seven Hollywood majors, including Walt Disney Company, Sony Pictures Entertainment, Metro-Goldwyn-Mayer, Paramount Pictures Corporation, Twentieth Century Fox Film Corporation, Universal Studios, and Warner Brothers. On January 29, 2002, the Government of India Ministry of Commerce and Industry, Department of Commerce, issued Public Notice No. 64/1997–2002, which announced the end of the quota system: "(i) Import of cinematograph feature films and other films (including film on video tape, compact video disc, laser video disc or digital video disc) shall be allowed without a license" (Government of India 2002).

The USTR has also imposed sanctions on occasion: "In April 1992, the President suspended duty-free privileges under the Generalized System of Preferences (GSP) for $60 million in trade from India. . . . Benefits on certain chemicals . . . were withheld from India, increasing the trade for which GSP is suspended to approximately $80 million" (www.ustr.com). The USTR's actions are not only directed toward increasing film quotas but toward systematically opening this sector, along with a variety of other trade-related sectors, to U.S. investments. It monitors the progress of IPR- and audiovisual (AV)–related domestic legislations, exerts pressure on the government to lift control restrictions, monitors anti-free-trade activities, and follows through on its intent to use bilateral and multilateral means to open this sector to U.S. capital. In the case of motion pictures, the USTR is currently involved in negotiating the lifting of domestic barriers to trade, including precensorship certification of films, the fees involved, entertainment taxes, the import of film/video publicity material, and the ceiling of $6 million for remittances by foreign film producers for balance-of-payment reasons (USTR, www.ustr .com; for more details, see Thomas 2003).

Bollywood, inclusive of its regional manifestations in South India, is a significant basis for Indian popular culture. Like most popular culture, the Indian variant reflects a mixture of deep conservatism and a politics of the possible. It nurtures an elite star system but is also deeply inscribed in the cultural narratives that the majority of Indians relate to. The values that it espouses are often out of sync with Indian reality, and yet, there are always popular films that problematize issues related to governance, citizenship, consumerism, and the human predicament. I would argue that in spite of its many contradictions and its resolute grounding in a market economy, Bollywood is a reflection of global cultural diversity. Therefore, it is worth protecting. While I am, on the one hand, critical of Bollywood values, I am equally, if not more, critical of the predatory nature of global Hollywood.

So, what are some of the threats posed by Hollywood? First, the presence of Hollywood needs to be seen as a threat to the plural nature of film production in India. This industry employs a couple of million people—from the billboard artist to the stars, and while it can be argued that the film industry in India needs to be professionalized, it remains a uniquely Indian industry, with a variety of distinct characteristics and cooperative traditions of film production. Although it is true that Hollywood in India will have to Indianize in order to survive (like MTV India), its control over film memory (ownership of film archives), film production, film distribution, and broadcasting outlets places it at a distinct advantage over the domestic industry. Second, there are issues related to the sanctions-based political economy of change that is being imposed by the MPAA and the USTR. Third, there is the issue of reciprocity; it is very difficult for the Indian film industry to break into Western markets. There have been a couple of successful crossover films, like *Lagaan* and *Bend It Like Beckham*, but these are not strictly Bollywood productions.

ENFORCING THE INTELLECTUAL PROPERTY WRIT

The tightening and strengthening of copyright enforcement with respect to domestic cultural products, film in particular, has also become part of MPAA's New Delhi–based, Indiawide operations. It would seem that such a prioritizing will, in the long run, also ensure the protection of Hollywood films in India. The reason for MPAA's involvement in copyright protection of local film products becomes clearer when seen against the investments made by one of its members, Sony Pictures' Indian wing, Colombia Tri-Star India. It was the first Hollywood company to earn in excess of 100 rupees crore at the Indian box office, and India now ranks among the fifteen top film markets for Sony. The company earned 30 percent of its income from the production of Indian-English films and 70 percent from film distribution. Hollywood share in the Indian film market is around 10 percent, and this needs to be seen against the 300 rupees crore loss suffered by Bollywood in 2003 (Gumaste 2003). Furthermore, Sony Entertainment TV, launched in October 1995 in the Indian subcontinent, has bought rights to three hundred Hindi films and secured exclusive rights for cultural and sporting events in India. Sony also hosts the top-rated show *Aahat,* currently has access to and owns fifteen hundred hours of exclusive programming, has invested millions of dollars in dubbing Hollywood films into Hindi and in the making of local feature films, and is also involved in making profits from its Sony music label. Similarly, another member of MPAA, Twentieth Century Fox, a subsidiary of News Corporation, is also poised to break into the film market with twenty productions per year. With such investments at stake, India can look forward to the active involvement of the MPAA in the matter of copyright enforcement. There is, of course, a major commercial reason for copyright enforcement that has to do with the global cross-sectoral marketing of products. These developments and the emergence of strong contenders in the domestic software and entertainment businesses, along with the entry of global players and North–South alliances supportive of copyright protection, have led to the emergence of a new culture of intellectual property (IP) in India consonant with the global IP regime.

The Indian government has attempted to harmonize its IP legislations with the Trade-Related Aspects of Intellectual Property (TRIPS) treaty and international copyright legislations. The range of policy changes that have recently been administered to India's intellectual property regime, along with policy changes in related areas such as telecommunications, is a clear indication of the extent to which a global proprietary agenda has become a significant aspect of India's social and economic future. The pace of accommodation with the TRIPS treaty has accelerated during the last two years. India had become a signatory to the Paris Convention and the Patent Cooperation Treaty on December 7, 1998, and had earlier become a signatory to the Berne Convention and the Universal Copyright Convention. Recent legislative changes that will have a direct impact on IPR in India include the following: the Patent (Amendments) Act, March 1999; the Copyright (Amendment) Act, December 1999, which conforms to the Berne Convention on Copyright and Related Rights; the Trademark Act, 1999; the Geographical Indications of Goods (Registration and Protection) Act; and the Designs Act,

2000, which is in compliance with TRIPS agreements on industrial designs. Other bills currently being debated in parliament include the Information Technology Bill, 2000, the Semiconductor Integrated Circuits Layout-Design Bill, and the Convergence Bill, which will address regulatory issues related to the convergence of communication, IT, and broadcasting (Thomas 2001).

In light of what is a grossly unequal power play, there is little that India can do to forge domestic trade policies in line with domestic requirements. A case in point is the ruling (March 29, 2003) on foreign news-channel up-links from India (Gopalakrishnan 2003).[2] The Union Cabinet has imposed a cap of 26 percent on foreign investment in news channels that wish to up-link from India, a ruling that has the potential (at least on paper) to dent the ambitions of Rupert Murdoch's Star News channel. However, if this ruling is contested at the World Trade Organization (WTO) as an instance of an unfair trade practice or barrier, it is more than likely that the Indian government will be forced to rescind its policy or face retaliatory measures. This is no light threat, for as the media critic Shalini Venturelli has observed,

> Under the supranational regulatory system, environmental policies can be invalidated as trade barriers, anti-concentration competition policies that ensure information diversity can be invalidated as trade barriers, cultural policy to provide pluralism in cultural expression can be invalidated as trade barriers and even constitutional guarantees of political rights, communication rights, and human rights as expressed in communication policy and social policy can be contested on grounds that they act to constrain international trade. (1997, 63)

MEDIA DEMOCRATIZATION IN INDIA

The term *media democratization* is typically multiaccentual, in the sense that it is used to denote (1) the creation of media environments responsive to the needs of people, (2) diverse, accountable, responsive mainstream media, and (3) the space for and use of people's media. It is not a stand-alone option but an essential aspect of the democratization of society.

Media democratization has never been a top priority for successive Indian governments. In fact, broadcasting, which remained a state monopoly until 1990, continues to be deemed the property of the state, to be used to extend the electoral advantage of the incumbent government. While there have been some moves to reform the media in postindependent India, these have been half-hearted attempts, and the reports of the many commissions set up have invariably been shelved. There is no dearth of official reports, and some very good recommendations related to public broadcasting, for instance, by the Joshi Commission, the setting up of an autonomous broadcasting council by the Verghese Commission, and the Hegde Commission's report on local radio, are all gathering dust. Even the ruling by the supreme court in 1995, the highest

court in India, that broadcasting is public property has not led to any percepti-
ble, propeople policies related to broadcasting. In fact, the period from 1995
onward has been characterized by the parceling out of broadcasting between
the state and an increasingly small coterie of private firms.

Perhaps the only example of a state-generated attempt to democratize
communication that is indirectly supportive of media democratization is the
Freedom of Information Act enacted in 2002. This act recognizes that the
right to information is a fundamental human right. While it does include provisions that override restrictions to public information contained in the Official Secrets Act, a number of its provisions are negated by those contained in
the Prevention of Terrorism Ordinance (2000). Amulya Gopalakrishnan
(2003), in an article in *Frontline*, highlights some of the limitations of this bill:

> The Freedom of Information Bill . . . excludes Cabinet papers, including records
> of the Council of Ministers, Secretaries and other officials. This, in effect, shields
> the whole process of decision-making from mandatory disclosure. The blanket
> exemptions for security and defense organizations have also been criticized.
> Another shortcoming is the absence of an independent review of refusals to dis-
> close information. . . . [T]he law provides for two internal appeals within the
> government machinery and, in addition, blocks access to civil courts. . . . [T]he
> lack of an independent monitoring committee . . . means that ultimately the de-
> cision to release information rests with the administration.

Nevertheless, this legislation remains an important landmark in the history of
people's rights to information, transparency, accountability, and informed governance. It has spawned a number of state-level information-rights initiatives—
in Tamilnadu, Delhi, Rajasthan, Maharashtra, Goa, and Karnataka. To be fair,
the impetus for the Freedom of Information Act was generated by a number of
citizen's movements. The National Campaign for People's Rights to Information, which to some extent was motivated by the example of a peasant movement's attempts to create local government accountability through public hear-
ings (the *Mazdoor Shakti Sangathan* [MKSS] in Rajasthan), played an important
role in advocating and lobbying for a national right to information (Kumar
2003). The government has also been involved in setting up rural and urban
telecenters throughout India; however, these initiatives are the technology-
driven results of government largesse and are not meant to disturb feudal constancy and entrenched, local establishments.

THE IMPETUS FOR MEDIA DEMOCRATIZATION HAS OFTEN BEEN GENERATED BY CIVIL SOCIETY

Media democratization in India supported by civil society is essentially of
two kinds: (1) the use of the media in India to initiate change in social and

economic structures and political processes, and (2) media activism aimed at media reform and the creation of alternative voices and alternative media.

From the beginnings of India's tryst with empire, modernity, and the mass media, there have been attempts at using the media for effecting institutional reforms, creating the space for dialog, and as a channel for popular protest. The best examples of the latter are political protest theater, which was used by a number of anticolonial institutions—for instance, the Indian National Congress and the Communist Party of India–related *Indian People's Theatre Association* (IPTA)—to mobilize public opinion against British rule. This tradition was of earlier vintage, best illustrated by Dinabandhu Mittral's *Nildarpan* (1872), a story of the exploitation of workers in indigo plantations by British planters. This was a highly subversive play, and in response to the rise in anti-British political activism, the colonial government enacted the Dramatic Performances Act (1879) to curb such expressions. During the 1940s and 1950s, political theater was used by the anti-Brahmin movement in South India. This was followed by a massive upsurge in the use of popular theater for democratic reform in the 1970s. This tradition—with its variety of styles and formats, some of which were based on a fusion of traditional theater with modern, agit-prop styles influenced by Bertolt Brecht, Augusto Boal, Paulo Freire, and local activists, such as Badal Sircar, as well as organizations such as the *Safdar Hashmi Trust*—continues to be a favorite medium for mobilization, awareness raising, and strategizing for change. It is widely used throughout India by women's groups, the environmental movement, Dalit organizations, and antiglobalization activists, among other nongovernmental organizations (NGOs) involved in social change. Popular theater is an inexpensive medium, and provided that it is adapted to local conditions, expressions, and rhetorical styles, it can be a potent tool for awareness raising and community organizing. In the state of Tamilnadu in South India, street theater (Terrakoothu) is routinely used by NGOs with varying degrees of success in issues related to health, family planning, AIDS awareness, and interfaith and Dalit solidarity/rights issues. There are also many examples of the use of alternative video and film for social mobilization—from Madhyam in Bangalore to the Magic Lantern Foundation in New Delhi. Audiences in India tend to be film literate, given the influence of Bollywood, and video machines are ubiquitous. Nevertheless, given the costs involved, the lack of trained video professionals, and poor-quality products, doubts have been expressed about the efficacy of many a video/film initiative.

Media activism aimed at media reform is of more recent vintage. The term covers the activities carried out by what can loosely be called the media-reform movement in India. This movement consists of NGOs and activists involved in old media and new, who use a variety of platforms, channels, and strategies to achieve the end of media democratization. There are a number of dedicated alternative media NGOs, from the Pune-based Abhiyavyakti, to Voices in Bangalore, the Manipal-based Asian Network of Women in Communications, and the Goa-based group Bytes for All, among scores of other NGOs throughout India. There are groups involved in media education (literacy), networks such as the Delhi-based Sarai, which provide a forum for a critical understanding of the interfaces between new and old media, online media-democratization portals such as The Hoot, along with a number of IT-centered initiatives involved in the democratization of knowledge. The many Internet-centered initiatives—inclusive of telecenters, Internet radio, Indymedia-type open-publishing ventures, institutions like One World South Asia—are relatively new, urban, and essentially technology driven. While there are some much-heralded examples from the field, including the telecenters in Pondicherry supported by the MS Swaminathan Foundation, these centers remain essentially contained examples for global consumption and have not led to any significant local replications.

One of the key battles related to media democratization in India is the freeing of the airwaves from both state and market imperatives—the battle for community radio. Despite the fact that radio use in India has been tied to entertainment, there is great potential for centering radio as a tool for democratization. There is no tradition of community radio in South Asia, with the exception of Sri Lanka and Nepal, where there are a few examples of NGO-run broadcasting. Currently, a number of NGOs in India are involved in narrowcasting; they have set up studios and trained people belonging to the local community but are restrained by the lack of an official directive from the central government licensing community radio. This includes the Voices-Myrada project Namma Dhwani (Our Voice) in Kolar District, Karnataka; the radio project started by the Deccan Development Society in Medak District, Andhra Pradesh; and the initiative undertaken by the *Kutch Mahila Vikas Sangathan*, a rural women's group in Bhuj District, Gujarat (Ninan and Mehta 1999). The state has initiated its own "community broadcasting" over its All India Radio network and currently licenses NGOs to produce community-centered programs that are broadcast over its local radio stations. However, these have limited value, given that content must abide by national development guidelines and priorities. Nevertheless, the opportunities for training and program production resulting from these initiatives need to be seen in a positive light, for these initiatives have contributed to nurturing future community-radio activists in India.

While there are rumors related to the impending "freedom" of the airwaves in India, this has not become official policy as yet. While there are a few notable spokespeople for community radio in India and isolated attempts at lobbying in New Delhi, the lack of an Indiawide movement has hampered the opening up of the airwaves to social sectors. This inability to forge a nationwide consensus on community media is emblematic of realities within civil society and the existence of differences due to ideology, the politics of funding, access to technology, and limitations to networking.

MEDIA GLOBALIZATION OR MEDIA DEMOCRATIZATION

So, what future is there for media democratization in India? While it is clear that centralized media governance remains an obstacle to effective civil-society lobbying for media democracy, the slow but steady federalization of Indian politics and the migration of power to local states within federal India offer possibilities for local lobbying on communication issues. Despite the fact that public broadcasting remains a function of the central government, a limited service has begun in the state of Andhra Pradesh. Public broadcasting, in other words, is being decentralized. This needs to be seen as a first step on the road to media democratization. There are other hopeful signs. Individual states have, for instance, enacted freedom of information bills. This is an important step on the road to information accountability and transparency of governance at local levels. There is also the possibility, in light of the manner in which the cable television industry established itself in India, that a few copycat, pirate community-radio initiatives will lead to a country-wide, community-radio wave. This is not an impossible scenario. The origins of community radio in Latin America are, in most cases, linked to earlier traditions of pirate broadcasting.

The Indian economy is slowly, but surely, becoming integrated with the global economy. While the Indian government has publicly affirmed its intent to slow down the pace of liberalization under WTO rules, the examples of the harmonization of IP laws in India with TRIPS and the government's inability to protect its film market against Hollywood imports, alluded to in this paper, point to the real limits to any exuberant celebrations of media democratization in India. While new technologies can and do present possibilities for reform, the absence of a political will and the dispersed nature of civil-society mobilizations suggest that media reform at a national level will remain, at least for the immediate future, a distant possibility. Galloping economic liberalization, one-dimensional development policies typified by the ostrichlike attitude adopted by the outgoing government in the face of mounting evidence of rural poverty, the BJP's disregard for the rule of law as highlighted by its attitude toward the Tehelka scam, and increasing media concentrations in the domestic market do suggest that media democratization in India will remain a difficult, and at times painful, process. Whether the Congress government will be able to deliver on its promise of growth with distributive justice remains to be seen. For the moment, the ordinary voter's disavowal of the image of "India Shining" does suggest that democratic India will be shaped by the majority of its citizens, rather than by the chosen few.

NOTES

1. Seventy-five farmers in Karnataka state (capital, Bangalore) have committed suicide since August 1, 2003, due to the nonviability of agriculture ("Six More Farmers End Life," *The Hindu*, September 3, 2003, 1).

2. It is interesting to observe internal differences within the government of India on this matter; while the Communications, Home, and Finance ministries were open to allowing a 49 percent cap, the External Affairs Ministry pushed for the 26 percent cap that prevailed. The Indian government is sensitive to critical news from the outside on issues related to local governance. The bloodletting in Gujarat did damage the BJP's image outside of India, and it would seem that the 26 percent cap is related to controlling coverage and content within "acceptable" limits. Also see "Foreign Equity for News Channels Capped at 26 Percent," *The Hindu International Edition*, March 29, 2003, 12.

REFERENCES

Carp, J. 1995. "Reality Calling." *Far Eastern Economic Review* (October 5): 60–62.
Chandhoke, N. 2003. "Governance and the Pluralization of the State: Implications for Democratic Citizenship." *Economic & Political Weekly* 38, no. 28: 2957–67.
"Foreign Trade Barriers." 2004. India, available at www.ustr.gov/assets/Document_Library/Reports_Publication/2004/2004_National_Trade_Estimate/2004_NTE_Report/asset_upload_file973_4773.pdf.
Gopalakrishnan, A. 2002. "Information by Right." *Frontline* 20, no. 1: 18–31, available at www.hinduonnet.com/thehindu/thscrip/print (accessed August 5, 2004).
———. 2003. "Media: Down-sizing Foreign Equity." *Frontline* 20, no. 8: 1–4, available at www.flonnet.com/fl2008/stories (accessed August 5, 2004).
Government of India. 1994. Schedule of Specific Commitments, General Agreement GATS/SC/42, 15 April 1994 on Trade in Services, 94-1040, available at http://docsonline.wto.org/GEN_viewerwindow.asp (accessed August 5, 2004).
———. 2002. Ministry of Commerce and Industry, Department of Commerce, Public Notice to be published in the Gazette of India Extraordinary, available at http://dgftcom.nic.in/exim/2000/pn/pn01/pn6401.htm; also available at http://mib.nic.in/ncinematograph/htm (accessed August 5, 2004).
Gumaste, D. 2003. "Hollywood Piece of Cake." Rediff.com, available at http://rediff.com/movies (accessed February 5, 2003).
IIPA. 2003. *Special 301 Report India*, available at www.iipa.com (accessed August 5, 2004).
Khare, H. 2000. "Wanted, Sensitivity." *The Hindu Online*, May 18, 2000, available at www.hinduonnet.com/thehindu/2000/05/18/stories/05182523.htm (accessed August 5, 2004).
Kumar, A. 2003. "Right to Information: Background and Perspective," available at www.infochangeindia.org/RighttinfoIbpprint.jsp (accessed August 5, 2004).
Kumar, S. 2003. "Making Sense of CAS." *Frontline* 20, no. 13: 1–11, available at www.flonnet.com/fl2013/stories/20030740002909900.htm (accessed August 5, 2004).

Menon, P. 2000. "Drought and Delayed Relief." *Frontline* 17, no. 10 (May 26): 130–33.

Ninan, S., and A. Mehta. 1999. *Internet-Based Community Radio in India: A Way out of the Regulatory Bottleneck.* Unpublished manuscript, available at World Association for Christian Communication (accessed August 5, 2004).

"Radio Report: Radio in India, Players in Different Centres." 2002. Available at www.exchange4media.com/e4m/radio/Radioindiareport_2.asp (accessed August 5, 2004).

Roy, A. 1999. *The Greater Common Good.* Bombay: India Book Distributors.

Sainath, P. 2000. "Reporting Poverty." In *Communication and the Globalization of Poverty,* 19–29. London: WACC.

Sekhar, A. S. 2000. "A. P. Farmers Sell Kidneys to Avoid Penury." *The Hindu Online,* May 16, 2000, available at www.hinduonnet.co/thehindu/2000/05/16/stories/0216000k.htm (accessed August 5, 2004).

Thomas, P. N. 2001. "Copyright and the Emerging Knowledge Economy in India." *Economic and Political Weekly* 36, no. 24: 2147–56.

———. 2003. "GATS and Trade in Audio-Visuals: Culture, Politics and Empire." *Economic and Political Weekly* 38, no. 33: 3485–93.

Venturelli, S. 1997. "Prospects for Human Rights in the Political and Regulatory Design of the Information Society." In *Media and Politics in Transition: Cultural Identity in the Age of Globalization,* eds. J. Servaes and R. Lee, 61–74. Leuven, Belgium: AccoLeuven/Amersfoort.

5

Changing Political Cultures and Media under Globalism in Latin America

Javier Protzel

We must approach Latin American media with prudence. A holistic focus tends to blur or implicitly efface the immense cultural and economic differences that mark the subcontinent, a problem common to many comparative regional studies. At issue in current social science research are such differences between sociological analysis and the study of international relations. When one of these disciplines intersects the other to form a common stream, differentiating vast cultural spaces becomes crucial, as is the case for Latin America.

Two facts are becoming undeniably characteristic of Latin American countries in this new millennium. On the one hand, global flows of finance, trade, migration, crime, and culture are reshaping (often decreasing) the autonomy of nation-states (Castells 1998, 271–305). Concomitantly, unsatisfied social demands arising from expanding-democratic citizenship coexist with the mostly free-market, export-oriented economic policies of trade and integration agreements like Mercosur and the Andean Community (*Comunidad Andina*), which are unlikely to solve major unemployment and poverty problems. On the other hand, Latino industrial cultures may be grounding Latin America in something more solid than old rhetoric. The lag separating the late formation of modern national cultures from the early legal origins of states has made vitally important the construction of national public spheres and struggles for power therein.

This chapter is not a thorough portrait of media and politics. It attempts only to provide some clues about the wide range of political cultures of the subcontinent and how they are being affected by general access to media, primarily but not only to television, inducing a profound transformation in both audiences and political systems.

INHERITING THE PAST

Current ownership of private sector Latin American media is deeply grounded in common traditions. Benedict Anderson's theory of "imagined communities" took South American republics as an example. The role of the press, he argues, was decisive. Newly shared sentiments of belonging to a fatherland were spread across extended territories, originating new national identities (2000, 77–101) Although this may be acknowledged, such discourses were validated only within the ruling literate groups.

It is also true that when the protracted independence wars (*guerras de independencia*) from Spain ended in 1824, liberal democracy, inspired by the Enlightenment, was the principle upon which the new nation-states were founded. Yet, social domination by local political leaders and landlords, as well as endless military interventions, thwarted such idealism, and in some cases there was even refeudalization. Two further points must be stressed here. First, patrimonialism persisted, based on land ownership, kin, and ethnicity, marked by leisure-oriented Iberic behavior and poor entrepreneurship. Second, this blend of patrimonialism and liberalism provided a distinctive setting for a diversity of political cultures, upon which print journalism and, later, electronic mass media would operate.

Cultural heterogeneity is not merely a messy mixture of symbolic referents; it generates social specificity, in this case a particular type of leadership and commitment. The local elites' unwillingness to assume austerity and a work ethic blended with a fascination for industrial progress and science. Regardless of the strength of tradition, Latin American countries manifested new realities, inasmuch as their foundational lag between nation and state bound them to the future. From Mexico to Chile, these countries emerged more as administrative and juridical entities than cultural ones. Internal inequalities and inconsistencies generated by Spanish and Portuguese colonial empires drove the people toward the "invention" of nations as new projects; in turn, different interpretative discourses were created in the interplay between political and class factions.

By the end of the nineteenth century, most of the existing nation-states had minimally developed legal and administrative backbones, facilitating considerable export-resource expenditure by emergent interest groups. Argentina, Chile, Mexico, and even Brazil (while still part of the Portuguese Empire) developed local bourgeoisies capable of controlling their economies, unlike Peru, Bolivia, or Venezuela, whose weaker ruling groups (*oligarquías*) favored mining enclaves and plantation economies, unsuitable for local capital accumulation. Where the local bourgeoisie flourished, civil society was emergent, along with early practices of political communication. Probably inspired by the nineteenth-century French conception of the liberal *homme de lettres*, journalists were frequently bound to politics as a civilian counterpart of the military warlord, a role in which they could still assume that of *caudillos* (conductors), mobilizing crowds and organizing conspiracies. Political journalism remained closely related to literacy and electoral rights. While countries with a considerable indigenous presence, like Mexico and Peru, had a small Spanish-speaking population, high rates of European migration to the South Cone states (Chile, Argentina, Uruguay) provided a different social composition. Argentina could boast 165 newspapers in 1880 and 345 in 1895, and while it was the fastest growing country, a consolidated press became a reality.

By the late nineteenth century, even the export oligarchies were gradually forced to yield to the advance of popular and middle-class parties and to the criticism of the oppositional press. The thin line separating the roles of the politician, the caudillo, and the journalist remains a permanent trait of Latin American political cultures.[1] In this period of intensified trade and raw material extraction, news agencies became important. Initially, the French Havas had exclusivity over all Latin American territories until the 1930s, when the United Press International and Associated Press took over. But it would be simplistic to reduce the role of the press to the defense of the conservative status quo. The overall conflict was neither strictly one of class struggle nor simply the search for material benefits. This outward development frequently triggered social protests against state administrations, highlighting their allegedly antinational behavior. While the Mexican Revolution left 250,000 dead in combat and 750,000 by hunger or disease from 1910 through 1920 (Krauze 1997), other countries, such as Chile and Argentina, achieved democratic representation and reduced landowners' and bankers' strength through a stabilized party system in 1920 and 1912, respectively. Venezuela's thirty-two-year dictatorship of Juan Vicente Gómez ended in 1935, resulting in a party system and the country's participation in the oil industry. These processes, also called the westernization of politics, cannot be understood without the press, which functions to provide information and construct political meaning. This gave paramount importance to public discourse and, accordingly, to the craft of journalism. Thus, radicalized, excluded, middle-class intellectuals joined forces with emergent rural or urban workers to struggle for political inclusion. National-popular movements (*movimientos nacional-populares*) leading to populist regimes were being born and with them ideological debates and different forms of control and censorship.

POPULISM AND THE MEDIA

Populism as a political form historically has been a part of the broader cultural stream of Latin American nation building. Mass media has set their material foundations, constructing the collective identifiers of a modern popular tradition (*moderna tradiçao popular*), using Renato Ortiz's term (1994). Media's comparatively early development was not a simple reproduction of political domination or of ideological influence coming from Western powers. Instead, populist regimes favored the absorption of traditional preindustrial local expressions, converting them into easily understandable mass culture to ensure integration processes, which in turn would "nationalize the state," closing the aforementioned gap between nation and state (Martín-Barbero 1987). In terms of social awareness, the role of the film industry was probably more crucial than that of the press.[2] Film, weekly sentimental novels, and the radio (Mazziotti 1996), which came to the forefront through the *radionovela*, reflected the private-sphere dimension of populist culture. However, after 1920, production from other regions became influential, primarily American films, but also news and advertising.

Yet, the duration and radicality of populist regimes and their mobilization of mass media varied considerably throughout Latin America. The Brazilian *Estado Novo* (new state) (1930–1945) deployed media control to enhance a mythical conception of the state and the personalization of power in Gétulio Vargas, establishing the *Departamento de Imprensa e Propaganda* (Press and Propaganda Department) for systemic indoctrination (Morán 1981).[3] During World War II, the Argentinean military administration's favorable attitude toward the fascist block entailed severe tensions with the United States, leading to restrictive measures that proved indirectly favorable to the local cultural industry. Immediately after World War II, the election of Juan Domingo Perón, a powerful member of the preceding junta, hastened national-popular media policies that were already ongoing, aiming to control the press and the radio, as well as to protect film production. On the other hand, Mexican commitment to the Allies and pressure from a friendly private sector forced a government withdrawal from intervention policies.

Three kinds of North American postwar influence on the media are relevant here. First, there are organizational and economic influences. A diversity of nationalist regimes, ranging from that of the late Gétulio Vargas in Brazil to the post–Lázaro Cárdenas administration in Mexico, were all conducive to the development of media networks consisting primarily of advertising-supported private radio. Indeed, they readily acquiesced to censorship and, hence, aligned themselves with the state, insofar as it served their corporate interests. Unlike the European system, these networks did not really operate as public services. Internal press competition trumped the old, elitist, politics- and business-centered conception of journalism, thrusting news-value and human-interest standards into prominence. As well, the United Press and Associated Press not only displaced the French Havas news agency, opening those markets to their subsequent hegemony, but they also ushered in new levels of competition, including a modernization drive in managerial methods. A second Americanizing influence was felt via intensified advertising through agencies such as McCann Erickson and J. W. Thompson, which entailed compliance with international standards for topics, genres, and formats. Such adaptations followed the good-neighbor policy imposed by the United States during and after World War II through the Inter-American System. Increased corporate investments from north of the Rio Grande generated the third, strictly ideological level of influence. The Office of Coordination of Inter-American Affairs, directed by Nelson Rockefeller, distributed information collected from U.S. networks and news agencies to some two hundred radio stations and more than twelve hundred daily newspapers. By 1949, 75 percent of international news in Latin America was controlled from Washington D.C. (Fox 1989).

THE GROWTH OF THE DOMINANT INDUSTRIAL CULTURES

During the cold war era, a number of governments turned to the Right politically. World War II had caused deprivation, especially in the rural areas of export economies like Argentina, driving rural dwellers into the cities. This created conditions for the assistance/client substratum of national-popular regimes. A new, more secularized approach to politics was evident under the soaring process of foreign investments. Yet, there were few substantial changes in political culture regarding leader-mass relations. These conditions did little to encourage support for public-intervention policies; after Vargas's suicide and Perón's downfall, mass-media landscapes were opened further to U.S. influence. Advertising expenditures increased, and concrete quotidian consumption put mass culture in the foreground. Mexico was the sixth country in the world to start regular TV broadcasting, in 1950, followed promptly by the rest of Latin America, with the exception of Bolivia and Chile, where TV would be inaugurated in the late 1960s. Throughout, broadcasting systems were virtually fully private and commercial, again with the exception of Chile and Bolivia, where TV fell under the purview of the universities. Colombia, meanwhile, established a mixed system of private concessions to private companies under public service criteria, long masking what are strictly commercial standards.[4]

The Latin American broadcasting structure was atypical compared to most TV systems around the world. Before the global privatization wave, there were only thirty-one countries whose national TV systems operated under commercial standards—sixteen of those were Latin American. But why was there a "foundational singularity," using Rafael Roncagliolo's term (2003, 32–33)? There may be several intertwined answers. First, there were neither long-term state intervention policies nor abundant assets to build strong public networks; the import-substitution model, which provided the economic foundation of populist regimes in Brazil, Argentina, and Peru, had gone into a profound crisis.[5] Second, the rise of U.S. television was profound. Widespread investment in media, namely from NBC, ABC, and CBS, developed with seeming ease, largely because of the already established influence of news agencies and brand advertising. This brought about technological dependency, programming and management expertise, as well as studio production techniques. Third, U.S. sales efforts were strategic and effective, insofar as they priced their programming competitively for local markets. Finally, there was a general miscalculation among local authorities regarding the political role TV might play. Unlike print journalism, it was considered solely an entertainment and money-making machine.

Obviously, as national audiences grew and social conflicts were openly broadcast, attitudes changed, entailing, in most cases, political pacts. While foreign programming and advertising in Latin America remained strong, the endogenous production of powerful countries like Mexico, Brazil, Argentina, and Venezuela was stimulated. With the well-known exceptions of Cuba, Chile during Salvador Allende's overthrown *Unidad Popular* government (1970–1973), and Nicaragua at the beginning of the 1980s, Latin American media complied with U.S. influence. Politically, at stake during the cold war were established government-aligned corporate interests—in short, the structural conservation of the American commercial system. The growth of national markets interconnected by microwaves or satellites renewed the internal stratification of Latin American industrial cultures, already long interlinked on a microlevel via film, Latino music (e.g., tango, bolero, mambo, cha-cha), and radionovelas. Again, the allegiance between established political power and oligopolistic media family groups became a common pattern under the umbrella of information technology. Let us then introduce them to complete our perspective on globalization and regionalization.

Televisa was one such powerful private network, founded in 1973 in reaction to eventual political constraint (Caletti 1989, 90–106; Orozco 2002, 216–20);[6] in turn, the ruling PRI (*Partido Revolucionario Institucional*) made Televisa its ally, resulting in real and virtual monopolies of political and media power. Horizontal and vertical integration around 1980[7] induced a remarkable increase of national production, reaching up to 80 percent of programming, more than 90 percent of total Mexican audiences, and a similar percentage of advertising revenue (Sinclair 1999, 41). Unlike Brazil and Argentina, the weight of the United States and the increase of the American Hispanic population logically induced expansion north of the Rio Grande under adequate technological conditions. That is why Mexico in 1984 was among the first countries to operate TV distribution by satellite, namely through the U.S.-based PanAmSat, the first satellite system authorized to compete with the Intelsat agency (Sinclair 1999, 107–8), presumably via the intervention of U.S. Ambassador John Gavin, a friend of both President Reagan and the Azacárraga family, which controlled Televisa.[8] After broadcasting initially to Peru, Televisa's area of influence grew to most of South America and to some European countries, and by 1993 it controlled the U.S. Latino network Univisión.[9] Exports of *telenovelas* alone topped one thousand hours to eighty-nine countries by 1998.

Brazil, on the other hand, experienced both explosive conflict and transnational capital growth under authoritarian administrations. As a result, communication policies were negotiated to reduce tensions between issues of national security and autonomy, the latter directed to develop sizeable national media capable of outward expansion. In both cases the TV systems were constructed on the solid ground of radio networks and on modern, urban audiences, which absorbed new cultural identity symbols, such as music, soccer, and radionovelas, the prelude to telenovelas. The Marinho Group founded what became the Brazilian giant Rede Globo by applying a general formula—management by small family groups financed through advertising, plus friendly relations with constituted power. This family, owner of the Rio de Janeiro newspaper *O Globo* and a radio network founded in 1944, commenced broadcasting TV Globo in 1965. It began as a small venture undertaken with the Time/Life Group, although the agreement was doomed to be breached in order to gain the support of the military regime. The timely convergence of public and private strategic interests thrust TV Globo toward success; by the early 1970s, it had surpassed all competitors, reaching an immense audience through government-sponsored Embratel's vast telecommunications network.

This process followed a strict criterion of creating content and building audiences, while keeping committed to the military administration. During the 1969–1974 regime of Gen. Garrastazu Médici, its daily news broadcasts reached more than fifty million people. Likewise, its broad support of the Brazilian soccer team stimulated national sentiments, making Globo a modern national symbol (Guimaraes and Amaral 1989, 159–60). Later, while still favoring dictatorship, the company improved the production of telenovelas to a "Globo-quality standard," which required sophisticated portraits of characters, innovative and socially critical plots, and frequent historical reconstructions shot outside the studios. The goal was to reach educated, upwardly mobile Brazilians and also to facilitate an international strategy owing to the Hispanic American predilection for heavy, stereotyped melodrama, popular among urban audiences and readers since the 1930s (Mazziotti 1996), which gave a definite advantage to Mexican and Argentinean telenovelas and a cultural discount to the Brazilian productions.[10]

Brazilian production increased from 48 percent of total national programming to 80 percent between 1978 and 1997. This consolidation is crucial for the understanding of Globo's might. On the one hand, it allowed for the recuperation of costs and revenues adequate to offer sophisticated products at reasonable prices per episode. On the other hand, it induced vertical integration in the 1980s, strengthening its dominant position enough to gain greater political autonomy from the military regime. Yet, while Globo's telenovelas became a prestigious choice for Latin American channels, almost 80 percent of its revenues were from Europe (Mattelart and Mattelart 1988, 111), where it could charge a higher per-chapter price. Globo's products were welcomed in most Central and Eastern Europe countries and even in China, reaching 130 countries worldwide by 2001.

Venezuela followed a similar pattern, with a family-controlled oligopoly. Grupo Cisneros, with assets worth U.S. $5 billion, controls the major producer and exporter Venevisión, founded in 1960 with the participation of ABC. This company has about half the national audience share, in competition against Radio Caracas Televisión (RCTV), owned by the Phelps Group (Fox 1989). Unlike Televisa and Globo, most of the Cisneros enterprises did not originate in communications, and its current investments are widely diversified. The Cisneros Group has entered publishing, music, advertising, and film production, as well as purchased TV stations in Chile and Puerto Rico, enjoying the advantages of vertical, and to a lesser extent, horizontal concentration.

THE DEBATE ON COMMUNICATION POLICIES

The expansion of entertainment business cultures was accompanied by an activation of social movements and their increased importance in mass politics. Despite their expansion, the great private corporations had yet to struggle against left-wing criticism; when they found themselves in the midst of the harsh political debates of the 1970s, they aimed to preserve their autonomy under the ideological umbrella of the free flow of information. While negotiations resulted from such confrontation, these were wars the corporate media has yet to lose. Even after the 1974 authoritarian confiscation of the main daily newspapers, the two private TV networks, plus the most important radio networks by Peru's leftist military government (1968–1980), there was minimal change in either the content input from transnational news agencies or TV fiction (Gargurevich 1987).[11] With the exception of this Peruvian-military national-popular government, Cuba, a brief 1971 junta in Bolivia, the military de facto administrations in Brazil, Argentina, Chile, and Paraguay, and the permanent monopoly of the ruling PRI in Mexico, there was a monolithic rightist landscape, which, according to specific national situations, covered more than twenty years, finishing with Augusto Pinochet's retirement at the end of the 1980s.

Two comments are relevant here. On the one hand, the expression of ideological differences were somewhat minimized by a common obsession with psychological war and the fear of an overflow of popular demands. Thus, until the early 1980s the overall issue was that of the conservation of power, rather than democratizing mass communications. Regardless of human rights violations and of the militarization of TV networks, the U.S. media continued backing the Argentinean dictatorship until its downfall in 1982, as was the case in Chile and Bolivia. Conversely, a double standard was practiced in Nicaragua and Panama through censorship of media coverage and illegal interventions of force. Ideological agendas concealed the gap, which increasingly separated the existing polities from the unsettled civil societies. Rightist (or even leftist, as in Peru) forms of authoritarian media control emphasized security issues, inspired by U.S. and French postwar doctrines conveyed to Latin American military officers who attended special courses at Forts Gulick and Bragg. Such strategies mostly preserved hierarchies but overlooked society as an equalitarian network of groups and individuals invested with rights.

On the other hand, core conflicts seldom registered amid the corporate and political interests, which controlled the access to public debate on communication policies. Until the 1980s there was in debates about media a misplaced emphasis on ownership. This failed to reflect what was really at stake—freedom of information and opinion, especially from and for emergent social groups. Instead, the light of the U.S.-USSR cold war struggle overshadowed these developments in the region. Yet, the mass media found their windows forced open beyond the vista of evening entertainment, soccer games, or edited official information to new scenes of social debate. In short, their positions changed as they found themselves part of a profound crisis of social representation.

Media criticism claimed state control as a solution, no matter how obviously that experience may have led to censorship or bureaucratic paralysis. After the era of dictatorships, the media faced problems of political legitimacy and credibility, which could only be solved by demonstrating greater autonomy during the ongoing transition processes. What was overlooked in the debate about legal matters concerning ownership and nationality was the nature of democratic control over the arbitrary use of media. Problems resulted from the social effects of each given set of regulations. For instance, Rede Globo's behavior during the oppositional mobilizations against the military regime and its support for the election of Tancredo Neves conveyed a clear message of commitment to general elections and identification with the Brazilian people. Globo gained legitimacy during the 1980s after withdrawing support for the military government upon its refusal to organize direct elections. By showing and using its autonomy, Globo acted, for practical purposes, as a sort of political institution (Fox 1989, 46).

In Mexico, Televisa played the role of government spokesperson in Trejo Delarbre's view (1996) during both the dubious 1988 elections and after the

1994 victory of Ernesto Zedillo, both times clearly favoring PRI. The electorate's gradual rejection of this party, which held power for six decades, was certainly influenced by the excessive propaganda broadcast by Televisa, contributing to its defeat in 2000 and indirectly to Vincente Fox's victory.[12] Chile's situation was substantially different. Although Allende's socialist government established the National Television Council (*Consejo Nacional de Televisión*) in 1970, which was intended as a public entity and not a government-censorship organ, the Pinochet military junta changed the rules. It modified the composition of the council (Fuenzalida 2002, 169–74), censoring the Televisión Nacional de Chile for years, until increased social pressure compelled the military in 1988 to organize a referendum on the future of the military regime.[13]

The political transformations in Latin America could not have been achieved without the political actors who contributed to the still unfinished process of democratization. Credit must also be given to Latin American communication research by reason of its limited position inside mainstream American theory, regardless of its intellectual qualities. Spanning the subcontinent were myriad discourses on mass communication and its discontents in the context—mutatis mutandis—of militarism, censorship, and rapid cultural change, as had been the case in prewar Germany. Definitely unsuited for a modern/traditional dichotomy or for characterization as inside/outside the West, critical thought traversed different ground. Neither purely academic nor militant, critical thought on Latin American mass culture could not be centered on the role of the state, and instead was decentered toward the people. Somewhat at the opposite end of the entrepreneurial media ventures of the subcontinent, they were concealed by the prevailing geopolitical discourses of the dominating world powers. Initiatives such as *comunicación alternativa* (alternative communication) and research projects on critical reception, among others, were overlooked, although they were partly included in UNESCO's McBride Report for a New World Information and Communication Order (NWICO). Yet, they served as pioneer experiments that are still alive.

TELEVISION AND THE PROBLEMS OF AUTHORITARIANISM

It would be naive to believe that since the 1980s global media networking itself has changed politics. Although increased exposure to international agendas is significant for greater audiences, it is more interesting to focus on social dynamics, rather than on content. Three intertwined topics concerning global scenarios affecting democratization in Latin America may be delimited: first, the role of TV as a commodity throughout the subcontinent; second, the crisis of political parties and development of media politics and corruption; and third, the ravages of neoliberal policies.

Significant parts of society remained excluded from literacy and political participation. Except for the South Cone countries, Costa Rica, and Cuba, the consolidation of TV audiences dates only from the 1980s. The return of Peru (1980), Bolivia (1982), Argentina (1982), Brazil (1986), and Chile (1990) to representative democracy after military regimes entailed a substantial modification of political structures. This late expansion of material conditions for modern citizenship occurred during *la década perdida* (the lost decade), named for its weak economy, albeit one with the unexpected consequence of new relations between civil society and political organizations. New and far bigger electorates, due both to migration trends and population increase, throughout more than a decade of suppressed elections altered the meaning of democratic life, with eagerness for fast economic results, mainly concerning social policies. High inflation rates, averaging 131 percent and 621 percent, successively, for each half of the 1980s, heavy, nonpayable, foreign debts, and a regression from a 5.5 percent to 3.7 percent share of world trade all contributed to cool the enthusiasm generated by the return to democracy (Ugarteche 1997, 54)

Argentina, Peru, and Brazil then experienced a vicious circle of social demands, salary increases, and budgetary deficits, leading to inflation, more frustration, and new social demands, which modified political organizations. The return to representative democracy also meant a shift from revolutionary methods of seizing power to electoral participation and rational discussion (Lechner 1990, 17–38), and general access to television played an important role here. Following regional vicissitudes, Latin American mass politics functioned territorially with extended party militancy managed at the local, provincial, and national levels, able to display diverse collective forms of demonstration to symbolize strength and exert pressure. Open television, however, changed this by virtue of its fast, low-cost, and efficient structure of intermediation with civil society. Moreover, if the classical target for populist activism had been the male urban or rural worker, the pluralization of the social subject induced new issues: struggles for space (i.e., the need for housing or occupying the streets for informal trade), community-managed low-cost food programs, and demands for gender equality, among others, generated an unforeseen and vast complexity.

Besides, an overall decomposition of the social fabric, with delinquency rates among the highest in the world, led to a gradual loss of the communitarian ties necessary to maintain political loyalties, as well as patrimonialistic submission. Within this frame, traditional parties entered a gradual decay. This fading of intermediate organizations generated a permanent social vacuum, resulting in a new type of partyless leadership, whose instrument is television (Zermeño 1989).

Two main elements need to be emphasized: leadership and institutional frameworks. First, political leadership eschewed ideological discourse for a new foundation in spin doctors and marketing procedures measuring volatile attitudes. Thus, the quest for power turns into business, since anyone who can afford a campaign can be a candidate. Emphasis must be given to the correlation between the newness of television among the lower classes, the lack throughout the subcontinent of previous democratic experience in matters of political marketing, and institutional fragility. This has greatly facilitated the possible success of a new kind of sympathy-centered leadership personality whose electoral breakthroughs no longer depend on concrete proposals but on leaders' looks and behavior when they announce these proposals in front of the cameras. The Brazilian case of Fernando Collor de Melo, ousted by corruption, is notorious. More examples include Abdalá Bucaram in Ecuador, Carlos Saúl Menem, who has run for president three times in Argentina, and Alberto Fujimori in Peru, all of whom, at one time or another, have been indicted. As a result, the question of whether Latin America is undergoing a process of globalization or Americanization of politics is as frequently raised among this region's academics as it is in some European countries.

However, if marketing techniques have been imported from the United States, as they have elsewhere, the institutional frameworks are undoubtedly original, embedded in core political cultures. In general, Latin American presidentialism does not establish the same kind of equilibrium between the executive and the legislative powers as it does in the United States or France. The caudillo mentality is not a matter of specific norms but, all the way around, a legally enforced reality, the survivor of nineteenth-century militarism and of patrimonialistic leadership. In societies that remain hierarchical, it may be reproduced in new versions through media politics; its current expressions may come from outsiders with contesting positions toward the party system. The aforementioned old proximity of the journalist to the politician reappears under different modalities through the influence held by the electronic media under free-market, oligopolistic, and mildly regulated conditions, with a might inversely proportional to the weakening of institutional relationships with civil societies, only partially active as they may be. If this distance is too wide, scenarios of concentration of power like Colombia's may appear.[14] Another consequence of concentrated power is the mutual distribution of advantages for the ruling elites and corporate classes. As indicated, the Mexican Televisa-PRI relationship might be the most exemplary, notwithstanding the use made by Globo of its prestige to protect F. H. Cardoso's candidacy in 1994 against Luiz Inácio Lula da Silva—this was impossible to repeat in 2002 due to the recovered strength of Brazilian civil society and the Brazilian Labor Party (PTB).

The rules established by a constitutional status quo do not alone certify the effective functioning of democracy. When formal mechanisms coexist with extended skepticism and demobilization after economic hopes have been repeatedly deceived, there is a shift from representative to delegative democracy. Guillermo O'Donnell asserts that most neoliberal Latin American governments were not really grounded during the 1990s on their popularity (defined as ideological identification with leadership) but rather on the people's disengagement from political commitments, accompanied by an award of blind confidence without any demand for accountability as long as a solution to the economic burden of the majority was provided (1995, 222–39). Postpopulist scenarios are frequent when social movements are met with a lack of motivation in the political process. The great disappointment subsequent to Argentinean president Raúl Alfonsín's postmilitary failure, due to uncontained hyperinflation, advanced the election date, generating an ideological void from which, in practical terms, power transferred to TV networks and electoral marketing agencies. The outcome was the election of Menem, a man who, notwithstanding his affiliation to the Peronist party (*Partido Justicialista*), was peripheral to the doctrinarian and hermetical style of the politicians from Buenos Aires.[15] He built his public profile both by trading on his status as a former political prisoner of the military and by appearing frequently on late-night TV shows with artists and sport stars. He did not hesitate to apply severe International Monetary Fund (IMF) structural-adjustment programs, namely by establishing the equivalence of the national peso with the U.S. dollar. The resulting unemployment rates, income differentials, and labor flexibility were overshadowed by the stabilization of the main macroeconomic indicators. The general acceptance of Menem's administration may be interpreted both as the illusion of reliable economic prospects, despite the inconvenience of neoliberalism, but also as the demise of active citizenship characteristic of delegative democracy, together with individualistic contempt toward political issues. But pegging the peso to the U.S. dollar led to the general economic collapse of the Argentinean economy. The subsequent restoration of confidence by the administration of Nestor Kirchner required candid self-criticism from the electorate and new demands for accountability.

The most extreme case of political submission of the media under conditions of delegative democracy is probably the Peruvian crisis, which concluded with President Alberto Fujimori's flight to Japan in November 2000. One year after the first Menem election, Fujimori, a low-profile outsider and *nisei* (second-generation Japanese immigrant), unexpectedly became president.[16] Like Menem, he faced general cynicism toward politics following a period of hyperinflation. Fujimori also successfully enforced IMF recommendations, ending fifteen years of economic stress, while virtually defeating the leftist insurgent group *Sendero Luminoso* (Shining Path).[17] Economic stability and internal security were reasons enough to afford Fujimori full popular confidence, fostering his 1992 auto–coup d'etat, based on a military-contingency operation planned before the elections.[18] He dissolved the parliament, reorganized the courts of justice under bribed judges, and seized the media with the approval of more than 80 percent of the public (Cotler 1994). According to military strategic planners, representative democracy needed to be replaced by a long-term disciplinary regime, whose examples were Malaysia and Pinochet's Chile.

Pro-Fujimori TV and press coverage, plus talk shows and other highly rated media events, were intensified in order to prepare for his fraudulent re-election in 2000. Only two months after his third inauguration, Fujimori's downfall was set in motion, ironically, by the media. A videocassette made public by a pay-TV opposition channel, showing the chief advisor of Peru's National Intelligence Service and the country's second most powerful person, Vladimiro Montesinos, bribing a member of congress to vote with Fujimori's block, triggered a huge scandal that in a matter of days unveiled other concealed evidence of corruption. Two months later, Fujimori's reign came crashing down as the congress appointed a provisional government charged to organize elections. The transition to democracy had thus begun.

Peru's case is pertinent because it illustrates three aforementioned topics related to current global scenarios. First, from a Third World perspective, the expansion of television is a global process but not primarily due to the worldwide broadcast of foreign programs. Rather, it stems from the recent generalization of national information networks in most nation-states, generating in each common mechanisms of political communication from which emerge similar genres and discourses in different world areas. In 1980, only 47 percent of Peruvian households had access to open television, a number that soared to 67 percent in 1993 and reached 80 percent when the *vladivideos,* which brought down Fujimori, were shown. However, by the end of the 1990s, the area's cable and satellite TV indicators remained very low, except for Argentina. So, beyond the fascination that intercontinental programming may have for minorities through cable pay-TV, politically, the incorporation of vast audiences into the public sphere of television is far more significant. Except for censorship, it is a new arena of struggle for democracy. And in the foreground, investigative journalism has assumed the role of utmost importance in the dawn of more active self-conscious civil societies (Waisbord 1999). Independent journalists' ability to uncover corruption is often more closely connected to civil society and recognized for its political efficacy than political parties.

Second, the crisis of Peruvian parties is a particular example of the volatilization of political identities, guided by a generalized perception of the failure or greed of their caudillos.[19] The same could be said, under otherwise dramatic circumstances, for the distressing Venezuelan scene. The success of Hugo Chávez was a popular answer to a long cycle of biparty alternation of the Comité Político Electoral Independiente (COPEI) (Christian-Democratic, center-right) and Acción Democrática (Social-Democratic, center-left) administrations, resulting in inflation and accusations of heavy corruption. The failure of those parties induced a violent class-oriented for/against polarization: Venevisión and RCTV (comprising 80 percent of national audiences), together with the middle class and corporate and public-sector labor unions, sided with the traditional parties; Chávez, on the other hand, is backed mainly by those most sensible to clientelism among the dispossessed and the military.[20]

Third, anomie and social decomposition are extensive in the daily lives not only of Peruvians but also of most Latin Americans. The virtual absence of media regulations or policies, along with harsh competition sustained by advertising under exclusively commercial criteria, has considerably deteriorated the quality of popular information and entertainment.

THE UNCERTAIN PROSPECTS

Global trends are having two effects on democracy in Latin America. First, the nation-state is being diminished. Beyond the logics of network society, its legitimacy decreases while political operators of late capitalism diversify—with media owners, consultancy agencies, corporate guilds, and illegal information and intelligence services all foiling the transparency of public life. Second, media diversification is substantially changing the scope of those ethnic majorities whose parents were restricted to local news and indigenous music on the radio. Besides creating national TV audiences, the reduction of broadcasting costs has brought forth the development of local media, especially radio programming by and for lower classes. The marginal investment necessary for operation, vis-à-vis subsequent advertising revenues, has allowed consistent degrees of autonomy. These possibilities of communicating local issues and defending regional identities are often overlooked by media studies. However, the audiences' fascination with new communication flows conceals the unfinished task of secularizing politics as a part of any democratization process to counteract the old penchant for caudillos, still deeply rooted in vast sectors of popular political cultures.

Extended coproduction and distribution are creating consistent fields of media consumption. Yet, this parallels a broader dynamic of fast corporate joint ventures with associates among the world's most powerful corporations. Digitalization, in addition to expandable markets and increased production-participation by telecommunications groups, increases complexity in the structure of the entertainment industry. Many examples can be given: Venevisión, indeed, has expanded in South America (i.e., controlling two Chilean TV channels) and is in partnership with the Hughes Galaxy Consortium for direct-to-home (DTH) broadcast, now in competition against Televisa. Likewise, Venevisión and Hughes operate in the United States as Univisión, sharing distribution in Central and South America. As well, there is an ongoing Sky News Corporation project in association with Globo, Televisa, and the American Theatre Crafts International (TCI). Furthermore, Globo is already into film coproduction with some Hollywood majors. The overall tendency of capitalism toward concentration and corporate control definitely does not contribute to media democracy (McChesney 2000). And as the fabric of investment and mergers gets permanently modified, middle-term forecasts concerning the consequences of free-trade agreements such as Mercosur, Comunidad Andina, or an enlarged NAFTA become hardly predictable. However, the semantic differential between Americanization and globalization is minimal among most Latin Americans.

Besides, the significant Latino commercial media north of the Rio Grande, sustained by the Hispanics' almost half-trillion U.S.-dollar annual expenditure capacity (Ben Amor 2001), is challenging reality. While it may convey southbound a greater economic dependency, it could also strengthen the cultural perspective of Latin America. The region must no longer define itself in terms of a mythic immobile tradition; it must assume the contemporary standard of a permanently evolving interculturality (García Canclini 1999).

An undefined, yet recognizable, Latino symbolic repertoire has developed without being a specific component of any particular national group, including American Latinos. Nonetheless, it is a contemporary intercultural reference for the whole region (Yudice 2004). Latino transnational networks via intrasubcontinent production and exchange are now common, creating a new, enlarged space for texts, sights, and sounds. No matter how uncertain the existence of a common Latin American cultural identity may be, the theoretical issue will only find answers in concrete solutions regarding the trade of those products and in public policies to countervail concentrated media power.

NOTES

1. Several important Latin American newspapers have a long history. Before founding *La Nación* in 1870, Bartolomé Mitre had already been president of Argentina, succeeding the long tyranny of Juan Manuel Rosas; in Mexico, the *porfiriato*, the long-modernizing Mexican administration of Porfirio Diaz, was stabilized in 1880 through subsidies to the press. The conservative Chilean daily *El Mercurio* was founded in 1827, based in Valparaiso. In 1880 it was purchased by the powerful Edwards family, who moved the administration to Santiago. *El Comercio*, still the most important Peruvian paper, dates its daily editions back to 1839. Another case is, of course, José Martí in Cuba.

2. The predominance of illiteracy facilitated a particular space for fiction. The importance of family ties in Catholic countries undergoing rapid social change and severe stratification engendered the mass popularity of the melodrama. If the myth of Latino romanticism became the exportable by-product of film and music, the overall

meaning conveyed to the lower class was both moral and positive. Mexican, Argentinean, and, to a lesser extent, Brazilian films from the 1920s through the 1940s showed local color and poverty as an attribute of heroes.

3. The *Estado Novo* was more of a strictly fascist regime. Strictly speaking, populism followed the aftermath of World War II with broader redistribution policies and popular participation.

4. Until 2003, Chilean television was public and education-oriented through state concessions that admitted advertising revenues. The main national network Televisión Nacional de Chile is a politically autonomous nonprofit service. Other networks are managed by universities, like the Catholic University of Chile. The Colombian system is similar, but with fully commercial concessions supervised by the Comisión Nacional de Televisión (National Television Commission). In Bolivia public service was the rule since its late foundation in 1969 until the 1980s.

5. The popular appeal of Perón's government was due to agricultural depression. With low external incomes resulting from poor international crops, meat and wool prices drove many peasants to the cities, mainly Buenos Aires. Vargas's *Estado Novo* was overthrown in 1945 by a military coup backed by U.S. Ambassador Adolf Berle. He was reelected.

6. Mexico's initial laissez-faire policy toward TV proved insufficient, particularly after the 1968 bloody repression of a student-led anti-PRI demonstration in Mexico City's Tlatelolco Square prior to the Olympic Games. Although private channels and radio stations gave free space to government information, the lack of a consistent public network eventually prompted the Echevarría administration to purchase Channel 13 to create IMEVISION. Private broadcasters responded defensively to the merger of Telesistema Mexicano and Televisión Independiente de México, which by the end of 1972 united Grupo Monterrey, Grupo Puebla, and Grupo Alemán, creating Televisa.

7. This foundational merger resulted in a segmented broadcast by four different TV networks, each specializing in different genres of entertainment and journalism, whose revenues brought about significant diversification: a daily newspaper (*novedades*), film industry (*televicine*), recorded music, video hardware, software production and distribution, and so forth.

8. The PanAmSat system was the outcome of President La Madrid's lost dispute with the Azacárragas, when he intended to take control of satellite TV broadcasting with the Morelos national project.

9. Televisa's programming in the United States has a prior history, years before the group was founded as such, through radio networks. During the mid-1970s the Spanish International Communication Corporation/Spanish International Network (SICC/SIN) group, controlled by the Azacárraga family, became the first national TV satellite network, ahead of CBS and NBC. During the 1980s, control of Univisión was shared with Hallmark.

10. The competing Mexican and Venezuelan telenovela models were "opposite" because they followed a Hispanic popular narrative tradition, the direct predecessor of which was, as mentioned, the low-cost radionovela, originating in Cuba, Mexico, and Argentina.

11. This authoritarian "experiment" undertaken by the *Gobierno Revolucionario de la Fuerza Armada* (Revolutionary Government of the Armed Forces) was meant

to provide a popular point of view, following Soviet standards. Nominally, newspapers were to be assigned to the "organized sectors of the population" (e.g., peasants, blue-collar workers), but in practice aimed to neutralize the harsh right-wing opposition, circulate propaganda, and keep the military in power.

12. The Fox election was due not precisely to his center-right affiliation but to his projects of redemocratization of the public sphere via television, which is seen as a historic transition. Since then, representative organizations oversee the functioning of television.

13. This included a small opening on TV for both yes and no campaigns, celebrated as a breakthrough by the opposition, which won the referendum, and the subsequent restoration of democracy in 1990. The military government had kept both the National Television Council and the university-based broadcast administration, although the presidents of the universities (*rectores*) were designated by the military, as was the *rector-delegado*. In 1990, a new law confirmed the public mission of Televisión Nacional de Chile, as well as its political and financial autonomy.

14. In spite of the actual autonomy achieved by Colombian television, the disconnection of state from society is so extreme that national unity becomes almost fictitious, allowing old elite families (often called *la clase política*) to continue controlling the administration and inheriting control over the media.

15. Menem had previously been governor of the minor province of La Rioja, where he groomed his unusual, informal attitude of visiting small towns and shaking hands with people.

16. His first election was, somewhat like Menem's, the result of a "new" style, except for the clamorous defeat of political marketing techniques. Fujimori ran against the famous writer Mario Vargas Llosa, well known as much for his neoliberal ideas as for his aristocratic, elegant eloquence. Vargas Llosa's campaign cost approximately sixty-seven times more than Fujimori's and received broad media support. The overwhelming difference in rhetoric and the excess of the Vargas Llosa TV ads resulted in a popular counteridentification with the nonfamous, nonwhite, nonrhetorical narrative of Fujimori.

17. The Shining Path was defeated with the capture of its leader, Abimael Guzmán, known as Chairman Gonzalo, who organized this Communist Party under strict Maoist standards. Considered the most lethal terrorist group in the world, approximately 900,000 Andean dwellers had to flee from the cross fire of the army and the *senderistas*, both responsible for abundant violations of human rights and some 70,000 deaths.

18. The coup was undertaken by high officers of the army, outlined in *Plan Verde* (green plan), a secret document prepared prior to Fujimori's election with authoritarian recommendations to prevent a leftist government.

19. The exceptions may be Brazil, with the clear victory of Lula da Silva's *Partido Trabalhista Brasileiro*, and Chile, where the *Convergencia* pact gives continuity to political life.

20. Unlike Fujimori's regime, the neopopulism of Hugo Chávez originated in the fully constitutional election of a broad majority, although he has worked against freedom of information and of speech and his presidential status was challenged by a referendum.

REFERENCES

Anderson, Benedict. 2000. *Comunidades imaginadas. Reflexiones sobre el origen y difusión del nacionalismo.* Buenos Aires: Fondo de Cultura Económica. Originally published as *Imagined Communities: Reflections on the Origin and Spread of Nationalism.* London: Verso, 1991.

Ben Amor, Leila. 2001. "Les médias latinos aux Etats-Unis." *Problèmes d'Amérique latine. Médias, représentations sociales et démocratie.* La documentation Française No. 43 (October–December): 85–106.

Caletti, Sergio. 1989. "Las politicas de comunicación en México: Una paradoja histórica en palabras y en actos." In *Medios de comunicación y política en América Latina. La lucha por la democracia,* ed. E. Fox, 90–106. Barcelona: Gustavo Gili.

Castells, Manuel. 1998. *El poder de la identidad,* Vol. 2 of *La era de la información. Economía, sociedad y cultura.* México: Siglo XXI. Originally published as *The Power of Identity,* Vol. 2 of *The Information Age: Economy, Society and Culture.* London: Blackwell, 1997.

Cotler, Julio. 1994. "Crisis política, outsiders y autoritarismo plebiscitario: El fujimorismo." In *Política y sociedad en el Perú. Cambios y continuidades,* 165–228. Lima: IEP.

Fox, Elizabeth. 1989. "Las políticas de los mass media en Latinoamérica." In *Medios de comunicación y política en América Latina. La lucha por la democracia,* ed. E. Fox, 19–54. Barcelona: Gustavo Gili.

Fuenzalida, Valerio. 2002. "La televisión en Chile." In *Historias de la televisión en América Latina,* ed. G. Orozco, 163–202. Barcelona: GEDISA.

García Canclini, Néstor. 1999. *La globalización imaginada.* México: Paidos, 1999.

Gargurevich, Juan. 1987. *Prensa, radio y TV: Historia crítica.* Lima: Ed. Horizonte.

Guimaraes, César, and Roberto Amaral. 1989. *La televisión brasileña: Una rápida conversión al nuevo orden.* In *Medios de comunicación y política en América Latina. La lucha por la democracia,* ed. E. Fox, 157–71. Barcelona: Gustavo Gili.

Krauze, Enrique. 1997. *La presidencia imperial. Ascenso y caída del sistema político mexicano (1940–1996).* Barcelona: Tusquets Editores.

Lechner, Norbert. 1990. *Los patios interiores de la democracia.* México: Fondo de Cultura Económica.

Martín-Barbero, Jesús. 1987. *De los medios a las mediaciones. Comunicación, cultura y hegemonía en América Latina.* Barcelona: Gustavo Gili.

Mattelart, Armand, and Michèle Mattelart. 1988. *El carnaval de las imágenes. La ficción brasileña.* Madrid: Akal/Comunicación.

Mazziotti, Nora. 1996. *La industria de la telenovela. La producción de ficción en América Latina.* Buenos Aires: Paidós.

McChesney, Robert W. 1999. *Rich Media, Poor Democracy. Communication Politics in Dubious Times.* Urbana: University of Illinois Press.

Morán, José Manuel. 1981. *A comunicaçao populista. Populismo, totalitarismo e políticas de comunicaçao: O referencial nazi-fascista.* In *Populismo e comunicaçao,* ed. J. Marques de Melo, 77–83. Sao Paulo: Cortez Editora.

O'Donnell, Guillermo. 1995. *¿Democracias delegativas?* In *Instituciones políticas y sociedad,* ed. Romeo Grompone, 222–39. Lima: IEP.

Orozco, Guillermo. 2002. *La televisión en México*. In *Historias de la televisión en América Latina*, ed. G. Orozco, 203–44. Barcelona: GEDISA.

Ortiz, Renato. 1994. *Mundializaçao e cultura*. Rio de Janeiro: Ed. Brasiliense.

Roncagliolo, Rafael. 2003. *Problemas de la integración cultural: América Latina*. Buenos Aires: Ed. Norma.

Sinclair, John. 1999. *Latin American Television: A Global View*. Oxford: Oxford University Press.

Trejo Delarbre, Raúl. 1996. "Prensa y gobierno: Las relaciones perversas." *Comunicación y Sociedad* 25/26: 35–56.

Ugarteche, Oscar. 1997. *El falso dilema. America Latina en la economia global*. Lima: Fundacion Friedrich Ebert.

Waisbord, Silvio. 1999. *Watchdog Journalism in South America: News, Accountability and Democracy*. New York: Columbia University Press.

Yudice, George. 2004. *The Expediency of Culture: Uses of Culture in the Global Era (Post-Contemporary Interventions)*. Durham, NC: Duke University Press.

Zermeño, Sergio. 1989. "El regreso del líder. Carisma, neoliberalismo y desorden." *Revista Mexicana de Sociología* 4, no. 1: 115–50].

6

Media in "Globalizing" Africa: What Prospect for Democratic Communication?

Arthur-Martins Aginam

AFRICA AND THE CHALLENGES OF DEMOCRATIZATION

There is hardly any question that democracy, whatever the model, has emerged as the dominant political ideology since the end of the cold war. Although previously much more entrenched in the liberal political cultures of Western Europe and North America, democratization has become a global trend and the key political buzzword since the 1980s. While Francis Fukuyama (1992) prematurely celebrated the triumph of liberalism as "the end of history," Samuel Huntington (1992) couched the resurgence of democracy as a "third wave." So prevalent is democracy today that it is now theorized as an idea that transcends the nation-state, with such terms as "global," "supranational," "cosmopolitan," "transnational," or "universal" variously used to explain its current form (Archibugi and Held 1995; Held 1993; Holden 2000, 1–2). Paradoxically, democracy as an ideal is "everywhere praised, yet nowhere achieved" (Blaug and Schwarzmantel 2001, 1) or as Claude Ake (1993a) would say, "we have always preferred the reputation of being democrats to the notorious inconveniences of practicing democracy." The apparent limitations, if not downright subversion, of the egalitarian ethos of democracy has in various political contexts led to such oxymorons as "democratic Leviathan" (Keane 1991), "praetorian democracy," and "revolutionary conservatives" (Bourdieu 1998, 52), the last in reference to Europe's predatory liberalism, which has subverted the welfare state system.

Yet, notwithstanding its obvious limitations and immense ambiguities as a complex and highly contested idea (Held 1996), many in the West have been resolute in forcing a particular neoliberal model of democracy on the developing world, and Africa is no exception to this trend. In the gospel of neoliberalism, democracy and market economics are not presented as distant cousins who could coexist in certain contexts and situations but more as Siamese twins, so inextricably linked that one can hardly exist independently of the other. Consequently, African nations are not only required to democratize (even if that means the periodic conduct of flawed elections) but, more importantly, to deregulate their economies, which is often a prerequisite for receiving any form of international aid and assistance (Ake 1993a; Herbst 1992). To African nations, the message from the West is unequivocal: it is necessary that they democratize but even more imperative that they deregulate their economies, and while manifestly flawed electoral processes can be tolerated (after all democracy takes time to root), the door of international development assistance will be slammed against them if they fail to embrace free-market policies. And that leads to the question, is Africa truly democratizing (Ake 1993a)?

Just like in other parts of the developing world, debates about democratization in Africa have always revolved around such weighty issues as

- The suitability of the liberal model among a people that are intensely communitarian in temperament (Ake 1993a; 1993b)
- The relationship between market economics and democratization, or more pointedly, whether globalization is antithetical to democratization or a necessary condition for it (Olukoshi 1998; Ake 1993b; Joseph 1993, 317–18)
- Whether Africa needs more of procedural democracy (elite politics) by way of multiparty elections or some radical transformation of the state to facilitate empowerment and participation (Ake 1993a; Arusha Declaration 1990)
- Whether Africa can afford to develop and democratize at the same time (Sen 1999, 146–59; Sorensen 1998, 64–92)

Space will not permit me to get into any detailed discussion of these contentious issues. Suffice it to say that quite often, free market democracy is presented as a one-stop solution to all social problems in the developing world, when, in fact, it engenders, even if sometimes unwittingly, tragic backlashes by fueling class and ethnic conflicts (Chua 2004).

Some believe that democracy, or, better still, democratic values, are alien to Africa and only wound their way to the continent by the accident of European colonialism. Nothing can be further from the truth. While some precolonial African societies were undoubtedly hierarchical and built around strong monarchies, others, like the Igbos of southeast Nigeria, were fiercely republican and abhorred any form of authoritarianism. This egalitarian ethos is best encapsulated in "the king in every person" worldview. Prior to the creation of warrant chiefs by the British in furtherance of their imperialist interests, the closest semblance to monarchs in most precolonial Igbo societies were priest-kings whose powers were limited to matters spiritual. Political decisions at all levels—clan, village, or town—were made through open and robust deliberative assemblies, where the right of all participants to speak and be heard was guaranteed (Njaka 1974; Uchendu 1965; Davidson 1998). This is, however, not to suggest a radical, all-inclusive political system. Just like classical Greek democracy and the eighteenth-century European public sphere that Jurgen Habermas (1989) romanticized, the Igbo example was mostly limited to adult male members of the community and excluded women and slaves. But, it at least helps debunk the myth that democratic ideals entered Africa through European colonialism. If anything, the communitarian edge of traditional African social life has been largely blunted by the excessive individualism of Europe's liberal model.

Thus, in contemporary Africa, there is much confusion about democracy as evidenced by the manifestly self-serving and often conflicting interests of its most fervent proponents. For instance, while the African elite sees democracy primarily as a means to political and economic power, international development agencies and Western governments view it as a resource for their free-market programs (Ake 1993a). Consequently, the continent's long-impoverished masses, already led to expect so much from democracy, are left high and dry. This is not surprising, as Africa's relevance in the global scheme of things hardly goes beyond the exploitation of her rich natural resources (e.g., oil, diamonds, uranium) and the cheap labor she provides the world economy.

This chapter critically discusses the contending visions of media in globalizing Africa, particularly between state, civil society, and, lately, capital. With a primary focus on radio broadcasting, the chapter argues that while pressures from Western governments and international donor agencies may have forced African states to partially open up broadcasting to private niche-market operators, cronyism in the issuance of such licenses, coupled with excessive state oversight, have combined to undermine its vaunted promise of providing a plurality of viewpoints so vital to the constitution of a democratic public sphere. Meanwhile, the civil society–backed public service model is hardly ever broached, raising concerns about the prospects, if any, of democratic public communication on the continent. I argue that this democratic media deficit can be partly mitigated by the establishment of strong, independent, and truly participatory community (rural) media that are distinct from localized outlets of public (state) or commercial operators.

STATE, CIVIL SOCIETY, MEDIA, AND GLOBALIZATION IN AFRICA: A BRIEF OVERVIEW

Most contemporary discourse of globalization usually begins with the late 1980s and early 1990s, when the United States declared victory following the cold war and sought to impose a new world order anchored on the twin pillars of liberal democracy and free-market economics. However, I adopt a historically expansive view of globalization that dates back to the imperialist adventures of European powers in colonial Africa, centuries-old developments that have continued to have grave implications for state–civil society relations on the continent. Apparently, finding their intense jostling for political and economic territories in Africa such an expensive enterprise, major European powers met in Berlin in 1884–1885, where they arbitrarily carved up the continent among themselves with no African input (Davidson 1974; Oliver and Atmore 1994). This was, for the most part, done with utter disregard for the primordial affiliations of the continent's various peoples. In many instances, homogenous ethnic nationalities were ripped apart, while historically antagonistic peoples with no common history or ancestry were lumped together under geographic state entities whose claims to nationhood were purely nominal. Evidence of this abounds in virtually all regions of Africa, where genocide and other forms of violent ethnic conflict have continued to impede the peaceful coexistence of neighbors, as well as any effort at development and democratization (Bourgault 1995, 21; Suberu 2001). For example, the colonial roots of the 1994 genocide in Rwanda that led to the death of hundreds of thousands of Tutsis are well documented (Mamdani 2001, Melvern 2000, Kukah 1998).

As a conquering force, the colonial state in Africa was essentially a "military-administrative unit," and the formal structures it bequeathed to the newly independent states were inherently "authoritarian in nature, and primarily concerned with issues of domination rather than legitimacy" (Chazan et al. 1999, 43).

With such inherited authoritarian structures of governance, politics in the newly independent African states became intensely adversarial, with the leaders seeking first the "political kingdom" at the expense of any genuine efforts toward the economic and social transformation of their societies (Ihonvbere 1998, 10). On the flip side of this, however, is the bestial nature of the African state, which rather than moderation encourages a politics of extremism (Ake 1993a).

The neurotic quest for state power and the unrestrained exercise of it engendered the corrosive culture of military rule, life presidents, and one-party states so prevalent in Africa until the early 1990s. Needless to say, whatever atrocities these regimes committed happened under the watch of their cold war benefactors, some of whom, today, are among the most ardent proponents of democracy and human rights.

Typically, an authoritarian political culture is never conducive to the development of civil society, which in the context of a democratic constitutional state refers broadly to "that complex and dynamic ensemble of legally protected non-governmental institutions that tend to be non-violent, self-organizing, self-reflexive, and permanently in tension with each other and with the state institutions that 'frame,' constrict and enable their activities" (Keane 1998, 6). Postcolonial Africa is no exception. Forced to confront a largely praetorian state, civil society in Africa has been, for the most part, uncivil, as its frequent invocation of primordial ethnic affiliations and recourse to violence in resolving conflicts (Ihonvbere and Mbaku 1998, 3) have led to what Celestine Monga (1996) aptly calls the "anthropology of anger."

To postcolonial African governments, the control of the mass media, particularly radio broadcasting, was vital to their consolidation and personalization of state power (Hyden and Okigbo 2002, 38). Even in the few places where the privately owned print media tried to provide alternative viewpoints from those of the state-run media, all sorts of draconian laws and arbitrary actions were used to muzzle them (Martin 1998; Ogbondah 2002). Prior to the 1980s, such publications (wherever they survived) belonged mostly to opposition politicians and parties whose brazen editorial partisanship in pursuit of some parochial interests were as troubling as the propagandist excesses of their state-run counterparts. However, with the growing agitation for democratization, the 1980s witnessed the growth of independent (non-state-owned) newspapers, established primarily as business interests and with the goal of advancing public discourse, albeit from a centrist perspective (Faringer 1991; Eribo and Jong-Ebot 1997). These would be followed by a number of populist and ideologically driven advocacy publications that manifest varying degrees of militancy. Such publications include Nigeria's *Tell, The News*, and *Tempo* and Zambia's *The Post* (Olukotun 2002; Ibelema 2003; Kasoma 1997). Opinions remain sharply divided as to the relevance of this adversarial brand of journalism, given these publications' irreverence for public officials and their penchant for sensationalism.

Yet, the battle for the control of the mass media in Africa has never really been as much about the print media as it is about broadcasting, particularly radio. To date, radio broadcasting remains the most popular form of mass communication in sub-Saharan Africa. This is particularly so, given that the vast majority (about 80 percent) of the population lives in the rural areas. Also, the relative cheapness of the medium, the low level of functional literacy (about 50 percent), and the prevalence of multilanguage states combine to give radio its preeminent status among other forms of mass communication (Ziegler and Asante 1992, 55; van der Veur 2002, 81–82; Daloz and Verrier-Frechette 2000, 180–81).

Radio broadcasting was first introduced in Africa by the colonial powers primarily to further their own imperialist interests and policies. While the British invoked the public service model, the French, in pursuit of their assimilation policies, adopted a centralized system that was much more susceptible to official manipulation. In either case, colonial broadcasting was primarily used in the service of empire, even as the British made some effort, particularly in the waning years of colonial rule, to bequeath a truly public service system to her colonies.

Such efforts were, however, wishful, as the newly independent states in no time turned the semiautonomous broadcasting corporations into government agencies, which left them very vulnerable to official manipulation (Eko 2003, 177–80; van der Veur 2002; Bourgault 1995, 69–70; Katz and Wedell 1978, 81). While some of these broadcasting institutions retained their original designation as corporations, they were in reality no more than the official mouthpiece of whichever regime was in power. Proponents of state control of broadcasting in Africa often justify it by pointing to the very complex and fragile nature of the continent's nation-states and the need for national unity and integration as the basis for any meaningful development. This line of reasoning was most sustained in the now much-savaged development-communication paradigm, which requires that the mass media literally be at the service of the state in its arduous task of nation building (Eko 2003, 178–79; Bourgault 1995, 21–22; Hyden and Leslie 2002, 8). For instance, short of an outright endorsement of direct state control of broadcasting in Africa, D. Ziegler and Molefi Asante (1992, 61–62) would rather have the governments direct the broadcasters by articulating "developmental goals in such a way as to persuade broadcasters to agree to those goals." Yet, by their own admission, even if they think it applies only to a minority of African states, such direction usually never comes by way of persuasion and argument but more by intimidation, fear, and torture. On (is "on" better here than "in"?) a continent that, until the mid-1990s, was largely ruled by despots—military and civilian (life presidents) alike—it's hardly surprising that such direction to broadcasters always came by way of force. The larger implication of the personalization of state power so prevalent in Africa is that there is hardly any distinction between the regime and the state, so much so that regime interest becomes national interest and regime security equates to national security. For instance, how democratic/participatory is the process that produced those "developmental goals" that the broadcasters are required to disseminate?

MEDIA AND GLOBALIZATION IN AFRICA: CONTENDING VISIONS

Democratization, or better still, the liberal model of it that is being foisted onto Africa by the West, appears to move along two parallel trajectories: the political and the economic. Robert Horwitz (2001, 38) describes this as "double transition: from authoritarianism to democracy, and from controlled or command economy to a market system more or less in line with the exigencies of globalization."

While the political track involves liberalizing the polity to facilitate multiparty elections and respect for the rule of law, the deregulation of the economies of such nations is promoted as a condition for fully actualizing the immense promise of the former. The conventional argument goes thus: there can be no true political progress without a corresponding economic growth, and such an economic growth can only be guaranteed in a deregulated, free-market system with little or no state intervention. Thus, a major plank of democratization is the privatization of hitherto state-controlled industries, which in the context of Africa includes key media and communication structures.

For instance, prior to the early 1980s, there were virtually no private (non-state) broadcasters operating in sub-Saharan Africa. However, by 1995, there were at least 137 private operators in twenty-seven countries, and many more stations have since come into existence. This was primarily brought about by sustained pressure from the World Bank (privatization is a major plank of its economic policies) and from Western nations that made deregulation a key condition for development aid (van der Veur 2002, 93). Faced with very few options, reluctant African governments signed up for the deal by marginally opening up the broadcasting and telecommunications sectors to private operators, even as they have continued to keep a tight reign on such operators, particularly the broadcasters.

In the context of globalizing Africa, three contending visions of the media are discernible. First is the deregulated free-market model canvassed by the West; second is the primarily public service, civil society–oriented model favored by UNESCO and African nongovernmental organizations (NGOs); and third is the mixed public-private model adopted (even if reluctantly) by many African nations in an effort to meet the basic deregulatory requirements of Western governments and international financial institutions. Horwitz (2001) refers to the third model, especially in the context of South Africa, as "negotiated liberalization."

Since the mixed private-public model appears to be the most prevalent of the three, I will discuss it in some detail, focusing especially on what form it has taken in two of the continent's more influential nations: Nigeria and South Africa. But first, a quick discussion of the other two visions.

Given the immense influence of radio broadcasting in Africa, it is highly unlikely that any African governments, regardless of their current democratic posturing, will embrace a totally deregulated broadcasting system without some form of strong state control or oversight. For such governments, broadcasting is too vital to the continent's power dynamics to be left to the unpredictable whims of a certain insidious army called "market forces." In many African countries, it is not unusual for key broadcast stations (public and private) to be guarded by heavily armed soldiers to prevent their takeover either by mutinous troops staging a putsch or by activists involved in some act of civil disobedience. There is the anecdotal case of President Ahmad Tejan Kabbah of Sierra Leone, who is said to have been stepping into the shower when he heard on the radio that he had been deposed as head of state (van der Veur 2002, 89). In short, the idea of a completely market-driven media never washed with African governments after they learned from colonial times that the control of the media, particularly broadcasting, is the beginning of political wisdom.

On the flip side of this entrenched statist approach to the mass media is the pluralistic model usually canvassed by the continent's NGOs and civil society groups. This rather progressive vision of the media found its first major expression in the May 3, 1991, Windhoek Declaration, which affirmed that an "independent, pluralistic and free press" is essential to Africa's political and economic development. Organized under the auspices of UNESCO, the declaration defined an independent press as one "free from governmental, political or economic control" and a pluralistic press as a monopoly-free media environment where as many publications as possible reflect "the widest possible range of opinion within the community." Much as this declaration referred exclusively to the print media, it still recognized the immense power of broadcasting on the continent and recommended the reconvening of another conference with a view to applying the same ideals to the broadcast media (UNESCO 1996). A similar declaration was also made in 1993 at the Panos Institute–sponsored colloquium on facilitating the growth of pluralist media and broadcasting in West Africa (Myers 2000, 92).

However, it was not until 2001 that the African Charter on Broadcasting was adopted by a group of NGOs, again in Windhoek. The charter sought to fill the void left by the first Windhoek Declaration by applying its ideals to broadcasting. Among its key demands are the establishment of a three-tier system of broadcasting (public service, commercial, and community), guaranteed independence for all public authorities involved in broadcasting and telecommunication regulation, a transparent and participatory spectrum-allocation and licensing process, the transformation of all government-controlled broadcasting outlets into public service stations, and adequate public funding of such stations that is not subject to the whims of government officials or politicians (African Charter on Broadcasting 2001).[1]

Despite these lofty and progressive ideals, I will, for lack of a better phrase, call this the "orphan model" of broadcasting, as no African state, not even South Africa, is known to be committed to pursuing such a public service approach.

This leads us to the third model of partial deregulation that a growing number of African countries have adopted as a part of the democratization process. Under this model, two distinct approaches have emerged. First is the state-private mix, where a powerful state broadcaster operates alongside localized, niche-market, private concerns, as is the case in Nigeria and in many other African nations. Second is the public service–private mix that emerged in South African following the end of apartheid rule. I will distinguish between these two approaches by briefly discussing the broadcasting cultures of Nigeria and South Africa.

In pursuit of its liberalization policies, the Nigerian military government in 1992 established the Nigerian Broadcasting Commission and charged it with licensing radio, television, cable, and direct satellite broadcasters, as well as the overall regulation of the broadcast industry (Ogbondah 2002, 61; Obazele 1996, 153). The consequent issuance of broadcasting licenses to a number of localized private operators in 1993 effectively marked the end of state monopoly of broadcasting in Nigeria. However, the state continues to exert dominance both through ownership of the national network and through editorial influence over the local private sector.

As already observed, the British toward the end of their colonial adventure in Africa tried to establish a public service broadcasting system. In the case of Nigeria, that culminated in the transformation of the Nigerian Broadcasting Service (NBS), established in 1932 as the mouthpiece of the colonial administration, to the Nigerian Broadcasting Corporation (NBC) (now the Federal Radio Corporation of Nigeria) in 1957. True to its public service mandate, the NBC was neither a part of the civil service nor directly controlled by the government, although a minister was answerable for the corporation in parliament. It was akin to something of a national trust and had no commercial inclinations whatsoever. The 1956 act that established the corporation charged it with providing "independent and impartial broadcasting services" that adequately promoted the "culture, characteristics, affairs and opinions" of the nation's federating units (Obazele 1996, 145–46). However, at independence in 1960, the first indigenous government became wary of the substantial autonomy the corporation enjoyed and sought to curtail it by placing the corporation under direct government control (Katz and Wedell 1978, 84). Ever since, successive Nigerian governments have abused the corporation, reducing it to their mouthpiece. Even under the present democratic dispensation, that policy has not changed in any significant way. Effectively sucked in by the state, Nigeria's national radio and television, as well as the regulatory agency, operate under the direct control of the Ministry of Information, with the appointment of their directors-general and board members being the exclusive preserve of the president on the advice of his minister of information.

While the National Broadcasting Code drawn up by the commission is replete with lofty public service ideals, such objectives remain illusory as there are no institutional mechanisms to guarantee the commission's independence. The same applies to the board, management, and editorial staff of the state-owned broadcasting corporations. The government in power has unlimited power over them in terms of appointments and budgetary allocation.

The Nigerian model prevalent in many African nations has merely opened up the broadcasting sector to private interests operating localized, limited-range FM stations in niche markets, while the state continues to wield national influence. In effect, state monopoly of broadcasting may have ended, but not state broadcasting itself.

While a few African countries have yet to approve private broadcasting, others practice de facto state monopolies by using exorbitant licensing fees and strict regulatory policies to discourage potential investors (van der Veur 2002, 89–92; Ogbondah 2002, 61). Proponents of the partial deregulatory (state-private) model celebrate its ability to facilitate a plurality of voices that will counter the propagandist monologue of the state broadcaster. While in principle, the liberalization of broadcasting could potentially help open up the discursive political realm hitherto controlled by the state, in reality, it may primarily serve just the urban-based elite and the economic interests of the operators, if no strong public service demands are imposed on them (Bourgault 1995, 68). For one, no commercial operator would want to invest in a market that is not viable. Countries like Benin Republic have tried to address this problem by having the Office of Radio and Television support local-language community broadcasts in five rural radio stations (van der Veur 2002, 94). Even then, most of the private stations favor music and entertainment/cultural programming over hard-nosed news and public-affairs commentary (Hyden and Okigbo 2002, 45; Daloz and Verrier-Frechette 2000, 183). Reasons for this are part economic (appealing to the lowest common denominator) and part political (taking extra care not to get into trouble with an overly snoopy, censorious state and risk losing licenses and investments). In respect of the later, the first group of private stations licensed in Nigeria in 1993 had to walk a straight and narrow path as officials of a despotic military regime kept a very close eye on their content.[2] Besides, it is an established fact that such licenses are usually issued to powerful interests and individuals sympathetic to the government in power, who can reasonably be counted on always to tow the official line (Carver 2000, 194; Bourgault 1998, 94; van der Veur 2002, 91; Eko 2003, 182).[3] Just as the mere conduct of elections does not equate to democracy, the licensing of private broadcasters may not automatically lead to a plurality of viewpoints. It may well be a case of many stations with the same voice—that of the licensor. As Daniel Hallin (1998, 162) has counseled, particularly with respect to broadcasting in the developing world, any effort to study media in a democracy must simultaneously look at power and access to the media, at what interests they serve, and at how they manage social plurality, all of which are implicated in the structure of power.

It must, however, be stressed that state broadcasting is not inevitably "evil," as some African experiences have shown. For instance, state broadcasters have always made some effort to reflect cultural diversity by broadcasting in as many languages as possible, some of which would make no economic sense to commercial operators (Eko 2003, 180; Fardon and Furniss 2000, 3–4). Quite often too, Rwanda is cited as the perfect contemporary example of the tragic consequences of the abuse of radio. While the general premise of that argument is correct, it is necessary to stress that the brazen use of radio to promote genocide began only after the country slid into anarchy following the April 6, 1994, death of the moderate Hutu president in a mysterious plane crash. Prior to that, the state was very instrumental in reining in the extremists and preventing them from blatantly using radio for genocidal ends (Carver 2000).

The second variant of the mixed model (public-private) framework can be found in South Africa where a relatively independent, even if financially hobbled, national public service broadcaster operates alongside localized private operators in a three-tier system of public service, commercial, and community broadcasting. The key difference between this and the Nigerian model is the presence of a national public service broadcaster as the flagship of the system. This was a by-product of the constitutional negotiations of the early 1990s that led to the end of apartheid minority rule in that country. The emergence of this model was a little fortuitous, as civil society groups exploited the deadlock between the ruling National Party's free-market approach and the African National Congress's (ANC) largely statist model to fashion a "post-social-democratic," public-private compromise that is neither state- nor market-heavy (Horwitz 2001, 45).[4]

Historically, broadcasting in South Africa has always been used in the service of the apartheid state (Minnie 2000, 174; Horwitz 2001, 38; Barnett 1998). However, the political reforms of the early 1990s, which culminated in the first multiracial elections in 1994, led to the reconceptualization of "the electronic media as a single public sphere at a national scale, providing a space for democratic communication and national unification" (Barnett 1998, 552). Consequently, in 1993, the South African Broadcasting Corporation (SABC) was transformed from a government broadcaster to a public service provider under an independent regulatory and policy-making body, the Independent Broadcasting Authority (IBA), which answers only to parliament. The reforms also led to the birth of several private broadcasters who are expected to help provide a plurality of viewpoints from across the segments of the deeply bruised and fragmented society (Maingard 1997, 260–71; Horwitz 2001, 38). To guarantee this plurality, the IBA Act imposed substantial local-content requirements on all operators, along with stringent cross-ownership regulations for prospective commercial operators, particularly with respect to the black majority who must be adequately represented in the ownership and operation of any such commercial undertakings (Horwitz 2001, 45). Under the act, broadcasters at all levels, public and private, are required to do public service by fostering national unification and reconciliation and facilitating democratic participation rather than exclusion (Barnett 1998, 553–55; Horwitz 2001, 46). But this grand public service vision was doomed from the outset by the seeming unwillingness or inability (depending on whom you ask) of the government to provide the funding the SABC needed to carry out its mandate effectively. Budgetary constraints, among equally competing national priorities like health and housing, meant the corporation had to rely almost entirely (about 80 percent) on advertising revenue, as its only source of public funding came by way of the paltry license fees paid by viewers (Horwitz 2001, 47; Barnett 1998, 560; Minnie 2000, 177). Thus, in a desperate bid to survive, the SABC has increasingly embraced market principles at the expense of its core public service values.

Beyond the funding crises is also the political threat posed by some hawks in the ruling ANC who have wrested the formulation of broadcasting policy from the IBA. That power is now vested in the Ministry of Posts, Telecommunications, and Broadcasting (Barnett 1998, 564). This could signal a return to the old, blatant partisanship in broadcasting, with its attendant consequences for an intensely fragmented country like South Africa.

Curiously, the visionary African Charter on Broadcasting was substantially modeled after the South African public service blueprint. Now that the immense promise of the latter is increasingly threatened, it is perhaps time to assess the prospects (if any) of democratic public communication in Africa.

GLOBALIZATION AND PROSPECTS FOR DEMOCRATIC COMMUNICATION IN AFRICA

Until the early 1990s, the manifestly authoritarian nature of the African state was the major impediment to media democratization on the continent. But with the current wave of globalization, capital is slowly but steadily emerging as a second key obstacle. In transitional societies, the media, in the words of Silvio Waisbord (2000), appear doomed "between the rock of the state and the hard place of the market." Deregulation has substantially changed the political and economic dynamics of Africa's media industry, particularly broadcasting. For one, democratization has fostered a less threatening media environment such that journalists can now practice their craft more professionally. As a result, citizens, more than ever before, have access to a variety of information from a range of sources (local and foreign) that could help them participate better in public life. At the institutional level, local broadcasters now enjoy far more opportunities to forge very beneficial partnerships and affiliations with their foreign counterparts (e.g., technical support, staff training, program exchange, distribution). However, in almost all cases, such partnerships preclude the life transmission of foreign media programs, which the regulatory agencies usually consider inimical to national interest and security. Also globalization has in some cases helped draw international attention to problems that are much more peculiar to Africa. For instance, the enormity of the health crises (e.g., malaria, HIV/AIDS, tuberculosis) on the continent prompted the Commonwealth Broadcasters Association (CBA) to devote its 2003 African regional conference to health communication, with a call on the heads of states of commonwealth countries to draw up an emergency health broadcaster's charter (Communiqué of the CBA 2003).

The end of state monopoly of broadcasting has also forced state broadcasters to become more creative in an effort to survive in an increasingly competitive industry (Eko 2003, 184–85; Fardon and Furniss 2000, 18).

Yet, many of these changes are limited to cultural programming and new technologies and hardly ever extend to critical public-affairs issues that diverge from the views of the government in power (Eko 2003, 184–5). From the foregoing, it would seem that the idea of democratic public communication is somewhat alien to Africa's political experience. The mass media in Africa has always been exploited by the state in the service of domination. Now with the growing influence of capital, the worst- and possibly best-case scenarios are either a two-pronged, frontal assault on the citizenry by both forces or the replacement of one hegemony (state) by the other (capital); either option impedes the constitution of a truly democratic public sphere. The very insidious nature of capital makes it even more threatening to the project of egalitarian democracy as it "exacerbates existing inequalities and results in a deep erosion of people's liberty to achieve self-empowerment" (Hamelink 1995, 31).

Scholars like Robert White (1995, 92) and Michael Traber (1993) have rightly argued that the key issue in the 1970s New World Information and Communication Order (NWICO) campaign was the democratization of communication and, more importantly, its transformation from a social need to a basic right, both for individuals and cultural groups. African governments were in the forefront of that effort. The paradox, though, is that while they sought a democratic public-communication system at the international level, they maintained a firm stranglehold on their nations' mass media, thereby undermining the very thing they were fighting for.

White (1995, 93) sees democratic public communication as an institutional mechanism that strives "to guarantee the right of all individuals and sub-cultures to participate in the construction of the public cultural truth." And by public cultural truth he means "the dominant consensus about what is true and what is the meaning of the history of the group or society at any given moment of time." Implicit in his definition is the need for such an institution to be open and accessible to all, to embody a plurality of viewpoints, and not to be beholden to powerful interests be they those of the state, capital, or dominant social groups. Put differently, democratic communication presupposes a two-way, dialogical, and participatory process that guarantees the right of all citizens and cultural groups, both as receivers and transmitters of information, or what Karol Jakubowicz (1993, 40) calls "send-ceivers." While most radical alternative media, by their egalitarian philosophy and social-movement ethic, operate largely by these ideals, democratized—better still, socialized—mainstream media denote a nonstate, nonmarket media organized as a public good in the social interest and in which the public has substantial influence in the formulation and implementation of its policies and programs (Splichal 1993, 11–12; Jakubowicz 1993, 46). Based mostly on European experiences, writers like Nicholas Garnham (1990) and James Curran (1996) have located such an institution within the broader public service paradigm and, more importantly, as the closest of all mainstream media institutions to the Habermasian public-sphere ideal.

But the public service model is not without its flaws, including its apparent elitism and moral paternalism, or what its critics label "nanny state broadcasting" (Humphreys 1996, 161). Yet, given the multiethnic and fragile nature of most African nation-states, a truly socialized public service system can facilitate genuine nation building and development quite different from the fraudulent type engendered by the modernization paradigm of the 1960s. Little wonder that the continent's NGOs have always preferred it to the prevalent and widely abused governmental broadcasting model, as well as to the advertising-dependent market model that "transforms programs into its own valets" and "works in favor of . . . businesses and against citizens" (Keane 1991, 80). Although much of contemporary Africa lacks the kind of strong democratic culture necessary to sustain a truly public service media, it nonetheless retains a normative appeal worth aspiring to. Instead of the wholesale replication of specific Western models, each nation should strive to adapt the system to its peculiar sociopolitical and economic realities. For instance, the widespread poverty on the continent rules out the license fee as a possible funding option, as the South African experience has shown. One way or another, the state has to play a key role in funding the system, even as there must be institutional mechanisms to protect it from the shenanigans of politicians and government bureaucrats.

COMMUNITY BROADCASTING AND THE
INTERNET AS DEMOCRATIC MEDIA

Not-for-profit community broadcasting, as distinct from decentralized public broadcasting, is a key component of the 2001 African Charter on Broadcasting. Such an enterprise, according to the charter, must be "for, by and about the community," with a "social development agenda" and an ownership and management that is representative of the community.

Community media can be theorized both in spatial and ideological terms. While the former refers to some limited geographic space (e.g., neighborhood), the latter speaks to a more dispersed notion of a community of people united by common interests, be they political, social, religious, and so forth (Jankowski 2002, 5–6). In Africa, though, the emphasis appears to be on the geographic, as community broadcasting tends to be synonymous with local or more pointedly rural broadcasting, regardless of ownership, organizational/management structure, and overall objectives (Jankowski 2002, 6; Ceesay 2000, 102). As a generic term, *local radio* encompasses both rural and community radios (Fardon and Furniss 2000, 9). However, not all community radios are rurally based, just as some rural radios do not necessarily qualify as community radios. Even the notion of geographic community is problematic, as such communities are often split along racial, caste, class, and gender lines (Myers 2000, 100).

Normatively, community radios are self-managed (internally democratic), self-financed, pluralistic, and participatory in nature, and they usually strive to afford every member of, or subgroup within, the community an equal opportunity in the communication process (Valle 1995, 209–10; Hochheimer 1993; Opoku-Mensah 2000, 165). However, in the context of Africa, such key elements as self-financing and self-management are usually downplayed, as the most successful stations are either operated by governments on behalf of the communities or are substantially funded by international organizations (Myers 2000; Ceesay 2000). While it is debatable to what extent these qualify as community media in the normative sense, it is hard to imagine how else they can survive over any reasonable period, given the debilitating level of poverty in rural Africa (Myers 2000). Such financial lifelines either from governments or international organizations usually have obvious political and strategic implications (Nombre 2000; Ilbuodo 2000; Ceesay 2000; Opoku-Mensah 2000; Daloz and Verrier-Frechette 2000, 185). Add to that the traditionally restrictive regulatory frameworks for broadcasting in Africa, and it becomes apparent why community broadcasters focus almost exclusively on development issues to the detriment of critical public-affairs programming. To their credit, such community outlets have since become the primary sources of information on a wide range of developmental issues, such as health education, family planning, new agricultural methods, conservation, skills acquisition, and more (Myers 2000, 97–98; Fardon and Furniss 2000, 9). And since rural Africa still embodies much of the continent's cultural essence, African broadcasters at large are increasingly making an effort to incorporate aspects of traditional African culture and presentational formats in their programming. Frank Ugboajah (1985) calls this attempt to ground the media in indigenous African forms "Oramedia." One notable example of this effort is the Village Palaver Tree, a kind of open-house program reminiscent of the village square, where the community gathers to discuss matters of common concern and resolve disputes (Ceesay 2000, 107; Eko 2003, 188). Laudable as such experiments may be, still lacking is the critical edge, especially with regard to the unfettered discussion of public issues and the expression of views that diverge from those of people in power. Just like the writers of old comedy, who threw brickbats not caring whose egos were shattered (Gassner

1954, 79), traditional African orature, especially the satirical genre, is as robust as it is irreverent in its task of social correction (Ebewo 2001; Okpewo 1992). For community broadcasting to truly empower the vast majority, yet marginalized, rural populations of Africa, it must go beyond the narrow confines of developmentalism to become a political project as well. The prevailing apolitical approach hardly goes far enough, as development problems cannot be effectively tackled in isolation from the political system that breeds them (Ake 1996). This calls to mind the frustrations of Don Helder Camara, the late Catholic archbishop of Recife, Brazil, and moral backbone of many of the region's liberation theologians, who once observed, "when I give food to the poor, they call me a saint; when I ask why the poor have no food, they call me a Communist." Since about 80 percent of the continent's population lives in the rural areas, independent community media have a vital role to play in facilitating grassroots development and empowerment.

In the early years of radio, Bertolt Brecht celebrated the dialogic potentials of the medium and the immense democratic promise it offered. Technically, that potential was never realized, as radio remains largely a one-way communicative apparatus. Today, such democratic utopianism has shifted to the Internet, given its interactive nature and emerging broadband potentials. But in Africa, factors like poverty, restrictive government policies, and the lack of basic infrastructure for its exploitation (Leslie 2002) have combined to undermine its democratic promise. And while the Internet may have expanded the range of information available to citizens, it has not dramatically influenced the course of democracy on the continent, largely because it remains an elitist medium accessible only to a tiny fraction of the urban population (Tettey 2001). As a democratic resource, it has been most useful to the continent's advocacy journalists and progressive social-movement activists in evading the restrictions imposed by despotic regimes. The conventional thinking is that the ongoing massive deregulation of the telecommunications sector will facilitate Internet diffusion in Africa. However, such hopes may well be misplaced as empirical evidence from the developing world has not shown any direct causal link between free-market policies, on the one hand, and social distribution of services and economic development, on the other (Audenhove et al. 2001, 24–25). Besides, the question is not so much about the potentials and availability of a technology as it is about whose interests it primarily serves. Despite its immense potential as a dialogical (two-way) medium of communication, the Internet will probably never have the reach, accessibility, and affordability that radio enjoys in Africa.

CONCLUSION

As Africa democratizes, it is becoming increasingly apparent that the West's liberalization policies, which drive the process, favor a commercialized, rather than a reformed, public service media system (Carver 2000, 194). However, the ascendancy of a commercial media system in Africa will depend largely on the extent to which the state is prepared to accommodate it. Either way, a democratized information and knowledge system, according to Chris Ogbondah (2002, 74), must be a major component of Africa's ongoing political transition. In pursuit of this, he argues, "there is the need for a legislative framework that will guarantee all constituent segments of society balanced access to government-owned media and other communication services" (2002, 74). It is one thing to pass such laws and another to implement them, for by his own admission, African political leaders are notorious for ignoring legal and constitutional rules, not least the ones they themselves have made (Ogbondah 2002, 55).

Much as legal and institutional means are necessary to have some form of a democratic media, an entrenched democratic ethos more than anything else is required to guarantee the success of such an enterprise. In other words, a truly democratic media cannot be legislated into existence. As White (1995, 100) argues, "once the values of democratic communication (become) the organizing logic of all social institutions, providing the 'script,' so to speak, for social roles of family, government, work, recreation, these values become the pervasive atmosphere of social relations." Given the continent's political experience, postcolonial Africa appears to be a long way from home in this regard. Yet, the immense normative appeal of such an ideal must continue to guide her quest for a just and truly democratic society.

NOTES

1. Progressive African NGOs, as concerned stakeholders, have always tried to influence the political and economic direction of the continent. This usually happens by way of far-reaching declarations on a wide range of issues, be they social, economic, political, environmental, and so forth. Sometimes such declarations emerge from conferences also involving African government officials and representatives of international organizations. But hardly ever do such recommendations get implemented. One such declaration is the African Charter for Popular Participation in Development and Transformation, adopted in 1990 by the African Peoples Organization in Arusha, Tanzania. Several African governments and UN agencies took part in that conference.

2. The routine live transmission of a BBC news report that the son of the now late Nigerian maximum ruler Gen. Sanni Abacha had died in a plane crash with a couple of his friends almost cost the local radio station its operating license.

3. In Equatorial Guinea, the only private station, Radio Asonga, is reportedly owned by the son of the president and Minister of Forestry Theodoro Mbazogo (van der Veur, 2002, 90).

4. For a slightly different account from Horwitz's in which the ANC, from the outset, supported an independent public broadcaster, see Jeanette Minnie (2000).

REFERENCES

African Charter on Broadcasting. 2001. In *Media Development*, 3/2001: 53–54.
Ake, Claude. 1993a. "Is Africa Democratizing?" The 1993 Annual Guardian Lecture, Lagos, Nigeria, December 11.
———. 1993b. "Rethinking African Democracy." In *The Global Resurgence of Democracy*, eds. L. Diamond and M. Plattner, 10–82. Baltimore: John Hopkins University Press.
———. 1996. *Democracy and Development in Africa*. Washington, D.C.: The Brookings Institute.
Archibugi, D., and D. Held, eds. 1995. *Cosmopolitan Democracy*. Cambridge: Polity Press.
Arusha Declaration. 1990. "The African Charter for Popular Participation in Development and Transformation," available at www.iss.co.za/AF/Regorg/unity_to_union/pdfs/oau/keydocs/popular_participation_chart.pdf (accessed April 24, 2003).
Audenhove, Leo Van, et al. 2001. "Telecommunication and Information Policy in Africa: The Dominant Scenario Reassessed." In *The Digital Divide in Developing Countries: Towards an Information Society in Africa*, eds. G. Nulens, N. Hafkin, et al., 17–53. Brussels: VUB University Press.
Barnett, Clive. 1998. "Contradictions of Radio Broadcasting Reforms in Post-Apartheid South Africa." *Review of African Political Economy* 25, no. 78: 551–70.
Blaug, Ricardo, and John Schwarzmantel. 2001. "Democracy—Triumph or Crisis." In *Democracy: A Reader*, eds. R. Blaug and J. Schwarzmantel, 1–18. Edinburgh: Edinburgh University Press.
Bourdieu, Pierre. 1998. *Acts of Resistance*. Cambridge: Polity Press.
Bourgault, Louise M. 1995. *Mass Media in Sub-Saharan Africa*. Bloomington: Indiana University Press.
———. 1998. "Nigeria: The Politics of Confusion." In *Communicating Democracy: The Media and Political Transitions*, ed. P. H. O'Neil, 79–101. Boulder, CO: Lynne Rienner.
Carver, Richard. 2000. "Broadcasting and Political Transition: Rwanda and Beyond." In *African Broadcast Cultures: Radio in Transition*, eds. R. Fardon and G. Furniss, 188–97. Oxford: James Currey.
Ceesay, Christine N. 2000. "Radio in Niger: Central Control Versus Local Cultures." In *African Broadcast Cultures: Radio in Transition*, eds. R. Fardon and G. Furniss, 102–9. Oxford: James Currey.
Chazan, Naomi, Peter Lewis, Robert Mortimer, et al. 1999. *Politics and Society in Contemporary Africa*. Boulder, CO: Lynne Rienner.
Chua, Amy. 2004. *World on Fire: How Exporting Free Market Democracy Breeds Ethnic Hatred and Global Instability*. New York: Anchor Books.
Communiqué of the Commonwealth Broadcasters Association (CBA). 2003. Africa Regional Conference, Abuja, Nigeria. September 2003.
Curran, James. 1996. "Mass Media and Democracy Revisited." In *Mass Media and Society*, eds. J. Curran and M. Gurevitch, 81–119. New York: Edward Arnold.
Daloz, Jean-Pascal, and Katherine Verrier-Frechette. 2000. "Is Radio Pluralism an Instrument for Political Change: Insights from Zambia." In *African Broadcast Cultures: Radio in Transition*, eds. R. Fardon and G. Furniss, 180–87. Oxford: James Currey.

Davidson, Basil. 1974. *Africa in History: Themes and Outlines*. Frogmore: Paladin.

———. 1998. *West African before the Colonial Era: A History to 1850*. London: Longman.

Ebewo, Patrick. 2001. "Satire and the Performing Arts: The African Heritage." In *Pre-Colonial and Post-Colonial Drama and Theatre in Africa*, eds. L. Losambe and D. Sarinjeive, 48–58. Trenton, NJ: Africa World Press.

Eko, Lyombe S. 2003. "Between Globalization and Democratization: Governmental Public Broadcasting in Africa." In *Public Broadcasting and the Public Interest*, eds. M. McCauley et al., 175–91. Armonk, NY: M. E. Sharpe.

Eribo, F., and W. Jong-Ebot, eds. 1997. *Press Freedom and Communication in Africa*. Trenton, NJ: Africa World Press.

Fardon, Richard, and Graham Furniss. 2000. "African Broadcast Cultures." *African Broadcast Cultures: Radio in Transition*, eds. R. Fardon and G. Furniss, 1–20. Oxford: James Currey.

Faringer, G. L. 1991. *Press Freedom in Africa*. New York: Praeger.

Fukuyama, Francis. 1992. *The End of History and the Last Man*. London: Hamish Hamilton.

Garnham, Nicholas. 1990. *Capitalism and Communication: Global Culture and the Politics of Information*. London: Sage.

Gassner, John. 1954. *Masters of the Drama*. New York: Dover Publications.

Habermas, Jurgen. 1989. *The Structural Transformation of the Public Sphere*. Cambridge, MA: MIT Press.

Hallin, Daniel C. 1998. "Broadcasting in the Third World: From National Development to Civil Society." In *Media, Ritual and Identity*, eds. T. Liebes and J. Curran, 153–67. London: Routledge.

Hamelink, Cees J. 1995. "The Democratic Ideal and Its Enemies." In *The Democratization of Communication*, ed. P. Lee, 15–37. Cardiff: University of Wales Press.

Held, David, ed. 1993. *Prospects for Democracy*. Cambridge: Polity Press.

———. 1996. *Models of Democracy*. Cambridge: Polity Press.

Herbst, Jeffrey. 1992. *U.S. Economic Policy toward Africa*. New York: Council on Foreign Relations Press.

Hochheimer, John L. 1993. "Organizing Democratic Radio: Issues in Praxis." *Media, Culture and Society* 15, no. 3: 473–86.

Holden, Barry, ed. 2000. *Global Democracy: Key Debates*. London: Routledge.

Horwitz, Robert B. 2001. "'Negotiated Liberalization': The Politics of Communications Reform in South Africa." In *Media and Globalization: Why the State Matters*, eds. N. Morris and S. Waisbord, 37–54. Lanham, MD: Rowman & Littlefield.

Humphreys, Peter J. 1996. *Mass Media and Media Policy in Western Europe*. Manchester, U.K.: Manchester University Press.

Huntington, S. 1992. *The Third Wave: Democratization in the Late Twentieth Century*. Norman: Oklahoma State University Press.

Hyden, Goran, and Charles Okigbo. 2002. "The Media and the Two Waves of Democracy." In *Media and Democracy in Africa*, eds. G. Hyden, M. Leslie, and F. Ogundimu, 29–53. New Brunswick, NJ : Transaction Publishers.

Hyden, Goran, and Michael Leslie. 2002. "Communication and Democratization in Africa." In *Media and Democracy in Africa*, eds. G. Hyden, M. Leslie, and F. Ogundimu, 1–27. New Brunswick, NJ: Transaction Publishers.

Ibelema, Minabere. 2003. "The Nigerian Press and June 12: Pressure and Performance during a Political Crisis." *Journalism Communication Monographs* 4, no. 4.

Ihonvbere, Julius. 1998. "Where Is the Third Wave? A Critical Evaluation of Africa's Non-Transition to Democracy." In *Multiparty Democracy and Political Change in Africa*, eds. J. Mbaku and J. Ihonvbere, 9–32. Aldershot: Ashgate.

Ihonvbere, Julius, and John Mukum Mbaku. 1998. "General Introduction." In *Multiparty Democracy and Political Change in Africa*, eds. J. Mbaku and J. Ihonvbere, 1–7. Aldershot: Ashgate.

Ilbuodo, Jean-Pierre. 2000. "Strategies to Relate Audience Research to the Participatory Production of Radio Programmes." In *African Broadcast Cultures: Radio in Transition*, eds. R. Fardon and G. Furniss, 42–71. Oxford: James Currey.

Jakubowicz, Karol. 1993. "Stuck in the Grove: Why the 1960s Approach to Communication Democratization Will No Longer Do." In *Communication and Democracy*, eds. S. Splichal and J. Wasko, 33–54. Norwood, NJ: Ablex.

Jankowski, Nicholas W. 2002. "The Conceptual Contours of Community Media." In *Community Media in the Information Age*, eds. N. Jankowski and O. Prehn, 3–16. Cresskill, NJ: Hampton Press.

Joseph, Richard. 1993. "Africa: The Rebirth of Political Freedom." In *The Global Resurgence of Democracy*, eds. L. Diamond and M. F. Plattner, 307–20. Baltimore: John Hopkins University Press.

Kasoma, Francis. 1997. "The Independent Press and Politics in Africa." *Gazette* 59, nos. 4–5: 295–310.

Katz, Elihu, and George Wedell. 1978. *Broadcasting in the Third World: Promise and Performance*. London: Macmillan.

Keane, John. 1991. *The Mass Media and Democracy*. Cambridge: Polity Press.

———. 1998. *Civil Society: Old Images, New Visions*. Cambridge: Polity Press.

Kukah, M. H. 1998. *The Fractured Microcosm: The African Condition and the Search for Moral Balance in the New World Order*. Nigeria: Faculty of Social Sciences, Lagos State University, Guest Lecture Series.

Leslie, Michael. 2002. "The Internet and Democratization." In *Media and Democracy in Africa*, eds. G. Hyden, M. Leslie, and F. Ogundimu, 107–28. New Brunswick, NJ: Transaction Publishers.

Maingard, Jacqueline. 1997. "Transforming Television Broadcasting in a Democratic South Africa." *Screen* 38, no. 3: 260–74.

Mamdani, Mahmood. 2001. *When Victims Become Killers: Colonialism, Nativism, and the Genocide in Rwanda*. Princeton, NJ: Princeton University Press.

Martin, Robert. 1998. "Notes on Freedom of Expression in Africa." In *Communicating Democracy: The Media and Political Transitions*, ed. P. H. O'Neil, 63–77. Boulder, CO: Lynne Rienner.

Melvern, Linda. 2000. *A People Betrayed: The Role of the West in Rwanda's Genocide*. London: Zed Books.

Minnie, Jeanette. 2000. "The Growth of Independence Broadcasting in South Africa." In *African Broadcast Cultures: Radio in Transition*, eds. R. Fardon and G. Furniss, 174–79. Oxford: James Currey.

Monga, Celestine. 1996. *The Anthropology of Anger: Civil Society and Democracy in Africa*. Boulder, CO: Lynne Rienner.

Myers, Mary. 2000. "Community Radio and Development: Issues and Examples from Francophone West Africa." In *African Broadcast Cultures: Radio in Transition*, eds. R. Fardon and G. Furniss, 90–101. Oxford: James Currey.

Njaka, Elechukwu N. 1974. *Igbo Political Culture*. Evanston, IL: Northwestern University Press.

Nombre, Urbaine. 2000. "The Evolution of Radio Broadcasting in Burkina Faso: 'From Mother Radio to Local Radios.'" In *African Broadcast Cultures: Radio in Transition*, eds. R. Fardon and G. Furniss, 83–89. Oxford: James Currey.

Obazele, Patrick. 1996. "Challenges of Radio Journalism and Management of Broadcasting in Nigeria." In *Journalism in Nigeria: Issues and Perspectives*, eds. O. Dare D. and A. Uyo. Lagos: Nigerian Union of Journalists.

Ogbondah, Chris W. 2002. "Media Laws in Political Transition." *Media and Democracy in Africa*, eds. G. Hyden, M. Leslie, and F. Ogundimu, 55–80. New Brunswick, NJ: Transaction Publishers.

Okpewo, Isidore. 1992. *African Oral Literature: Backgrounds, Character and Continuity*. Bloomington: Indiana University Press.

Oliver, Roland, and Anthony Atmore. 1994. *Africa since 1800*. Cambridge: Cambridge University Press.

Olukoshi, Adebayo. 1998. *The Elusive Prince of Denmark: Structural Adjustment and the Crisis of Governance in Africa*. Uppsala, Sweden: Nordiska Afrikainstitutet.

Olukotun, Ayo. 2002. "Authoritarian State, Crises of Democracy and the Underground Media in Nigeria." *African Affairs* 101, no. 404: 317–42.

Opoku-Mensah, Aida. 2000. "The Future of Community Radio in Africa: The Case of Southern Africa." In *African Broadcast Cultures: Radio in Transition*, eds. R. Fardon and G. Furniss, 165–73. Oxford: James Currey.

Sen, Amartya. 1999. *Development as Freedom*. New York: Knopf.

Sorensen, Georg. 1998. *Democracy and Democratization: Processes and Prospects in a Changing World*. Boulder, CO: Westview Press.

Splichal, Slavko. 1993. "Searching for New Paradigms: An Introduction." In *Communication and Democracy*, eds. S. Splichal and J. Wasko, 3–18. Norwood, NJ: Ablex.

Suberu, Rotimi. 2001. *Federalism and Ethnic Conflict in Nigeria*. Washington, D.C.: United States Institute of Peace Studies.

Tettey, Wisdom. 2001. "Information Technology and Democratic Participation in Africa." In *A Decade of Democracy in Africa*, ed. S. Ndegwa, 133–53. Boston: Brill.

Traber, Michael. 1993. "Changes of Communication Needs and Rights in Social Revolutions." In *Communication and Democracy*, eds. S. Splichal and J. Wasko, 19–31. Norwood, NJ: Ablex.

Uchendu, Victor C. 1965. *The Igbo of Southeast Nigeria*. New York: Holt, Rinehart and Winston.

Ugboajah, Frank O. 1985. "'Oramedia' in Africa." In *Mass Communication, Culture and Society in West Africa*, ed. F. O. Ugboajah, 165–76. Oxford: Hans Zell Publishers.

UNESCO. 1996. *Basic Texts in Communication: 89–95*. Paris: UNESCO.

Valle, Carlos A. 1995. "Communication: International Debate and Community-Based Initiatives." In *The Democratization of Communication*, ed. P. Lee, 197–216. Cardiff: University of Wales Press.

van der Veur, Paul R. 2002. "Broadcasting and Political Reform." In *Media and De-mocracy in Africa*, eds. G. Hyden, M. Leslie, and F. Ogundimu, 81–105. New Brunswick, NJ : Transaction Publishers.

Waisbord, Silvio. 2000. "Media in South America: Between the Rock of the State and the Hard Place of the Market." In *De-Westernizing Media Studies*, eds. J. Curran and M. Park, 50–62. London: Routledge.

White, Robert, A. 1995. "Democratization of Communication as a Social Movement Process." In *The Democratization of Communication*, ed. P. Lee, 92–113. Cardiff: University of Wales Press.

Ziegler, D., and Molefi Asante. 1992. *Thunder and Silence: The Mass Media in Africa*. Trenton, NJ: Africa World Press.

II

MEDIA AND DEMOCRACY IN GLOBAL SITES AND CONFLICTS

7

Globalization, Regionalization, and Democratization: The Interaction of Three Paradigms in the Field of Mass Communication

Kai Hafez

Through history democratization occurred in waves. An established model is to divide modern history into three major waves of the establishment of democratic systems: the first in the nineteenth century with the United States, Canada, Britain, France, Italy, and Argentina; the second after World War II with West Germany, Japan, India, and Israel; and the third beginning in 1974 with Portugal, Spain, and many other countries in Asia, Africa, Latin America, and Eastern Europe (Potter et al. 1997, 9). Today there is no consensus as to whether the third wave remains in motion or whether we are in the midst of a reverse wave. It seems obvious, however, that the dynamics of democratic transformations have slowed significantly over the last decade, with only a few exceptions, like Indonesia in 1998. Political development in large parts of Asia, Africa, and the Middle East is stagnating. Intermediate liberalizations in certain countries (e.g., Zimbabwe, Algeria) have suffered authoritarian rollbacks, with no regional spillovers of democratization spreading from individual countries.

Contrary to common wisdom, new media like the Internet and direct satellite TV have not yet proved to be strong forces of global democratization. Third-wave democratizations between the 1970s and the early 1990s occurred long before the massive spread of new communication technologies. Indeed, democratization has almost come to a standstill since the mid-1990s, when satellite TV became accessible to the general population in developing countries and a growing number of members of upper and middle classes started using the Internet. What seems paradoxical at first glance is, in fact, not easy to explain. Most analysts would agree that it is absurd to hold new media responsible for the failures of political transformation. Equally, it is difficult to assume that Internet and satellite TV are "technologies of freedom." Since there is no evidence that new communication has changed political systems, we will have to revise our theoretical assumptions and come up with more differentiated, less normative, and also more "modest" and realistic views on the processes of interaction between media and democratization.

To date, there has been little serious research done on the impact of new media on democracy in developing countries, with the exceptions of the work of Vicky Randall (1998), Peter Ferdinand (2000), and Adam Jones (2002). Most transformation theory in political science is policy oriented and largely neglects the media (Merkel 1994; Potter et al. 1997), although Eastern European trans-formations were amply analyzed (Aumente et al. 1999; Paletz, Jakubowicz, and Novosel 1995), as there was easy access to the newly found democracies. Yet, most literature is dedicated to the "consolidation" phase when democracy was technically introduced; again, scant attention was paid to the problems and strategies of the democratization of media working under authoritarian rule.

Since this chapter focuses on the interaction of democratization with glob-alization and regionalization, there are other useful types of communication research. Globalization literature, for example, is full of references to new media but seldom seriously reflects on political transformation in developing countries because of the focus on changes in Western political communica-tion (Tsagarousianou et al. 1998; Margolis and Resnick 2000). Work done on new media in developing countries is produced by area specialists like ori-entalists, who observe many developments but usually lack the theoretical perspectives in communication, rendering their work mainly descriptive (Hafez and Reinknecht 2001).

Only a few specialists on international communication have produced re-search directed both toward democratization and globalization, including regionalization (Sinclair et al. 1996; Page and Crawley 2001; Hafez 2003). Overall, this issue seems to be in an academic no-man's land situated at the crossroads of different disciplines and, thus, outside of each's respective realm of responsibility.

GLOBALIZATION, REGIONALIZATION, AND DEMOCRATIZATION: SOME BASIC MEDIA FUNCTIONS IN POLITICAL TRANSFORMATION

In order to assess the implications of globalization and regionalization on de-mocratization, we will first have to establish theoretical premises about the relationship between the media, communication, and democratization. Such political transformation usually goes through the following phases:

1. Authoritarian phase: The political process is monopolized by an elite that rules not on the basis of democratic procedures and legitimacy but by co-

ercion or force. The degree of authoritarian power varies; a useful distinction here is between so-called soft- (Algeria) and hard-authoritarian (North Korea) systems, because they allow for different degrees of media freedom.

2. Transitory phase: Political transition is characterized by either reformist or revolutionary processes away from authoritarian regimes. While the transition ends with the establishment of a democratic system, primarily characterized by free elections, a number of other criteria also need to be met.

3. Consolidation phase: Analysts agree that the consolidation of democracy is the longest and most complicated period. Consolidation includes the establishment of institutions like a constitution, parliament, or democratic media, as well as a stable political culture and vibrant civil society. Consolidation is prone to relapse because the authoritarian bureaucracy and societal values cannot be replaced from one day to another.

"Big" and "small" media, from TV, to radio, press, Internet, video, clandestine radio, and leaflets, can fulfill different functions, depending on the phases of transition. In the authoritarian phase, the government's monopoly on public information must be gradually lifted in order to allow the opposition to inform and mobilize the population for political reform.[1] Patrick H. O'Neil rightly argues that television has the capacity to galvanize people and likely has the largest mobilization effect (1998, 8). Its mobilizing ability aside, broadcasting is vulnerable to state intervention because the large technical equipment needed requires structural centralization. Since mass communication is an industrial process, individual dissidents, artists, or writers are sometimes more effective in opposing authoritarian rule than big media is.

The media's success in catalyzing democracy depends on a number of intervening variables that seem to favor the effectiveness of small over big media (Jones 2002, 17–72): First, the degree of state repression varies between authoritarian systems, depending on their aforementioned soft or hard status. In hard-authoritarian systems, like the former Soviet Union, only small clandestine media (like the famous *Literaturnaja Gazeta*) can exist. In soft-authoritarian systems, like Morocco, gradual press liberalization, sometimes including TV and radio, is allowed. Second, the state of society and culture plays an important role. Since illiteracy reduces the spread of political ideas, we must concede that the easy control of TV by authoritarian governments thwarts mass mobilization. Third, the existence of private, nonstate capital that can be used for media activities is crucial. The least-developed countries (LDCs) have a much lower capacity to substitute state capitalist control of the media sector than richer authoritarian societies. Privatization, on the other hand, is no guarantee of liberalization since richer elites in the developing world are closely intertwined with ruling autocratic elites. Fourth, the influence of the media on political transformation increases with the number and quality of ties existing between the media and oppositional groups and other civil society elites. The media might be more effective in articulating alternative views and mobilizing people for transition if their positions are in line with the political programs of existing groups or networks. Fifth, the state of journalism is important since its professional development is usually limited in predemocratic countries. Professional ethics and education are not only blurred by political imperatives but also by mechanisms of self-censorship.

Most factors influencing the media in the authoritarian phase also play an important role in the phase of transition. However, for media, conflicts within elite ranks—as during the tenures of Mikhail Gorbachev or Iranian president Mohammad Khatami—are important because soft-liners usually provide a certain degree of protection for a semiliberalized media system. Taboos are downgraded, and the relationship between big and small media changes. In periods of transition, the role of big media increases due to elite protection.

The phase of consolidation is surely the time of the big media. Free of authoritarian intimidation and restrictions, the media usually develop rapidly, as has been seen in countries like Indonesia, while the country is at the same time a case for the structural instability and the dangers inherent in consolidation. Latin America is in many ways proof that exploding commercialization after years and decades of state control can lead to immediate media concentration that again limits the capability of the media to function as a fourth estate (Waisbord 2000).

EXTERNAL FACTORS OF MEDIA DEMOCRACY

Figure 7.1 shows a simple model incorporating the various phases of transformation, the intervening variables of society, and the dimensions of the media activity:

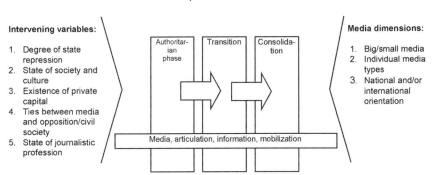

Figure 7.1. Media and political transformation.

This chapter primarily analyzes the third media dimension: national and/or international orientation. The question is whether the global or regional orientation of the media and consumer has an impact on the relationship between the media and political transformation. Further, is the international sphere really an activating media dimension facilitating political opposition, civil society, and the media to counterbalance state intervention or societal obstacles (intervening variables), and does it improve their capacity to articulate alternative political views and mobilize the people for democratization?

Margaret E. Keck and Kathryn Sikkink rightly argue that when individuals or groups are refused certain rights by authoritarian governments, they seek international connections and organize networks, causing boomerang effects by creating external pressure on national processes of transformation (1998, 12ff.). Since the right to express one's opinion can be restricted, individuals, political groups, or even journalists and the media may seek external support by channeling domestic news into world public opinion, activating network support for journalists in danger, directing world attention to domestic problems, or soliciting assistance in the form of pressure from foreign governments or the United Nations.

Potential interaction processes between the national and international sphere are, for example,

1. Groups or individuals (e.g., dissidents, intellectuals) use the Internet to form advocacy networks, thereby reversing the news flow and political pressure of their own government.
2. Political activities by groups or individuals are covered by the international media, which may effect world public opinion.
3. Big media introduce a topic on the news agenda, which is picked up by foreign media and international news agencies, sometimes mediated by information networks on the Internet.
4. Dissidents (e.g., journalists) might be supported by international nongovernmental organizations (NGOs), which can activate political pressure both on their home governments and the dissidents' government.

These are only some of myriad interaction processes that can take place between the national and the international realms. The following will concentrate on the first and second examples, followed by an elaboration on how mainstream global or regional media (big press, TV, and radio) can be conducive to democratization in authoritarian countries and under which circumstances small media like the Internet do or do not pose a vital alternative.

POLITICAL OPPOSITION AS COVERED BY GLOBAL MEDIA:
THE SPIRAL OF SILENCE OF DEMOCRATIC REPRESENTATION

It has become common for many globalization scholars and analysts to assert that the globalization of mass communication has taken a central role in political transformation. O'Neil is but one of many authors who assume that transborder flows of news influence world politics: "Already we have seen multiple examples in which the internationlization of mass communications has influenced the course of political change" (1998, 12). O'Neil offers two examples: the political changes in Eastern Europe and the Chiapas revolt in Mexico. The latter uprising and political movement highlights the role of the Internet and civic networking, which will be discussed later. Eastern European transformations have often been considered TV revolutions, but that argument suffers from inconsistencies in need of clarification. It is certainly true that the 1989 political events in Eastern Europe were constantly televised globally and that this kind of concentrated agenda setting could have spurred the political dynamics of that time.

However, those events were broadcast on national media systems because, in 1989, few European households, let alone Eastern European ones, had access to satellite TV. And the same holds true for access to the foreign press. With the exception of the German Democratic Republic, audiences in Eastern Europe had very limited opportunities to watch on TV their own or their neighbors' revolutions. The role of oral and nonmediated communication in such situations should not be underestimated: people met in marketplaces and joined in as demonstrations started and things snowballed. Furthermore, Eastern Europe received a tremendous push from Gorbachev's reforms from the mid-1980s (DeLuca 1998). The media operated amid political transition, which had already reached countries like Hungary, among the first to revolt in 1989. Furthermore, international TV only covered the political events after the movements and revolts had already broken out. It is impossible to draw conclusions from this situation for political transformations in a strictly authoritarian, low-context situation.

The effects of global TV on democratization seem rather limited, since the so-called third wave of democratization has waned as the presence of satellite and global TV expanded. One of the major reasons is that many democratization processes are only marginally represented on global TV. Case studies of the coverage of the Middle East on a prestigious German national news program show that it is often not the democratic opposition, but rather violent and extremist Islamist or nationalist political groups, that get the most attention (Hafez 2002b, 134ff.). Comparing German press coverage of Turkey and Egypt, the Kurdish extremist party PKK gained tremendous coverage in the 1990s; however, it stalled in the Turkish parliament, coming up against the governing parties and opposition in a well-established (though, at times, insufficiently consolidated[2]) democratic system. In contrast, Egyptian secular and leftist parties and forces (e.g., the Wafd Party, the liberal-socialist Tajammu, and the Misr Party) were almost completely marginalized in the German press in favor of coverage of Islamist extremists. Further analysis of German or other Western TV coverage would surely offer even clearer results. While extremist radicals like the Egyptian Jihad al-Islami are constantly in the news, most Egyptian parties and even large NGOs have never, ever appeared on Western TV.

There certainly exists a functional symbiosis between the extremists' desire for publicity and media interest in conflict and violence, a theme often analyzed (Wilkinson 1997; Nacos 1994). However, regarding political transformation, it seems more important to understand that moderate opposition receives limited coverage in the international media when there is a soft-authoritarian state not yet in a period of transition but developed enough to show vestiges of opposition.

Thus, with opposition rarely represented in international media, there is diminished international attention and minimal democratizing pressure from outside forces (governments, world public opinion, etc.). While it seems paradoxical, under certain conditions, media systems from countries that pretend to support democracy in fact pay less attention to democratic opposition than the ruling authoritarian governments against which the opposition struggles. In these cases international media and authoritarian governments prevent the articulation of alternative political views that could ultimately mobilize for democracy. If the relationship between international media and extremists is a functional symbiosis, then the relation with moderate opposition forces under pretransitory, authoritarian conditions is a spiral of silence regarding democratic articulation. When individuals or groups become dissidents and fulfill the criteria of sensational news, this situation can change briefly. But on a daily basis, democratic movements are of little interest to global media.

Interestingly, when theorizing media representation of political "challengers," Gadi Wolfsfeld speaks not of democratic movements or democratic parties but of protest movements. Those movements, he argues, need the media for mobilization, validation, and enlargement (Wolfsfeld 1997, 77). But protest is hardly possible under authoritarian rule, limiting Wolfsfeld's theory to democratic or liberal political systems. It is almost impossible for moderate opposition to initiate open protests like demonstrations to garner the attention of the global media. If they do—consider Burmese human rights activist and Nobel Prize–winner Aung San Su Chi—there may be a steep personal price to pay for becoming international media stars.

If this spiral of silence regarding moderate opposition and the global media's structural inability to positively effect democratization sounds very pessimistic, at least three important qualifications must be made:

1. The alleged underrepresentation in the global media is not sufficiently verified through country studies and comparative research.
2. While the global media representation of democratic oppositional forces might be deficient, the global media can have a positive democratizing influence through the "demonstration effect" of representing other democracies.
3. Oppositional TV and radio programs and foreign broadcasting services producing specific programs in local vernaculars can have a positive effect on political transformation.

Some foreign broadcasters show a clear orientation toward compensating for deficits of the national authoritarian media systems by giving oppositional forces a voice (Groebel 2000). But subsuming foreign broadcasters like Voice of America under the phenomenon of global media, as O'Neil (1998, 11), for example, has done, is questionable. Foreign broadcasting is based on the very old concept of mostly the big Western, but also other, states seeking news hegemony over certain world areas.[3]

REGIONAL COMMUNICATION: THE DECISIVE LINK BETWEEN GLOBALIZATION AND DEMOCRATIZATION

For the last decade, social scientists have debated what they perceive to be an emerging "new regionalism," a popular term for increasing regional economic and social interactions that are informal, nonhegemonic, comprehensive, and multidimensional (Breslin et al. 2002; Schirm 2002). While "old" regionalism was clearly dominated by government-to-government relations, new regionalism is based on networks of society-to-society interactions, including such diverse phenomena as regional political networking by NGOs or regional transborder media dissemination and consumption.

John Sinclair, Elizabeth Jacka, and Stuart Cunningham maintain that today the growth of regional media markets is even more significant than the spread of anglophone globalization (Sinclair et al. 1996, 12f.). Their vision is one of geolinguistic subregions like South Asia or Latin America incorporating Western influences and generating new national or regional products, including TV news and films, thus dominating Western "cultural imperialist" globalization.

In fact, the number of mostly private TV and radio broadcasters in Asia, Africa, Latin America, and the Middle East has multiplied. New cultures of news production have been established through a mix of Western-style news formats, domestically oriented news agendas, and various degrees of liberalization under both soft-authoritarian and already democratic conditions. "Globalization gone regional" is an indirect, albeit key, effect of global media on political transformation. However, regionalization is also a double-edged sword, since much of the news and political information is not completely free. Is regionalization, therefore, a catalyst for or a barrier to democratization?

A good example of regional adaptation of transnational TV formats is the famous Arab network Al-Jazeera in Qatar. In the few years of its existence, it has become the most important Arab TV news network. Al-Jazeera has achieved what global networks have failed to do: stimulate a democratic discourse in the Arab world through daily coverage of regional problems like the Gulf wars or the Arab-Israeli conflict and by broadcasting open and outspoken debates among various political sectors on national and regional affairs. While Al-Jazeera's coverage can be criticized for certain biases, like all other networks, including CNN and the BBC (Ayish 2002, 143f.), overall it is pluralist in nature, and its programming plainly advocates democracy.

Success stories like those of Al-Jazeera are based on the fact that they operate transnationally but remain in a more or less homogenous cultural and linguistic environment. Satellite transmission allows such media to bypass national authoritarian information control and all other intervening variables identified in the "Globalization, Regionalization, and Democratization" section above as important for the development of democratic media in an authoritarian context. Furthermore, the commonality of language facilitates widespread acceptance of regional programming in countries throughout the region. While Western media can be received by many consumers, they are understood only by small English-, French-, or other-language-speaking elites. Regional formats, however, have a potential to reach larger audiences and to be more popular; therefore, they have greater potential for political mobilization (Sakr 2001; Hafez 2001; Sreberny 2001; Hafez 2002a).

There are parallel but contradictory developments in global communication nowadays. One is the spread of English as a common language; a tendency strong on both the Internet and TV (e.g., English programs on Nile TV). The other is the revitalization of indigenous languages, as in India, for example, where dozens of programs in Hindi and other languages have come into existence. Many regions in the world show similar regional, transborder effects, including the Arab world, Latin America, and South Asia, among others. While Europe may be more integrated economically and politically, a "European media" hardly exists because languages are too diverse.

Comparing those regions, it becomes clear that in both Latin America and India, democracies were established before there was democratic TV and (at least big) radio. In the Arab world, however, the case of Al-Jazeera points to the opposite trend. Qatar is an economically vibrant small state whose ruler wants to transform his emirate into a trading hub of the Middle East. Emir Al-Thani, who founded the network in 1996, is not a political reformer, because Al-Jazeera is not allowed to cover domestic issues of Qatar critically, although it can do so regarding other Arab governments. Rather than being the product of domestic political reform, Al-Jazeera is an instrument of the emir for shaping his country's image as a modern state.

South Asia is another example of the regionalization of satellite TV. Indian TV—for example, the various programs offered by Zee TV—is influential in Pakistan, Nepal, Bangladesh, and Burma. Pakistani advertisers even place advertisements on Zee TV to reach domestic customers (Page and Crawley 2001). Other Indian channels, like Asianet, are directed toward the Malayalam-speaking viewers of South India and to the Indian diaspora in the Persian Gulf region (Wildermuth 2000, 225). One might argue that the bulk of Indian TV productions are commercial and entertaining, rather than political, like Al-Jazeera's, which challenges Arab authoritarian rule. However, Manas Ray and Elizabeth Jacka have observed that the Bangladeshi government, representing a very small stratum of the super rich in that country, fears that the middle-class lifestyle and consumerism represented in Indian films could cause social unrest in a country that, for the most part, is extremely poor (Ray and Jacka 1996, 96). Also, Indian broadcasting challenges the Islamic law that the Bangladeshi upper class uses to play down class differences and which in the past dominated state TV and radio.

Latin America and the Caribbean are further examples of regionalization. The English-speaking Caribbean has for decades been a testing ground for regional, transborder broadcasting flows. Even before satellites, authoritarian states like Cuba were never able to prevent the influx of broadcasting from neighboring countries. Consumers always had access to media other than that which was officially sanctioned (Brown 1996, 43ff.). In contrast to much commercial media in South Asia, Caribbean regional broadcasting always comprised news outlets, helping consumers to interpret domestic and regional political events.

In Latin America, regionalization has taken on various forms that are more or less conducive to political transformations. The most renowned trend is the commercialization of Latin American TV by a handful of media enterprises like Globo and Televisa, which in many countries are closely associated with the ruling elites. The result is a lack of political information and independent critical views. Advocates, therefore, look to small and alternative media networked in regional cooperation to cope with the commercial sector and help to build democratic media for the consolidation of democracy (Suárez 1996, 51).

In parts of the world where political development is stagnating, economic motives are key factors pushing for the opening of media systems. Despite players like Rupert Murdoch, global media capital has been scantily invested in Africa, Asia, and the Middle East. The business activities of most media tycoons are regional rather than global. Italian prime minister and media tycoon Silvio Berlusconi, members of the ruling family in Saudi Arabia (Boyd 2001), the German Bertelsmann empire, and many others who dominate media markets around the world are more regional than global players. The sole exceptions are Euro-American media mergers and financial transactions. But even seemingly global players like Murdoch generate only about 10 percent of their business outside the Euro-American-Australian formation (Balnaves et al. 2001, 60). Transnationalization of Asian media capital, for example, remains low because international firms face many political and cultural risks. Western business is not keen to invest in parts of the world with limited markets. Therefore, media capital, one of the intervening variables for the development of democratic media, is mostly national or regional in nature.

When the globalization debate started in the 1990s, analysts tended to neglect or underestimate the regional dimension of future developments. The concepts of the "end of the nation-state" and the "globalization of communication" left no room for a third, intermediate layer. What is needed, therefore, is a new theoretical approach to the national-regional-global nexus in the field of media and political transformation.

Does regional broadcasting really serve as a catalyst for those potential cultural impulses that global TV has failed to send out? Does it fully compensate for the spiral of silence, in which the secularist, nonviolent opposition at times seems to be banned?

Samuel Huntington's idea of a "clash of civilization" addressed the issue of regionality, but Huntington was wrong in assuming that cultures as such are antagonistic forces. However, it would be correct to argue that hegemonic forces within any nation or region—autocratic regimes, traditional patriarchal or religious leaders, and so forth—can be hostile toward globalization; thus, regional communication is often established as a countervailing force against global influences and intended to filter out, for example, prodemocracy news from outside a country. In the 1990s, Saudi Arabia established an empire of Arabic TV networks that were modern in their style of presentation but remained restricted in many sensitive political-news areas. Critical statements about the Saudi Arabian government or even the king or any "friendly government" on a Saudi TV network are impossible.

Such regionalization is deterring people's attention from much more diversified programs, such as Al-Jazeera. Marwan M. Kraidy is right when he argues that most regional TV in the Arab world allows no access to NGOs or the political opposition, which remain isolated from mainstream TV discourse (Kraidy 2002, 15). Here we have established the representation of the opposition as one of the main theoretical criteria for a positive link between

media and democratization. The bulk of the new Arab TV channels and programs, however, are owned and dominated by private capital that is intertwined with the ruling elites and, therefore, politically controlled and hardly
conducive to democracy.

While there is real potential for regional communication to support democratization, in reality many regional broadcasters prefer a modernized
version of status quo communication.

THE ZAPATISTA EFFECT? MYTHS AND REALITIES ABOUT CIVIC
NETWORKING AND THE MOBILIZING EFFECT OF THE INTERNET

The small medium of the Internet obviously plays a completely different role
at the intersection of globalization, regionalization, and political transformation. Most intervening variables show a positive balance:

1. Liberalization granted by the state: It is not easy for governments to
   control the Internet.
2. The existence of private capital: The Internet is a low-budget medium.
3. Ties between oppositional groups and the media: The Internet offers
   every group a chance to present itself since there is no "mediator," like
   the journalist, acting as gatekeeper.
4. The state of the journalistic profession: This is irrelevant for the same
   reason as for number 3.

Moreover, the media dimensions (see figure 7.1) have tremendous potential
since the Internet is an integrated medium that comprises big and small media (e.g., the press is also on the Net) and allows both national and international political strategies.

Rather than idealizing the Internet, one has to come to terms with a number of problems. There is one intervening variable in our theoretical model
that can easily limit the effect of the Internet: the state of society and culture
(variable 2). Problems related to this matter have been amply discussed under the rubric of the "digital gap" or "digital divide." In reality, that gap is
multiple. There are many differences in Internet access between developing
and developed countries, between the rich and the poor in each country, between metropolitan and rural areas, and between younger and older generations. In communication related to political transformation, these gaps can
accumulate, leaving merely a thin layer of young, urban, well-educated, and
politically conscious people and groups, who compose political communication on the Internet. Traditional (e.g., religious) institutions and many
mainstream organizations (like trade unions) have only minor standing on
the Net, overshadowed by small groups of young political activists. Mean-

while, there are much larger constituents of traditional and more established political-social formations.

We must also acknowledge that the Internet is a so-called pull medium in that it necessitates an active search for political information. TV, radio, and the press, on the other hand, are push media because they offer a selection of news for consumption. Therefore, Internet-based political information is mainly used by information elites. Nevertheless, the debate about the digital gap between the North and South is often misleading since many of the discrepancies are more quantitative than qualitative. Most of the intervening variables that we have theoretically defined allow, or even necessitate, elite behavior by private capital, the opposition, and journalists. While private capital might be satisfied with the mainstream development of regional TV, political parties and other oppositional forces are rarely articulated in the mainstream media of many countries.

But the Internet demonopolizes access to political information, creating new discourses about democratization. If we assume that national big media are restricted in authoritarian states and that international repercussions are limited by language barriers, and if we also assume that opposition forces have a limited presence in the global media, then we must conclude that the Internet offers huge potential for political representation. Its messages can be formulated in English or other languages and, thus, receive global attention. Since the Internet gives political groups and individuals a voice, the degree of differentiation in political articulation is significant and incomparable to anything big media could offer. Also, it is interactive by nature and, therefore, a place where dense political discourses can take form and transcend borders in a way unimaginable for classic, small-media-like leaflets.

In principle, the specific constellation of intervening variables allows the Internet to exert vital functions for political transformation, mainly political articulation and information. At the same time, uneven Internet access—the so-called digital gap—severely limits its capacity to exert the other vital functions of the media in political transformation: the mobilization of people for political movements. Both the unequal representation of political organizations and the limitations of Internet access severely reduce the Internet's mobilization effect. The Internet is unable to directly attract the attention of the masses for political purposes and is instead confined, for example, to inter-elite mobilization of NGOs and their sympathizers. But is elite mobilization really a new phenomenon? Political opposition forces like the African National Congress in South Africa and many other movements have had a mass mobilizing effect on people long before the Internet came into existence.

It might therefore be correct, as Lawrence K. Grossman claims, that in Africa, for instance, the Internet enables "tens of millions of widely dispersed citizens to receive the information they need to carry out the business of government themselves" (Grossman 1996, 6). However, Dana Ott and Melissa Rosser are equally correct when conceding that

> The statistical data, although preliminary, suggests that there is a measurable link between political and economic freedom and access to the Internet in Africa. It must be remembered, however, that association is not the same as causation. . . . Some would argue, in fact, that the causal arrow might point in the other direction, namely that political and economic freedom are, in fact, promoting the Internet, rather than the converse. . . . Considering the relative newness of the Internet to Africa, our ability to determine its impact on other development sectors is still in its infancy. (2000, 152)

Even though an analysis of Internet content points to the existence of new political discourses and a new brand of political information, the current literature is unable to prove the existence of significant effects of the Internet on political and democratic mobilization. Case studies, like the one on Indonesia, that indeed suggest a close connection between the Internet and mobilization have not taken place in a purely authoritarian context but rather describe a society already in the midst of rapid political transition. In situations where political change is already at hand and societal freedoms are growing, the Internet serves as a pin board for the coordination of activists and the advancement of the political program of an already strong political movement.

To summarize, the Internet often helps the articulate political elites, but it seems questionable that it can mobilize the masses. Analyzing the Palestinian Internet, for example, Peter Schäfer concludes that the Internet has not improved the coordination of political activities among Palestinian NGOs or other forces trying to mobilize people for political action. Coordination is still exerted through traditional channels (e.g., face to face), while the Internet is perceived as a forum for lively, but often contradictory, discourse (Schäfer 2004, 62, 89). The same holds true for authoritarian countries like Saudi Arabia, where cassette tapes remain the most effective communication tool of the opposition because they reflect Saudi oral culture and the limited literacy among the Saudi population (Fandy 1999, 144).

The last point to be analyzed is the international dimension, the third of the media dimensions of the media-democracy-relations in our theoretical model (see figure 7.1). How effective is the Internet in helping to create international alliances? Through the Internet, political activists can funnel relevant information in regional or global networks of like-minded or interested people. Keck and Sikkink (1998) speak of a boomerang effect of political communication. If communication between the ruler and the ruled in a certain country is blocked, political messages from civil society and the opposition can be sent out of the country and return through outside political pressure on the ruling government; this pressure can be exerted by other governments, through international NGOs, and over myriad other channels.

The international link of political communication on the Internet is often labeled the "Zapatista effect" (Cleaver 1998; Randfeldt 1998). The Zapatista rebellion in Mexico received worldwide attention through its presence on the Internet. A closer look at that effect, however, shows that international mobilization of political activism occurred under very specific conditions. The Zapatista effect was created through an alliance between an indigenous national-liberation movement and the global movement against neoliberalism. The Chiapas revolt was made into a symbol for the struggle against an unjust world order. Other provinces in Mexico with similar problems did not get the same attention, and it was not the Zapatistas themselves who created the massive Internet presence; rather, such initiatives came from outside and were only later coordinated with the Zapatista leadership. Thus, it would be naive to believe that messages sent out by indigenous political movements would automatically resonate with international advocacy networks and create boomerang effects of external pressure for democratic developments. Rather, such international alliances are characterized by many specific conditions.

The case of the Palestinian autonomous area is another example. Schäfer has observed that the Internet has improved the communication of NGOs and other political forces with the rest of the world. The most valuable contribution, according to Schäfer, are daily information newsletters by a number of human rights NGOs on casualties from the Israeli-Palestinian conflict (Schäfer 2004, 54). There has also been improved interaction within the Palestinian diaspora and between the Palestinian territories and the diaspora (Schäfer 2004, 89).

But it is hard to see how the Internet could have had a positive effect on the internal political mobilization for democracy within the territories. Many oppositional individuals and groups that were banned from the censored Palestinian mainstream media express themselves on the Internet. But the second intifada uprising that started in 2000 and resulted in anti-Israeli and antigovernment demonstrations is only the result of any Internet presence to a very limited degree since mobilization occurs through oral communication or traditional political communication (e.g., pamphlets). Boomerang effects informing global audiences about the problems of Palestinian democracy do take place, but there is no evidence that this information has had an effect on international or domestic policy makers, including international or national NGOs, or that such messages have changed the course of events in the Arab-Israeli conflict, simply because that conflict has for decades been prominent in the international media and the effects of a single medium can hardly ever be isolated by scientific means. Unlike the Zapatista case, Palestine has not been made the symbol of an Internet-based antiglobalization movement; therefore, the effects of the Internet are very hard to discern.

Although single-medium effects on politics can hardly ever be elaborated by scientific means, there are many other examples of countries where it is at least very likely that the Internet has had positive effects on democratic developments. When Tunisian journalist Tawfiq Ben Brik started a hunger strike to protest for freedom of opinion, the Internet witnessed a wave of protests, long before the global mainstream media placed the issue on the agenda. Also, Taliban Afghanistan was the target of feminist campaigns. It is noticeable, however, that a directly mobilizing effect of the Internet, in the sense of measurable policy changes, protests, or the like, seems limited to specific campaigns that have created very short-lived alliances of the global civil society. Nevertheless, the Internet in those cases has seemed a vital alternative to the other media.

CONCLUSION

It is undisputable that the new technological developments of satellite TV and the Internet have tremendously increased the flow of transborder communication. However, there is no automatic link between such interconnectedness and a positive effect on the political transformation and democratization of authoritarian countries.

Global media, both transnational TV networks like CNN and national programs received from outside the country, have a demonstration effect on authoritarian states. They open windows of information about other political systems, providing role models for better political practice in other countries. Direct positive influences on the transformation of authoritarian systems are limited because moderate opposition forces of the respective countries are seldom represented in the global media system, except in extraordinary events. The idea that global TV and radio could bypass authoritarian media control and bring critical voices into these countries must be qualified by the fact that the presence of global media from outside a certain country or region do not guarantee permanent, long-lived, or in-depth coverage of the national politics of authoritarian countries.

Regional TV, radio, and the press have a greater impact than global TV on political transformation because the content is politically and culturally more adapted to transformatory needs. Media capital flows are more regional than global in outreach, and regional TV and radio production and consumption in geolinguistic entities like South Asia, the Arab world, or South America are growing faster than global programming. Very often, however, regional media are dominated by political and business elites who allow media modernization only as long as the political status quo is not in danger. Because, even in regions with a higher number of authoritarian systems (Africa, Middle East, Asia), political systems differ in their approaches to political issues, regional transborder transmission of TV and radio very often does have an opening effect on public political communication. However, small media like the Internet are, in principal, more functional than big media in influencing political transformation in the authoritarian phase. The medium has great potential to serve as a platform of articulation for oppositional views. The same is true for national-global interaction. Boomerang effects do occur in the sense that Internet messages are transmitted from national to international advocacy networks and the world media. Direct political mobilization of NGOs, foreign governments, and other political forces, however, is most likely to be successful if campaigns can be based on alliances of national oppositional forces and established global political movements (like the antiglobalization movement), which are not always existent.

NOTES

1. Revolutionary developments are not conceptualized in this chapter.
2. For example, the Turkish military has at many points in recent history intervened in democratic decision making.
3. I recently finalized an evaluation project on the Arab, Turkish, Farsi, Dari, and Pashto radio programs of the Deutsche Welle, the German foreign broadcasting service.

REFERENCES

Aumente, Jeraume, Peter Gross, Ray Hiebert, Owen Johnson, and Dean Mills. 1999. *Eastern European Journalism.* Cresskill, NJ: Hampton Press.
Ayish, Muhammad I. 2002. "Political Communication on Arab World Television: Evolving Patterns." *Political Communication* 19, no. 2: 137–54.
Balnaves, Mark, James Donald, and Stephanie Hemelryk Donald. 2001. *The Global Media Atlas.* London: The British Film Institute.
Boyd, Douglas A. 2001. "Saudi Arabia's International Media Strategy: Influence through Multinational Ownership." In *Mass Media, Politics and Society in the Middle East*, ed. K. Hafez, 43–60. Cresskill, NJ: Hampton Press.
Breslin, Shaun, Christopher W. Hughes, Nicola Phillips, and Ben Rosamund, eds. 2002. *New Regionalisms in the Global Political Economy.* New York: Routledge.
Brown, Aggrey. 1996. "In the Caribbean, a Complex Situation." In *Media and Democracy in Latin America and Caribbean*, ed. UNESCO, 40–47. Paris: UNESCO.
Cleaver, Harry M. 1998. "The Zapatista Effect: The Internet and the Rise of an Alternative Political Fabric." *Journal of International Affairs* 51, no. 2: 621–40.
DeLuca, Anthony R. 1998. *Politics, Diplomacy, and the Media: Gorbachev's Legacy in the West.* Westport, CT: Praeger.

Fandy, Mamoun. 1999. "CyberResistance: Saudi Opposition between Globalization and Localization." *Society for Comparative Study of Society and History* 41, no. 1: 124–47.

Ferdinand, Peter, ed. 2000. *The Internet, Democracy and Democratization.* London: Frank Cass.

Groebel, Jo. 2000. *Die Rolle des Auslandsrundfunks: Eine vergleichende Analyse der Erfahrungen und Trends in fünf Ländern* [The Role of Foreign Broadcasting Services: A Comparative Analysis of Experiences in Five Countries]. Bonn: Friedrich-Ebert-Foundation.

Grossman, Lawrence K. 1996. *The Electronic Republic: Reshaping Democracy in the Information Age.* New York: Penguin.

Hafez, Kai, ed. 2001. *Mass Media, Politics and Society in the Middle East.* Cresskill, NJ: Hampton Press.

———. 2002a. "Mediated Political Communication in the Middle East." *Political Communication* 19, no. 2: 121–24.

———. 2002b. *Die politische Dimension der Auslandsberichterstattung* [The Political Dimension of Foreign Reporting]. Vol. 2. Baden-Baden: Nomos.

———. 2003. "Globalisierung und Demokratisierung in Entwicklungsländern: Die Informationsrevolution hat die 'dritte Welle der Demokratisierung' verpasst" [Globalization and Democratization in Developing Countries: The Information Revolution Has Missed the "Third Wave of Democratization"]. In *Neues Jahrbuch Dritte Welt*, eds. J. Betz and S. Brüne, 39–52. Opladen: Leske and Budrich.

Hafez, Kai, and Gottfried Reinknecht. 2001. "Medien, Politik und Entwicklung in Asien, Afrika und Lateinamerika: Eine Auswahlbibliographie" [Media, Politics, and Development in Asia, Africa and Latin America: A Bibliography]. *Asien, Afrika, Lateinamerika* 29, no. 6: 637–58.

Jones, Adam. 2002. *The Press in Transition: A Comparative Study of Nicaragua, South Africa, Jordan, and Russia.* Hamburg: German Overseas Foundation.

Keck, Margaret E., and Kathryn Sikkink. 1998. *Activists beyond Borders: Advocacy Networks in International Politics.* Ithaca, NY: Cornell University Press.

Kraidy, Marwan M. 2002. "Arab Satellite Television between Regionalization and Globalization." *Global Media Journal* 1, no. 1, available at http://lass.calumet.purdue.edu/cca/gmj/SubmittedDocuments/Kraidy.htm (accessed July 1, 2004).

Margolis, Michael, and David Resnick. 2000. *Politics as Usual: The Cyberspace "Revolution."* Thousand Oaks, CA: Sage.

Merkel, Wolfgang, ed. 1994. *Systemwechsel* [System Change]. Vol. 5. Opladen: Leske and Budrich.

Nacos, Brigitte L. 1994. *Terrorism and the Media: From the Iran Hostage Crisis to the Oklahoma City Bombing.* New York: Columbia University Press.

O'Neil, Patrick H. 1998. "Democratization and Mass Communication: What Is the Link?" In *Communicating Democracy: The Media and Political Transitions*, ed. P. H. O'Neil, 1–20. Boulder, CO: Lynne Rienner.

Ott, Dana, and Melissa Rosser. 2000. "The Electronic Republic? The Role of the Internet in Promoting Democracy in Africa." In *The Internet, Democracy and Democratization*, ed. P. Ferdinand, 137–55. London: Frank Cass.

Page, David, and William Crawley. 2001. *Satellite over South Asia: Broadcasting Culture and the Public Interest.* New Delhi: Sage.

Paletz, David, Karol Jakubowicz, and Pavao Novosel, eds. 1995. *Glasnost and After: Media and Change in Central and Eastern Europe.* Cresskill, NJ: Hampton Press.

Potter, David, David Goldblatt, Margaret Kiloh, and Paul Lewis, eds. 1997. *Democratization.* Cambridge: Polity Press.

Randall, Vicky, ed. 1998. *Democratization and the Media.* London: Frank Cass.

Ray, Manas, and Elizabeth Jacka. 1996. "Indian Television: An Emerging Regional Force." In *New Patterns in Global Television: Peripheral Vision*, eds. J. Sinclair, E. Jacka, and S. Cunningham, 83–100. Oxford: Oxford University Press.

Rondfeldt, David. 1998. *The Zapatista Social Netwar in Mexico.* Report prepared for the United States Army, RAND Arroyo Center. Santa Monica, CA: Rand.

Sakr, Naomi. 2001. *Satellite Realms: Transnational Television, Globalization and the Middle East.* London: I. B. Tauris.

Schäfer, Peter. 2004. *Internet als politisches Kommunikationsmittel in Palästina* [The Internet as a Means for Political Communication in Palestine]. Hamburg: German Institute for Middle East Studies (Deutsches Orient-Institut).

Schirm, Stefan A. 2002. *Globalization and the New Regionalism: Global Markets, Domestic Politics and Regional Cooperation.* Oxford: Polity Press.

Sinclair, John, Elizabeth Jacka, and Stuart Cunningham, eds. 1996. *New Patterns in Global Television: Peripheral Vision.* Oxford: Oxford University Press.

Sreberny, Annabelle. 2001. "Mediated Culture in the Middle East: Diffusion, Democracy, Difficulties." *Gazette* 63, nos. 2–3: 101–19.

Suárez, Luis. 1996. "Mass Communications and the Major Challenges." In *Media and Democracy in Latin America and Caribbean*, ed. UNESCO, 48–53. Paris: UNESCO.

Tsagarousianou, Roza, Damian Tambini, and Cathy Brian, eds. 1998. *Cyberdemocracy: Technology, Cities and Civic Networks.* New York: Routledge.

Waisbord, Silvio. 2000. "Media in South America: Between the Rock and the State and the Hard Place of the Market." In *De-Westernizing Media Studies*, eds. J. Curran and M. Park, 50–62. New York: Routledge.

Wildermuth, Norbert. 2000. "Satellite Television in India." In *Neue Medien und Öffentlichkeiten* [New Media and Public Spheres], ed. S. Brüne, 212–37. Vol. 2. Hamburg: German Overseas Institute.

Wilkinson, Paul. 1997. "The Media and Terrorism: A Reassessment." *Terrorism and Political Violence* 9, no. 2: 51–64.

Wolfsfeld, Gadi. 1997. *Media and Political Conflict: News from the Middle East.* Cambridge: Cambridge University Press.

8

Constructing Collective Identities and Democratic Media in a Globalizing World: Israel as a Test Case

Dov Shinar

GLOBALIZATION, DEGLOBALIZATION, COLLECTIVE IDENTITY, AND THE MEDIA

Contemporary sociopolitical iconography is richly populated with images and narratives of collapsing empires and emerging collectives, of reframed ideologies and religions, and of new boundaries, social constructs, and communication networks. The construction and dissolution of collective identities are major components of these images and narratives, particularly in the wake of 9/11 and the war in Iraq. A new agenda for social research and policy has resulted from these changes, formulated in several conceptual frameworks,[1] highlighting issues such as the dialectics between the multiple processes and expressions of globalization and the resistance it meets in myriad processes of deglobalization, as well as the meanings and functions of rights, representation, democracy, and democratization in the interaction of collective identity with processes of globalization and deglobalization, democratization and dedemocratization. Also at stake are concerns such as contexts for analyzing collective identity: imperialism, nationalism, decolonization, psychohistory, geography, religion, politics, culture, and new patterns of state/market, public/private, and central/sectorial relations, as well as the changing roles of media as mechanisms for social definition, integration, and the spread and transformation of democracy, particularly in the context of shaping, preserving, and changing collective identities in a globalizing world.

Deglobalization is a relatively recent construct used to study reactions to globalization. Ranging from diffuse states of mind to system, community, and nation building, concepts of deglobalization have appeared in socioeconomic analyses (Bello 2002), in community-organizational contexts, such as Stuart Hall's "counter politics of the local" (1997, 40), and in sociogeographic frameworks, such as Brazilian social geographer Milton Santos's reintroduction of fragmentation and territory as defining concepts of collective identity (2002). Economist Walden Bello, for example, while stronger in his criticism of globalization than in delineating concrete alternatives, attacks the South's resubordination to the World Bank, International Monetary Fund, World Trade Organization, G-8, and World Economic Forum, among others. Bello proposes utilizing the crises of contemporary capitalism to weaken the legitimacy of these structures, deconstruct them, and set up a vaguely described blend of deglobalized national economies with pluralist global governance.

Hall also eschews concrete alternatives. He interprets deglobalization as a psychocultural process linked to decolonization. Departing from the premises that "the return to the local is often a response to globalization" (1997, 33) and that decolonization involves the discovery of a specific self, he concludes that "when the unspoken discovered that they had a history which they could speak . . . languages other than the languages of the master . . . the world begins to be de-colonized" (1997, 35). This relevance of fragmentation is explored by Santos, who sees the local as a manifestation of counterglobalization and deglobalization as "the rupture of political-territorial links, with the ambition to create new boundaries and new states" (2002, 11).

ISRAEL AS A DEGLOBALIZED ENTITY IN A GLOBALIZING REALITY

This discussion of deglobalization highlights its relations with various processes of globalization and their interaction with identity and democracy, both in general and with reference to the media. This chapter focuses on the conditions and constraints that affect the forging of collective identities in multiple frameworks of globalization and deglobalization, on the role of the media therein, and on the relationship between identity and democracy in the contexts of the tribe, community, nation, the other, and the world.

The need for self-definition is inherent in every society; in Israel, the creation of a collective identity is intensified because of its history and the ways in which it was established and has survived. The development of an Israeli identity is a clear case of deliberate deglobalization, in which a nation-state has been carved out from a centuries-long diaspora. The conceptual background of "invention of tradition" (Hobsbawm and Ranger 1983) and of "imagined communities" (Anderson 1991) allows for juxtaposing Hall's and Santos's concepts with the Zionist creation and development of a particular cultural and territorial self. Moreover, in line with Hall's insight—that "movements of the margins . . . retreat into their own exclusivist and defensive enclaves . . . [in] a rediscovery of identity which constitutes a form of fundamentalism" (1997, 36)—the Israeli case illustrates how a shared sense of identity, a prerequisite for political democracy, can turn into fundamentalist chauvinism, marginalizing more democratic versions of collective identity.

Amid the Diaspora, Jewish identity was understood via affinities to a universal religion and global community but without a particular territorial dimension. This has led Jews and non-Jews to perceive this identity in diffuse terms.[2] The question of whether the Jews are an ethnic, religious, or national minority has never been fully answered, and their contrasting orientations—isolationist/assimilatory, religious/secular, Diaspora/state—have been largely ignored. The establishment of the state of Israel disrupted this perception on multiple fronts. Since 1948, traditional identity has interacted with a deglobalizing ideology based on territory, namely, the creation of a Jewish state in the promised land. There has been a sociocultural transformation, the emergence of a new type of Jew—free, productive, attached to the land, creator and bearer of an egalitarian society, and bearer of a renewed secular culture. Finally, there has been the revival of the Hebrew language as symbol and vehicle of this consciousness.

Thus, Israeli nation building has been typified by a pendulumlike interaction between globalizing and deglobalizing pressures: on the one hand, more than two thousand years of Diaspora gave Israel's historical, religious, linguistic, and cultural character a global orientation; on the other hand, with the Zionist movement beginning in the late nineteenth century, deglobalizing motives typified the gradual building of Israel. In both vision and practical expressions—immigration, settlement, and other nation-building efforts—the "return to Zion" was consistently presented as a deglobalizing project. Lacking, however, in economic viability and always dependent on foreign military and economic aid, the Zionist project and Jewish state never abandoned their global attachment to the Diaspora or to other allies. Also, as an immigrant-settler nation, like North and South America, Australia, and South Africa, Israel's identity building had to draw on global sources.

DEFINING PROCESSES AND DILEMMAS IN THE CONSTRUCTION OF AN ISRAELI COLLECTIVE IDENTITY

Several "defining processes" have served to trigger the emergence of serious existential dilemmas in Israel's deglobalization. The pioneering ideology that typified Israel's early years was replaced in the 1960s by processes of normalization, a process that triggered the appearance of some emergent dilemmas. These conflicting values strongly challenged the then-embryonic democratic consensus.[3] The early collectivist, puritan, secular ideology was challenged by globally inspired materialism, permissiveness, and individualism, as well as by the sectarian outlook represented by radical settlers in the occupied territories, their chauvinist-irredentist promised-land narrative, and ultraorthodox religious currents. This sectorialization trend has intensified considerably since the early 1990s with the influx of new immigrants, mostly from the former USSR, now comprising some 20 percent of the population. Furthermore, religious Jews have accounted for a similar percentage. Finally, the Arab-Israeli population is now an influential identity-elated factor, also making up 20 percent of the population. The self-perception of many of them as Palestinians has converged with their Israeli citizenship, highlighting another budding dilemma.

A second trigger was the activation of a swinging political pendulum. Disrupting the tradition of some thirty years of left-wing predominance, the nationalist right-wing Likud Party came to power between 1977 and 1984, when it was replaced until 1990 by a national right-left Unity government. The Likud returned to power in 1990, was replaced in 1992 by a left-wing Labor government, and returned from 1996 to 1999. It was replaced again in 1999 by Labor and in 2001 by a National Unity coalition, returning to power in 2003. While reflective of democratic shifts of power, this trend has certainly not enhanced the stability needed for the definition of a collective identity or for significant democratization.

New economic trends are another trigger. The alternation of violence and peacemaking has been expressed in the change from a flourishing economic climate in the mid-1990s to a persisting severe crisis since September 2000. Meanwhile, "globalization" has become a popular catchword, together with "liberalization," "privatization," "concentration," and "incorporation." These neoliberal policies, as has happened around the world, have eroded the former Israeli welfare state, opening a wide economic gulf, among the most severe found in democratic countries. These processes contextualize most "defining dilemmas" in the construction and change of an Israeli collective consciousness.[4]

The first dilemma concerns the coexistence of two mutually exclusive identities—secular and religious—that affect all spheres of life. The former is the civil identity of a modern state, run by the customary laws of open, Western societies, and focused on the concept of citizenship, citizen's rights and duties, and voluntary participation. This is the state of Israel, anchored constitutionally in written laws and civil society norms. The latter is a tribal-religious identity, prescribing that *Eretz Israel* (the land of Israel) should be ruled only by Jews, according to Jewish law, and that the fate of non-Jews should be like that of biblical tribes. Israeli democracy has not devised institutional mechanisms to resolve this split personality or managed to put these questions on the public agenda.

A second existential dilemma concerns the ability to survive and the right to exist and has important implications for a democratic climate. Created by immigrants who differed in almost every sense from the inhabitants of the land, Israel has always had to face problems of existential security, resulting from its demographic inferiority, basic rejection by the local population, and dependence on foreign aid. Doubts over Israel's ability to survive were compounded by the trauma of the Holocaust, in which most families of immigrants were exterminated, with survivors comprising the majority of immigrants in the early years. While other immigrant-settler societies have achieved security through the extermination or assimilation of local populations, the Jewish society did not have the will or the power to do that. Thus, security problems were not resolved with the establishment of the state, and doubts persisted about Israel's ability to survive and its right to exist.

The question of legitimacy has been more complex, mostly because Zionism—modern, secular, and obliged to universal egalitarian values—could not come to terms with Palestinian national aspirations. The earlier failure to define the conflict as a class struggle common to both sides, one that would be resolved in due time, forced Zionism to look for other solutions to the problem of legitimacy, such as the adoption of Old Testament imagery and language. This linkage of nationalism with religion exploded in the wake of the 1967 war, when Israel's military might converged with its existential anxiety, and its new control of the ancient biblical land where Palestinians lived. As a result, land conquest has become a daily reality of political and administrative measures, military action, and settler hooliganism.

The military victory of 1967 temporarily eased problems of existential anxiety and legitimacy as euphoric confidence grew out of ancient symbols of land and messianic salvation, largely ignoring the decline of Israel's legitimacy and the erosion of its democracy. The 1973 war revived the anxiety and need for legitimacy. Only the strength of North American Jewry and the support of the United States allowed Israel to overcome isolation during the 1970s and 1980s. The Oslo Agreements in the early 1990s provided solace, but this has been shaken by a new round of ongoing violence, particularly since September 2000.

The combined effect of existential anxiety and legitimacy problems is manifested by the state of siege mentality that has become a built-in psychological identity component. Security and economy concerns have always been typical of Israel.

Arab threats to use military force to prevent the establishment of a Jewish state, and to exterminate it if established, have been a perennial motif of the Israeli ethos. The Arab League boycotted companies that traded with or invested in Israel, practically imposing a regional economic blockade. Austerity policies and harsh measures were taken to resist the boycott, leading to severe restrictions. The siege atmosphere was gradually eased with the advent of more liberal economic policies, increased international trade, peace agreements with Egypt and Jordan, and the establishment of regional commercial links. The vision of a new Middle East emerged in the 1990s, marked by globalization, privatization, and competition. Thus, global corporations entered the Israeli market, accompanied by large foreign investments, joint ventures, and international partnerships. Nonetheless, this has been punctuated by the eruption of the intifada in the fall of 2000, by 9/11, and by the war in Iraq, renewing a sense of isolation, disapproval, and shrinking international ties.

ROLES OF THE MEDIA IN THE INVENTION, CONTINUITY, AND CHANGE OF GLOBALIZED AND DEGLOBALIZED IDENTITIES

Ideological strife characterized the Israeli media in the early years of the state with newspapers serving mostly as mouthpieces of the major parties. In the 1960s, a more professional, privately owned press emerged, featuring structural, financial, and professional codes of conduct adapted from the West. The privatization of the press and its control by big commercial corporations, assisted by political and business levers that did not always function in the service of the public interest, was completed in the 1990s. The two most popular newspapers are usually supportive of harsh governmental actions in the intifada and anti-Arafat policies. The only quality newspaper (*Haaretz*) has been moderately critical. This has been accompanied by an economically weaker trend of decentralization, expressed by a flourishing local press in Hebrew, Russian, and Arabic, which is more critical of the government than the national press.

Radio broadcasting began in the 1930s under the British Colonial Office. The news was strictly controlled, and programming was conducted in Hebrew and Arabic. When the state was established in 1948, radio was put under the Ministry of the Interior and later the prime minister's office. Linguistic minorities were served in Arabic and in languages spoken by new immigrants.

Established in 1965 as a public agency modeled on the BBC, the Israel Broadcasting Authority (IBA) has sought to eliminate direct government control and satisfy a wide range of needs through radio and television, the latter introduced in 1968. These goals were achieved only in part. Political, ethnic, religious, and gender-based groups, among others, have often complained that their media needs are not being satisfied. Professional and financial problems, management crises, and labor unrest have served to justify this situation and allow for increased governmental control. Concomitant with the weakening of the IBA and with an economic neoliberal stance are pressures to rearticulate the media system under "open skies" and deregulation principles.

In electronic media there has been outstanding growth since the late 1980s: private cable TV appeared in 1989, regional private radio stations in 1996, and satellite broadcasts in 2002. Channel 2 began broadcasting in the early 1990s, operated commercially by three independent programming and news companies, with a third TV open channel commencing operations in 2002. Since then, a limited media market and serious economic crisis have caused both public and commercial broadcasting, particularly TV, to operate under constraints of political and big-business control, ranging from direct government intervention to economic pressures from commercial interests. Manifestations include the appointment of management in programming and in the manipulation of the news, creating a dangerous climate for media democracy.

As possible media examples of Hall's and Santos's theories, the first pirate radio stations, which used to broadcast in the 1970s from vessels anchored outside Israeli waters,[5] have branched out to include dozens of religious radio stations and satellite TV broadcasts of weekly religious lessons, pop music stations, and pirate radio and cable-TV stations broadcasting in Arabic and Russian. A pirate industry of homemade, illegal, audio- and videocassettes, operated by Israeli-Palestinian partnerships, markets Middle Eastern and international music and local and imported soap operas.

This background at least partially explains the active role of the media in both influencing and reflecting the ideological, professional, and organizational shifts in Israel's climate. The media play three key roles at this crossroads of identity and democracy: the expression and reflection of identity symbols and rituals; the representation of images and narratives of deglobalized and global identities; and the participation in processes of democratization and dedemocratization.

Media Expressions of Identity Symbols and Rituals

Likely unparalleled elsewhere, one of the most-observed secular rituals in Israel is reading, watching, and listening to the news. Initially, there were hourly newscasts of five to ten minutes during "normal" times (when there were no official wars or major security events); in the 1960s, four hour-long news magazines were added, and later there were newsflashes on the half hour. Since the 1980s this pattern has become entrenched on Kol Israel (The Voice of Israel), controlled by the IBA, and the army-operated Galei Zahal (IDF-Waves). On television, nationwide open-broadcast channels 1, 2, and 10 transmit at least three regular daily newscasts of thirty to sixty minutes each, supplemented by longer magazines. Such news consumption rituals can be explained by immediate needs. Against a psychohistorical background of constant physical threat, surveillance of the environment became a basic need. The growth of this practice into a national addiction can be considered as part of Israel's existential-anxiety syndrome.

A second role for media in forging an Israeli collective identity is the symbolic naming of media organizations. Like the names given to media in other

newly independent states, the name Kol Israel is a clear deglobalizing identity symbol. Radio channel 7 uses the meaning of the number seven in Jewish tradition. Other symbolic names include the Holy Channels, radio stations run by an ultraorthodox movement on behalf of a global Sephardic[6]
sense of belongingness, and Tchelet (Blue), a cable TV channel aired legally
in 2003 by less-orthodox traditionalists.

DEGLOBALIZED DIMENSIONS OF MEDIA REPRESENTATIONS

The media contribute to the articulation and dissemination of collective identity through the construction, production, and transmission of images, narratives, and myths. Three major strategies are employed by the media to represent deglobalized national identities in Israel. Two of them—staging media
events, holidays, and celebrations and mobilizing the media—refer to an Israeli deglobalized identity as a whole. The third strategy has to do with the
articulation of narrower needs, in which the media are levers for representing subidentities.

   The first major strategy is the staging of media events (Dayan and Katz
1992)—the representations of identity rituals. Israeli existential anxiety and
need for legitimacy are powerful triggers for this type of mediated identity
construction, emphasizing popular narratives and myths related to grief,
courage, and victory. Memorial occasions are a key site of media representation of grief, namely through events like remembrance days for Holocaust
victims and for those who have fallen in war and during acts of terrorism.
Combined with wide media coverage, the loud, shrill sound of the sirens an-
nouncing the beginning of these memorial days vividly symbolizes a defining moment of identity strengthening. Permeating the live coverage of acts
of terrorism and victims' funerals, a journalistic style has developed that goes
beyond political commentary into the domain of human and collective values. Such coverage emphasizes solidarity, steadfastness, heroism, and historical, sometimes mythological, precedence. Also, religious memorials fuel
media events, as does the remembrance of the destruction of the first and
second temples, during which prayers at the Wailing Wall are broadcast live
and reported by the printed press.

   Courage and heroism—promulgated via mythological slogans like
"Masada shall not fall again" or "never again"—are widely represented and
reenacted by the media. The first example refers to the myth of Masada, a
fortress in the Judean desert besieged by the Romans during the Jewish rebellion in the first century AD, which was eventually captured when occupants, it is believed, committed collective suicide to prevent falling into enemy hands. "Never again" refers to a symbolic oath taken by Jews in and
outside Israel with reference to the Holocaust.

Victory is another major motif. For many years, Israel's Independence Day was a popular participatory event celebrating the establishment of the state and victory in the 1948 war. In recent years, the celebrations have been increasingly mediated. Films, talk shows, and entertainment programs depict memorial episodes. Official ceremonies are broadcast, including military parades,[7] the awarding of the Israel Prize, and the International Bible Contest. Also Jerusalem Day, marking the unification of the city, has become a media affair, rather than a popular celebration.

In the Arab sector, an evolving particular identity increasingly identifies Israel's Independence Day with the *Nakba* (disaster), marking the defeats suffered by Arabs in 1948 and since.

Thus, the media have been highly instrumental in deglobalizing, nationalizing, and secularizing Israeli life. The Zionist movement reinvented Jewish holidays, emphasizing secular interpretations of ancient biblical times, together with their religious Diasporic meanings. Passover is an example. The reinvented version of the Passover meal in the kibbutz, with its particular narrative that combines Jewish history, new humanity, and the cycle of nature and agriculture, has been read, sung, danced, and performed on radio and, later, television holiday broadcasts. The mobilization of the media on behalf of the government is a second major strategy for the representation of a deglobalized national identity. Notwithstanding efforts to protect the media from governmental influence, journalists and media organizations have maintained close ties with official sources; the effect is that in recent years, the Israeli media have displayed many instances of orthodox loyalty in publicizing and defending governmental and military positions, while ignoring acts of repression.

At the same time, media performance vis-à-vis the government and the public has become an arena of deeper public scrutiny and debate between ideological or patriotic deglobalized loyalties and universal professional media norms and duties. Since the invasion of Lebanon in 1982, a fierce debate has taken place between these positions, namely, whether the media are free to criticize the government during war. Prime Minister Ariel Sharon, then Israeli minister of defense, has always maintained that the media have not been patriotic enough. Nevertheless, important components of the Israeli media willingly rallied behind the government during the initial phase of the war in Lebanon; with the first Gulf War, protests were meek when radio channels were unified under the wing of the Israeli Defense Forces spokesperson, silencing some critical voices. In addition, there is evidence of government-led media mobilization during the two intifadas (1987–1992 and 2000–present), peace negotiations and treaties between 1992 and 2000, and the most recent war in Iraq (Wolfsfeld 2003; 2004; Dor 2004).

The third media strategy is the articulation and satisfaction of subidentities. It was first employed in response to the communication needs of immigrants in the early years. Together with the partisan climate of the time, this need produced governmental radio broadcasts and newspapers in the immigrants' languages.

In the 1990s, when the wave of immigration from the former USSR again demanded extensive communication, this practice reemerged, replacing the government and party officials who had controlled the media in earlier years with professional journalists from among the new immigrants.

Another example is the coverage of *Yaum al-Ardh* (Land Day), which has become an integral component of the Palestinian national narrative within and outside the borders of Israel. Marking the March 30, 1976, killing of six Israeli Arabs by soldiers and police in a series of protests over the confiscation of Arab land, this day is annually observed by Israeli Arabs. It has symbolized their grievances against governmental policies. Land Day has often been marked by general strikes, mass rallies and demonstrations, marches, the chanting of antigovernment slogans, and waving PLO and Syrian flags, Hizbullah banners, and the posters of the late Egyptian president Gamal Abdel Nasser and of former Iraqi president Saddam Hussein. At times, remembrance ceremonies have been accompanied by violent riots and clashes with police. The heavy coverage by local and foreign media and the participation of Jewish solidarity movements have given Land Day the dimensions of a media event with wide public acknowledgment and legitimacy in the Israeli and foreign media.

GLOBAL DIMENSIONS OF MEDIA REPRESENTATIONS

Media globalization has become more significant in Israel since the 1980s, adding some features to the shrinking deglobalized media scene.

Ideology has played a significant role in Israel's media globalization. One of its expressions is the typical nation-building tension between local expression and mobilization around national goals and the opening by the media of "windows to the world." The introduction of television typically illustrates this process. Starting in 1950, a fierce public debate erupted, in which government officials, private groups, and international foundations advocated the introduction of television not only for nation building and education, but for opening windows to the world and improving Israel's international standing. Yet, a group of old-guard politicians and educators, led by "founding father" David Ben Gurion, opposed television, arguing both against the promotion of consumer values, which contradicted nation-building needs, and against cultural, educational, and social downgrading. The debate continued until Ben Gurion was no longer prime minister; in 1966, television was introduced via an educational station under the supervision of the Ministry of Education and funded by the Rothschild Foundation.

Israel Television went on the air in 1968 through a task force in the prime minister's office, with the official objective of bridging the gap between Israel and the Arab world and Palestinian population following the 1967 war. Shortly after its inception, television became part of the IBA. The original ratio of airtime in Arabic and Hebrew was reversed, and Western-produced programming comprised the broadcast backbone. Globalization has intensified in recent years, as demands to increase and diversify sources of televised news and the need to "open the skies" to more varied contents have resulted in the introduction of additional television channels. Along with online media, these channels symbolize the final downfall of ideological obstacles to media globalization in Israel.

The media have also become symbolic outlets for reducing Israel's isolation. The process took off in 1960 with the introduction by Kol Israel of a second radio network, Hagal Hakal (The Light Wave), to transmit international music and talk shows. Sponsored by advertising, the network has been highly popular since its inception. Hagal Hakal and its followers introduced a global component to the extremely deglobalized Israeli collective consciousness. Israel's assiduous participation in the Eurovision song contest became another source of national popular pride, perhaps matched only by the victories of Israeli basketball teams in European leagues.

GLOBALIZATION OF MEDIA ORGANIZATIONS

Globalization has affected many changes in Israeli media, like a vanishing ideology, a changing economy, and technological advancement. The decline of the partisan press and its full privatization under the control of a few families have reached global dimensions, with Israeli correspondents sent abroad, syndication with foreign newspapers, and the publication of Israeli Hebrew newspapers abroad, directed at the large number of emigrants. Radio and television have moved from the educational/nation-building domain to the economic sphere, expressed by their adherence to the "ratings culture." The globalization of Israeli broadcasting has differed little from that of other countries, featuring ratings-oriented structures and content, including locally produced and imported talk shows, light entertainment, game shows, soap operas, *telenovelas*, and advertising.

This situation has affected public broadcasting in particular. Regardless of the protracted introduction of private broadcasting, the IBA was caught unprepared and did not change its traditional monopolistic mentality. The resultant innovative content and style of the new broadcasters severely reduced the IBA's audience. When public broadcasting finally decided to face the new challenges, it became engaged in a hopeless ratings competition, while lacking the resources needed for expensive talent or production budgets. This public display of weakness promptly attracted political pressures, expressed by the appointment of government officials and supporters to IBA-governing bodies and to the radio and television programming staff, as well as by fully mobilizing the broadcasting of sensitive matters, such as the collapse of the Oslo peace process, the realities of occupation, the intifadas, and the wars in Iraq.

IN THE EYES OF THE WORLD

In the eyes of the world, the media have scrutinized Israel's behavior, evaluating its might and right. The legions of foreign correspondents covering Israel reflect global interest in the area. Contrary to some powerful Western criticisms of the global media, especially of the mainstream American media's pro-Israel biases, many Israeli officials and citizens and Diaspora Jews have accused the world media of developing particular expectations of Israel. Against a historical image of Jewish weakness in the Diaspora, some assume that the use of power by a Jewish state has been both unexpected and difficult to accept by the media. Thus, say the critics, both the euphoria of the Western media over Israel's unexpected military victories, particularly in 1967, and the criticism of its excessive use of force against Palestinians might have resulted from such expectations.

Some evidence supports claims that in Middle Eastern reporting, facts are often made to fit familiar paradigms for the sake of a good story and that the media have been involved in interpretation and storytelling rather than fact gathering (Said 1981; Itzhak, Roeh, and Ashley 1986; Shinar and Stoiciu 1992; Dor 2004). Such factors have contributed to a shift in media tones and narratives, particularly since the 1982 invasion of Lebanon, when some Israeli researchers observed a particular emphasis on Israel's role as villain to the Palestinians' victim. Researchers Roeh and Ashley (1986) mention inaccurate casualty counts, partial selectivity with respect to sources, one-sided and excessive terminology, and lack of context. Also, some correspondents report that the coverage of peace actions and demonstrations in Israel has been minimal, in favor of "running off to the front-line" (BBC Freedom Forum 2001).

Also some Israelis have alleged that there are double standards in Western reportage, and some argue that Israel has been singled out. For instance, a CNN viewer, commenting on an interview conducted by CNN's Aharon Brown with Mideast scholar and director of the Mideast Forum think tank Daniel Pipes (Levi 2002; Pipes 2002) about an Israeli bombing in Gaza in July 2002, asks, "What about Dresden, Hiroshima, Berlin, Kabul and Kosovo?" (CNN, July 2002). And, mentioning the skimpy coverage of atrocities in the Sudan, the president of the American Anti-Slavery Group asks in the *Boston Globe*, "Why is Israel, and not Sudan, singled out?" (October 5, 2002).

A comparison of reporting on Israeli violence in the occupied territories and on the U.S. killing of civilians in Afghanistan has criticized the double standard of the politically correct concept of "collateral damage" (Committee for Accuracy 2002).

Israel has been busy explaining itself. Claims of Jewish humanity and respect for human rights have usually failed to convince the global media to trust (let alone accept or praise) Israeli behavior. Existential anxiety and the "never again" motif are other Israeli arguments that have failed to win legitimacy. Contrasting media images of Israel have thus been produced, ranging from aggression to self-defense, from oppressor to victim, and from democratic state to adherent of state-sponsored terrorism. This reflects a basic cleavage, expressing shifting identity images. The argument that, as a member of the family of nations, Israel should not engage in occupation has been countered with the view that Israel acts in its own self-defense; furthermore, there is the sense that "the entire world is against us anyway, so what the hell, we'll do what we deem right."

Before 1967, sympathy for Israel was expressed by the Western media through images of heroism, the conquest of the desert, scientific progress, assistance to the Third World, and Israeli democracy. Since then, global media images of Israel have increasingly emphasized occupation, oppression, and the infringement of human rights. Close ties with the United States have added negative shades to Israel's image in the rest of the world, where it has been identified with neoimperialist forces and as "Little Satan." Whether the erosion of Western media sympathy toward Israel results from alleged lack of fairness toward the Arabs, as argued by Edward Said (1979; 1981) and Noam Chomsky (1999), from the growing protest against the United States and its allies, or from other reasons, the increasing criticism of Israel is shared by the North American and the European media.

Thus, for the 2002 Dishonest Reporting Award, AP, CBC, CNN, MSNBC, NPR, the *New York Times,* Reuters, and the *Washington Post* were given dishonorable mentions (Dishonest Reporting Award 2002), reflecting in many ways a study conducted on the German press's Middle East coverage ("Mideast Reporting"). Furthermore, the analysis of "conflict discourse" in German newspapers discloses negative portrayals of Israel and Israelis, critical terminology, anti-Semitic discourse, and a paternalistic tone. German journalists express cultural superiority, based on the achievements of their democracy, while Israel is presented as irrational and dangerous.

Depictions of Israeli behavior in the West Bank Jenin refugee camp, during the Defense Shield operation in March 2002, illustrate the status of Israel in the world media. Two films produced on the topic[8] have provoked a heated debate since late 2002, focusing on an alleged Israeli massacre, countered by an official UN report that denies it. The Israeli actor and director Muhammad Bakri produced *Jenin, Jenin,* which expresses harsh criticism and depicts negative images of the state, of its army, and of individual troops. The film was distributed outside Israel, and some Israelis saw it in private screenings. After having been scheduled and announced for TV broadcasting in late 2002, the airing of the film inside Israel was prohibited, following a decision by the government-controlled Council for Film and Play Criticism, a civilian version of military censorship. On the other hand, one year after the events in Jenin, Channel 1 aired *Back to Jenin*, directed by the French journalist Pierre Rechov, a documentary entirely loyal to the Israeli official position.

These films are clearly directed to mobilize international public opinion in favor of their positions through manipulating the images of Israel and Israelis, Palestine and Palestinians.

DEMOCRATIZING AND DEDEMOCRATIZING COLLECTIVE IDENTITIES AND THE MEDIA

The major characteristics of Israeli identity and their media reflections clarify some complexities of democratic identity and media. The existential anxiety, quest for legitimacy, and isolation felt by Israel and Israelis have become part of their collective identity, as much as have the coexistence of civil and tribal identities and of a deglobalized consciousness seasoned with global elements. They have been displayed in the Israeli and the international media. Four basic questions emerge from the interaction of these factors on the relations of globalization, collective identity, democracy, and the media: What happens when military might originally developed for self-defense is used for territorial occupation and for the oppression of large populations? Does it reduce existential anxiety and help to win international legitimacy? How do these processes affect the democratic mechanisms developed in Israel vis-à-vis Israeli Jews and Arabs, and Palestinians? Finally, what are the relations between the Israeli collective identity and media democracy and democratization?

A historical lesson recognized by generals, politicians, and intellectuals provides the answer for the first two questions: the more military might has been used for occupation and oppression, the higher the levels of existential anxiety and the lower the levels of international legitimacy. Thus, the goal of the 1982 Israeli invasion of Lebanon, the defense of Israel's northern border against PLO attacks, turned with time into an increasingly futile effort by the occupiers to defend themselves against the raids of local forces, while northern Israel came under increasing threat of enemy incursions and bombardments.

In a similar vein, the occupation and reoccupation of the West Bank and Gaza strip has reduced Israel's security, as well as its international recognition and legitimacy. The aftermath of the war in Iraq and American impotence in controlling violence reconfirm this lesson.

The response to the third question is another result of experience: the discrepancy between particularistic sentiments (such as biblical heritage and security traumas, based on military might) and universal democratic values has produced a "selective democracy" regarding Arab Israelis and a severe anti-democratic climate in the occupied territories. A "nation of masters" emerged, with a triple personality: first, a majority of Israeli Jews enjoy more or less equal democratic rights in a business-as-usual climate; second, in order to suit their needs, the same majority has been manipulating the democratic rights of the Arab Israeli minority; and third, as occupiers, the same majority has been applying a rule of unlimited might over a large Palestinian population, denying human and civil rights.

These democratic and undemocratic dimensions of the Israeli identity are clearly reflected in the response to the fourth question about the relations between Israeli collective identity and media democracy and democratization. The constitution and organization of media structures are crucial for democratic collective identities. Decentralized, open media and participatory channels serve broad interests and universal values, democracy, and democratization. On the other hand, centralized media and restricted channels serve narrower interests, particularistic values, and thus lower levels of democracy. The resulting media performance is important for societal character and functioning.

This has been true for Israel within the parameters of the triple structure of Israeli identity and democracy: internal democracy for Israeli Jews, manipulative democracy for Israeli Arabs, and no democracy for Palestinians. General processes of media democratization, particularly in the Jewish sector, have included a tradition of refraining from publishing government-owned newspapers, protecting broadcasting from direct governmental control, multiplying news sources, enhancing a media public sphere, empowering voiceless groups through pirate and legal channels, and opening windows to the world.

Threats to media democratization have included some well-known constraints on the media, such as the rule of the few and the rule of the ratings, compounded by local expressions of global processes, such as neoliberal policies, market capacity, and the use of political pressures to circumvent lawful regulation. Neoliberal tendencies have been expressed in pressures to abolish public broadcasting, given its low ratings, financial difficulties, and mismanagement. Originating in the political right wing and utilizing the populist argument of freeing the population from license fees, these pressures advocate the privatization and commercialization of the IBA, practically eliminating public broadcasting and replacing its democratic cultural and social commitments with market interests.

The problem of market capacity has been expressed in the public debate over the introduction of a second commercial television channel. This was approved by the government with the formal objective of enhancing the democratization of the media market through increased competition between commercial operators in a market populated hitherto by one public and one commercial channel. Soon after Channel 10 went on the air in 2002, its operators, among others, realized that the market was too limited to allow for advertising and programming on two commercial channels: the older one lost some of its revenue but not its market command, while the ratings and advertising volume on the new channel remained flat.

This situation demonstrates some structural limitations of media democratization. Accusations of "Berlusconization" (i.e., the use of economic and political pressure to act outside lawful regulation) permeate the debate over the third television channel. The main investors in the channel—first, an Israeli real estate magnate who made his fortune in the South American oil business and, later, a U.S. millionaire supporter of Finance Minister Benyamin Netanyahu—were accused of planning to use the channel as a lever to build a media business empire and to amass political power through buying out other channels, à la Silvio Berlusconi in Italy. This reflects another potential danger for Israeli media democracy.

Within the manipulative democracy of the Israeli-Arab sector, broadcasting services in Arabic were until recently in the hands of official channels such as the IBA under the heavy influence of surveillance and intelligence agencies. Arab entrepreneurs, who took advantage of the relatively liberal laws on the freedom of expression inside Israel, have recently added private press organizations to the hitherto partisan printed press.

Also, pirate radio and television have been growing, demonstrating once again that there is no way to suppress expressions of identity, even in imperfect democracies.

The Palestinian media have been less fortunate. Before the establishment of the Palestinian Authority, Israeli occupation authorities did not allow Palestinian broadcasting and exerted harsh censorship on Palestinian newspapers. Nevertheless, they were published in Israeli-annexed Jerusalem because this guaranteed at least some protection by civilian courts, while publishing in the occupied territories put the publishers and journalists under unlimited military control and jurisdiction. Radio and television were introduced when the authority took charge in 1994. Together with the press, they have been operating under heavy official control.[9]

CONCLUSION

This chapter highlights some aspects of the new agenda created in recent decades by changes in societies, values, and communications. The construction of collective identities, particularly in Israel, has served as a basis for the discussion of globalization and democratization processes. An important building block in this framework is the perception that particular collective identities result from deglobalization, namely, antiglobalization resistance. This view has produced stimulating insights on the interaction of various forms of globalization and democratization in general and both of and by the media in particular.

Focusing on Israel does not exclude the use of this analytical framework in other cases. On the contrary, others can benefit from the kaleidoscopic nature of the Israeli reality and from the opportunity to learn through dissecting its anatomy. Still in the making, Israeli identity allows for an examination of its parts, as well as an analysis of its whole. And the fluid, yet immature, Israeli democracy invites comparison, perhaps because it is neither perfect nor universal.

At least five parameters presented here can contribute to further analyses. Three of them emphasize collective identities, and two focus on the media. The first is the awareness of change, presented in the discussion of the transformation of Jewish identity under the impact of Zionism and the establishment of Israel and of the dynamic change in typical features of Israeli identity, such as basic values, existential anxiety, and the need for legitimacy. The second parameter is the awareness of interaction as demonstrated in the interplay of various types of globalization (e.g., traditional Diaspora, modern, postmodern) and deglobalization. Multidimensionality is the third parameter, expressed in the coexistence of global and deglobalized identities, of civil and tribal identities, and of might, right, and fear. The fourth and fifth parameters are applications of the former to the media. The fourth has to do with the roles of the media in globalization and deglobalization as presented in the discussion of globalized and deglobalized dimensions of media representations of identity. The fifth deals with the relations of collective identity, democracy, and media tendencies as expressed in the discussion of democratizing and dedemocratizing collective identities and the media.

NOTES

1. See, for instance, Benedict Anderson's *Imagined Communities: Reflections on the Origin and Spread of Nationalism* (1991); Michael Ignatieff's *Nationalism, Nation-state, and Nation-building* (1993); Benjamin Barber's *Jihad and McWorld* (1995); Pascal Bruckner's *Xenophobic, Universal, and Cosmopolitan Strategies* (1996); and Dov Shinar's "Re-membering and Dis-membering" (1996).

2. Including supranational rabbinical edicts (such as the ban on polygamy, by Rabbi Gershom ben Judah in Germany in about AD 1000); global networks of economic assistance, such as the American Jewish Joint Distribution Committee; and international educational agencies, such as the Alliance Israelite Universelle.

3. For discussions of these conflicts, see S. N. Eisenstadt, *The Transformation of Israeli Society* (London: Weidenfeld & Nicolson); B. Evron, *Jewish State or Israeli Nation?* (Bloomington: Indiana University Press, 1995); D. Horowitz and M. Lissak, *Trouble in Utopia: The Overburdened Polity of Israel* (Albany, NY: SUNY Press, 1989); U. Ram, *The Changing Agenda of Israeli Sociology* (Albany, NY: SUNY Press, 1995). Also Kimmerling's works, mentioned below, are highly illustrative.

4. The Kimmerling/Morris debate (B. Kimmerling, "Benny Morris' Shocking Interview," *Logos Journal* 3, no. 1 [Winter 2004], available at www.logosjournal.com/kimmerling.pdf), and B. Kimmerling, *The Invention and Decline of Israeliness: State, Society, and the Military* (Berkeley: University of California Press, 2001), clarify these dilemmas.

5. Including the now defunct left-wing Voice of Peace and the very much alive right-wing Channel 7, a settlers' station practically legalized.

6. Sephardic Jews are those from Spain, North Africa, Southern Europe, and the Balkans, while Ashkenazi Jews come from Eastern and Central Europe.

7. The military parade in 1968 was the opening broadcast on Israel Television.

8. A third film, *After Jenin*, directed by Jenny Morgan, was produced by a British independent crew and premiered internationally at the 2002 Vancouver International Film Festival. *Ajtiah* (invasion) is a fourth film, directed by Arab-Israeli director Nizar Hassan and funded by Swedish Television in 2003. Both are highly critical of Israel.

9. In fact, the Palestinian daily *Al Kuds* is still published in Jerusalem. Excellent overviews of the Palestinian media are Nabil Khatib's *Media Landscape in Palestinian Autonomous Areas*, 2002, available at spirit.tau.ac.il/socant/peace/psp/downloads/6%20- %20Khatib%20Nabil.pdf, and *The Structure of the Palestinian Media*, lecture given at the Palestinian Media Seminar, February 7–8, 2003, Maale-Hahamishah, Israel, available at spirit.tau.ac.il/socant/peace/psp/downloads/Khatib.rtf (accessed October 1, 2004). Adel Sanara's "Media as a National Class Tool for Oppression," excerpted from *War, Lies & Videotape: How Media Monopoly Stifles Truth*, ed. Lenora Foerstel (New York: International Action Center, 2000), is an illustrative critique of Palestinian printed and electronic media).

REFERENCES

Anderson, Benedict. 1991. *Imagined Communities*. London: Verso.

BBC Freedom Forum. 2001. "Reporting the World Seminar: Are We Getting The Story?" March 21, http://213.232.90.139/clients/rtwhome.nsf/seminarwrapups/ (accessed October 1, 2004).Barber, B. 1995. *Jihad Vs. McWorld*. New York: Times Books.

Bello, W. 2002. *Deglobalization: Ideas for a New World Economy*. Black Point, NS: Fernwood.

Bruckner, P. 1996. "The Edge of Babel." *Partisan Review* 43, no. 2: 242–54.

Chomsky, N. 1999. *Fateful Triangle: The United States, Israel, and the Palestinians*. Cambridge, MA: South End.

Committee for Accuracy in Middle East Reporting in America. 2002. *Geraldo Rivera's Double Standards*. March 13, available at http://www.camera.org. (accessed October 1, 2004).

Dayan, D., and E. Katz. 1992. *Media Events: The Live Broadcasting of History*. Cambridge, MA: Harvard University Press.

Dishonest Reporting Award. 2002. Available at HonestReporting.com, at http://www.honestreporting.com (accessed October 1, 2004).

Dor, D. 2004. *Intifada Hits the Headlines: How the Israeli Press Misreported the Outburst of the Second Palestinian Uprising*. Bloomington: Indiana University Press.

Hall, S. 1997. "The Local and the Global: Globalization and Ethnicity." In *Culture, Globalization, and the World-System*, ed. A. D. King, 19–39. Minneapolis: University of Minnesota Press.

Hobsbawm, E., and T. Ranger. 1983. *The Invention of Tradition*. Cambridge: Cambridge University Press.

Ignatieff, M. 1993. *Blood and Belonging*. Toronto: Penguin.

Levi, J. 2002. "What about Dresden, Hiroshima, Berlin, Kabul and Kosovo?" User comment on article "*The Aftermath of Attack in Gaza*," by Daniel Pipes, July 28, 2002, available at http://www.danielpipes.org/436 (accessed October 1, 2004).

"Mideast Reporting on the Second Intifada in German Print Media, with Particular Attention to the Image of Israel." Report of a project carried out by the Duisburger Institut für Sprach- und Sozialforschung (DISS) on behalf of the American Jewish Committee's Berlin office, n.d., available at www.ajc.org/InTheMedia/Publications Print.asp?did=539 (accessed on October 1, 2004).

Pipes, Daniel, Mideast Forum director, interviewed by Aharon Brown. 2002. *CNN Newsnight with Aharon Brown*. CNN, July 25, available at http://www.danielpipes.org/article/436 (accessed October 1, 2004)

Itzhak, Sharon, I. Roeh, and S. Ashley. 1986. "Criticizing Press Coverage in the Lebanon War: Toward a Paradigm of News as Storytelling." In *Communication Yearbook*, 117–41. Newbury Park, CA: Sage.

Said, E. 1979. *Orientalism*. New York: Vintage.

———. 1981. *Covering Islam*. New York: Pantheon.

Santos, M. A. de Souza, and M. L. Silveira, eds. 2002. *Territorio: Globalização e Fragmentação*, Sao Paulo: HUCITEC & AnnaBlume.

Shinar, D. 1996. "Re-membering and Dis-membering Europe: A Cultural Strategy for Studying the Role of Communication in the Transformation of Collective Identities." In *Globalization, Communication, and Transnational Civil Society*, eds. A. Sreberny-Mohammadi and S. Braman, 89–103. Cresskill, NJ: Hampton Press.

Shinar, D., and G. Stoiciu. 1992. "Media Representations of Socio-Political Conflict: The Romanian Revolution and the Gulf War." *Gazette* 50, nos. 2–3: 243–57.

Wolfsfeld, G. 2003. "The News Media and the Second Intifada." *Politics* 6, no. 4: 113–18.

———. 2004. *Media and the Path to Peace*. Cambridge: Cambridge University Press.

9

The Iraq Conflict and the Media: Embedded with War Rather than with Peace and Democracy

Jan Oberg

ROOTING POLITICS IN A SURREAL MAKE-BELIEVE WORLD OF GOOD AND EVIL

The Iraq conflict, war, and occupation can be interpreted as a tragic illustration of an essential absurdity of our times: democracies fight wars allegedly to promote democracy but end up undermining it both at home and abroad. In the process, they frustrate the citizenry and undermine the very idea and enabling environment of independent media.

War and democracy do not go well together. When democracies go to war, noble motives are usually brought forward, but the conduct of the war itself, which always serves certain interests, unavoidably puts the democratic ethos at risk. Wars force citizens in democracies to accept that a smaller group of people makes decisions with larger consequences than in any other situation. In times of war, media freedom is reduced, either through censorship or self-censorship.

But the war on Iraq was different in several ways. Even before it started, the largest-ever prewar antiwar movement had been initiated. However, most governments in Western democracies chose to ignore it. Indeed, it seems to me that this was the first war in which actual reality was not only influenced or overshadowed by a manipulated, virtual reality but in which the bonds between the two were deliberately cut. Neither the decision makers behind the war nor media-consuming Western citizens in general had a decent understanding of the real Iraq. Iraq was an information black hole. The Iraqi people, society, and culture were made invisible. The monster enemy called Iraq, a designation that served to explain and legitimize the war, became a virtual, imagined—perhaps psychologically desired or necessary—evil enemy. This war's preparation was more Orwellian than most.

It's nothing new that wars go hand in hand with a certain amount of manipulation and distortion of reality, but at least some decision makers used to know quite well what reality was and used manipulation, deception, and partial or complete lies to cover it up. In the case of Iraq, we witnessed something new: the war relied basically on invented reality bites and imaginings, and this virtual reality suspended actual reality. Warring nations fell into their own propaganda traps.

This could not have happened without certain psychological distortions that I believe could be found in both the U.S. and Iraqi leadership. Both lived more in their own worlds—sharing quite a few similarities, such as irrationality, autism (i.e., not really processing information coming from the real world), group think, psychopathological projections, and eschatological assumptions—than in the world with the rest of us.

Iraqi media, as well as mainstream Western media, mistook their leaders for rational players. While that can be expected in authoritarian regimes, free media could be expected to practice investigative journalism and break through to some empirical reality. Regrettably, they remained uncritically inside what could appropriately be termed the military-industrial-media complex, one that is not known for transparency or for inviting in investigative reporters.

The very concept of politics will be defunct if psychologically constructed images of good versus evil are allowed slowly, but surely, to displace analysis, facts, and a grounding of opinions in reality. I believe that the media in what are usually termed democracies will have to decide at some point whether to contribute mainly to pathology and eventual, unavoidable, unspeakable globalized destructiveness or to side with the majority voices of reason, analysis, compassion, and decency.

It is true that there is an ever-growing number of media. Apart from daily newspapers, radio, and television, there has been an upsurge in local radio channels, television networks, and Internet websites. The larger mainstream media assortment available to the average media consumer, however, grows more uniform by the day. Diversity and pluralism give way to politically correct, standardized images of a generalized truth. This truth is constructed by what is covered, what is ignored, and what is deliberately covered up and left untold. Of course, there is high and low quality within the mainstream sector; of course, there are different types of editors, journalists, and reporters. Speaking in fairly general and sometimes impressionistic terms, I do appreciate such differences in what follows.

Having said that much, it would be unfair to seek the causes exclusively in the individuals working in the media and their professional performance. There is a larger system of media styles, corporate practices, and schools of journalism. There are the interests of the owners and the influence of media consultants who tell the media what is likely to work and what is not. There are the market-related interests; media rely on advertisements and commercials; news and articles have become commoditized, and stories must be sold in a tough market place. And there is the politics of it all: some media are politically independent, some are party related, some see themselves as mainstream and politically correct, and others see themselves as alternative and as challenging conventional wisdom. In times of war, in particular, loyalties are tested.

Finally, by way of introduction, two things must be emphasized. First, the thrust of this chapter is not to determine the causes of media performance since I am not a media expert. Rather, it is to describe what mainstream media did before, during, and after the war on Iraq. Second, while media structures can be tight and society's larger structures, in which all media play a part, must be taken into account, the fundamental importance of the individual media person's professionalism, creativity, investigative mind, risk taking, and even civil courage should never be underestimated. I believe it would be beneficial to the world if there were more investigative and peace-oriented media people who saw their job as a calling.

In an admittedly impressionistic manner, this chapter (written in June 2003) focuses on selected elements of the interplay between the Iraqi conflict cycle—conflict, warfare, and postwar occupation (the latter sometimes euphemistically called peace building)—and the media coverage of that cycle.

This chapter contains my subjective judgment about the media based on my two, two-week fact-finding missions to Iraq in May 2002 and January 2003 and, more generally, on my on-the-ground experience with media and war in the Balkans since 1991. This chapter provides some comparisons between "actual" reality as I have perceived it in Iraq and virtual reality as I have monitored it.

Finally, this chapter is based on my own experience as a (voracious) media consumer and peace researcher doing media work and contributing to opinion formation in various public audiences. A good two months before the war on Iraq broke out, I gave some eighty public lectures and media interviews in Iraq, Japan, Germany, Denmark, Norway, Sweden, Turkey, Holland, and Finland. The media I covered ranged from Japanese newspapers with a readership of twelve million and CNN International to my local Lund student radio and town hall meetings.

PREWAR IRAQ IN THE MEDIA

What was the general image of Iraq, of the enemy of the United States and the West in general, until the war broke out? What were the implicit images of ourselves? According to Johan Galtung's classic conflict-analysis triangle, a conflict consists of and should be analyzed in terms of *A*, *B*, and *C* (attitudes, behavior, and contradiction), the elements of a conflict, and of course the parties involved, *P*.

The Attitudes in the Media

Since only human beings can have and demonstrate attitudes, the study of attitudes requires that we go and ask the conflicting parties what they think and feel about themselves and others and listen to how they define what the conflict is about. Western media monitored the attitudes of the Bush regime, other Western governments, and the Western-dominated UN Security Council and gave them plenty of coverage. But, there was virtually no coverage of the attitudes of the Iraqis.

The image Western consumers could not help but get was this: Iraq consisted of basically one mustached dictator garbed in various uniforms and role-playing outfits, including strange hats, shooting guns in the air with one hand or watching military parades and puffing cigars. He and his cronies had done and did only bad things to their own people and were only up to mischief when it came to their neighbors, the Middle East (Israel in particular), Europe, and America. In short, they were evil and dangerous, deserving to be punished.

The concrete accusations circulating in the media were, among others, that the country had invaded Kuwait (one of the few facts) and, thus, was ready again to invade her neighbors; the country had weapons of mass destruction (WMD) and would soon be able to threaten the world with nuclear bombs; it was a dictatorship (another fact) and a one-party system that prevented democracy and freedom not only there but in the region; the Iraqi leaders harbored terrorists; they had "gassed their own people" (Bush); and they did not comply with UN Security Council resolutions.

Little of this was investigated, questioned, or qualified by mainstream media. Of course, no journalists could have gone to Iraq and returned with the proof that Iraq, say, did not have WMD, but investigating the history and talking with relevant Iraqi institutions could have helped any unprejudiced journalist to evaluate the quality of the information obtained from only one party in the conflict.

Quite a lot of the work could also have been done without going to Iraq. For instance, anyone could have browsed the CIA's website to find out roughly how strong Iraq and the United States and United Kingdom were, at least measured by military expenditures. For instance, what the Transnational Foundation for Peace and Future Research (TFF) wrote on March 11, 2003, could have been found out by any investigative reporter:

President George W. Bush believes that Iraq represents a threat to the whole world. Here are the facts: US military expenditures are estimated at around US$ 400 billion, or about half those of the whole world. According to CIA's website, the military expenditures of Iraq are US$ 1.3 billion or roughly 0.3 per cent of those of the US [www.cia.gov/cia/publications/factbook/geos/iz.html#Military]. The military expenditures of the UK are US$ 32 billion, also according to CIA. Taking these simple facts into account, we get the following ratios: Iraq:US = 1:308, Iraq:USA+UK = 1:332.

In addition, the US and UK have about 200,000 troops and very advanced equipment near Iraq and they plan to be able "if necessary" to use nuclear and chemical weapons against Iraq. Iraq has no troops or weapons close to the UK and US and it has no nuclear weapons.

Imagine that the figure 1:332 had been repeated as many times as the accusation that Iraq had WMDs and threatened the world. To put it undiplomatically, a trip to Iraq or a few minutes of surfing the Internet would have been to take steps away from parrot reporting, or repeating the master's voice and leaving untold what it omits, toward professional, proactive, and investigative journalism.

Perhaps the worst injustice done to the Iraqis was to ignore their suffering due to the sanctions imposed on them by the UN Security Council in 1991.

Shock is the only word that can describe my reaction to what I experienced when I visited Iraq for the first time. In spite of being a media consumer and deeply engaged in international affairs, I had been ignorant of the change in the Iraqi society from the late 1980s to the present, caused predominantly by these sanctions. This is not the place to delve into the sanctions issue per se or what caused the suffering of the Iraqi people, but I think that the reports and statistics compiled by various UN organizations (all obtainable at the time from the UN missions in Baghdad) offer clear-cut evidence on two dimensions: the sanctions in and of themselves caused the death of between five hundred thousand and one million Iraqis, and the death rate was particularly high in the first half of the 1990s (www.transnational .org/pressinf/2003/pf173_Sanctions_moral.html).

Most media consumers did not know some of the basic facts: Iraq itself paid for food and medicine by means of its oil revenues, and Kuwait received 25 percent of the oil income as war damage compensation (and then served as a U.S./U.K. base in the latest war on Iraq). Grossly underreported also was the fact that Saddam Hussein's regime provided free education and free health care to everybody and that literacy, health, and other human indicators ranked far above virtually all other Arab states in the late 1980s. The living standard in Iraq, one of the potentially richest countries in the world, had before the war fallen to a level similar to Lesotho's. And almost half of its twenty-four million people were children and youths under the age of sixteen.

It is reasonable to assume that most people could have been better informed about such important facts had there been more investigative reporting. Leading media could have provided us with documentaries about Iraqi and Arab history, the Mesopotamian cradle of our own civilization, the historical role of the West throughout the Arab world, and about Arab religion and ways of thinking.

Another virtually absent perspective was this: what did we Westerners know about Iraq and what did the Iraqis know about the West? It was mind-boggling to me to discover the general knowledge of and fascination with the West in Iraq, compared to the fearful images here of Islam and the Arab world. Many ordinary Iraqis speak English or French; many in the once-existing, but now demolished, middle class received their higher education in Western countries and have developed a taste for its culture. Indeed, as I have argued, there are many similarities between Iraq and the West (see "Similarities between Bush and Hussein and between the U.S. and Iraq" at www.transnational.org/pressinf/2003/pf179_BushHussein_similar.html).

Every night you could watch American action films, dramas, and videos on television in Baghdad. The book bazaars were full of (more or less old) Western textbooks, dictionaries, weeklies, fiction, and novels by Western authors. During my visit in January 2003 in particular, I experienced this peculiar mixture of fascination with everything Western and fear of what that same West was about to do to their country.

Therefore, to put it crudely, people in the West were the relatively ignorant and uninformed party. We displayed conflict illiteracy. If we believe that knowledge and information may, under the best of circumstances, bring human understanding and reason and increase the chances for peaceful conflict resolution, then mainstream media in general did a considerable disservice to us all.

Without intending to, I perhaps made a little contribution to humanizing the image of Iraq. In between meetings and interviews during my fact-finding missions, I like to take pictures of people and places. I do it partly as a hobby, partly because it makes for a nice memory, and sometimes to assist my memory upon return. Given the discrepancies between what I felt was the generalized mainstream media image of Iraq and my own observations on the spot, I decided to share some of these photos by posting them on TFF's website under the title "Iraqi Faces and Surfaces 2002–2003" (www.transnational.org/photoseries/iraq/photo_iraq_index .html). The series shows street life, bazaars, lots of portraits, life in cafes on a Friday, mosques, people in shops, as well as some people in power that we had interviewed in Baghdad, Basra, and Babylon.

Much to my surprise, this series created a larger response on the Internet than anything we wrote about Iraq. Thus, I learned that certain pictures can contribute to preparing people for war, while others can help us see the human dimension and recognize that "they are like us" or "these children are innocent." That makes war more difficult to start.

The Behavior of the Conflicting Parties in the Media

The parties (*P*) and behavior (*B*) that the most influential media covered were predominantly those of the Bush regime, the weapons inspectors in Iraq, the Iraqi regime's statements (written off as slightly mad and, thus, neither commented on or analyzed) and, finally, the deliberations in the UN Security Council. The activities covered were mainly bellicose speeches, ultimatums, and the military buildup. All of this is something you can take pictures and shoot films of. Filming attitudes (*A*) or the root causes of the conflict—the contradiction (C) and the stuff it is made of—is much more problematic as it requires much more prior knowledge and creativity.

Another way of putting this is that violent behavior attracted much more media attention than political, negotiated, or peaceful initiatives. Perhaps that is not so strange; after all, war was "the only plan in town." No government delegations were sent to Baghdad (the pope's three cardinals were the only ones), and there were no known high-level contacts, meetings, or negotiations between the U.S. and Iraqi governments. Whoever produced alternative conflict-resolution or mediation plans belonged to the nongovernmental organization (NGO) world.

The actors mentioned above had in common the use of verbal, political, or (the threat of) military violence. Their behavior and political body language vibrated with threats, accusations of lies and cheating, name calling such as "evil," demonization (by both Bush and Hussein), demonstrations of contempt, issuing of ultimatums, and the making of "peace" proposals that were known in advance to be unacceptable to the other side.

Most of the media's behavioral focus was on formal motives rather than interests, on goals rather than means, seldom making the link between the two. If U.S. interests had been in focus, one would have expected the media to look into issues such as these:

- With rapidly increasing U.S. dependence on imported oil estimated to be 75 percent in fifteen years, what is their interest in Iraq's oil?
- Does the United States have an interest in keeping the European Union and Russia weak when it comes to intervention capacity?
- What are the economic benefits for the United States in general and for the military-industrial complex in particular of having a war rather than not having it?
- How could an intervention in Iraq be interpreted in the light of various scenarios for the future world system that may exist in the minds of strategists in Washington?

- How is a U.S./U.K. occupation intended to influence countries like China, or Asia in general?

The official Western motives were of course good: to rid the world of a dictator, to free the Iraqi people, to spread democracy, to protect America, to combat terrorism, to stop the proliferation of WMD, and so forth. In contrast to its interests, Western motives related well to the individualization of complex conflicts (i.e., focusing on a person or regime rather than on issues). Individual traits transferred to complex issues offer an opportunity for the viewer and listener to identify, to relate to something that is well-known from everyday life.

Thus, the Balkans were, to a large extent, about Slobodan Milošević, Somalia about Siyad Barre and later Mohamed Farah Aideed, and 9/11 and Afghanistan about Osama bin Laden and Mullah Omar. From the viewpoint of the West in general, Iraq was Hussein, and it was about Hussein. Quite forceful, deep-seated psychic energies can be actualized and projected further to collective hatred against certain individuals. And, indeed, it is hard to convince people of the necessity of a war without a favorite hate object that appears threatening.

In politics, motives and goals are manifest, while interests are rather untold or latent, which means neither that decision makers are unaware of such interests nor that interests are not the primary objectives of policies. Rather, interests are just less visible and virtually never stated openly.

The Conflict and Its Root Causes in the Media

With a few exceptions, the mainstream media definition of what the Iraq conflict was all about turned out to be isomorphic with what Western leaders told the world it was about. But hardly any war has been so characterized by a lack of knowledge and experience with the country, on the one hand, and hard sell, propaganda, and inventions and lies, on the other.

The West at least had embassies, diplomats, contact groups, mediators, and the like in, say, the Balkans. If they wanted to, they could find out a few things about the "other side." There were innumerable meetings between Western diplomats and Milošević. Much the same goes for the Israel–Palestine conflict, Northern Ireland, and North Korea.

Not so in the case of Iraq. Comparatively, as has been pointed out above, Iraq was a black hole. To put it crudely, it was difficult to challenge the master's voice on what this conflict was about. It would have required investigative reporting in Iraq and attentive listening to Iraqi high-level people and citizens. From my own experience, the conflict was, to them, about something rather different than what was stated by Western politicians and media. The fear of being seen as "pro-Saddam" made it impossible for most media to point out that Iraq may have a point here and there, too, and that it takes two to have a conflict—a restraint bordering on self-censorship.

Incidentally, my organization, the TFF, was one of the very few research institutes that invested time (one month in total) in Iraq on fact finding during the ten months leading up to the outbreak of the war. Very few of the experts and commentators brought into Western radio and television studios during this conflict had any up-to-date knowledge based on personal experience about what was going on in Iraq and how people there thought and felt. Without that, however, it is professionally impossible to understand the conflict as a conflict.

So, in terms of knowledge and personal experiences from and with "the enemy," the Iraq conflict, war, and occupation were absolutely unique. The information black hole provided the vacuum into which imagined problems, accusations, stereotypes, exclusions, propaganda, misinformation, and worse could be poured. As stated in the introductory remarks, virtual reality could substitute for actual reality. There was more constructed reality and less empirical reality than in almost all other wars of recent years.

THE WAR ON IRAQ IN THE MEDIA

There are several ways in which media coverage of the war itself was unique. First, many journalists were embedded with the invading forces and operated under the direct rules set up by the invading forces. Thus, the media were closer to the events than ever before. I believe this embedding had both positive and negative effects. Being so close—for instance, filming nervous, young American soldiers shooting right into civilian cars at a checkpoint, filmed from a soldier's shoulder—does convey something important and may add to the truth about war, including its dilemmas and cruelty. (And in this case, U.S. authorities could not deny the tragedy or accuse Iraqi civilians of the shooting.)

It also presents evidence of journalists and film crews who bravely took huge personal risks in an attempt to do what they considered to be a better job. Al-Jazeera, for instance, had its offices bombed and staff killed by the United States. One can hardly underestimate the extent to which the media war and the military war have become intertwined.

But, it also raises the professional question as to whether reporters should accept all the limitations set up for them before they can be embedded with the forces. Obviously, it cannot take place according to any other criteria and rules but those of the military; impartiality is definitely lost, and being embedded with the winner means taking the winner's perspective.

A second new feature in the coverage of this war was that one could follow the war on a series of non-Western Internet and satellite news services—foremost among them being Al-Arabyia and Al-Jazeera. This time some Western media also invited non-Western colleagues into their studios, had their editors interviewed, reviewed their editorials, and used footage from their stations. Also remarkable was how German and especially French media deviated from those replaying the master's voice. In general terms, one can say that mainstream Western media covered the war and the American viewpoint in particular, while Arab and other non-Western media covered the suffering and the military failures.

Third, quite a few Western media should also be commended for featuring facts and discussions about the role(s) of media in war: the "media in the media," the conditions of war reporting, and the roles of independent channels and news sources. It is now fairly easy to witness the media deliberately contrasting views and news about which the media consumer is left to form an opinion. This type of metadiscussion and self-reflection should be welcomed. It may signify that lessons have been learned over time and that the media have recognized that today's media consumers require quality, are conscious of complexity, and have a variety of competing media, not least the Internet and satellite TV, to choose from.

Arguably, these points represent important improvements in covering war compared with the first Gulf War and the bombings of Bosnia and Yugoslavia. One reason may be that, long before this war started, public opinion around the world was skeptical or outright negative. Media that tried to present this war as unproblematic, or simply as "right," would have been counted out by concerned audiences who had become more politically aware from one war to the next. We are all able to—and many do—find out more about the world out there these days, although the coverage of foreign and global affairs has shrunk in many media. Moreover, we have witnessed how propaganda and lies have been shot down almost instantaneously.

In addition, the prewar propaganda machines of the United States, the United Kingdom, and their few political allies did not do a convincing job. Many saw George W. Bush and Tony Blair as pathetic, intent on not listening, and repeating themselves, mantralike, to an embarrassing extent. Somehow, the "story" was too thin in proportion to what was at stake. People who would normally have supported the United States with enthusiasm and admiration dropped out early. For instance, not even major allied leaders or loyal media editors managed to muster anything but a tired comment on Colin Powell's seventy-minute-long exposé to the UN Security Council about Iraq's WMD.

And then, the war itself went wrong on several accounts. Journalists who believed seriously in all statements made by uniformed (military as well as civilian) "coalition" spokespeople and talking heads to the effect that this war was going according to plan would have been considered amateurs by their peers. There were too many cases of friendly fire and stray bombs causing civilian dead and wounded to be explained away.

It was significant that Michael Wolff, a journalist from *New York Magazine*, while attending the U.S. Central Command (CentCom) press briefing on March 28, said, in effect, "At the end of the day, what you tell us at these briefings doesn't help us to know anything. What is the purpose, really?" After which, the world press gathered in the room applauded spontaneously. NATO spokesman, Jamie Shea, somehow had had an easier task when the bombs were raining down over Yugoslavia.

Something had indeed happened. The militarily strongest, the invader who professed to do good and eradicate evil, did not stand a chance of winning the media war in the eyes of the majority in the West. Neither did they win the hearts and minds of the Iraqis, who conspicuously did not line the roads, as predicted, to greet their "liberators" with flowers. This time the imbalance between virtual and actual reality had become too big to be credible.

What was not new was the male-dominated focus on the *war* rather than the *conflict*, as has been argued above. Coverage of the war focused on the weapons, the battles, the drama, and (occasionally) on the human suffering. While the media had cared little about Iraq as a society and culture before the war, Iraq hit the front pages the moment the United States started the war; CNN International presented virtually twenty-four hours of coverage. It was as if nothing else was happening in the world, which, in passing, represented a gross injustice to problems and (larger) suffering happening simultaneously elsewhere.

It is fairly easy to point out cases where the media made mistakes and took psychowarfare propaganda for fact, where deliberate frauds were not investigated, and so forth. This is not the thrust of this chapter, but a few examples of everyday reporting during the days of war are provided. Below, I extract materials from a series of about fifty articles that I wrote between the outbreak of the war on March 20 and the end of May 2003 entitled *Think Freely about Iraq. Comments about Operation Iraqi Freedom and the Media* (see www.transnational.org/forum/meet/2003/AT_WAR_IRAQ.html):

- Around March 26–27, the media jumped on a British hoax that there was an uprising in Basra against the regime and for the invaders. However, to everyone's surprise, it took three weeks for the British to secure Basra, long before which the story about the uprising had died down.
- On March 27, 2003, Tony Blair argued at a press conference at Camp David that 450,000 children had died in the last five years from preventable diseases and malnutrition due to the character of Saddam Hussein's brutal regime. Donald Rumsfeld had said something similar the

day before. Unfortunately, not one UN report supports this argument. Since extremely few mainstream journalists have bothered during the last twelve years to investigate the complexities of the sanctions and the Oil for Food program, no media person asked what Mr. Blair meant or on what he based his statement.

- Iraqi infrastructure was deliberately targeted during the first Gulf War on Iraq. Water and electricity systems were destroyed and people suffered from day one of the war. But few media investigated why and what purposes it served. I was in Basra in January 2003, and I met no one who was thirsty and, although there were occasional problems with the electricity, a few minutes here and there, there were no permanent power cuts and there was no need for the International Committee of the Red Cross to come in and restore water to Basra. The water and electricity supply is usually destroyed to starve out the people, to wear down their resistance psychologically and physically. Then, the gallant invaders can move in as humanitarian agents. In other words, a thirsty population "begs" the merciless aggressors, who use and humiliate civilians in their warfare, to bring the most essential thing in life, water! Few mainstream media gave it the angle it ought to have had: that it was a gross violation of the Geneva Convention. But almost all gave wide coverage to U.S. officials who were upset that American prisoners of war had been shown on Al-Jazeera!

- Wild exaggerations were made (and thus no documentation provided) concerning the warm welcome of American troops in "one city after another." In the *Financial Times* of April 3 (p. 2), the forces have already entered: "Warm welcome for US soldiers as coalition forces enter Najaf." Citizens clapped and cheered as a company of U.S. soldiers walked through the center of town, we are told. But the article, written by Charles Clover in Najaf, presents only two witnesses to support this assertion: Lt. Col. Marcus De Oliviera, who says that the citizens of Najaf "evidently no longer fear the bad guys who were controlling this place" and one Hadi, a middle-aged man on a street corner. Clover does not bother to ask who he is. Hadi is the witness to the asserted truth about the popularity of the invaders—the only one, unfortunately.

- On April 2, 2003, the *International Herald Tribune* carried a report by Jim Dwyer, who was embedded with the 101st Airborne Division near Al Hillah. He reports, "It was possible Monday [March 31] to drive 50 kilometres north from An Najaf toward Baghdad and not see a single, living person other than U.S. soldiers." The road was littered with the hulls of pickup trucks and taxicabs fired on by the U.S. forces. Then he writes, "As for the occupants of several of those cars—targeted as paramilitary forces loyal to Saddam Hussein—their bodies were sprawled on the ground nearby."

This is embedded war reporting at its worst. One wonders where the civilian farmers and shepherds were, the people who used to live there. Dwyer writes that the Iraqi countryside was "all but devoid of ordinary life on this beautiful spring day." Investigative reporting would ask, where have they disappeared to, when, and why? Perhaps Dwyer did not know that Iraqi families live on food rations delivered to stores all over Iraq. Families can get their monthly ration only at the local shop in the municipality or town where they live and have no right to a ration anywhere else. They must have been extremely frightened to run away.

Embedded with the military, he can't just jump out and ask the first civilian he sees. But my question is, does he bother to understand the fate of the civilians or must his perspective be that of the military? Please also take note of the fact that Dwyer takes for granted—in a sentence—that trucks and taxicabs must have been paramilitaries if they were targeted by the U.S. forces.

- One of the main media hoaxes was the fall of the Saddam statue in Fadus Square. When it happened, I happened to question its authenticity. Here follows my comment from April 10, in response to the question, where were the Iraqi masses when the Saddam statue fell in Fadus Square?

> Today's leading media story is the one about the Saddam pedestal that fell to the ground in Fadus Square. The IHT carries a big picture on the front page; John Vinocur writes on p. 3 under the headline "Iraqis' celebrations help justify the war." TV beams joy from the Arab street. George W. Bush says he is pleased and Donald Rumsfeld compares it with the fall of the Berlin Wall. Dick Cheney says it all proves that the military plan has been a "brilliant success."
>
> No doubts on their side. John Vinocur took self-congratulatory platitudes to new heights. The Arab street was cheering and throwing shoes at the carcass there in Baghdad. An American flag covered Saddam's head, hoisted by a clambering U.S. Marine. An Arab then brought an Iraqi flag to replace it, he reports—sitting in Paris. An "irrefutable justification [of the war is] coming to hand. A war continuously challenged as illegitimate and unnecessary in the international community and the United States has undergone a profound change of course," he tells us excitedly. "This almost instant de facto legitimization appeared enormously powerful. BBC reporters described both 'a straitjacket coming off and a taste of freedom' seizing people in many parts of Baghdad."
>
> The *Financial Times* gave it the headline, "World watches as *Saddam* falls into the Baghdad dust" [my italics as it was a statue and not Saddam himself]. It had an amazing close-up on its front page of the U.S. Marine who "drape[d] the stars and stripes on a Saddam statue before its destruction." For sure, it's a great photo. Paul Eedle in Baghdad writes that "dozens of cheering Iraqis, delirious with sudden, unaccustomed freedom, surged forward to dance upon the wreckage of their ruler."

But, sorry to say, I think this story smells like a staged media event. Here is why:

1. Most of the pictures are close up. If there was a huge crowd for the world to see, some television station or photographer would have taken pictures of those masses.
2. I have been to Fadus Square and know that there are good photo opportunities to be had of masses of Iraqis.
3. The reports talk about "dozens" of people. Baghdad has 5 million inhabitants!
4. I cannot find interviews with the Iraqis who hammered on that statue.
5. It's a bit strange that it is an American soldier who climbs onto the statue with an American flag if the scene is meant to be an Iraqi celebration of Iraqi liberation.
6. I do not see pictures of the Iraqi flag that some reports mention.
7. With hundreds of other statues all over Iraq and thousands of pictures, murals, etc., we have seen relatively few pictures of Iraqis destroying those images.
8. Fadus Square is just outside the Palestine Hotel where about 150 international journalists were working.

BBC produced a photo series on its website about the event. Picture number 2 shows you an empty street near the Saddam statue which stands in the middle of the round square. See for yourself here: http://news.bbc .co.uk/2/hi/in_depth/photo_gallery/2933629.stm. It is strange that the fall of one single statue in Baghdad has been acclaimed in so many bombastic words at a time when the invasion forces have not provided any evidence that they have found, arrested or killed a single Iraqi leader.

I, for one, am neither convinced that the event was genuine nor that it has any significant resemblance to the fall of the Berlin Wall or the fall of Hitler or Stalin, as Rumsfeld would have us believe: "Saddam is taking his place alongside Hitler, Stalin, and Ceausescu in the pantheon of failed, brutal dictators" . . . .

Is this a surrogate event? A media event to "de facto legitimize" the war? And, if it is a genuine event, isn't its significance blown out of proportion?

A few days later, the *Information Clearing House* and other sources provided the relevant pictures and analyses that confirmed my suspicions. See, for instance, www.informationclearinghouse.info/article2838.htm. What you see in these pictures is that Fadus Square was closed off by military vehicles, allowing only a few to get near the statue. It is hinted that some of the people were brought in and could have been from Ahmed Chalabi's exiled, CIA-supported, armed fighters.

- The same media that profess to be very concerned about human rights and endorse war as a means to provide human rights have cared surprisingly little when the occupier has violated the human rights of Iraqis.

From a human rights perspective, there was, indeed, room for question when Iraqi leaders, who had not been proven guilty of any crimes, were depicted as "Wanted" on a (tasteless) deck of cards, hunted down, taken away, and heard from no more. I happen to have met with three of them, Tariq Aziz, Amer Al-Saadi, and Hoda Amash. On April 13, when Gen. Amer Al-Saadi turned himself over to the American forces after repeating that Iraq had no WMD and that he, as Saddam's leading scientific adviser, had told the truth to Hans Blix the whole time, I wrote,

> It is now terribly important that the media and others keep an eye on what happens to General Amer, where he is taken to and how he is treated. It is very important that General Amer is protected by keen media attention. It is very important that the media and others keep on asking US and British officials questions about their search for Iraqi WMD. General Amer's freedom of speech, and that is what must be preserved, could be very awkward for the invaders. This top official's statement after "liberation" that Iraq does not have WMD may not be so popular.

I suspect that this story is yet another example of how difficult it is for media people to give various stories the right relative weight in their coverage—and of how short the public's attention span is.

- With a view to humanitarianism and human rights, one wishes that Iraqi lives had been evaluated using the same standards as American lives. One has only to think of the coverage given to the "rescue" operation of U.S. Private Lynch, a story that later turned out to be an extraordinary piece of stage-set propaganda. It went unnoticed in the entire press that Dr. Hoda Amash was treated with blatant racism virtually everywhere, being called "Mrs. Anthrax" without the slightest evidence that she ever participated in producing anthrax or other biological weapons. I was stunned by CNN presenting her first as "Dr. Germ" and later as "Mrs. Anthrax." The only footage, repeated over and over, showed her in a green uniform walking upon an American and Israeli flag and greeting, fist raised, a huge crowd of Baath Party youth. It was also stated that Hussein had her father killed. He was an old friend of Hussein's and, at the end of his career, served as the Iraqi ambassador to Finland. I haven't seen that killing confirmed anywhere. The other part of the story was that she got her Ph.D. in the United States and that she could be useful as a guide to the WMD we have been told that Iraq's old leadership has been hiding.

The same story was featured in almost all the international media and on their websites. Given this media coverage, I ask myself whether anyone can get a human impression, or image, of this woman? Imagine what kind of feeling the name "Mrs. Anthrax" raises among Americans. Her association with biological weapons is pure conjecture, allegation, or guilt by association. Since then, there has been no media interest in the fate of these individuals. One wonders whether, if they are still alive, they will ever get a fair trial.

These are merely examples of more or less subtle media manipulations. It deserves mention that representatives of CentCom always had three lines of defense when civilians were killed: (1) we did not do it, (2) pockets of groups loyal to Hussein or soldiers dressed in civilian clothing could have done it, and (3) we will investigate it.

None of these investigations have appeared on CentCom's website, and virtually no journalists have kept an eye out for stories about fulfillment of these promises. Indeed, one is reminded of what seventeenth-century French aristocrat Marie de Medici once said: "It is enough that a lie is believed for three days—it has then served its purpose."

POSTWAR IRAQ IN THE MEDIA

Among several postwar media foci, the following three are particularly important. First, a sharp eye focused on the peace-building process is needed, in this case, on the occupying U.S. administration and U.S./U.K. forces and their activities and interaction with the Iraqis. Second, we need to investigate what were we told in the period leading up to the war and what actually happened and is happening? Third, we need to deepen our understanding of Iraqi society, to catch up on the dimensions missed in the prewar coverage and learn some lessons.

My argument is simple: if the media's prewar performance was poor, and if during the war, it was a mixture of good and bad, the immediate postwar media coverage of the Iraq conflict was poor.

Even the media that had questioned the justifications for and conduct of the war stopped asking critical questions about this colonial-style occupation. And, sadly, so did the public. With critical public opinion gone, the media went back to business as usual.

When the invasion fighting died down and CentCom stopped giving daily briefings, the media packed up and went home. We have seen the same pattern in Bosnia, Serbia/Kosovo, Macedonia, and Afghanistan.

The media interest in Iraq rapidly faded. SARS, North Korea, and each country's local affairs took over. Over the summer of 2003, we were back to where we were months ago: with very few journalists in Iraq and almost no media interest in the sanctions or the points of view of the Iraqi citizens. Without the drama of bombing, troop movements, killing, friendly fire, physical injuries, and uniformed people giving press, or PR, briefings, the interest in the area vanished. Only larger globalized media such as CNN International and the BBC stand out here as noteworthy exceptions.

Why do the most influential media systematically embed themselves in the war system rather than in peace, democracy, and freedom? Why is 90 percent of their coverage and attention directed at the violence and the war and not at the underlying conflicts? Why do they not practice conflict and peace reporting and, whenever there is a conflict, only practice violence reporting? What are the structural, psychological, political, and economic reasons behind this type of reporting?

Perhaps, at least, we should stop deceiving ourselves with the words we use. Perhaps we must begin to question the concept of a free media, if the main freedoms the most influential media choose to practice are the freedom to not investigate and not to question the war system of their own society, the freedom to be as biased as they please, and the freedom not to investigate what is not officially stated.

If the West professes to spread democracy the way the United States and Britain did and do in Iraq, perhaps it is time to highlight the role of all acts of violence—not just those of the officially designated enemies, but also our own. In contrast to dictatorships, democracies ought to find violence problematic.

TOWARD A BALANCED MEDIA COVERAGE OF WAR AND PEACE

If one respects the view that the finest task a media person can perform is to come as close as humanly possible to a balanced, unbiased, and complex truth, it follows that he or she should neither seek to promote violence nor peace as such, since that would be perceived as unprofessional among peers and biased among media consumers.

Despite my personal preference for peace journalism, this chapter does not advocate for that approach per se. It does insist that we need a better balance than the one observed during this war on Iraq—I say this in my capacity as a peace and conflict researcher, a media consumer, someone who goes to places war reporters travel to and who expresses himself through media. To put it crudely, whatever the complex reasons, the fact is that the majority of the mainstream media promoted war—directly as well as indirectly—to a much higher degree than they promoted its alternatives, and that should be of concern to the media producers as well as consumers.

There seem to be three logical ways to do things better in the future: to increase peace-oriented media work, to reduce war-oriented media work, or to do both.

Throughout this chapter, I have made an implicit assumption. In order to improve the balance in favor of peace journalism and reach a higher level of truth, I recommend that the media take the following steps.

1. Deal with the conflict, its A, B, C, and P, and focus less on violence.
2. Cover not only motives but also investigate deeper-lying interests.
3. Focus less on individuals and demonizing mechanisms; focus more on history and socioeconomic dimensions.
4. Define the parties in a broad manner and give all sides a fair hearing; focus not only on leaders' but also on citizens' perceptions.
5. Be curious about the many ways in which the same issue can be seen because of different positions in the world, different cultures and norms, and different ranks within the same system.
6. Listen to what is not stated, not argued, and not done, but could be; focus on potential and latent aspects of the larger truth(s), never repeating the obvious rhetoric unquestioningly.
7. Focus more on human beings than on weapons and the conduct of war; do not accept that all norms of civilization can be ignored in times of war (i.e., watch out for dehumanization and civilizational decay in the heat of violence).
8. Remain critical not only of the official enemy but also of your own side; remain independent and avoid becoming a loudspeaker for the master's voice.
9. Finally, remain passionately distant from the violence; never succumb to or be carried away by a fascination with politicomilitary power, technological power, and their violence; focus on intellectual and moral power.

Peace reporting requires imagination and creativity. Imagine for a moment that the media had covered the postwar situation in roughly the same manner as they covered the war. In that case, journalists would have been embedded with Jay Garner's U.S. Office of Reconstruction and Humanitarian Assistance and, later, with the Coalition Provisional Authority (CPA)—one journalist would be placed within each department as they were with each military unit. There would be a camera showing how the CPA people work, contact local people, and negotiate and solve conflicts with them. We would get a sense of how they treat the Iraqis.

They would have to answer questions from trained journalists, such as, Why do you build peace this way? Why have you chosen these particular types of Americans to run Iraq? What is your understanding of democracy? How do you feel it differs or overlaps with that of the Arab Iraqis and the Kurds? How is it different from what you thought when you arrived?

Journalists would know as much about peace and development as they do about the weapons of war. They would know peace concepts as well as they know weapons designations.

There would be in-depth coverage of the postwar traumas, the sick and the wounded, the cases of postwar suicide. We would learn about the long-term human consequences after sanctions, war, and destruction.

Professional reporting would result in interviews with all kinds of representatives of this fascinatingly complex country; we would finally find out about the situation of women, youth, and children, of ordinary people with whom the media can talk freely now that Hussein is gone. The main focus would be on civil society in a broad sense. Thus, we would acquire more knowledge about the many and different ways in which Iraqi men and women helped each other, supported and sheltered each other, and about how much fundamental goodness there is in and among people. We would see the courageous people, the peace heroes, or peace lords. We would see how people today are helping each other recover, over and above the so-called help of the Americans. Documentaries about the history, culture, and religion of Iraq would finally appear as public education on our screens.

The media would go to schools and hospitals (aspects that have disappeared completely now). Imagine a journalist "adopting" one school somewhere in Iraq, talking with teachers, pupils, and parents, then talking with the American administration about that particular school's recovery—not the physical reconstruction in itself but the healing of that school community as a whole. We would get an impression of the lovely children and their families, their potential, their hopes and fears, and how they get by.

Media would promote dialog and reconciliation, too. We would see intensive discussion, panels, and dialogs among American and other Western scholars, on the one hand, and Iraqi and other Arab scholars, on the other. If these didn't take place by themselves, they would be brought about by the larger media. Intentionally or not, the media contribute to war by conveying propaganda, psychowarfare, and disinformation; why should they not also contribute to peace? Nothing would prevent the BBC, CNN International, and all the rest from bringing people together to help bring about mutual understanding and reconciliation.

A balanced mass media working together with upgraded peace reporting would radiate genuine respect, empathy, and sympathy for living people and not use them as an illustration or highlight them when they are dead. This improved media would convey images and a vision of peace and the potential strength of people and of civil society. It would convey hope and, thus, a willingness worldwide to get involved. And isn't this exactly what democracy is all about?

Whether intended or not, war reporting makes violence legitimate, somehow natural. Too much war reporting and too little, or no, peace reporting is unprofessional. Our world needs to be better balanced. Why not begin by making the necessary changes in the media world?

10

Global Media Governance as a Potential Site of Civil Society Intervention

Seán Ó Siochrú

ISSUES AND DYNAMICS IN MEDIA AND COMMUNICATION

A point of departure for this chapter is the increasingly globalized nature and dynamics of communication media. Evidence for this abounds, for instance in the reach of global media corporations and the proportion of national media they control, the marketing and dissemination of homogenous or routinely modified content worldwide, the widespread diffusion of a single market-based regulatory model, and the emergence of a largely uniform global regulatory regime under the World Trade Organization (WTO).

Similarly a campaign to reform communication cannot succeed if its focus remains solely at a national level. It must from the outset consider global issues and build a global base. This is not to argue that in all cases intervention should be exclusively at the transnational level. The national and local remain key arenas of struggle, in their own terms for what can be achieved there but also because governments are the gatekeepers of influence in many international institutions, and contexts and activities must thus first persuade governments on their own turf. Conversely, a transnational campaign lacking local roots and direction cannot succeed in the long term. These roots can be fed through a campaign network, direct membership, alliances, or by other means, but they must be present and ultimately must drive the transnational activity.

What are the main fears relating to media and communication, as expressed by voices of civil society, that reverberate globally?

Below, these are grouped into four overlapping domains,[1] compiled from a number of sources, including advocacy campaigns and literature critical of trends in media and communication.[2] Some concerns are not new—they were already raised in the debates in UNESCO and elsewhere in the 1980s—but many are also peculiar to the dominant economic paradigm and to the emergence and convergence of digital technologies.

This is merely a first aggregation and is not the result of a rigorous process. It is intended to illustrate some sense of their interdependency and suggest at least one schema by which they can be aggregated in a manner that puts the risks involved, and implicitly the opportunities, to the fore. Chapter 14 argues that one of the main challenges facing a transnational media campaign is precisely to undertake a rigorous and regionally differentiated process in the context of the need to frame the issues for advocacy purposes.

Following a description of these domains, I extract some common dynamics and characteristics as evidence of their interdependence and, hence, of the need to address them at the transnational level. A further section takes a highly speculative look at a possible future scenario, one in which the negative aspects of the identified trends are taken to their, albeit unlikely, extreme. I conclude with a review of the main actors likely to be involved in preventing such a scenario from coming into being.

Four Domains of Concern

The Growing Failure of Media in the Public Sphere

Within the liberal-democratic tradition claimed by most Western societies, the public sphere is the arena in which general interaction and deliberation about society and polity are practised, where civil society discovers and exercises its political and social self-understanding. It encompasses the press, television, public demonstrations, discussion, e-mail lists, and a myriad other forms. The essence of the public sphere is that it is where people openly and transparently debate on the basis that they can be convinced by reason, by the rationality of argumentation, and not by rhetorical appeals or through the suppression or distortion of information. A distorted public sphere, controlled by narrow interests, can obfuscate and conceal injustice, smother voices of dissent, and place insurmountable barriers in the path of would-be campaigns. The result is heightened social tensions and inequities, with all that they entail.

The idea of the public sphere is thus closely linked to that of civil society itself. Those suffering under dictatorships and repression can barely glimpse such an ideal, focusing instead on the task of constituting an autonomous civil society free from state control. In liberal democracies it is a partially realized ideal, the basic parameters and role achieving varying degrees of realization and recognition. The notion must thus find distinct cultural moorings and articulation to suit the broader structures of representation and participation.

In recent decades concern has switched somewhat from state censorship and control toward commercial and corporate control and the transformation of media into a commodity. The main underlying dynamic is the imposition of a neoliberal model on media through, for instance,

- Media liberalization, one effect of which is to accelerate concentration of ownership nationally and of cross-ownership of media as in the United States, United Kingdom, and many other European countries
- The "marketization" of the media sector, in which media corporations subsume all other goals under that of profit maximization, in which advertising revenues play a growing role and in which the subsidy of public service media comes to be regarded as a distortion of market forces
- The emergence of global media conglomerates wielding enormous financial, marketing, and even political power and controlling ever larger slices of media markets
- The absence or suppression of effective international regulation of the activities of these conglomerates and of external cross-border media such as satellite television that can dictate to national regulators

These all conform to the standard neoliberal model, which is blind to the characteristics of a public sphere and holds that the market is capable of delivering on society's media needs. Even as a civil society begins to coalesce in countries emerging from feudal or modern dictatorships, and the notion of the public sphere appears on the horizon, the newfound freedom is subtly spirited away under the noses of an unknowing populace. Commercially driven globalized media are undermining existing models of public service media, are largely replacing previously state-controlled media as a low-cost, politically unthreatening option, and, in the global South, are sweeping away or transforming public-minded media traditions or filling a media vacuum and quickly becoming the norm.

A particularly dangerous hybrid is also in evidence around the world. Driven by the confluence of interests between politicians seeking to gain or retain power and media corporations, it leads to seriously worrying cases of apparent collusion, conflict of interest, and covert alliance between sections of industry and politicians in countries as diverse as the United States, the United Kingdom, Russia, India, Thailand, and Venezuela. From very different starting points, accommodations between neoliberal capital and political elites are potentially hugely damaging to the public sphere since at their core is a drive to distort public information systematically in favor of specific sectoral interests.

The Propagation of a Single Worldview: Individualist Consumerism

The second major concern targets the role of media in the propagation of a single worldview, consumerist capitalism and a global market economy. Fears are expressed not only by many nongovernmental organizations (NGOs) but by many governments of the South and indeed some in the North. The focus here is not on the political health of a country per se, but on the role of media and communication in promoting a worldview—consumerism and individualism—and its economic, social, and cultural counterparts as human relationships become mediated through the market.

Several issues intertwine here. One is the role of media in the formation of individual identity, especially of young people, and how individuals position themselves in relation to their surroundings. Aggregated up to the level of the community as a whole, this can have an enormous impact on community identity and social divisiveness. In traditional societies, with the imposition of this worldview comes the denigration and destruction of cultural traditions, which, though claimed by none to be ideal, are denied the possibility of further evolution in the context of cultural continuity. Fractures introduced between social groups in this cultural reformation, especially through the exclusion of the majority of the poor as irrelevant to the media (as neither sellers nor purchasers), lead to further reinforcement of deep-seated and persisting division. The net effect is that an emerging consumer society in practice displaces an emerging civil society. And at a metalevel, a fundamentally unsustainable way of life and worldview takes hold.

The underlying dynamics are driven largely by the general characteristics of neoliberal logic outlined above, but they are manifested in specific ways. The forceful entry of global capital into new markets in the South puts a special value on advertising, particularly of international brands. This, combined with the low level of disposable income in poorer countries, means that corporate advertising budgets are the main funders of mass media, aiming to create markets and manufacture new needs. News reporting and current affairs tend to be displaced by lifestyle journalism.

Facing demands from powerful governments and corporations and outmaneuvered by unregulated satellite, many governments acquiesce, striking a deal with the global media corporations. Mounting pressure from the WTO aims to eliminate borders to media investment and commodification, irrespective of cultural or social implications. With its ratchetlike effect, a real concern is that room for maneuver will disappear, leaving media corporations free to reshape culture and society according to their imperatives.

The Enclosure of Knowledge: Copyright and the Public Domain

A third area of concern is the privatization of information and knowledge itself, the benefits of human creativity being mediated through the profit-maximizing strategies of the copyright industries and mass-media corporations (Ó Siochrú and Girard 2003).

Copyright has been driven for the past few decades by the copyright industries of film, television, radio, publishing, music, and software. They significantly influence how people can appropriate and use information, and ultimately media, and the scope and vitality of the public domain. They have a strong global dimension since the completion of the WTO's Trade-Related Aspects of Intellectual Property (TRIPS) agreement, which essentially subjugates the various treaties gathered together under the World Intellectual Property Organization (WIPO). Over the past couple of decades, under TRIPS, the period of copyright control has been systematically extended to a total of fifty years after an author's death and to seventy years in the trend-setting United States. Furthermore, TRIPS imposes a single uniform version of copyright, irrespective of the level or nature of a country's development. Most importantly, with TRIPS the copyright industries now control the most powerful enforcement instruments available to any nonsecurity agency, with the authority to impose massive fines on countries and prison sentences on individuals. Efforts to introduce audio-visual products into successive WTO rounds are certain to continue, and in the meantime audio-visual obligations are being cumulatively imposed through bilateral and regional agreements.

The digital age offers a further opportunity to deepen corporate control of information, starting with the Digital Millennium Act and the WIPO Copyright Treaty. Electronic distribution, encryption, and digital-rights management are already severely curtailing "fair use" for educational and general social-development purposes. And pressures to assert copyrights and trademarks on the Internet are being felt by all levels of users.

The Erosion of Civil Rights in Electronic Communication

Finally, a fourth group of concerns relates to growing surveillance, censorship, and direct repression pursued both by governments and the corporate sector (Privacy International and GreenNet Educational Trust 2003; Ó Siochrú 2003).

Government censorship of electronic information, usually at the point of the Internet service provider (ISP), is very real and growing more effective. In some places, an ongoing cat-and-mouse game is played between NGOs and governments as each tries to outwit the other in controlling the flow of information. In a few countries, such as China, Vietnam, and Tunisia, Internet activists are jailed.

Levels of surveillance have recently increased greatly, both in terms of technological capability and political will. Troubling legal frameworks originating in the United States since the 9/11 attacks in New York and Washington are being replicated around the globe. A vast array of national and international laws and conventions being set in place give enormous powers to governments and secretive, sometimes unaccountable, agencies to monitor the full range of communication instruments, especially digital communication. ECHELON, Carnivore, Terrorist Information Awareness, the U.S. Patriot Act, and the Council of Europe's Convention on Cybercrime may be just the first wave, and the ripples are being felt throughout the world. "Purpose creep," where the purpose is gradually extended to include other goals, is a major concern in the context of intensified international collaboration, data retention, surveillance, and monitoring of online environments in attempts to counter cybercrime and terrorism.

Corporate censorship can be more insidious since it can be more difficult to identify and to grapple with. Corporations involved in Internet delivery, such as ISP and bandwidth providers, engage more extensively in self-censorship, ultimately based on commercial priorities but with secondary effects on a variety of actors.

Underlying and Common Features

Can common features be gleaned from this multidimensional palette of concerns? More specifically, is it possible to identify dynamics or interrelations that suggest that these domains can collectively constitute a coherent focus of a transnational campaign?

Certainly a common underlying dynamic is easily discerned in some. The neoliberal model of largely unregulated capitalism, open markets, and private ownership is behind the first three. Wielding enormous political and economic power, its logic is forcefully impressed upon every barrier it meets, such as resistance to the destruction of the (nascent) public sphere, attempts to protect cultural diversity, or efforts to deploy the fruits of human creativity optimally for the greater social good. The need to maximize profits and to create the ideal conditions, for this leads endeavors to sweep aside such obstacles and to transform the world in its own image and to suit its needs.

The fourth area is somewhat different. The erosion of civil and human rights in electronic communication is driven not primarily by commercial gain (though there is an indirect element of that) but by broader geopolitical forces. It is partly associated with "traditional" state repression of a people, as in China, Tunisia, Vietnam, and elsewhere, but the growing trend is not just national but international and is driven by the United States and its allies in the interests, they claim, of national and global security. The United States and its allies work closely with the neoliberal corporate regime by creating a positive environment globally and in ensuring it benefits from the spoils of war. But the motivation and dynamic go beyond corporate needs and can even enter into contradiction with them.

Yet, the identification of a common dynamic behind these domains need not imply that they constitute an appropriate subject for a transnational campaign. The dominant neoliberal paradigm of contemporary capitalism is also responsible for environmental destruction, growing global inequity, and so forth. While a grand coalition may eventually emerge to counter this logic, this will happen only if in each area opposition and alternatives can be articulated and mobilized around.

A second source of coherence from a transnational campaign perspective might be that, in terms of the subsectoral dynamics and actors, the four domains are closely interrelated and interdependent. A high degree of apparent interconnectedness might lead those mobilizing around one aspect to question what is happening in adjacent areas: concern with one has the potential to lead to concern with another, and so forth. This in turn might contribute to the emergence of coherence between the domains from the perspective of affecting change. In other words, such interconnectedness means that, on the one hand, it is impossible to deal with each domain in isolation, and on the other, it is possible to gain leverage in one domain by working on another.

A high degree of interrelatedness of actors and dependencies is indeed present, perhaps not surprisingly.

In terms of corporate actors, global media conglomerates have a strong presence, especially in the first three. The same mass media corporations seeking to undermine public service media and to commodify the media market are also busy clearing the cultural and ideological ground for global market-driven consumerism. They see it as two sides of the same coin: clearing away "unfair competition" in the form of public media subsidies and "market constraints" in the form of regulation, and at the same time building up a market for themselves through promoting consumerist capitalism among the middle classes. The former has an added emphasis in the North, while the latter is foremost in the South.

In copyright, mass-media corporations also have a major stake and huge influence, but they are joined by others. The copyright industries include television, film and video, radio, and newspapers, but they also include music, educational publishing, and software. Between them, they are the major drivers of the continued extension of copyright, in depth and breadth, and in building the global enforcement regime in place today. The latter group is also especially involved in the shift to digital media and pursue encryption and the move to contractual access to information, restrictive forms of digital rights management, and the erosion of fair use. Major global corporations have extensive interests and influence across many of these areas. And behind them all is a small number of powerful governments who have relentlessly pursued the interests of the copyright industries in global fora.

Electronic space is, again, exceptional, but there are strong links to the other actors. ISPs, Internet bandwidth retailers (who effectively operate a global oligopoly), and search engines constitute the critical intermediaries between government restrictions and end users in electronic space. Many of these, such as AOL, are tied into the same media corporations. And the tendency of such corporations to practice self-censorship and to profit from commercial surveillance and data mining is growing. Nevertheless, governments remain the main actors here.

At the level of international governance, examined in more depth in the next section, there are also clear linkages. At the fulcrum of many key concerns is the WTO as the major global actor imposing a market logic across the board. It plays the lead role in copyright and in conventional publishing, defines the international regime in telecommunication and ISPs, and potentially has a major role in audio-visual media. There are others, but the role of WTO puts it far ahead as a target for advocacy in the first three domains.

Thus, there are interdependencies between the actors. First is a relatively small number of governments pursuing the interests of their media and copyright industries, a couple of which also pursue geopolitical strategies for global economic and military dominance. Second are the media and copyright industries themselves sprawled across the full range of sectors after years of megamergers and acquisitions, as well as their various associations that enable them to coordinate their considerable powers to impact global politics. Third is a small number of intergovernmental organizations, principally but not only the WTO, which are utilized by these actors and actively collude to propagate their worldview and their communication regime.

This lends some support to our claim regarding the difficulty of tackling many issues in isolation. For instance, the copyright regime has been moving in only one direction for the past few decades, toward strengthening the rights of owners. Any attempt to change this, whether in terms of reversing the erosion of fair use, reducing the period of copyright, introducing greater flexibility, or addressing the enforcement regime, is likely to meet with the full opposition of all those concerned, both corporate and government. Any breach of the copyright front would likely be taken as an attack on the system as a whole and its rationale and would thus meet concerted opposition. Further, copyright is seen by these interests as simply a part of the overall intellectual property-rights regime, a central building block for continued corporate dominance globally. A similar argument could be made regarding attempts to regulate media at a global level—they would meet with the full force of opposition from all actors.

Thus, a prima facie case can be established that the concerns about media and communication outlined above are linked though subject matter and dynamics and through a relatively small group of mainly transnational actors closely interacting to pursue overlapping international agendas. It is offered as a tentative basis for why these four domains (or some variation of them) can strategically be considered as a whole in terms of an international advocacy network or campaign.

THE INTERNATIONAL POLICY/GOVERNANCE CONTEXT

Further consideration of the transnational-governance context might inform our later consideration of how a transnational campaign might in practice grapple with these issues. A small set of governance institutions constitute key arenas in which these issues are played out and in which such a campaign may operate (Ó Siochrú, Girard, and Mahan 2002).

As mentioned earlier, I do not underestimate the importance of national arenas, both in their own right and as essential mediators between civil society and international change. The activities of national governments are, however, increasingly mediated through and subject to international bodies.

Chief among the institutions involved in the governance of media and communication, although such a claim could not have been made even twenty years ago, is the WTO. It now straddles key areas of communication and is set to extend its mandate further.

First, the WTO, through the efforts of the United States especially, wrested copyright from WIPO with the TRIPS agreement in 1995. The set of international agreements incorporated into WIPO with its formation in 1970, the Berne and Paris conventions reaching back nearly 120 years, form the baseline upon which TRIPS builds. And build it has, in a number of directions. The TRIPS agreement virtually eliminates the flexibility of intellectual property right (IPR) regimes that had hitherto been recognized as a necessary component of development. Under TRIPS, flexibility to tailor IPRs to national requirements is greatly reduced.[3] The duration and breadth of copyright is fixed at a very high level as compared to previous norms in most countries: an author's lifetime plus fifty years. The copyright industries include the world's largest media corporations, and the WTO underwrites and enforces their rights in TRIPS signatory countries.

Second, under the Uruguay Round and the General Agreement on Trade in Service (GATS) agreement, the provision by governments of support for magazines, periodicals, and other non-audio-visual services was deemed to be discriminatory and faced threat of strong financial or trade sanctions. This was confirmed by the WTO dispute panel in a famous case taken by the United States against Canada in the mid-1990s on "split-run" magazines. Implicitly, it ruled that some media companies are less in the business of selling products to audiences than in the business of selling audiences to advertisers. An attempt was made in the Uruguay Round to lay down similar rules for film, video, television, and audio-visual products but failed due to

European and other opposition. It is back on the table, however, at the Doha round of negotiations and will remain so.

Third, since the shift away from monopolistic national providers to liberalized international suppliers, the telecommunication sector is governed by the trade paradigm of the WTO. An area of interest here is universal service policies, by which governments can oblige cross-subsidization from large business users and urban areas to domestic and small users and rural areas. The WTO agreement permits this only where it does not interfere unduly with competition—a vague formulation yet to be tested. The move to trade is also leading to the redundancy of the International Telecommunication Union's (ITU) accounting rate system and to a net loss of foreign earnings for some of the poorest countries (Ó Siochrú 1997).

But what is unique about the WTO and what makes it so attractive to the powerful countries is how it governs. In usurping these activities from others and incorporating them under its various agreements, it subjects them to a new form of governance. For the WTO has at its disposal some of the strongest policing and enforcement powers ever ceded to an intergovernmental body by governments, and it uses them extensively in copyright, media trade, and telecommunication. Furthermore, signing up to the WTO has a ratchetlike effect—it is, in practice, impossible to row back on agreements, even as their full implications become clear, even when circumstances change, or even when promises of reciprocal beneficial action go unfulfilled. The contractual structure of WTO agreements is also conducive to bilateral pressures and coercion, a source of regular complaint from southern governments.

Other organizations have not, of course, been left without influence. For instance, although WIPO is largely sidelined by the WTO, the WIPO Copyright Treaty entered into force in 2002. Designed to bring copyright into the digital-network era, it covers such areas as outlawing efforts to circumvent encryption of copyrighted material.[4] However, many are concerned that extending copyright into the digital era cuts, in practice, into fair use, the accepted means to enable limited public use of copyrighted material prior to expiration.[5] WIPO also has various responsibilities in relation to Internet domain names, including arbitrating ownership disputes.

The ITU also retains responsibility for several narrow, but important, areas. It is the venue in which governments settle the allocation of radio spectrum across borders, terrestrially and via satellite, for the purposes of telephony (mobile and fixed), data, television, radio, and others. The use of spectrum is coordinated to prevent interference and border spillover; and slices of it are allocated to different uses and users. Since it is regarded as a scarce public resource,[6] allocating it among users is an important and contentious issue internationally. The ITU also allocates satellite orbital slots, including the valuable and scarce geostationary orbit; another function is to develop standards for telecommunication networks and equipment, including protocols, which can be highly contentious since they are linked to struggles for market control.[7] The ITU is also concerned with extending telecommunication to less industrialized countries but has only very limited means to do so. Finally, it is worth noting that the ITU was the lead UN agency for the World Summit on the Information Society held in Geneva in December 2003 and will play the same role in Tunis in 2005; this summit covers a number of areas of relevance here.

UNESCO, on the other hand, has much "softer" responsibilities, but they extend to many areas of social concern. It is important less for its formal powers and enforcement capacities than as a forum for voluntary cooperation on (usually noncontentious but necessary) issues of mutual concern across a wide area. UNESCO in its early decades was instrumental in many conventions, declarations, and congresses, overseeing agreements on issues such as the exchange of audio-visual content for educational use, cross-border direct-broadcasting satellites, and copyright exemptions for development purposes. In the late 1970s to mid-1980s, it came to the fore as a debating arena for global communication issues in the context of the New World Information and Communication Order (NWICO).[8] Its fingers were badly burned on this, however, as cold war politics and the entrenched positions of some of the major powers eventually led to the defeat of voices calling for more open and democratic global media flows and structures (see chapter 1). UNESCO has never fully recovered in terms of facilitating vibrant and diverse debate, and indeed, the United States announced only in 2001 its intention to rejoin UNESCO after leaving in the mid-1980s.

In 1995, the UNESCO-sponsored World Commission on Culture and Development put forward some significant proposals regarding media, raising the idea of a tax on the use of spectrum, the proceeds from which would be utilized for internationally distributed noncommercial programming and for questioning the growing concentration of media ownership. However, it is probably indicative of UNESCO's broader constraints that these proposals failed to be ratified, or even discussed, at the follow-up intergovernmental meeting in 1998. Although it continues to support progressive media initiatives and to sponsor debate at a lower level, current negotiations on U.S. reentry will probably ensure that UNESCO is unlikely in the foreseeable future to become a major forum for open debate or dissenting views.

A newcomer is the Internet Corporation for Assigned Names and Numbers (ICANN). Established in 1998, its main job is to manage the process of assigning names and numbers for the Internet, an issue that has gradually taken on huge commercial and legal significance. ICANN initially saw itself as primarily technical, but its management of IP addresses and of the Domain Name System (DNS), which ultimately controls routing of Internet traffic, quickly moved into economic, political, social, and even cultural domains.

ICANN is interesting not just for what it does but for how it does it. It is constituted as a nonprofit private-sector corporation under Californian law, designed to allow the U.S. Department of Commerce to maintain ultimate control over the DNS (which it still does). This places it in the nongovernmental sector. Its governance is still in flux and is the subject of a task force set up for the second phase of WSIS. At-large membership (i.e., Internet users who have registered for the process) did initially have the opportunity to elect several directors, the rest coming from the initial board and nominated by associated organizations. But this was later unceremoniously scrapped and at-large membership reduced to a more or less advisory capacity.

Other lesser-known organizations are also involved with the Internet.[9] The Internet Engineering Task Force (IETF), for instance, sounds highly technical, but its work in defining the new Internet Protocol (called IPV6) could have significant long-term implications in terms, for instance, of surveillance and the commercialization of the Internet.

Regional-level institutions are also relevant. The EU, for instance, has its Television without Frontiers and Database Directives, the North American Free Trade Agreement (NAFTA) encompasses cultural agreements, and the Council of Europe in 2001 oversaw the Cybercrime Treaty; all of these institutions deeply influence media and communication. Apart from their impacts in their own right, regional agreements (and, indeed, national legislation in powerful counties such as the United States) are often early battlegrounds for matters that are later pushed up to global governance structures. Other intergovernmental organizations, such as the Organization for Economic Cooperation and Development (OECD) and the G8, are also important loci of collaboration between governments (in these cases, of the wealthier countries) in coordinating and implementing shared policy and in providing the research and ideological backup for their shared worldviews.

But governance does not just take place in intergovernmental organizations. Corporations, for instance, take a very keen interest in how media and communications are governed and lobby actively for various forms of self-governance through various associations and assemblies. Other forms of what amount to unacknowledged self-governance activities include, for instance, many examples of international censorship of Internet content by bandwidth backbone providers and by global ISPs.

These, then, are some of the players in global governance, and a quick glance at their areas of influence reveals again the reasonably coherent dynamic behind many of the trends in recent years, that of the neoliberal interpretation of capitalism. Driven mainly by the United States, but also supported in key aspects by the EU and others, governance structures have been transformed to fulfil capitalism's needs. In media and communication, the goals are clear: their commercialization through the elimination of government monopoly, government ownership, and of market distortions designed to achieve cultural or other social goals; the elimination of all barriers to market entry (except where they suit the dominant interests); and the annexation in perpetuity of society's knowledge into private ownership. The move toward the digital realm and the growth of the Internet are regarded as opportunities to impose these goals in electronic space, at the same time opening new opportunities for U.S. ambitions of military and political dominance.

THE FUTURE: PEERING OVER THE EDGE

I conclude with a speculative glance to the future, or at least one possible future. What would happen if the trends outlined above continued unchecked for a sustained period?

In such a scenario, commercial and liberalization logic would permeate virtually the entire media and communication sphere, nationally and internationally, largely at the expense of the social, cultural, and political dimensions of that sphere. Multinational industry would reign, and the UN system would gradually be displaced by an ever more powerful WTO, closed intergovernmental clubs of powerful governments, and private-sector allies. This would lead to the hollowing out of the public sphere, a contraction of the public domain, the severe weakening of human rights in the digital domain, and an extension of the private sphere and of the economic rights of those who can afford to exercise them.

At the macro level, this would require the resolution of current struggles concerning, for instance, the WTO and Bretton Woods institutions in favor of the neoliberal approach, with little structural change and emerging governance needs settled in compliance with the market-driven status quo.

For the media and communication sector, structural conditions and regulation of this scenario would include the following:

- Unimpeded global trade in media and cultural products, with no protection on the basis of cultural, social, or environmental outcomes.
- A fully enforceable and all-embracing intellectual property regime that stifles creativity and diversity and yields huge rewards for corporate owners.
- The virtual elimination of universal service instruments in telecommunication that are deemed to interfere with competition and the operation of the market.
- Heightened commercialization and looser regulation of radio, television, and other mass media, with public service media compelled to compete in the marketplace.
- The commercialization of spectrum terrestrially and in space, selling it to the highest bidder.

- The gradual extension of industry self-regulation in emerging media subsectors.

Were these trends to gain inexorable momentum, other global stakeholders would face stark choices. The UN system would be forced to choose between accommodating itself to the new world order and risking redundancy, becoming cash strapped, and lacking the internal capacity to devise and enforce alternative development- or human rights–based agendas.

Less developed countries, similarly, would probably find themselves divided between a majority that believes it has no option but to join in, on the one hand, and on the other, a minority that objects and so is sidelined from the globalization process or perhaps suffers the full rigor of what it has already signed up for. A few of the larger countries might attempt, with some perhaps succeeding, to gain a permanent and lucrative foothold in the industry—though paying the same ultimate price as everyone else.

Civil society, realizing the dangers too late to mount effective opposition, would find itself more or less excluded from this domain altogether, mere spectators as the global media circus rolls on.

The medium-term outcomes of such a scenario might be as follows:

- The number of media channels and sources available grows, especially from international sources by direct satellite broadcast and other means.
- Within these, diversity of program content diminishes and quality falls.
- Media ownership and content portfolios concentrate and centralize further.
- Public service media disappear or dwindle to become niche providers.
- Support measures for local, community, and people's media disappear in the clamor for market sustainability.
- Public-domain information shrinks as lucrative parts are hived off to profit-making concerns; copyright is ever more restrictive and digital-rights management denies even the right to fair use.
- Infrastructure and new services in telecommunications grow but are confined mainly to urban and business markets, leading to ever-growing disparities and inequities.

Brought to its (unlikely) ultimate conclusion, media and communication in a few decades could be expunged of fundamental dissent and criticism, with an entire generation having grown up knowing little else, not just incapable of autonomous political action but unaware of the concept and practice. The gap between those with access to media and those without would accentuate the already great economic inequalities; media content and information would become the property almost exclusively of giant corporations, which would keep creativity and diversity on the short leash of profit maximization.

Most insidiously, the process would slowly but surely transform the very wellspring of ideas, people's creative capacities, in the end yielding a self-perpetuating cycle that stifles genuine diversity and is purged of all dissent and nonconformity (except that which is profitable).

The circle is complete; the end point feeds back to the beginning. A consistent and coherent pattern of domination impels media in a downward spiral to a new Information Dark Age.

CONCLUSION: A CONSTITUENCY FOR CHANGE

Such a future is not inevitable, however. To be sure, building an alternative will not be easy. The issues outlined above regarding media and communications are difficult, if not impossible, to pick off on their own, through narrowly focused individual national or even international campaigns. Something broader is needed that can both encompass a wide range of diverse, but interconnected, issues and bring them to an international and global level.

This additional element I believe is a transnational advocacy network pursuing a campaign in media and communication.

Where will such a campaign find its constituency? Which groups and organizations might be willing to get involved? The introduction to this book touches on these issues, and related work offers an excellent starting point (Hackett 2000). For the purposes of this chapter, I will distinguish between three sets of potential actors.

The first is likely to be at the forefront of such a transnational campaign and includes those whose focus is already directly on one or more aspects of media from a progressive perspective. Among them are several international associations of community media and electronic networking, international campaigns and networks, national and transnational advocacy NGOs focusing on human rights aspects (Internet rights and communication rights), international professional associations, international trade unions and labor organizations, direct-action and "hactivist" groups, alternative media with a global scope, and a few national social movements. Despite recognizable differences between them in their specific analyses and proposals around media and communication, their general rights-based orientation and rejection of both totalitarian states and unregulated corporate dominance would suggest an alliance is in principle possible. Such groups are already coalescing.

A second group comprises noncore actors in the sense that either their horizons are currently limited to the national level or their interest in media and communication, although transnational in focus, is secondary or only a small part of their central agendas. This category would comprise similar types of entities as those identified in the core group, but with a primary focus on issues such as intellectual property rights in general, sustainable development, indigenous peoples, women's issues, and so forth. If a transnational campaign is to be effective, it will be necessary to attract the support of these groups.

A third set might be considered resource organizations, willing to provide different forms of backing for such a movement. These include some foundations, donor agencies, intergovernmental agencies, and others whose general concern for social development might, with the emergence of a transnational network, translate into a specific concern in the domain of media.

It is through the cooperation of these three groups, gradually extending outward from the core group, that the basis of an effective transnational campaign, and an alternative future, may be built.

NOTES

1. A fifth domain could be included here, although it might stretch the rationale somewhat, namely, the issue of affordable access to, and the capacity to use effectively, information and communication technologies. This is sometimes referred to as the "digital divide," although the term derived from a narrow interpretation focusing mainly on infrastructure provision. A succinct argument is made in CRIS (2004). A transnational campaign should consider whether to include this, and indeed other, areas.

2. These include the CRIS Campaign, Voices 21, and others.

3. "The Paris and Berne Conventions . . . allowed considerable flexibility in the design of IP regimes. With the advent of TRIPS, a large part of this flexibility has been removed. Countries can no longer follow the path adopted by Switzerland, Korea or Taiwan in their own development" (U.K. Commission on IPRs 2002, 23n6).

4. In December 1996, after the WIPO Diplomatic Conference, a new treaty was adopted: CRNR/DC/94—WIPO Copyright Treaty (www.wipo.org/eng/diplconf/distrib/94dc.htm, accessed October 7, 2004). It was ratified by a sufficient number of countries in 1992 to bring it into force.

5. The U.K. Commission on IPRs concludes, "An important concern here is that developing countries will come under pressure, for instance in the context of bilateral agreements with developed countries, to accede to the WIPO Copyright treaty, or even to adopt stricter prohibitions against circumvention of technological protection systems and effectively thereby reducing the scope of traditional 'fair use' in digital media." (U.K. Commission on IPRs, 2002, 118n6).

6. It can be argued that spread-spectrum technologies are greatly reducing the element of scarcity, a fact that could have serious repercussions for spectrum governance in the future. These technologies can make much more efficient use of a given bandwidth.

7. The recent open wireless standard, IEEE 802.11b at 2.4 GHz, known as WiFi, now being used by NGOs and communities to build autonomous wide-area net-

works is a good example of a standard releasing unanticipated potential (although this was developed by the Institute of Electrical and Electronics Engineers).

8. There are many publications on this. For a retrospective review, see Vincent et al. 1999.

9. The Internet Architecture Board (IAB) oversees technical development and formed the Internet Society (ISOC), a body of coordinating professionals. WIPO, by agreement with ICANN, is a key body in resolving domain name disputes.

REFERENCES

Communication Rights in the Information Society (CRIS). 2004. "Issue 9: Universal Access to Telecoms," available at www.crisinfo.org/content/view/full/175 (accessed October 7, 2004).

Hackett, Robert A. 2000. "Taking Back the Media: Notes on the Potential for a Communicative Democracy Movement." *Studies in Political Economy* 63: 61–86.

Ó Siochrú, Seán. 1997. "The ITU, the WTO and Accounting Rates: Limited Prospects for the South?" *Javnost: The Public, Special Edition* 4, no. 4: 47–57.

———. 2003. "Global Governance of ICTs: Implications for Global Civil Society." Report prepared for the Social Science Research Council (SSRC), available at http://www.ssrc.org/programs/itic/governance_report/index.page (accessed October 7, 2004).

Ó Siochrú, Seán, and Bruce Girard. 2003. "Information Wants to Be Free." Paper given at the International Telecommunication Union Visions Conference, Geneva, available at www.itu.int/visions (accessed October 7, 2004).

Ó Siochrú, Seán, and W. Bruce Girard, with Amy Mahan. 2002. *Global Media Governance: A Beginner's Guide.* Lanham, MD: Rowman & Littlefield.

Privacy International and GreenNet Educational Trust. 2003. "Silences: Censorship and Control of the Internet," September 10, available at www.privacyinternational.org/survey/censorship (accessed October 7, 2004).

U.K. Commission on Intellectual Property Rights. 2002. *Integrating Intellectual Property Rights and Development Policy.* London, available at www.iprcommission.org (accessed October 7, 2004).

Vincent, Richard, Kaarle Nordenstreng, and Michael Traber, eds. 1999. *Towards Equity in Global Communication: MacBride Update.* Cresskill, NJ: Hampton Press.

III
MODALITIES OF
DEMOCRATIZATION

11

Beyond Wiggle Room: American Corporate Media's Democratic Deficit, Its Global Implications, and Prospects for Reform

Robert W. McChesney and Robert A. Hackett[1]

Hackett: The American media system is often held up as a democratic model for the world. But you see a massive democratic deficit. In your writings, you have exhaustively documented the structure of U.S. media: a growing degree of concentration, conglomeration, and convergence; the extension and deepening of commercial logic throughout the media system; and the secrecy and indeed corruption of government policy making. You have also presented some of the negative consequences of these structural features for democracy and culture in America. For people unfamiliar with your work, could you summarize your critique?

McChesney: The first point is that media systems are not naturally the province of capitalist investors to maximize profits. Moses didn't hand the tablet to Thomas Jefferson, who handed it to Jack Welsh at General Electric, saying, "Thou shalt rule the media; this is the wish of God or democratic theory." All the great media companies today are in fact the result of government subsidies and policies, often quite lavish, made in the public's name but without the public's consent. The founders of the United States instituted a series of policies to build what they called a free press, because it was foundational to their notion of democracy. And there was no conviction whatsoever in the first several generations of this nation that a free press simply meant letting wealthy interests make as much money as possible and then have the government get out of the way. This is a recent viewpoint that accords with the growing power of self-interested corporations or wealthy individuals that dominate our media. It was understood that if you just let wealthy people run the media system, it would serve only wealthy people, not viable democratic self-government.

So, the government in the first several generations of U.S. history established extensive subsidies to spawn a diverse media system. The two most significant were printing subsidies to most leading newspapers of the day and postal subsidies. Over 90 percent of the post office's business was sending out newspapers; it was basically the press's delivery system. Newspapers were charged just a fraction of the actual mailing cost, to subsidize them. James Madison favored charging no fee whatsoever; he regarded any charge as a form of censorship that would eliminate dissident views, which would be unable to survive if they had to pay the full price. The connection between media policy making, media subsidies, and a diverse marketplace of ideas in which citizens could engage and govern their own lives was a standard view. In fact, congressional debates throughout the first half of the nineteenth century were never to increase the postal fees on publications, but how much to decrease them. There was always a strong movement, especially from populist and progressive elements, to eliminate any charge whatsoever.

So, this is our real tradition, and the problem we face in the United States today, and I think around the world, is that we have the same sort of policies now as in the first three generations of the Republic, but without the public's consent. We have tremendous subsidies and monopoly licenses being granted through the gifts of radio and TV channels at no charge to huge companies, monopoly privileges for satellite cable franchises, and copyright, which is a government-created and -enforced monopoly system. All of these are tremendous subsidies, which have built up a commercial media system, but most Americans have no clue about them. That's what the protest movement about media ownership has been about in 2003—changing the calculus so there is public involvement.

So, we have a media system that has been instituted without any public debate or ratification and that has been set up primarily to make money for the handful of very large private companies that own much of our media. The question then becomes, is this system going to generate the highest quality of democratic discourse? Will it do what the founders of the Republic clearly stated, when they wrote the First Amendment, was the necessary role of the free press in our society? I think the evidence is overwhelming. Maximizing profits for these firms generates lousy journalism. It makes perfect sense. If I was a shareholder in Viacom, General Electric, or News Corporation, I would want them to do exactly what they're doing—maximizing my return. Increasingly, doing what is traditionally regarded as high-quality journalism that improves civic discourse is clearly lousy for business: it costs money, it doesn't bring in a lot of revenue, the benefits go not to the company but to the whole society. The rational thing for these companies to do is to lowball the journalism, spend fewer resources on it, and avoid antagonizing people in power because nothing good will come out of that for a corporation. That's why we get the journalism we do. Scholarly research demonstrates these problems in case study after case study, but that is the foundation for understanding why we have this situation.

Hackett: To summarize, you have identified three key problems: first, the system disproportionately serves and reflects the interests of the wealthy; second, communication policy is made in secret without public participation; and third, it does not maximize the quality of democratic discourse and engagement with public issues. Notwithstanding such corporate control, however, there seems to be a crisis in recent years in corporate media, following the dot-com crash: a certain divestment or retreat from the grand dream of convergence, massive debt loads, and so on. Can you update us on these trends, and their implications?

McChesney: Since 2000, since the AOL/Time-Warner and Vivendi/Universal deals, the bubble has burst, and the synergy model that was held up as how media firms were constructing their empires in the 1980s and especially in the late 1990s has been repudiated as a false promise, a model that no longer works and will be discontinued. But this repudiation, the new line served up since 2001 that these deals proved that synergy was an unworkable principle, went too far. For starters, the AOL/Time-Warner and Vivendi/Universal deals didn't really fail because of synergy, in other words, because the parts they were assembling couldn't work together. In both cases, the firms hadn't been together long enough to see if they could make the parts mesh. Both deals became problems within months of their consummation, primarily because each entity had vastly overpaid for the assets and gone deeply into debt, then got clobbered when the stock market bubble collapsed. Those were management issues and problems of the business cycle, independent of the question of synergy. Most of the Vivendi media properties have been sold to, or merged with, General Electric, the NBC unit, but if you look at the specific pieces in both AOL/Time-Warner and Vivendi, the individual media units are still fairly profitable, and the assets have considerable value.

Having said that, the idea of synergy, of building vast arrays of vertically integrated conglomerates, where you have disparate media interests put together and where the profit whole is larger than the sum of its profit parts, did not work as well as its most flamboyant presentation. It's going to work better for some than for others; there's going to be some experimentation. For example, in the mid- to late 1990s, it was widely held that professional sports franchises could be a very lucrative part of media empires, but since then Disney, Murdoch, and AOL/Time-Warner have, I think, all sold off their teams. They just simply didn't contribute to the media empire in the way that each of those companies imagined. Does that mean that synergy doesn't work? No, it means that not all types of empire building necessarily work.

Moreover, there is no sense that, as a result of the AOL/Time-Warner and Vivendi/Universal deals' problems, we are seeing a breakup of big media companies or a fire sale of assets. Only Vivendi and AOL/Time Warner are unloading assets, and that is exclusively because they have to pay down debt; the assets themselves are lucrative, which is precisely why they are able to sell them.

Furthermore, the media companies that are doing the best in the world in recent years are Viacom and News Corporation, two of the five massive, vertically integrated conglomerates. The reason for their success is their very astute job of mixing and matching assets to produce a form of synergy. Viacom has an exceptional ability to commercialize every aspect of its media operations, be it MTV, CBS, Nickelodeon, or Infinity Radio, and then to link them together. It's the same with News Corporation and Disney, although in the case of Disney, there is experimentation going on. At one time, Disney thought it would build its own retail chain; at its high point, it had seven hundred or more stores globally, but I think now Disney has concluded that it's more profitable to use other retailers and simply to produce the material and hand out licenses for Disney characters, rather than to try to do the final retail sales too. That doesn't mean that synergy doesn't work; it means that not all forms of synergy work.

Hackett: In analyzing the U.S. media's democratic deficit, you and other critics note an escalation of hypercommercialism and a related decline of the public service ethos in journalism as more and more media are owned by profit-driven conglomerates. That seems to imply that you are using as an evaluative standard the public service ethos of what Daniel Hallin called American journalism's period of high modernism. Yet, like Yuezhi Zhao and me in *Sustaining Democracy? Journalism and the Politics of Objectivity*, you have also been critical of the older traditions of professionalism and objectivity in journalism in that they subtly embed corporate and commercial ideologies and imperatives. Are you actually critical of both contemporary infotainment and the older "Walter Cronkite" era? What alternative model do you offer as a benchmark?

McChesney: Indeed, I am critical of both. I have never said ownership can explain everything about journalism, but neither have I argued that professionalism in journalism is the solution to the problem. I think that both issues, ownership and professionalism, contribute to an understanding of why our journalism is the way it is and what needs to be done to improve it. The starting point for both aspects of the critique, of ownership or commercial pressures on journalism, as well as of the limitations of professionalism, comes from an understanding that both grow out of the same fundamental problem that emerged in the United States in the late nineteenth century and crystal-lized by the early twentieth century, namely, concentrated private control, supported by advertising, over the main units then producing journalism—newspapers. At the time, newspapers still had that old partisan legacy, the idea that their journalism should represent the politics of the owner. It's one thing to have highly partisan journalism in a commercial market if you've got ten or fifteen local daily newspapers, which was often the case in the major American cities in the nineteenth century; if the citizens didn't like the exist-ing papers, the citizens could put out another one without an inordinate amount of money. Then, having hired, partisan journalism is understandable for a democratic society.

The problem that hit the United States at that time was the combination of stridently partisan journalism in noncompetitive markets with only one, two, or three newspapers in the community and high barriers to entry so that only other very rich people could enter the market, and even they couldn't sur-vive economically in most cases. In that environment, partisan journalism becomes very controversial and leads to a crisis for the system because it looks like powerful owners are able to use their monopoly power to impose their views on the public, which has little recourse.

That environment helps explain the rise of professional standards, of neu-tral, nonpartisan journalism, between 1900 and 1920, although it didn't really become the rule almost everywhere in American journalism until midcen-tury. Professionalism, rather than being a counter to private ownership, was in fact a strategy of private owners to maintain monopoly control effectively, while lending legitimacy to the news product that they were controlling. I think that's a more accurate way to get at the power relations between pro-fessionalism and owners than to see them as purely adversarial. They are closely connected issues. A democratic critique of journalism has to address both, to suggest the weaknesses built within the professional code of jour-nalism as it emerged in the United States in the first half of the twentieth cen-tury, as well as the obvious contemporary ways that journalism is being warped by commercial pressure.

Hackett: What for you then is the alternative? Is it a more participatory model, like the civic journalism movement, which wants to see journalism become more proactive in engaging publics and stimulating community di-alog? Or is it alternative media, or the BBC notion of public service broad-casting?

McChesney: I don't know if there is one answer. I'm not a big fan of civic journalism in practice; I might be in principle, but in the real world of the United States, civic journalism is a pathetic movement. It's trying basically, as far as I can tell, to go into a newsroom and say to journalists, Americans can't do anything about the owners and the advertisers. We're not going to have a union; we're going to take the existing allocation of resources and power structure, and with the limited autonomy and resources you have, we want you journalists to alter your practices, but we don't want you to do anything that's politically controversial that upsets people in power.

More broadly, you try to look at institutional perspectives that generate a type of journalism that facilitates public awareness and involvement in public life. A partisan system like the United States had in its first seventy-five years and that other countries have had, with extensive public subsidies to keep a fairly wide array of diverse viewpoints alive, could well generate a very high quality of public life. Does that mean that's the model we should use today in the United States? Not necessarily, but it suggests that having a well-subsidized range of diverse viewpoints isn't a bad thing in a democracy; it might draw people into public life. While pure objectivity is nonsensical, there is value in having journalism that strives to be accurate and not bombastic. So, I think we can have different types of journalism, a combination system. But ultimately, we must always connect the types of journalism we have to the structure of the system and the policy to put the structure in place.

Hackett: How has the aftermath of 9/11 changed or complicated the role of media in American democracy?

McChesney: 9/11 initially was such a shock to most Americans, certainly to me, that it was widespread to say 9/11 had changed everything, but you don't hear that much anymore. In the case of media, the initial response was, we can expect our journalism to stop covering idiotic stories about celebrity scandals and shark attacks and really start to talk about serious international politics and terrorism so that Americans know what the heck is going on and so we are prepared for this sort of event. This was a widespread sentiment expressed, for example, in a very damning book by *Washington Post* editors Downing and Kaiser, right after 9/11. The studies that I've seen so far indicate that for a brief period after 9/11, there was an increase in what is called hard news and international coverage, but now journalism has gone right to where it was on 9/10 and earlier.

So, I don't think our media or journalism have become appreciably better since 9/11. In 2002–2003, we have had arguably the darkest episode in the history of modern U.S. journalism. If the 9/11 attack was supposed to teach us anything about journalism, it was that superficial journalism was no longer acceptable; it doesn't give us the ability to understand the world. And if that's the case, then the journalism on the Iraq war is nothing short of a disaster. That might not be entirely an accident. When you look at the way the current administration in the United States has dealt with 9/11, it has used it, in my view, in a very cynical manner to push its particular political agenda, to justify all sorts of policies totally unrelated to 9/11, whether it be trying to reduce taxes and regulations on wealthy Americans whose businesses support the administration or pursuing aggressive militarist foreign policy with nations that have nothing to do with terrorism or 9/11, or simply drilling for oil in the Arctic. Whatever positive lesson the American people might have learned has been lost in the rampant opportunism of this administration concerning that day.

Hackett: You are referring to the failure of American journalism to raise critical questions about the invasion of Iraq or the war on terrorism. How would you connect the political economy of America's corporate media with that failure?

McChesney: There's no simple direct line from ownership to news content; there is a line, but it is complex, and it zigs and zags. Crucially, the way to understand press coverage of foreign affairs in the United States is to understand the nature of the professional codes that journalists use, with their strong reliance upon official sources as the basis for legitimate news. Especially on a subject like foreign policy or war and peace issues, the legitimate bases for news are people in power, Republicans and Democrats, especially in the executive branch, but also in Congress. Journalists basically report on what official sources are debating. This is truly one of the great weak spots of professional journalism; it really imprisons journalists because, if they try to raise an issue that no one in power is talking about, they have a very difficult time; it looks like they're bringing in their own opinion—they are no longer being "objective"; they are being subjective or partisan.

And that is a starting point to understand the generally weak coverage of foreign policy, historically, not just in the Iraq war, because at least in the United States, both the Republicans and the Democrats, the business community, and what's called the foreign policy establishment all tend to agree in a handful of areas. One of the things that they all agree upon is that the United States, and it alone, has the right to invade any country it wants to at anytime. No other country in the world has this privilege unless the United States deputizes it. This principle is never up for grabs in the U.S. media; only the timing of invasions is. But a journalist can't really question that because nobody in power does. And this is a problem in a free society, because for a significant number of Americans, having to invade other countries routinely does not make a lot of sense. It is something many Americans would like to see discussed: why exactly are we always doing these invasions.

So, that is the starting point probably for understanding press coverage of the Iraq war—a very weak Democratic opposition, a powerful administration pushing its case, and a journalism that reflects this because this is what the official sources look like. But having said that, first, the professional code of objectivity is clearly related to ownership issues as we discussed earlier, and second, and most important, there are also strong and dubious connections between the largest media firms, especially the TV-owning firms, press coverage, and news-policy issues. It seems more than a coincidence that the companies that were leading the rah-rah cheers for this war are also strong supporters of this administration and are now going to this administration looking for regulations to be relaxed on their behalf. There are coincidences of interest, which work on a number of different levels. That's why I said earlier that there's not a direct line between ownership and content. The U.S. government not only deregulates or loosens regulations for media firms at home to make them more profitable, but it is also their number one advocate globally, creating global trade deals and other instruments that suit the interests of the transnational media firms and establish commercial media marketplaces. So, it's a very complementary and symbiotic relationship between large corporate media and the U.S. government.

How do you test this though? Where's the evidence that some corporation is banning antiwar views and fostering prowar rules in order to improve its business with the government in power? You're not going to find many smoking guns. You're putting together all sorts of seemingly unrelated facts; you create a picture with all of this information that points in a certain direction and suggests plausible explanations. But it is striking that in these companies, antiwar voices are almost never heard unless they are being ridiculed by a host for questioning our "maximum leader" or unless the level of dissent is within the confines of what is being said by official sources. To be sure, I think you'll see that dissent growing. Months after the invasion of Iraq, U.S. press coverage has become somewhat more critical toward the occupation in Iraq largely because the official sources are getting somewhat more critical; the war has not worked out as the administration claimed it would. But that is still a far cry from democratic journalism; it's still handcuffed by what people in power are communicating to journalists.

It has led to an ironic situation. In Britain and Australia, we see the public broadcasters being chastised for being too critical of their governments, governments that supported the invasion of Iraq; and we have always been told in the United States that public broadcasting is bad because it is too close to government and will just regurgitate the governing party's line. Ironically, public broadcasting appears to have more distance from governments than our commercial broadcasters do. Commercial broadcasters seem to be lackey media, certainly on this issue.

Hackett: Let's turn to some of the global implications of your analysis. Debate abounds over the validity and meaning of the concept of globalization—for example, whether globalization is a real process, whether it is historically new and distinct, whether nation-states are still powerful actors, and much else. Those are enormous questions, which I can't expect you to address here, but could you sketch where you stand on the concept of globalization and how you see the media fitting into that framework?

McChesney: I need to study this issue more, but I think in the early and mid-1990s, there was a common and growing belief, which certainly influenced me, that the great trend globally was toward unfettered capital markets with investors being able to move their capital to any country they wanted, undermining the ability of nation-states to interfere with capital, leaving a kind of capital feudalism, with the U.S. government constituting the military or power force to push such capitalism through all over the world. This perspective of globalization as global capitalism run wild with industrialists sitting in the driver's seat went against the traditional geopolitical assessment of power, which is built around nation-states and conflict and rivalry between the United States and Western Europe, or Japan, or Northeast Asia; this traditional view emphasized how capitalists use nation-states as their agents and how there was conflict between the dominant economic interests in these areas. In the first scenario, capitalists of the world basically unite; capital can flow anywhere, and the nation-states are less important. The second scenario still emphasizes the nation-state. I think in the 1990s a lot of people, mesmerized by globalization, fell into the first perspective. Now, however, while that fear of universal capitalists is still there, it has become more evident, with this battle over a global trade deal since Seattle in 1999, that there is nothing whatsoever natural about the global free market or global flow of capital and business services. It requires an extraordinary range of regulation and deals put together and constructed by governments. There's no level, free market playing field; it's very much a politicized project. That is where I lean. Since 2001, we have had a further reassessment of this idea of relatively powerless nation-states; it has become clearer that a notion of globalization that doesn't factor in the role of aggressive U.S. military involvement around the world isn't going to get us very far. Depending on what sort of theory of globalization we have, we have perhaps a different emphasis on how we see media and communication plugging into the system.

Hackett: Because, of course, you have written with Ed Herman in *The Global Media: The New Missionaries of Corporate Capitalism* (1997) and in your *Rich Media, Poor Democracy: Communication Politics in Dubious Times* (1999) that the emerging global media are ideological as well as economic handmaidens of globalization understood as pancapitalism.

McChesney: Yes, Ed and I saw the global media system as developing out of neoliberal policies that made it easier for firms to cross borders and as driven by capitalism and the pursuit of profit. But also, we saw the content of global media as clearly ideological, with built-in biases sympathetic to or comporting with the needs of neoliberal capitalists and their global order. I still think that's true.

Hackett: So, given that view, what implications does the architecture of the U.S. media system have for communication and democracy elsewhere in the world?

McChesney: I think it has a lot of implications because, first, if we look at the global media system, based on my calculations a few years ago of the rank orders of all the leading firms in terms of size, I'd say that roughly half the dominant media firms in the world are based in North America, mainly the United States. So, if you dominate the United States, you're dominating the world in many respects. Second, of the eight or nine first-tier conglomerates in the world, the ones that own the film studios, that have operations from every corner of the planet—Sony, Viacom, General Electric, News Corporation, Disney, Bertelsmann—these companies, even those owned outside the United States, all have significant U.S. interests. The U.S. market is crucial to them, so they bathe in American culture and politics, and they have close and important relations with the U.S. government. So, the commanding heights of the system are all strongly linked to the United States, even if the companies are not based there. Third, even in countries that have distinct local media not connected to the United States or owned by Americans, and sometimes these can be rather large (Globo in Brazil, Televisa, some European companies), they generally tend to have important relations with the largest dominant firms that do have strong U.S. links, and the system is increasingly linked together. Having said that though, there is wiggle room within countries with regard to policy. How much depends on the country; there's more in Italy or Japan than in Ghana, but there is wiggle room.

Hackett: More generally, let's consider the implications for democratization processes. What is the connection between global media and politically authoritarian regimes in the South? Advocates of media globalization, and some others besides, argue that the export or diffusion of Western programming and models of media professionalism and organization have a liberalizing impact on Third World and ex-Soviet "transition" societies, and therefore should be supported. What do you make of their case?

McChesney: The argument that commercial media come in and undermine authoritarian regimes is a long-standing one. I think originally it was based on a vision of a free press not controlled by authoritarian governments coming and supporting democratization and giving people information they wouldn't otherwise have about what is happening in their country. But in practice, the global, commercial media system and the journalism it brings in tend not to offer much coverage of local affairs. Except for the BBC, in the English-language media at least, it's not necessarily going to be rigorous journalism; rather, it's going to be like U.S. network journalism, emphasizing celebrity, entertainment, plane crashes, and so on—not much journalism critical of people in power, especially those in the United States and the West. So, the argument loses some of its theoretical muscle when you go from the classic notion of a free press in a democracy exposing how the powerful operate and telling the truth so that citizens can act on it, to the actual current system.

So, the argument has been revamped. It now focuses on the connection between consumption-oriented lifestyles, political democracy, and the removal of authoritarian regimes. The idea is, when people see fast cars and half-undressed women as their idols, when they want to shop until they drop and have nose rings and enjoy the good life of the West, they won't want to live in a repressive situation. On the surface, I'm not sure that the link between consumerism and democracy is always there. I think one test of this is going to come in China, where these tensions are beginning to play out (as discussed in chapter 3). We'll see how democratic they are.

Hackett: One could argue that the global media are liberalizing social mores vis-à-vis patriarchal traditional cultures, but that is not necessarily the same as participatory democratic government.

McChesney: I don't know how it's going to shake up, but the same trends that are held up as possibly liberating in authoritarian areas, especially in Asia, are trends that I would consider largely depoliticizing in American culture. So, we should not exaggerate their potential for politicizing other countries when they aren't doing that here.

Hackett: In light of your critique of the American media system, I'd like to turn to the question of reforming the media. First, what do you see as the connections or relationship between democratic media reform and other social and political change? In their book on so-called transition societies, *Media Reform: Democratizing the Media, Democratizing the State*, Monroe Price and his colleagues argue that political democratization seems to proceed mainly independently of media reform; media reform is a possible, but not inevitable, by-product of that change and, on its own, doesn't necessarily have a catalytic effect. By contrast, John Downing and his colleagues argue in *Radical Media: Rebellious Communication and Social Movements*, as does Kai Hafez in this book, that even small media can influence political change at pivotal moments, especially when they operate in conjunction with social movements or at specific historical conjunctures. If American media were reformed, what difference would it make to political outcomes?

McChesney: I don't think you can say that if you get media reform, you automatically get better public education, better environmental regulation, better social security, or whatever. But what you do get is a better chance to have a decent public discussion about those issues, and then a better chance that public discussion will lead to tangible reform. What those reforms will be, one can't predict, but the theory is that they will reflect the interests of a broader section of the population than policies that are currently drawn up, at least in the United States, largely by private interests behind closed doors. So, you would have more public input into policy, but any range of policies could grow out of it.

Hackett: In the context of the United States, how realistic is it to assume that media reform would generate more progressive politics or socially just policies? It is arguable that there is a rationalist bias in progressive thought on the media, which suggests that if only "the people" knew the truth, it would set them free? The concept of hegemony, which doesn't play a large role in your own writings, suggests otherwise.

What would you say to political and cultural pessimists, who doubt the possibility of mass-based, progressive, populist politics in the United States, who suspect that the masses could more easily be mobilized to fascism than to progressive political change, given the apparently deep level of nationalist identification with U.S. imperial power, post-9/11 security paranoia, and much else in American political culture? What is the potential to actually mobilize people around media reform or any other progressive reform issue?

McChesney: I think that is a difficult question to answer. It's a hypothetical situation, to take the population of this country as it is today, and then just change the media so you have a nonprofit, noncommercial system with lots of local control and the like, and then ask, would that transform the people's consciousness. Would we suddenly have a high voter turnout, more political involvement, and commitment to getting rid of injustice? I doubt it. But it's such a hypothetical question because you would never get to a point of changing the system until it was part of a process, a movement of politicization.

So, a certain amount of political organization and activity and change in people's consciousness would be involved before you could have a reformed media system that might generate further progressive political outcomes. That sounds like dodging the question, but any other way to pose it paralyzes you. Perhaps for progressives in the United States and maybe all of the West, the idea that people can organize against powerful, entrenched interests and improve the situation has become lost to us because we haven't won anything significant for a generation or more. That defeatist mentality sees the internal barriers as so high that social change is really unthinkable, as people have internalized too many of the regime's values. My experience, and I don't want to exaggerate it, is that while problems of hegemony seem overwhelming in seminar rooms and bars when you're talking hypothetically, when you actually start doing the organizing out there, and people actually get a sense that they can change things for the better, then the problem doesn't seem so insoluble. You go from defeatism to optimism. It's not all or nothing; things can change.

Related to that, a lot of that defeatism is built on a particular vision of the human species—that we're basically consumers: that it goes in one end and out the other end, that what defines us and our motivations are the two ends of our body, and that everything we do is ultimately based on this narrowly crafted, self-interest, marginal utility model of the human race. That vision is very inaccurate. Only in times of depoliticization or social inactivity does it make more sense.

Strikingly though, in times of political activity, as we see this year in the United States, and as I have seen at other moments of my life, especially in media, people can see themselves not simply as consumers but rather as citizens. That shift means, in the case of the media, that people can appreciate the social value of a particular type of program, even if they don't watch it themselves, and that the funding in a society for media shouldn't be exclusively determined by personal taste. To give an analogy, I personally rarely travel to a U.S. national park. In my limited free time, I'd rather go to Cleveland and watch a football game. Now, by this defeatist consumer mentality, that would be a clear sign according to "wise people" like George W. Bush and Milton Friedman that because I don't favor national parks, we may as well pave them over and build football stadiums, something I enjoy spending money on. But that would be a complete misreading of me. As a citizen, I support expanding national parks, and I'm willing to pay for them through taxes. I or my kids may never go to one, but it's a bigger, more important issue than me and my own children. I think that is where media activism takes off. People understand that there are bigger social issues that go beyond their personal consumption of the media. When that happens, it gets very exciting because then everything changes.

Hackett: You have written that a media-reform movement needs to be spearheaded by movements and organizations of the Left, since only they can develop a consistent analysis and strategy to confront the American media system's fundamental problems, primarily, commercial logic and corporate dominance. Yet, as you also note, a successful media-reform movement would need the support of social sectors far beyond the Left and, partly for that reason, needs to focus on "content-neutral" reforms. If so, that raises a host of strategic questions. Are there media-reform issues that span the political spectrum? Do we need a self-identified movement for media reform, or can it be achieved through the energies of existing movements making it their common, although secondary, concern, as you suggest in your books?

McChesney: Theoretically, you aren't likely to have a viable media-reform movement unless it is part of a broader politicization of society, with more popular involvement in politics. I doubt that media reform is a sufficiently strong issue to have legs on its own. At the same time, I think that a media-reform movement has to be autonomous; it just can't be a subset of broader political movements. We have learned in the United States—I think it's true worldwide—that you need organizations and individuals committed to working expressly on media reform. Why? Beside the fact that it's the only way it will get the attention it deserves, media issues can have a tremendous and nearly unique organizing potential. One reason is that it is a fairly heterogeneous area; in the United States, there are probably about forty different issues you could work on under the rubric of media reform. It's not like campaign-finance reform, where if you don't win a complete victory, the loopholes will be big enough to destroy whatever you have achieved. By contrast, in media reform you can win incremental issues. You can win a fight on low-power FM radio, on copyright, on media ownership, and you can preserve it; it can't be taken from you. That's one great thing about it as an organizing tool. Or you can get allies to work on specific fights that go outside the progressive constituency. Even people who don't share the progressive values that I and most media reform activists have are often very interested in issues. They don't like their children marinated in advertising, they don't like the lack of localism in their radio, for example, and they will come aboard and work, sometimes aggressively, on certain issues. They might not support the entirety of media reform; they may only agree on three of forty possible issues, but you can work with them on those three and not on the other thirty-seven. So, in sum, you need a distinct media-reform movement, but ultimately it's got to be part of a broader movement.

Hackett: Can media reform successfully mobilize people when so many people are drawn to media activism, if at all, around issues of media representation of their own particular group? Don't they need to see something for themselves?

McChesney: Good point; it has always been difficult taking what seems like an abstract set of issues and making them resonate with people's immediate concerns. But it has been most heartening this year in the United States to see how well people do get it as soon as they understand that it is a legitimate issue and more than a purely academic concern. If I say to someone in a community, instead of having three companies own the twenty-five radio stations in your town—with all three companies based in New York or Texas and all three bombarding you with lots of advertising and with the same fare that they broadcast on their hundreds of other stations—wouldn't it be cool if all twenty-five of those stations were owned by twenty-five different people, and because of that, logically many of them would come from this community. To start from that assumption doesn't say anything about how the content is going to change necessarily, but what's been striking this past year is how many people are smart enough to say it would likely get better if we did that, that it couldn't get worse.

Hackett: Is there a political barrier to left-oriented parties taking up the issue of democratic media reform? They may fear losing some of whatever access they have to corporate media. You yourself have written about how Labour in Britain, for instance, has retreated on this issue in exchange, in effect, for more favorable treatment by Murdoch's press.

McChesney: I think that parties and progressive political groups need to approach this issue because it is important in a variety of ways. It's not just that it affects them negatively if there is bad corporate-run media, although that's the most pressing thing, but also that plain lousy journalism and lousy media in general undermine the character of society. That's why this issue cuts across political lines. It's a pressing issue, like the environment. A progressive party not only has to weigh that issue on a political calculus but also has to understand that if we do nothing about the environment, our species isn't going to be here in a hundred years. Media is similar to that; it doesn't have quite the effects on our physical environment that ecological policies do, but it certainly does on our political environment. So, it has to be an issue; it can't be ignored, and it's not going to get better on its own. The question is how you raise the issue and how you approach it. Until this year, I would have said that politicians raising this issue were sacrificing themselves because it seemed like there was very little gain and a lot of cost. That political equation has apparently reversed now, a situation unthinkable a year ago.

Hackett: You are referring to the upsurge of media activism in the United States during 2003, in response to the proposed further relaxation of media ownership ceilings by the Federal Communications Commission (FCC), changes that would increase the levels of permissible control of national broadcasting markets by a single company and allow much greater cross-media ownership in individual cities. That upsurge was evident in the November 2003 Media Reform conference in Madison, Wisconsin, which was initiated by the organization Free Press, which you cofounded with journalist John Nichols. Can you update us on your views of the prospects for media reform in light of these developments?

McChesney: In fall 2002, if someone had said that there is going to be a massive uprising against relaxing media ownership rules in the United States, I would have said I didn't see how it could happen, for all the reasons that you and I know so well: it's not an issue people know about, it's not covered in the news media, all the politicians are on the take, most people don't care about it, it's too abstract, people are happy watching reality TV shows, and so on. All of these reasons have evidence of some kind to support them, but what's happened since January 2003 has really been quite extraordinary by historical standards. By our most recent count, more than three million people have written, telephoned, e-mailed, or signed a petition protesting the relaxation of media ownership rules. Members of congress say this is the second most widely discussed issue among constituent feedback this year, behind only the Iraq war. From my own experience, I doubt issues of media policy or ownership have ranked in the top hundred in the U.S. Congress before 2003; the amount of air you have to put in a truck's tire would have ranked higher. So, it's a world historic event in U.S. media politics.

Hackett: What do you think would account for that? Is it because politically conservative groups are behind it as well as progressives?

McChesney: Not entirely, although that was one key factor. As a historian, I can say that twenty years from now, it is going to be easier to look back and see what crucial pressures were really driving this, and it's difficult to give a nuanced perspective now. But I think that clearly what has happened in radio in this country over the last seven years, the absolute destruction of radio broadcasting with the relaxation of media ownership rules in 1996, was foundational to getting a lot of people upset and willing to move. A lot of people have become aware that the Telecommunications Act relaxed the ownership rules so a company could own as many stations as it wanted nationally up to eight in the largest market, and the FCC has been lax in its regulations, so some companies get away with owning a lot more local stations that that legal limit. And we have seen a total turnover in U.S. radio broadcasting in the past seven years. I don't know the exact percentage now, but about two thirds or more of all radio stations have been sold to a handful of giant companies dominating radio broadcasting; usually two or three companies dominate each local market, with the maximum being six, seven, or eight stations each. The amount of advertising shot up to about seventeen to nineteen minutes an hour, instead of twelve minutes, which it was a decade ago. The amount of localism has nosedived, and there is much less local coverage because companies can make so much money using standardized fare out of the central office. So, radio, which should be our most decentralized, or open, accessible medium, has become arguably our most centralized due to this corrupt policy change, one that was never debated in Congress or committee, that was just snuck into the bill by a powerful lobby.

Hackett: And you think that may be what mobilized people who never considered themselves part of the Left?

McChesney: Clearly, because that is a tangible way for people to get it. You can say, look, these guys want to do to television and newspapers what they have done to radio, which is not popular. I think this is one of the reasons why conservative groups really jumped on this issue, like the National Rifle Association, like some of the religious groups, like [conservative columnist] William Safire of the *New York Times*. The idea of having huge companies, especially out-of-town companies, gobbling up all the media in towns like

Jackson, Mississippi, and one or two companies owning the newspapers, all the TV and radio stations, the billboard concession, the cable system—a lot of people just said this doesn't make sense. There is no justification for that in conservative philosophy.

Hackett: Because they themselves take the idea of competition and the free market seriously, perhaps that was a mobilizing factor too?

McChesney: Yes, and one other thing: the power of the media companies that get these licenses, their power to get these policies enacted on their behalf and with impunity, was always predicated on the fact that no one else knows about these debates; they were top secret, off limits. The general public was led to believe that our media system was somehow a natural order of things. As soon as people realized that a government policy had let a company have all these radio licenses, that it wasn't natural law, then it was like everything changed.

There were other issues too. On the Left, the crucial issue mobilizing millions of people on media issues was the war in Iraq because President Bush was advocating and selling this war in fall 2002 and spring 2003. He was making a number of emotive arguments about Saddam Hussein and the Iraqi government with regard to weapons of mass destruction and links to terrorism, as well as insinuating that there were links to the 9/11 attacks. I think a number of Americans were greatly disturbed that the news media weren't doing a very sufficient job of challenging the administration to provide evidence to support these claims, that in fact several news media were rabid proponents of the president's position and going out of their way to crush any critical opposition to it, specifically Rupert Murdoch's News Corporation, which owns Fox News; Infinity Radio, which is owned by Viacom; Clear Channel Radio; and Cumulus, the radio chain that banned the Dixie Chicks for being critical of the president.

So, I think the press coverage had a lot to do with the media activism because activists concerned about this war were seeing that the companies that were most rabidly prowar, that were not letting dissidents have a voice, were the same companies leading the lobby for loosening up media ownership rules so they could buy more and more media. Activists said, we shouldn't let these people who do such a lousy job control even more of our media. It really led moveon.org, Code Pink, and a number of other progressive groups to make the issue of stopping the FCC from relaxing media ownership regulations a high priority.

There were other bases for the campaign that emerged in 2003. You also had a "good government" element that was just concerned about the decline in the quality of journalism and civic life and connected it to these big media conglomerates' having so much power. You saw organizations like Consumers Union, or a better example still, Common Cause, a large civic organization, which had never shown an interest in media issues in its history, suddenly making this the number-one issue they were working on, and it wasn't a leadership initiative; it was membership driven. Hundreds of thousands of members were getting alarmed and wanted to get involved. In fact, the head of Common Cause told me that in her experience, no other issue had galvanized her membership so much. It wasn't simply progressives or liberals or even moderates; it cut across the political spectrum and also included people who weren't very political. Musicians, artists, and music fans jumped on this issue because the enormous wave of ownership consolidation in radio has led to what many people see as more commercialism, less localism, less on-air musical diversity—to a standardization of content. No one liked what happened to radio after 1996, whatever his or her political views.

When elements of the political Right became very active to oppose the rule changes, that was the interesting wrinkle. Rank-and-file conservatives around the country shared that concern with everyone else. The National Rifle Association accordingly became one of the most active groups opposed to the FCC in 2003, not because the leadership initiated such opposition, but because the rank and file did.

Hackett: Speaking more broadly, in our research on democratic media activism, Bill Carroll and I identify four main fields of activity: building "independent" media; finding the openings for progressive messages within existing corporate media; developing audiences' capacity to deconstruct and critique media institutions and texts, through, for example, media education or culture jamming; and building coalitions for reforming the very structure of the media system and state policy toward it.

So, as we see it, media reform is one aspect, although a key one, of a broader process of media democratization. Do you agree that these cover the main aspects of media democratization? What do you see as the relationship between them and their relative priorities?

McChesney: I think you are right that they do all go together. The focus of our new organization Free Press is primarily one aspect of that, which is to put out proactive policies for structural reform of the system, then to go out and try to mobilize broad popular support for them on the principle that organized people are the only way to beat organized money. Be proactive and try to change things for the better—regarding ownership, public broadcasting, copyright, on a whole range of issues. To those who want to do independent media, who don't really care about policy, I'd say, fair enough, we need independent and alternative media, but don't kid yourself. This system is entirely based on policies. The marginalization of independent alternative media isn't happening because your ideas are naturally alternative or unpopular but because the system is built to make it very difficult for alternative media to survive. It's built to satisfy the interests of the dominant firms, and you've got to stand up and fight for the heart of the system, or else you're just accepting the corrupt system that makes you marginal. I think independent media is really a key part of the policy movement. In effect, a number of the policies are all about trying to find ways to creatively subsidize and enhance an independent, nongovernmental, noncommercial media sector. So, I think it's related that way.

Also, as an ancillary effect, the more success we have raising hell trying to change the current commercial system, the more media companies are going to be paying attention to this. They'll look out their windows and see a hundred thousand people protesting rather than eight lawyers in the hallway. It can only improve the quality of the system from within. Most importantly, to the extent that we are able to generate viable independent noncommercial media, we are going to be able to really strongly influence the nature of the media market in a given country.

Hackett: You do argue that media reform is pivotal to media democratization.

McChesney: If we don't structurally change our media system everything else is bullshit. It's just not going to happen. To be sure, what can happen is this: in times of social upheaval, when progressive forces get much more powerful and a branch of the elites may be much more sympathetic, then even within the commercial system, you might get an improvement—more movies, more sympathetic music. You saw that in the United States in the 1960s and 1970s. So yes, there is wiggle room in that regard, but I don't think that is sufficient. The limits to how far you can go are narrower today in some ways than they were thirty years ago. We need desperately to have a structure that does justice to the full range and talents of the whole population, not just of those who own these companies.

Hackett: To conclude, do you see the possibility of international coalitions for democratic communication or of working at the level of international policy making around media reform?

McChesney: I think that it's indispensable, mandatory. My emphasis was working on the national level in the United States, but already, just starting the group Free Press and working this year, our biggest campaign outside of the immediate FCC media ownership was with regard to the Free Trade of the Americas and global-trade deals, because if these deals go through as their proponents hope, they may well include provisions that will override any national efforts to regard media as cultural institutions and not simply as commercial entities. That will undercut all of our work at the national level in the United States or your work in Canada or that of anyone working anywhere. This is a global fight. We all have to come together here to make sure that media are not simply subsumed within the global capitalist market system and treated as just another commodity. If we lose that fight, all our other fights are irrelevant.

NOTE

1. Interview conducted and edited by Robert A. Hackett, October 2003.

12

Globalization, Communication, Democratization: Toward Gender Equality

Annabelle Sreberny

> Promote gender equality and empowerment.
>
> —Goal 3, Millennium Development Goals, 2000

> The politics of recognition is but the handmaiden of the politics of redistribution.
>
> —Walby 2001, 129

Analysis of communications and democratization tends to divide into two broad bodies of work. One nostalgically laments the demise of Western democracies with their declining rates of political participation, weak citizenship, and conglomeratization of media corporations and the consequent flattening out and "dumbing down" of the ever-elusive public sphere. The second focuses on the obstacles on the road to the democratization of authoritarian polities and the acquiescence or complicity of media in the maintenance of nondemocratic political structures; here, often, the public sphere is both the lamp that lights the way to democracy and the idealized marker of its achievement. In both, the national framing of big media and strongish states is taken for granted, democracy is essentially constructed as a set of formal practices, and the public sphere is a knowable phenomenon. Both are well represented in this volume.

There is, however, another orientation to the terrain of communication and democratization. This explores alternative communications practices to the corporate and mainstream, analyzes the rise of new social movements as articulations of the process of democratization, and takes seriously the new transnational spaces of political and communicative activism, thus challenging the territorially bounded frames of reference that still prevail in communication studies. There are growing clusters of work around "radical media" (Downing et al. 2001), "alternative media" (Atton 2001), "citizen's media" (Rodriguez 2001), and "small media" (Sreberny-Mohammadi and Mohammadi 1985), as well as around transnational networks (Castells 1996), transnational social movements (Smith, Chatfield, and Pagnucco 1998; Cohen and Rai 2000), and global political activism (Naples and Desai 2002). Yet, still the significance of communications is omitted from transnational political analysis, while descriptions of communicative practices often evacuate their political implications.

Media are many things, including technologies, tools for communication, spaces for the articulation of political voice, as well as autonomous arenas of struggle. I utilize what I call the four Rs of democratization—rights, representation, recognition, and redistribution—to understand contemporary processes of civil society building and its global extensions. I then explore the complex triumvirate of globalization, communication, and democratization specifically in relation to gender equality and empowerment, the United Nations' third millennium goal. I provide a historical analysis of the development of global women's networks, especially in the substantive areas of media and communications technologies, and examine their current politics in relation to the World Summit on the Information Society (WSIS). Using this substantive body of material, I flesh out a terrain of missing argument in the debates about communication and democratization. I argue that a gender lens is crucial to the articulation of a more holistic analysis of global issues that includes the democratization of communication, the communication of democracy, and the emancipation of the world's women.

RIGHTS, REPRESENTATION, RECOGNITION, AND REDISTRIBUTION: AN EXTENDED VISION OF DEMOCRATIZATION[1]

Rights are central to democracy, especially of the liberal variety, as well as to global processes of democratization. Indeed, democracy is measured not only by formal practices of accountable government and free and fair elections at the state level but also by the practice of a panoply of civil and political rights and of associational autonomy known by the shorthand of "civil society" (Potter et al. 1997, 4). Such rights include the obvious, specifically political rights to vote and to stand for elective office, the more communicative right to free expression, and the social right to form independent associations (Dahl 1989; Potter et al. 1997). Indeed, participation and integration are increasingly seen as part of an expanded sense of citizenship that goes well beyond the formal and the national to embrace many forms of activism and to foster a sense of global solidarity (van Steenburgen 1994; Falk 1994).

The international debates around rights are still strongly waged. Are they universal or West-centric? Do they value the monadic individual over collectivities? Does law increasingly recognize firms as economic actors with rights but not cultural groups, minority languages, marginalized peoples? How is the international architecture of rights to be made to work? What are the prohibitions that prevent abuse of rights, and what are the penalties when that happens? The recent establishment of the International Criminal Court in The Hague immediately saw the global hegemon, the United States, ask for certain exemptions—so might can avoid rights and responsibilities rather than acknowledge them.

The rights debates are particularly relevant in two areas: the contentious debate about communication rights in the information society and the acknowledgement of gendered rights, where there has been significant progress. Communication rights have been a central theme within the debates around the WSIS to be held in Tunis in 2005. In a manner redolent of debates in the late 1950s about the role of media in development and the 1970s debates around the New World Information and Communication Order (NWICO), a technological determinism that sees information technologies as simple solutions to a narrowly defined notion of development has been articulated in WSIS debates dominated by the interests of big states and big business. Civil society organizations have organized around the struggle for communication rights that does not separate information technologies from media and that continues to link a set of rights together, including linguistic rights, freedom of speech, intellectual property, and public-sphere concerns. Many constituencies, including indigenous people, labor, and gender groups, are involved. The Communication Rights in the Information Society (CRIS) campaign had a powerful presence at WSIS in Geneva in December 2003, and its outputs include a Charter on Communication Rights as well as a guide to communications rights (http://www.crisinfo.org, accessed October 7, 2004). Here I focus on the gender elements of this debate and connect this dimension with longer struggles to articulate women's rights.

Even liberal democracies have been intransigent toward women's demands for full citizenship, leading many analysts to argue that "the sovereign nation-state has not been associated with democracy for women" (Dickenson 1997, 107). Women's "democratic deficit at the level of the nation-state" (Dickenson 1997, 111) has been taken up both at a macrolevel global feminist network of solidarity that has transformed liberal democracy and also through the development of microlevel, grassroots "communities of fate" (Dickenson 1997, 111) below the nation-state level. Long and difficult struggles by women in local, national, regional, and international fora have meant that specific gender rights were finally adopted into the panoply of human rights adopted in Vienna in 1993. Concerted political and policy-oriented activity by women over many decades has achieved the recognition by the global community that gender equality is central to the development process (Steans 2002). Targets for universal access to basic education and for reducing maternal mortality were set in Cairo in 1994; the development summit in Copenhagen in 1995 added targets about primary health care and malnutrition, and World Social Summit on Development +5 in Johannesburg in 2000 reaffirmed the development goal of universal primary education for boys and girls alike by 2015. By 2003, 171 countries had ratified the UN Convention on the Elimination of All Forms of Discrimination against Women (CEDAW), which requires governments to take action to promote and protect the rights of women. The Fourth World Conference on Women in Beijing in 1995 produced a platform for action that highlighted twelve areas where action is needed in order to achieve gender equality, rearticulated in the Beijing Plus-Five international platform in 2000. Global campaigns fight against trafficking in women and children (www.hrw.org/about/projects/traffcamp/intro.html, accessed October 7, 2004), while others focus on various forms of violence against women (http://web.amnesty.org/actforwomen/index-eng, accessed October 7, 2004)

The concept of human development reworked a vision of development equated solely with economic growth to a focus on people and has been further refined to include a gender-related development index (GDI) and also a gender empowerment measure (GEM), both of which include indices of women's participation in economic and political life (hdr.undp.org).

Thus, in formal terms at least, through their articulation in programs and plans for action at various UN conferences and the commitment of governments toward achieving these goals, a certain global consensus on gender equality and women's human rights has been achieved (UN Development Fund for Women [UNIFEM] 2000). All global issues, including economic development, democratization, and cultural production, have gender implications, and globalization cannot be understood without acknowledging gender inequalities.

The second R, representation, always carries its double meaning of both political process and of mediation. The political struggles alluded to above clearly include moves toward the global enfranchisement of women, toward increasing the proportion of elected women in parliaments, and toward tackling the glass ceilings of limited political advancement for women. Sometimes, too, better-functioning democracy needs to adjust the mechanisms of formal political participation in order to improve representation. UNIFEM's 2003 analysis of "the progress of the world's women" suggested that the rise in women's share of parliamentary seats was mainly due to special measures such as quotas and not connected to the relative wealth or poverty of a nation.

In the sense of representation as mediation, global media concentration clearly poses a threat to cultural diversity and political empowerment. In many countries, there are ongoing struggles against sexist and distorted depictions of women, of gender relations, and of sexual expression in mainstream media. Another strategy is to develop alternative media to represent ourselves and to use communications technologies as tools of democratization to foster the diversity and participation blocked by the professional and political dynamics of the mainstream. Representing ourselves in text and image, finding a voice, may well lead to better political representation by giving women the confidence, articulacy, and support needed to run for office.

The third R, recognition, is essentially about mutuality—a dialectic through which one is recognized and knows that the other recognizes one. We hear each other, exist together, coexist. The significance of women's media developments and information and communication technology (ICT) use is to develop spaces where women can talk among themselves, find a voice, articulate concerns and demands, and receive recognition from each other, as well as mutual support in the many struggles beyond the politics of sorority. As A. Honneth (2001) argues, "The first and crucial claim of the dialectic of intersubjective recognition . . . is that the formation of one's being as a human being with particular characteristics, traits, qualities and features, in short the establishment of one's self understanding, is inextricably dependent on recognition or affirmation on the part of others."

There is a growing articulation of the relationship between recognition and redistribution, based on the understanding that struggles for political and cultural rights are dependent upon certain material rights. In the speedup of processes of globalization, the gaps between the richest and poorest in the world have never been more evident and are partly made more transparent through globalized flows of information gathering and dissemination. The UN Human Development Report reminds us that "amid the wealth of new economic opportunities, 2.8 billion people still live on less than $2 a day. The richest 1% of the world's people receives as much income each year as the poorest 57%. And in many parts of sub-Saharan Africa the lives of the poorest people are getting worse" (UNDP 2002, 2). The billions of pounds spent on the war with Iraq could have been spent on primary schooling, clean water, basic sanitation, adequate food, and disease prevention. It costs only about £2 billion (about U.S. $3.6 billion) to feed all the world's starving for a year, and £1 billion to provide clean water for five hundred thousand people.

Globalization theorizing has been pretty gender-blind, while gender inequality remains a profound structuring element within most societies, often exacerbated by global processes. In economic terms, only 1 percent of the world's assets are in the name of women; 70 percent of people living in abject poverty, on less than $1 per day, are women; women are still earning only 78 percent of what men earn, and women also remain significantly underrepresented in higher-paid, higher-prestige sectors of the workforce. In political terms, of the 186 UN-recognized countries, only 11 are headed by women; in only 8 countries do women hold 30 percent or more of the seats in parliament. Only 13 percent of members of national parliaments world-wide are women; only 7 percent of the world's cabinet ministers are women. In 1995, Sweden became the first country to have an equal number of women and men in ministerial posts, but that has since dropped below parity for women. In social terms, 543 million of the 854 million illiterate adults in the world (2000) are women, and 183 million of the 325 million children not in school are girls. In many countries the targets for reduction of infant, child, and maternal mortality have slipped, and a growing number of women are infected with HIV/AIDS (*Human Development Report 2001* 2001).

Identity politics are not simply new; nor are they at odds with struggles for material redistribution. Indeed, improved social and economic practices tend to foster political democracy, and the normative idea that members of a democracy must have the chance for social esteem, for recognition of achievement, can be the basis for demands for redistribution. The debates about the information society in preparation for the WSIS summit in Geneva in December 2003 continually prioritized access. Without better distribution, if not redistribution, of global technological resources, the entire WSIS debate makes little sense. As S. Walby (2001, 129) has written, in a sentence that acts as the epigram of this chapter, "the politics of recognition is but the handmaiden of the politics of redistribution."

Thus, rights, representation, recognition, and redistribution can be thought of as the four Rs of democratization, and women's activities around these four elements have been developed through a complex network of organizations that articulate the local, national, and global spaces of political participation. Women's media and communications activities are significant organizational and cultural activities in their own right, as well as the spaces in which further articulation of concerns can take place. Furthermore, this articulation is no longer constrained by the national political environment, not always the most conducive space for women. The virtual linkages of new communications technologies have helped to expand the spatialization of democracy. The burgeoning number of nongovernmental organizations (NGOs) and civil society organizations (Boulding 1988) are often active at the most localized, grassroots level and coordinate activities at the global level, functioning at many "levels" at once. Indeed, the multiple spatialities of activism confound any simple hierarchy of these political arenas: the local is not always the place to start activities; the global is not more important because it is the biggest arena; sometimes achievements at the global level can have profound impacts at the local level; and sometimes the national level seems to be most intransigent to change.

So, globalization has had contradictory impacts in relation to gender. On the one hand, the greater transparency and emergent global criteria appear to take gender more seriously, and some regulatory regimes, at least at the global level, are more gender sensitized. On the other hand, there is ongoing differential access by gender to power and resources, often exacerbated by global processes. Among the Millennium Development Goals (MDGs), agreed to by world leaders in September 2000, Goal 3 calls on nations specifically to promote gender equality and empower women, and there are gender implications in most of the other goals.

Yet, if women do not continue to highlight the gendered implications of global issues, few men will. N. Hertz (2002) noted that at the World Economic Forum and World Trade Organization (WTO) debates, concern about gender was hardly evident. Women have been actively pursuing an agenda for gender equity for decades, if not centuries. Much of the achievement of women's transnational movements has been to build the consensus and discourse at the global level, among institutions of the UN system, about gender equity and the engendering of global issues.

FROM THE GRASSROOTS TO OPTIC FIBER: WOMEN NETWORK GLOBALLY

The significance of transnational feminist activities has been recognized by social theorists as prefiguring the "network society" (Castells 1996), as exemplifying "globalization from below" (Falk 1994), as evidence of the existence of "global civil society" (Sreberny 1998), and as a prime example of "global advocacy networks" (Keck and Sikkink 1998). Women's movements are a key exemplar in the body of work on "new" social movements, despite enjoying long histories. In the field of communications and information, women's alternative networks have been busy for decades building up from grassroots organizations into national and regional structures to create a "network of networks" (Sreberny-Mohammadi 1998), "transnational feminist networks" (Moghadam, forthcoming) or "a world of networks in which there are many leaders but no one person or group who does everything" (Walker 2002).

Communication is fundamental to these processes: as practices of networking, of articulation, of political action. Media and information technologies are also central as the tools and infrastructures of connectivity, as spaces for debate, as channels of voice. Mediated spaces are where the four Rs are articulated and how they are spread.

Women have long recognized and utilized the power of new technologies, including the Internet, e-mail, and fax, together with older media such as print, "snail mail," and the telephone to build networks of solidarity around events and issues, potentially connecting grassroots women's organizations to centers of decision making and facilitating the participation of ordinary people not only in local and national civic politics but also in global issues as members of transnational social movements (Sreberny 1998; Harcourt 1999).

Women have been active builders of transnational networks. In building networks, and networks of networks, global feminism has developed ways of linking grassroots, local, national, regional, and global levels of activity together. I'll just pause to note that the word "women" always signifies both too little and too much, and there is a danger of a too-easy essentialism that claims women's similarity across socioeconomic, political, and cultural boundaries. It is vital to remember that "the shaping of gender identity and the ways women experience subordination are connected and mediated by other core variables such as race, class, age and generation, sexual orientation, history, culture, and colonialism" (Riano 1994, 35). Transnational processes have thrown up debates—still ongoing—about resource and power differentials among the world's women, and the power differentials between women need to be addressed as much as those between women and men. Agonistic communication is part and parcel of the internal democratization of women's networks, working through concerns about race and class, about Western privilege and cultural assumptions, constituting a key element of the internal politics of networking (Rai 2003).

REPRESENTING OURSELVES: BUILDING NETWORKS

Women's media and communications have been among the substantive foci of women's networks for many reasons. Gender critiques of mainstream mediated content led to demands for more adequate representation, for better recognition of women's concerns and viewpoints, for redistribution of decision-making roles and more gender-equitable employment practices, and for communication rights (communicative versions of the four Rs). Women have developed many forms of alternative media as channels and means of expression of women's voices, as the practices of recognition.

Communications has been the focus of a great many organizations and the practice of all, so that media-centric groups have become central to the general process of networking. Many networks have had a specifically media focus, including the Caribbean Association for Feminist Research and Action (CAFRA), Trinidad and Tobago; Women's Action for New Directions (WAND), Barbados; SisterLink, Australia; Institute for Women's Studies in the Arab World (IWSAW), Lebanon; and FEMNET at African Women's Development and Communication Network, Kenya. Organizations such as the International Women's Tribune Center (IWTC) in New York were set up as central clearinghouses of information about women's activities globally. IWTC also publishes the *Tribune* and manages Women, Ink, a marketing and distribution service funded by UNIFEM (www.unifem.undp.org, accessed October 25, 2004), which subsidizes distribution to the South by sale of publications in the North. Isis International, operating out of Santiago, Chile, and Manila, Philippines (www.isiswomen.org), was established as an NGO in 1974 as a women's information and communication service, supporting "the empowerment and full participation of women in development processes through the formation of networks and channels of communication and information." Isis has a global network, and its resource centers house a range of publications and audio-visual materials produced by southern women; as with so many of these projects, it has readily migrated onto the Web, making its resources even more widely available.

There are regional networks like Asia Network of Women in Communication (ANWIC) in New Delhi, which publishes *Impact* and aims "to mobilize Asian women, through communication, to achieve a more equitable and just social order recognizing the diversity present in the region." There are also networks operating within a religiocultural milieu like Women Living Under Muslim Law (www.wluml.org), an international network of solidarity that publishes a quarterly news sheet, as well as monographs on varied topics, including violence against women, reproductive rights, and disenfranchisement. They have strong links with women's groups in the North (Women against Fundamentalism in the United Kingdom) that focus on the dilemmas of women in minority ethnic groups whose voices are often not heard by the dominant culture.

Much of this information and communication networking emerged from the UN World Conference on Women in Nairobi in 1975, which established the Women's Decade. WOMENET, consisting of ten key networks based in nine countries, was established with the express purpose of sharing research and exchanging information around the world quickly. WOMENET regularly produced a wealth of materials including quarterly journals, news magazines, and newsletters; books, booklets, and comics; posters and postcards; resource kits, manuals, and training resources; occasional papers, research papers, and bibliographies; and news features and videos. The facilities used to produce this formidable array of materials at the time varied widely from the most basic (hands, pens and pencils, typewriters) to the most high-tech (computer, VCR, photocopier). Distribution channels also varied widely from domestic and international mail and delivery services, cars, telephones, and meetings and workshops, to fax, modem, e-mail, and the Internet.

The Association for Progressive Communications' Women's Networking Support Programme (APCWNSP) began in 1993 (www.apcwomen.org) as part of the preparation for the Fourth World Conference on Women. They trained women in the use of e-mail and the Web and raised awareness about the urgency of broadening media and communications concerns to include the new ICTs, addressing women's access to ICTs and women's participation in the determination of how such technologies are designed and deployed. The Beijing conference was a formative moment; the change of venue for the NGO forum triggered concerns about the possibility for effective lobbying at the official conference, prohibited meaningful plenary sessions, and offered limited telecommunications facilities. Global women produced a powerful response. The latent network structure was galvanized into action, including the Global Fax-net (Gittler 1996; Frankson 1996; Harcourt 1999). During the conference, APCWNSP implemented a women-led initiative that provided Internet access, electronic communications, and information services and support to over thirty thousand women attending the conference and the NGO forum. One of the main goals of this initiative was, as APCWNSP says, to "demonstrate to other women this new technology was appropriate for and could be maintained by women."

Many further transborder debates and consultations among women have since happened online in international "virtual fora" like Global Knowledge 97, Beijing Plus-Five, and the Women 2000 conference. In such online discussions and elsewhere, many barriers to actually achieving the goals set in Beijing have been articulated. These include, among others, enduring cultural values, societal norms, and religious beliefs that place lower value on the contributions, work, ideas, and lives of women and girls; the problem that women and gender equality are poorly represented in decision making and policy making; and the fact that the impacts of trade liberalization, globalization, and privatization are contradictory and uneven, with disproportionate numbers of women being negatively affected.

REPRESENTING OURSELVES: WOMEN IN MEDIA

For many decades, also, women have voiced specific concerns about the media, including the stereotyped and traditional images of both women and men; the huge amount of sexist and pornographic imagery available, and the invisibility of women in news stories. Media was one of the focal points of the 1995 Beijing process, and in 2003 the UN Commission on the Status of Women renewed its concerns about the processes and content of global media (www.un.org/womenwatch/daw/egm/media2002; ods-dds-ny.un.org/doc/UNDOC/GEN/N02/760/05/PDF/N0276005.pdf?OpenElement; both accessed October 25, 2004).

One suggested solution has been to improve the gender balance in employment. Attempts have been made to compile data about women's employment in the media, yet there remains an acute lack of empirical data, even from Western industrial societies. Some suggest that increasing the number of women employed in the media does not in itself translate into qualitative differences in programming or a radically altered news agenda of priorities. In Asia, the growing number of women journalists "has not made a significant change in the content, style or presentation of information. News decisions are still made by men even if news is increasingly reported and edited by women. . . . [T]he employment of women has not radically altered news agendas or priorities" (Balakrishnan 1994, 42) So, gender equity in employment can be a useful goal, "a 50% ideal women constituency in the industry" (Balakrishnan 1994, 45), but one that needs to be operationalized at every level and in every area of media employment.

The concern about stereotypes has focused on the narrowness of the range of representations of women in the media and sexually objectifying or violent gender imagery—women as objects of the male gaze, male sexuality, and male violence. An important argument is that such concerns are not about censorship but about human rights, including the right to be represented appropriately. In regard to information genres, such as news, there is another set of concerns that center on the question, where are the women? Stories about women are rarely treated as newsworthy; news is urban-centric and women are still sidelined into stereotyped roles with far fewer women than men presenting or appearing in factual programming. It is not that there are definable women's issues but rather that media should try to reflect women's perspectives on all issues. Women are everywhere, and women's perspectives in regard to political and economic, indeed all, issues must be heard. Another argument is that it is often the "invisible barriers" of attitudes, biases, and presumptions that hinder women, so assertiveness training and support groups within organizations can help women feel less isolated and alienated and empower them to try to act differently and produce difference. Women's professional organizations such as the International Association of Women in Radio and Television (IAWRT) network (www.iawrt.org) also provide international solidarity and support.

These arguments have been articulated for a long time, and as one indication of their ongoing significance, two new academic journals, the *International Feminist Journal of Politics* and *Feminist Media Studies*, focus in different ways on analyses of these processes.

REPRESENTING OURSELVES: WOMEN'S ALTERNATIVE MEDIA

Deciding to "represent ourselves," women have actively developed many forms of media appropriate to local needs and circumstances. Such media include the following.

Alternative publications have been created, including newspapers, journals, magazines, and newsletters, as well as occasional monographs and leaflets. By 1990, Isis International already had a directory called *Third World Women's Publications* that listed over three hundred publications.

Particularly influential were *Sister* (Namibia), *Speak* (South Africa), *Asmita* (Nepal), and *Tamania Mars* (Morocco) (Lewis 1993). The latter began in 1983 as a magazine collective by women from a left-wing political party, was organized democratically, and published articles by men. It established a rallying point to fight against patriarchy, specifically the personal statutes of Moroccan law, and worked for human rights and a more just and egalitarian society. It was the catalyst for discussions on the origins of women's subordination, carried out surveys, discussed previously taboo topics such as prostitution and repudiation, and examined the broader contexts of family, the economy, education, and law. Its work culminated in the establishment of a Women's Action Union in fifteen locations across Morocco, and it inspired the establishment of other publications such as *Nissa al Maghrib* (Morocco), *Nissa* (Tunisia), and *Fippo* (Senegal) (Lewis 1993).

A number of alternative women's press services supportive of a feminist press have developed around the world, including *DepthNews* in Asia, the *Women's Feature Service* based in New Delhi (www.wfsnews.org), which grew out of Inter Press Service, *WINGS* in the United States (www.wings .org), and a women's news agency, *FEMPRESS*, in Chile (www.fempress.cl). *Women's ENews* provides e-mail news to subscribers (www.womens enews.org).

Alternative broadcasting, film, and video have been used in many local contexts to help define women's and communities' identities, to develop skills and weaken fears, to remember, and to build for the future. Examples include video use by the Self-employed Women's Association (SEWA) from 1984 in India (www.videosewa.org) and video and radio among indigenous women in Bolivia and other parts of Latin America. The Feminist International Radio Endeavor (FIRE) in Costa Rica aimed to "give voice to those who never had one"; FIRE conceived of radio as a process of meeting, dialog, and participation with other women and puts great store in the transformational power of women's personal testimonies (www.fire.or.cr).

One early model of good practice was the Development through Radio Project in Harare, Zimbabwe. In 1988 the Federation of African Media Women–Zimbabwe (www.famwz.org.zw) provided rural dwellers with access to national radio by participating in the preparation of development-oriented programs based on their own needs and priorities. The programs were part of the regular schedule of the national education-and-development channel of the Zimbabwe Broadcasting Corporation. Radio listening clubs, overwhelmingly female, were organized in rural areas to discuss imbalances in the distribution of and access to resources, from land to decision making, that women faced and to see if media could promote access to other resources. Clubs listened weekly to a half-hour tape compiled by the broadcasters from all the tapes submitted by the clubs. The clubs then recorded their own responses and the appropriate government minister, businessperson, or donor-agency representative was invited to respond to the issues raised. This process spawned over forty radio listening clubs, and the practice was extended to include men and adolescents also.

FROM NETWORKING TO WORKING THE NET

Increasingly, through processes of digitalization and deregulation and the growing convergence between media and "new" communications technologies, women's concerns about media have become refocused toward ICTs. Communications technologies are significant tools of networking, making transnational communication progressively faster, cheaper, and more accessible to more people, although many still remain outside their loops.

Networking has been hugely facilitated by access to the Internet and e-mail, making more specific links and targeted projects possible. The Women and Environment Network forged links between its Canadian base and African researchers; Mujer a Mujer, a Mexican-based women's collective concerned with free trade and structural adjustment, coordinated projects in Mexico, Canada, the United States, and Nicaragua. There are a variety of electronic bulletins (*Women Envision* by Isis; SEAWIN, South East Asian Women's Information Network in the Philippines) and countless feminist Listservs and discussion groups, many of which function under the aegis of the Association for Progressive Communication (APC; www.apc.org). A range of current 2004 projects for gender empowerment are celebrated on the Global Knowledge website (www.globalknowledge.org).

The strategic use of ICTs in support of women's actions and agendas does many things. It helps bring more attention to issues of concern to women. It reinforces solidarity campaigns. It can enhance traditional women's networking activities. It can be used to defend the rights of women to participate equally in civil and public life. The APC Women's Networking Support Programme (APC-WNSP) works with women and their organizations to integrate the use of ICTs in a way that strengthens women's capacities, improves information flows within their organizations, empowers individual members to do their work, and improves their organization's overall ability to achieve its strategic objectives. Strategic use also involves harnessing ICTs to organize and transform information into knowledge and communicating that knowledge to a wider global community to promote the development of cultures that are based on values of equality, freedom, and justice, including gender equality.

As I write in 2004, a major focus of debate and organization is the nature of the information society itself and its gendered dimensions, triggered by the WSIS held in Geneva in December 2003 with the final meeting to be held in Tunis in Autumn 2005 (www.geneva2003.org/wsis/indexa01.htm).

WSIS: GENDERING THE AGENDA ONCE AGAIN

In December 2003, representatives of global civil society and women's organizations once again tried to intervene in a global process, the WSIS, to get their agenda of issues concerning the role of communications in development included. Once again, the politics of the process threatened to overwhelm the politics of the content, which had to do with actually developing an accessible, transparent, and publicly accountable information environment that works for people and not simply for profit.

WSIS (discussed in detail by Ó Siochrú in chapter 14) is the first summit process to include civil society in the process of deliberation. There is no unanimously accepted definition of "civil society," but WSIS has started with a broad and inclusive definition and then defined "families" of civil society entities according to various criteria. The families were clustered into three main groupings: professionals (academia, science and technology, media, and creators and active promoters of culture), constituent bodies (cities and local authorities, trade unions, parliamentarians), and social groups (NGOs and social groups with special needs, such as youth, women, indigenous populations, the disabled, etc.; advocacy groups; and multistakeholder partnerships). One real danger was that women were positioned as a "special needs" group rather than a gendered perspective being used throughout the deliberative process. And while gender balance was acknowledged as important to the functioning of the process, that, too, is not identical with adopting a gender lens. So, women were once again involved in two parallel political processes: to be included in the WSIS process itself and to be able to help define and set the agenda of issues. And once again, women-centered and gender-focused activities were quite plentiful (if one knew where to look for them).

The WSIS Gender Caucus (www.genderwsis.org) was concerned to position gender issues in WSIS and to ensure that gender advocates were involved in every aspect of the planning and implementation of the WSIS. The Women of Uganda Network, WOUGNET, reflecting the increasingly important role of African women activists, has taken onboard the development of the gender caucus websites and hosted the electronic debates (www.wougnet.org/WSIS/genderstatement.html). Many of the preexisting organizations and networks described above were strongly involved, while others were established. Their aim is a world information society that contributes to human development and gender equality. So, once again there is no shortage of women's voices, analytic materials, detailed case studies, international organizational support, NGO involvement, and grassroots need. Can the international community hear? With what ears will it listen?

It seems clear that there is a need not only to analyze the specific relationships that women have with technology in different sectors and in different national and cultural locations, but also a more general need to understand the relationship between gender and communication. Norris (2001, 92) has noted that broader patterns of social stratification "shape not just access to the virtual world, but also full participation in other more common forms of information and communication technologies." In addition, both governments and industry are pushing the twin processes of digitalization and convergence, and it makes less and less sense to debate media in one forum and information technologies at another. Internet radio and video-streaming, broadband delivery, connectivity through television, and video-messaging on mobile telephony are the most obvious examples of converging technologies of diffusion that carry content and reach into households, and more is to come. Connectivity, content, and communications technologies are blurring together (Gallagher 2002). Thus, if women are to gain equality of design, access, use and representation, we need more coherent and more broadly conceptualized strategies.

GENDER, NET-WORK, AND AN INFORMATION SOCIETY

In all of these activities, communications technologies and content have not only been tools for the achievement of other issues, but issues in their own right. Volumes of work focus on gender and representation and recognition in the media sphere. In the ICT field, there has been an important shift from a concern about "women and technology" to trying to understand "gender in technology" (Faulkner 2001). Indeed, Sorensen argues that it is vital to understand how "gender and technology is co-constructed," which implies that "exclusion is not an accident, but it is not predetermined either" (2002, 11). Slowly a better understanding has developed of the need for a gendered lens in relation to ICTs in both developing and developed contexts.

APCWNSP has usefully identified the most critical concerns in achieving gender equality and women's empowerment in the areas of ICTs:[2]

Access and Control

Neither women's access to ICTs (the opportunity to use ICTs) nor their control of ICTs (the power to decide how ICTs are used and who has access) are equal to men's. Diverse factors, including gender discrimination in jobs and education, social class, illiteracy, geographic location (North or South, urban or rural), mean that most of the world's women still have no access to ICTs, and as information dynamics accelerate their migration toward the Internet, people without access are bound to suffer greater exclusion.

But connectivity in itself is not enough, since know-how is equally or more important than access itself. Criticism has been expressed of ICT development programs that concentrate excessively on access to technology and information sources, as though it were sufficient to provide women with computers and modems for them to resolve their development problems.

Education, Training, and Skill Development

Obstacles here include the continuing higher illiteracy rates for women in developing countries; that the design of software that often does not respond to the needs of women and girls; that training methods are often ad hoc, alienating and not customized to women's needs; and that there are profound gender and cultural barriers to women's access to careers in technology.

APCWNSP suggests, "Learning practices for women should be extended to girls and women, made gender-sensitive (making training women-specific, ensuring ongoing user support, and mentoring in the communities where women live) and deepened (for women as users, technicians, policy- and change-makers)."

Industry and Labor

The growing ICT sector in many parts of the world offers employment opportunities for women, particularly in data entry, medical transcription, geographical information systems, and software production. But there are still powerful gender and age factors at work.

Labor is highly sex-segregated with women occupying disproportionately the lowest paid and least secure jobs. And while telework, flexi-time, and work-from-home arrangements bring women into the labor force, these are areas where women have few rights, meager pay, and no health, social or job securities. Involvement in the wage economy in the public sphere doesn't necessarily alter the family division of labor, so that women find themselves with dual or triple burdens. Poor working conditions, long hours and monotonous work routines associated with ICTs are often injurious to women's health and also entail environmental and other costs. Employment issues of concern to women working in technology relate to contractual terms, intensification of workloads, wages, training, and health and safety such as VDU hazards and repetitive-strain injuries.

On average, women are paid 30 to 40 percent less than men for comparable work. A 2001 ILO employment report revealed a "digital gender gap" with women underrepresented in new technology employment in both developed and developing countries. It also found that patterns of gender segregation were being reproduced in the information economy: "Although pay inequality exists between those who have ICT skills and those who do not, pay polarization also exists within ICT use itself. This polarization is often gender-based" (cited in APCWNSP). But women in India have increased their share to 27 percent of professional jobs in the software industry, while in the 1990s thousands of women obtained jobs in the data-processing sector in the Caribbean and elsewhere. The age divide among women is serious. While young women with familiarity with English are picking up the new service-sector jobs, a vast number of over-thirty-five-year-olds have been made redundant, either because they are in declining industries or have outdated skills.

Content and Language

Issues around content include the language used, the culture encoded and the nature of the representations constructed. These resonate with older debates about stereotyping and sexism in media portrayal. On the web, the dominance of English is particularly pronounced. Language barriers to information access require the development of applications like multilingual tools and databases, interfaces for non-Latin alphabets, graphic interfaces for illiterate women, and automatic translation software.

Power and Decision Making

Although more women have jobs and expertise with ICTs, they lag behind men in access to decision making and control of resources. Whether at the global or national levels, women are underrepresented in all ICT decision-making structures, including policy and regulatory institutions, ministries responsible for ICTs, and boards and senior management of private ICT companies. Most often decision making in ICTs is treated as purely technical (for male experts), rather than political, where civil society viewpoints could and should be considered. Deregulation and privatization of the telecommunications industry is also making decision making in this sector less and less accountable to citizens and local communities, further compounding issues of decision making and control of resources for women. Again this parallels long-standing debates within media studies about the lack of women in the higher echelons of publishing, broadcasting, and cultural policy making (Gallagher 1995). Beale (1998) has argued that cultural policy itself should be seen as a technology of gender with a similar implication of coconstruction and antiessentialism that runs through Sorensen's argument.

Representation is important in creating the conditions and regulations that will enable women to maximize their possibilities of benefiting from ICTs, and ensuring the accountability of the institutions that are responsible for developing ICT policies. More egalitarian representation would help create the conditions and regulations to enable women to maximize their possibilities of benefiting from ICTs, and to ensure the accountability of the institutions that are responsible for this valuable resource.

Privacy and Security

Privacy, security, and Internet rights—including secure online spaces where women feel safe from harassment and enjoy freedom of expression, privacy of communication, and protection from "electronic snooping"—are also significant for women. The Internet has fostered the creation of private online spaces that often spill over national boundaries, an important democratizing part of its diffusion, vital for empowering exploited and victimized sections of society and well utilized by women.

But national legislation, such as the Regulation of Investigatory Powers (RIP) Act in Britain, the Wiretapping Act in Japan, and most recently the Homelands Security Act in the United States all potentially threaten private Internet communication, and may destroy democracy in the name of defending it against terrorism and cybercrime.

The interception of Internet communications is also justified to the general public as necessary for combating the sexual exploitation of women and children, and to combat the activities of racist groups. But it is the creation of private spaces, where the victims of abuse can discuss between themselves and with others they trust and have chosen to talk to, that has, in fact, proven to be the most powerful weapon against both sexual exploitation and racial oppression.

Trafficking, Pornography, and Censorship

The use of the Internet for pornography, sexual exploitation, or hate literature is of great concern to women, although there is no consensus about freedom of expression and censorship. Some women want technologies that filter content and track down creators and clients of pornographic websites; others see this as itself an infringement of rights that could be extended to limit other forms of freedom of expression. In a context of considerable debate, what is clear and must be a priority is that women are informed, aware, and involved in the discussions and debates that must take place.

The Internet has allowed the voices of ordinary citizens and organizations lacking strong financial resources to be heard. With an estimated one billion users by 2005, the Internet provides a unique public sphere where decisions that shape people's lives can be freely debated and considered. It allows small groups and individuals, men and women—previously working in isolation from one another—to communicate, network, share information, and prepare actions in an unprecedented manner. ICTs must be made available to all at an affordable cost and the development of infrastructure must ensure that marginalized groups are not further disadvantaged. This should be the strategic starting point for all concerned with gender equality and social transformation. In a globalized world that often undermines localized democratic institutions, the Internet provides an essential means for defending and extending participatory democracy. The Internet and ICTs can strengthen diversity and provide a platform for a multitude of voices, a pluralism of ideas and opinions, and a place for cross-cultural exchange. But this can only be true if developments preserve and enhance local and regional linguistic diversity and civil society has a voice in the policy formations that regulate control and ownership of the Internet.

The range of issues covered here is wide, and reflects more endemic patterns of inequality than simply in the domain of ICTs. As P. Norris (2001, 91) has argued, "the heart of the problem lies in broader patterns of social stratification" so that access to, use of, and influence over ICTs follow a standard pattern of inequality. Tellingly, K. H. Sorensen (2002, 16) argues from a review of the literature that much more attention has been paid to mechanisms and dynamics of exclusion than to inclusion, so the real challenge remains exactly how inclusion is to be achieved.

The WSIS Gender Caucus keeps repeating that the significance of ICTs for development and the growing demand for the extension of the benefits of the information society to all rest on the understanding that ICTs are an instrument for achieving economic and social goals and are not simply an end in themselves. The Gender Caucus stresses the need for an intersectional approach that considers the diverse needs and perspectives of women and focuses on unequal power relations—not just between men and women but more fundamentally between rich and poor, North and South, urban and rural, empowered and marginalized. The Gender Caucus summarized the final key recommendations for action (www.genderwsis/recommendations) as

- Gender as a fundamental principle for action
- Equitable participation in decisions shaping the information society
- New and old ICTs in a multimodal approach
- Designing of ICTs to serve people
- Empowerment for full participation
- Research, analysis, and evaluation to guide action

It is more than evident that the four Rs ripple powerfully through these analyses.

CONCLUSION

The long and dynamic history of women's global activism has provided very useful experience for promoting gender concerns within the civil society debates about the WSIS, itself part of the process of including gender within regimes of global governance.

The Gender Caucus was one of the best organized and best networked, with clear demands that gender advocacy and a gender lens be involved in every aspect of the planning and implementation of the WSIS. The women-centered approach in relation to media has focused on the need for better and more adequate representation, both in content and in employment arenas (Gallagher 1995), and is coupled with the need for recognition and empowerment of women's voices (Sreberny 2002). Recognition is not at odds with struggles for material redistribution; rather, the chance for social esteem and achievement can be the basis for demands for greater equality (Honneth 2001). Gender-sensitive approaches argue about the social construction of gendered positions through the processes of developing, diffusing, and utilizing communications technologies. But women still often lack critical mass and presence at international fora; and it is still a rare occasion for men to recognize the issue of gender equality voluntarily. That means not forsaking the "women in media/technology" argument for the "gender and technology" one but pursuing both together; the rhetoric needs to be supported by action (Sreberny 2004).

The networking revolution has diffused very rapidly: It took the telephone seventy-five years to reach fifty million people, but the Web took only four years. The e-economy is growing rapidly, so the digital divide is not just about a lack of connectivity but has implications for economic growth and sustainable development (InfoDev 2000). The mere existence of a gap in levels of ICT services between rich and poor across and within countries is not an automatic reason to argue that ICTs should be placed near the top of the development agenda. After all, poor countries also have fewer factories, fewer cars, fewer schools, fewer doctors and nurses, and a lower caloric intake per capita than wealthy countries. But the growing gap is a cause for concern because the gap is larger in ICT provision than in other areas; there is evidence of an ICT-related poverty trap since ICTs are increasingly important for taking part in global exchange, and countries without sufficient access will be excluded from the international trading system. The rapid convergence between telecommunications, computerization, and media, helped by digitalization and supported by both governments and industry around the world, means that it makes less and less sense to debate media in one forum and information technologies in another. That is true for the entire WSIS debate and especially true for women's concerns.

What do women want? remains a good question—and one that only women can answer, although we won't all necessarily want the same things. Everywhere women are still struggling to free themselves from the shackles of repressive traditions, ignorance, sexist ideas, and machismo. Globalization, democratization, and communication processes are both built around and further articulate the four Rs (rights, representation, recognition, redistribution) and will find full expression only with gender equity. The future is global, participatory, and more gender equal. Women still hold up half the sky!

NOTES

1. This section draws on Sreberny 2002.
2. The following section draws heavily from the material prepared by APCWNSP, available at www.apcwomen.org/gem/icts (accessed October 7, 2004).

REFERENCES

Atton, C. 2001. *Alternative Media*. London: Sage.

Balakrishnan, Vijayalakshmi. 1994. "Indigenous Social Norms and Women in Asian Media." In *Women Empowering Communication*, eds. Margaret Gallagher and Lilia Quindoza-Santiago. Bangkok: WACC/IWTC.

Beale, A. 1998. "Cultural Policy as a Technology of Gender." In *Ghosts in the Machine: Women and Cultural Policy in Canada and Australia*, eds. A. Beale and A. van den Bosch. Toronto: Garamond Press.

Boulding, E. 1988. *Building a Global Civic Culture*. Syracuse, NY: Syracuse University Press.

Castells, Manuel. 1996. *The Rise of the Network Society*. Oxford: Blackwell.

Cohen, R., and S. Rai, eds. 2000. *Global Social Movements*. London: Athlone.

Dahl, R. 1989. *Democracy and Its Critics*. New Haven: Yale University Press.

Dickenson, D. 1997. "Counting Women in: Globalization, Democratization and the Women's Movement." In *The Transformation of Democracy?* ed. A. McGrew, 97–120. Cambridge: Polity Press.

Downing, John D. H., with Tamara Villareal Ford, Geneve Gil, and Laura Stein. 2001. *Radical Media: Rebellious Communication and Social Movements*. Thousand Oaks, CA: Sage.

Falk, R. 1994. "The Making of Global Citizenship." In *The Conditions of Citizenship*, ed. B. van Steenbergen. London: Sage.

Faulkner, W. 2001. "Women, Gender in/and ICT: Evidence and Reflection from the UK," SIGIS, available at www.rcss.ed.ac.uk/sigis (accessed October 7, 2004).

Frankson, J. 1996. "Women's Global Fax-net." *Journal of International Communication* 3, no. 1: 102–10.

Gallagher, M. 1995. *An Unfinished Story: Gender Patterns in Media Employment*. Reports and Papers in Mass Communication 110. Paris: UNESCO.

———. 2002. "Women, Media and Democratic Society: In Pursuit of Rights and Freedoms." Paper prepared for the United Nations Division for the Advancement of Women Expert Group Meeting on Participation and Access of Women to the Media and the Impact of Media on, and Its Use as, an Instrument for the Advancement and Empowerment of Women, Beirut, Lebanon, November 12–15, available at www.un.org/womenwatch/daw/egm/media2002/reports/BP1Gallagher.PDF (accessed October 25, 2004).

Gittler, A. 1996. "Taking Hold of Electronic Communication." *Journal of International Communication* 3, no. 1: 85–101.

Harcourt, W. 1999. *Women @ Internet*. London: Zed Press.

Hertz, N. 2002. "Women on the Edge: Globalization and Gender." LSE lecture, December 3, audiotape, available at www.lse.ac.uk/collections/globalDimensions/globalisation/hertz/Default.htm (accessed October 25, 2004).

Honneth, A. 2001. "Recognition or Redistribution? Changing Perspectives on the Moral Order of Society." *Theory, Culture and Society* 18, nos. 2–3: 43–57.

Human Development Report 2001. 2001. "Making New Technologies Work for Human Development." Oxford: Oxford University Press.

InfoDev. 2000. "The Networking Revolution: Opportunities and Challenges for Developing Countries." InfoDev working papers, World Bank, June.

Keck, M., and K. Sikkink. 1998. *Activists beyond Borders: Advocacy Networks in International Politics*. Ithaca, NY: Cornell University Press.

Lewis, Peter. 1993. *Alternative Media: Linking Global and Local*, Reports and Papers in Mass Communication 107. Paris: UNESCO.

Moghadam, V. Forthcoming. *Globalizing Women: Gender, Globalization and Transnational Feminist Networks*.

Naples, N., and M. Desai, eds. 2002. *Women's Activism and Globalization: Linking Local Struggles and Transnational Politics*. New York: Routledge.

Norris, P. 2001. *Digital Divide: Civic Engagement, Information Poverty and the Internet Worldwide*. Cambridge: Cambridge University Press.

Potter, D., D. Goldblatt, M. Kiloh, and P. Lewis, eds. 1997. *Democratization*. Cambridge: Polity/Open University Press.

Rai, S. 2003. "Networking across Borders: The South Asian Research Network on Gender, Law and Governance." *Global Networks* 3, no. 1: 59–74.

Riano, Pilar, ed. 1994. *Women in Grassroots Communication*. Thousand Oaks, CA: Sage.

Rodriguez, C. 2001. *Fissures in the Mediascape*. Cresskill, NJ: Hampton Press.

Smith, J., C. Chatfield, and R. Pagnucco, eds. 1998. *Transnational Social Movements and Global Politics: Solidarity beyond the State*. Syracuse, NY: Syracuse University Press.

Sorensen, K. H. 2002. "Love, Duty and the S-Curve: An Overview of Some Current Literature on Gender and ICT," SIGIS, available at www.rcss.ed.ac.uk/sigis/public/D02/D02part1.pdf.

Sreberny, A. 1998. "Feminist Internationalism: Imagining and Building Global Civil Society." In *Electronic Empires*, ed. D. Thussu. London: Arnold.

———. 2002. "Gender and the Politics of Recognition." Special plenary on Women in Communication Scholarship: Achievements and Aspirations, IAMCR Conference, Barcelona, July.

———. 2004. "WSIS: Articulating Information at the Summit." *Gazette* 66, nos. 3–4: 193–201.

Sreberny-Mohammadi, A. 1995. "Women, Media and Communication in a Global Context." Paper presented to UNESCO meeting on Women and Media: Issues of Access and Decision-Making, Toronto, May.

———. 1998. "Feminist Internationalism: Imagining and Building Global Civil Society." In *Electronic Empires*, ed. D. Thussu, 208–22. London: Arnold.

Sreberny-Mohammadi, A., and Mohammadi, A. 1985. *Small Media, Big Revolution.* Minneapolis: University of Minnesota Press.

Steans, J. 2002. "Global Governance: A Feminist Perspective." In *Governing Globalization: Power, Authority, and Global Governance,* eds. D. Held and McGrew. Cambridge: Polity Press.

van Steenbergen, Bart, ed. 1994. *The Conditions of Citizenship.* Thousand Oaks, CA: Sage.

Walby, S. 2001. "From Community to Coalition: The Politics of Recognition as the Handmaiden of the Politics of Equality in the Era of Globalization." *Theory, Culture and Society* 18, nos. 2–3: 113–36.

Walker, A. 2002. "Women's Communications Strategies: Utilizing ICTS and Strategic Alliances Worldwide." Paper prepared for United Nations Division for the Advancement of Women Expert Group Meeting on Participation and Access of Women to the Media and the Impact of Media on, and Its Use as, an Instrument for the Advancement and Empowerment of Women, Beirut, Lebanon, November 12–15, EGM/MEDIA/2002/EP.9, available at www.un.org/womenwatch/daw/egm/media2002/reports/EP9Walker.PDF (accessed October 25, 2004).

UNIFEM. 2000. *Progress of the World's Women.* New York: UNIFEM.

13

Peace Journalism: A Global Dialog for Democracy and Democratic Media

Jake Lynch and Annabel McGoldrick

The U.S.-led attack on Iraq in 2003 propelled several urgent questions to the top of the global agenda. Above all, do we want to embark on another world war—an all-encompassing "war on terrorism" that, according to its proponents in Washington, could last for decades—imposing by force a "new American century"?

If it is to be of any value at this time, democracy must mean the world's peoples deciding for themselves whether they and their governments should join in—or seek alternative ways to navigate the mingling currents of resource issues, security, identity, and development that will likely direct the course of international politics in the coming decades.

According to the liberal theory of press freedom, this is where the media should help. John Stuart Mill, in the most famous liberal tract of all, "On Liberty," writes, "The peculiar evil of silencing an expression of opinion is that it is robbing the human race; posterity as well as the existing generation; those who dissent from the opinion, still more than those who hold it. If the opinion is right, they are deprived of the opportunity of exchanging error for truth: if wrong, they lose, what is almost as great a benefit, the clearer perception and livelier impression of truth, produced by its collision with error" (Hargreaves 2003). In liberal terms, therefore, the democratic use to make of free expression is to animate, and bring about a collision of, alternative views and propositions as to how progress can be made. This is vital when people in powerful positions put forward policies—like war—that they propose to implement "in our names." Then, the journalist's mission, in a liberal democracy, is to speak truth to power, thereby equipping readers and audiences to assess those policies—and, in so doing, to discern truth from error—for themselves.

This theoretical framework raises a number of important questions. Do the media really behave in this democratic way? Or are certain expressions of opinion routinely, perhaps systematically, omitted in favor of others? If so, what kinds of opinions are they, and how do they come to be silenced? What might be the consequences for democracy of silencing them?

PEACE JOURNALISM

It is in this context that peace journalism is put forward as an indispensable concept in any discussion where the terms "media," "globalization," and "democracy" occur together. Its utility is fourfold:

1. As a mode of analysis, identifying cumulative patterns of omission and distortion in the reporting of conflicts
2. As a springboard for assessing the consequences of these patterns, both in terms of the understanding they convey to the public and their influence over the course of events in conflicts
3. As a source of practical alternative methods and approaches to the reporting of particular conflicts
4. As a rallying point for contestation, a challenge to what is becoming a homogenized global news discourse, and a campaign for change capable of uniting reform-minded journalists and activists across different media and different countries

Table 13.1, originally created by Professor Johan Galtung, one of the founders of peace studies as an academic subject, gives the characteristics of peace journalism and its corollary, war journalism (Lynch 1998).

IRAQ

Throughout the year or so after the start of September 2002, one story dominated the news in virtually every part of the world. Others, including widespread and needless poverty, AIDS, thirty-plus active wars, and catastrophic global warming, all had to take second billing to the U.S.-led invasion of Iraq, the buildup, and the aftermath.

The choice of story makes a telling comment about where the power to set the global news agenda is concentrated. Of course, the way the story, once chosen, was covered contains many more choices. Here the concept of war journalism is employed as a diagnostic tool to identify patterns of omission and distortion in the choices made.

Table 13.1.   Galtung's Characteristics of War Journalism and Peace Journalism

Peace/Conflict Journalism	War/Violence Journalism
I. Peace/Conflict-oriented	*I. War/Violence-oriented*
Explore conflict formation, x parties, y goals, z issues	Focus on conflict arena, two parties, one goal (win), war general zero-sum orientation
General win–win orientation	Closed space, closed time; causes and exits in arena, who threw the first stone
Open space, open time; causes and outcomes anywhere, also in history/culture	Making wars opaque/secret
Making conflicts transparent	"Us–them" journalism, propaganda, voice, for "us"
Giving voice to all parties; empathy, understanding	See "them" as the problem, focus on who prevails in war
See conflict/war as problem, focus on conflict creativity	Dehumanization of "them"; more so the worse the weapon
Humanization of all sides; more so the worse the weapons	Reactive: waiting for violence before reporting
Proactive: prevention before any violence/war occurs	Focus only on visible effect of violence (killed, wounded and material damage)
Focus on invisible effects of violence (trauma and glory, damage to structure/culture)	
II. Truth-oriented	*II. Propaganda-oriented*
Expose untruths on all sides/uncover all coverups	Expose "their" untruths/help "our" coverups/lies
III. People-oriented	*III. Elite-oriented*
Focus on suffering all over; on women, aged, children, giving voice to voiceless	Focus on "our" suffering; on able-bodied elite males, being their mouthpiece
Give name to all evildoers	Give name to their evildoers
Focus on people peacemakers	Focus on elite peacemakers
IV. Solution-oriented	*IV. Victory-oriented*
Peace = nonviolence + creativity	Peace = victory + ceasefire
Highlight peace initiatives, also to prevent more war	Conceal peace initiative, before victory is at hand
Focus on structure, culture, the peaceful society	Focus on treaty, institution, the controlled society
Aftermath: resolution, reconstruction, reconciliation	Leaving for another war, return if the old flares up again

The following takes, briefly, each of the components in turn:

- *War/violence-oriented:* A famous cover of *Newsweek* magazine in September 2002 counterposed the faces of Presidents Saddam Hussein and George W. Bush, separated by the question, in stark type, "Who will win?" This is a perfect example of the "two parties, one goal" formulation that is a defining characteristic of war journalism—and one that will instantly be recognizable as typical by anyone who has followed this story over the years in virtually any medium.
- *Propaganda-oriented:* The period leading up to war was marked by a dramatic increase in official rhetoric about "lies" emanating from the regime of Saddam Hussein over its record on weapons of mass destruction. This was enthusiastically picked up and amplified by most global media, especially in the United States and United Kingdom, even to the point where the headlines exaggerated the case governments themselves were making.
- *Elite-oriented:* Discussions about possible undeclared motives for the war, alternative means for bringing about "regime change" in Iraq, and the possible illegality of military action were three examples of important news angles generally blotted out by blanket coverage of leaders reiterating familiar demands and positions.
- *Victory-oriented:* When President Bush flew on to the deck of the aircraft carrier U.S.S. *Abraham Lincoln* with much fanfare on May 1, 2003, his announcement that "major combat operations are over" was generally reported as the end of the war. Only afterward, as a violent and traumatic summer wore on in Iraq, was that claim increasingly questioned.

This analysis will concentrate mainly on U.K. media for two reasons: one of happenstance—because it is most familiar to us, based as we are in the United Kingdom—and the other having to do with patterns of global communication flows that make London arguably the world's most influential media capital. News organizations headquartered here, like the BBC, Reuters, the *Financial Times*, the *Economist*, and the *Guardian*, not to mention CNN's biggest office outside Atlanta, have a global reach.

Moreover, training organizations like the BBC World Service Trust, Reuters Foundation, Thomson Foundation, and others have come to the fore in spreading the precepts and methods British journalists (are supposed to) employ to those in other countries—an undertaking that has grown into a multi-million-dollar industry in the years since the end of the cold war (Howard 2003).

As to whether, and how far, the patterns set by such organizations are now discernible in the coverage offered by indigenous media in other parts of the world, to offer any authoritative view on that question would exceed the scope of this chapter.

We do, however, offer some insights from a survey carried out in the period leading up to and including the invasion of Iraq by the journalism think tank Reporting the World (RtW). We quote some of the comments and findings in passing, as an indicative—rather than scientific—accompaniment to the observations made in this chapter.

In the survey, reporters and editors were asked to assess how far the media in their own countries—and, for those in developing or transitional societies, the international media—were managing to live up to the ideals inscribed in the liberal theory of press freedom. If the reporters, editors, producers, and others deemed the media were not, or not completely, living up to their ideals, they were also asked to discuss in what way and to comment on any difficulties they themselves had encountered in doing their own jobs as they believed they should be done.

THE BBC GUIDELINES

Putting these ideals into practice would entail different approaches in different settings. One of the most influential formulations, which puts it in a way that many journalists in many countries would recognize as having at least some validity for them, is to be found in the BBC's *Producer Guidelines*.

It is, in essence, a reworking of the classic liberal theory. The document echoes Mill's own phrasing with its call for a "full range" of arguments to be "tested" against each other.

From *Producer Guidelines*:

- Viewers and listeners should receive "an intelligent and informed account of issues that enables them to form their own views."
- To this end, journalists should "ensure that a full range of significant views and perspectives are heard," especially in dealing with "major matters of controversy."
- "There are generally more than two sides to any issue" and "no significant strand of thought should go unreflected or under-represented."

From the supplementary *War Guidelines*, issued in January 2003:

- "Enabling the national and international debate remains a vital task."
- "All views should be reflected in due proportion to mirror the depth and spread of opinion. We must reflect the significant opposition in the UK (and elsewhere) to the military conflict and allow the arguments to be heard and tested."

So, how did U.K. media perform, on these criteria, before, during, and after the U.S.-led invasion of Iraq? What were the key arguments in favor of war, and to what extent did journalists manage to test them? Consider five essential propositions:

1. The crisis—later, the war—is really "about" Iraq's weapons of mass destruction.
2. These represent an authentic and current threat to both regional and world security.
3. The only way to rid the world of this threat is regime change.
4. Regime change is also the only way to improve the humanitarian situation in Iraq.
5. The only way to bring about regime change is war.

This analysis focuses on two key periods when, it could be argued, the onus was firmly on journalists to help the public discern truth from error and to help equip them to form their own views.

In the prewar period, Britain had, as it were, a decision to make: whether to go to war or not. We argue that the prevalent war-journalism conventions ensured that nonviolent options were systematically underreported and consequently undervalued, that this distorted the decision-making process and amounted, therefore, to an important abrogation of democracy.

Then, after the war, journalists' job was to help readers and audiences to form a clearer perception and livelier impression of whether the policy had, in retrospect, been a good one, one that should form a blueprint for responding to conflicts and crises in times to come.

PREWAR

We have already suggested that testing the prowar arguments would require some sense that they were being brought into "collision"—to use Mill's word—with countervailing propositions. Were they? This was only really case with regard to the third point listed above, which states that bringing about regime change was the only way to neutralize any threat from Iraq's supposed weapons. The French, German, and Russian governments led a "coalition of the unwilling" with their case that, as long at UN weapons inspectors were in Iraq, the threat could be adjudged as under control.

Contrast that with the first proposition. Two opinion surveys last year found different ways to ask British people the same thing—what do you think it's really about? In the first survey for Channel 4 Television, respondents were presented with a menu of alternatives. The security explanation topped the poll, with 22 percent, but only by a narrow margin from the most popular alternative view. Fully 21 percent told pollsters they thought it was really all about oil.

The second survey for the Pew Research Center, framing the question in a different way, found the oil theory shared by fully 44 percent of the British and large majorities in many other countries. Far from being "reflected . . . to mirror the depth and spread of opinion," this view was largely absent as an analytical factor in coverage by mainstream media of the buildup to war. The very occasional television reports on this angle were usually confined the periphery of the schedule—two by the BBC, for instance, appeared on the early morning *Breakfast* and late-evening *Newsnight* shows.

Perhaps the most visible signifier of the view that the drive for war originated in a determination to install and maintain compliant governments in the world's main oil-producing region came in the form of placards and banners carried at London's biggest-ever demonstration, held on February 15— one of over six hundred around the world. The slogan "no blood for oil" carried over from the buildup to the Gulf War in 1991. Now, it remained in evidence throughout 2003 on thousands of posters at bus stops and on lampposts, where they had been pasted by activists organizing for the demonstration.

The wave of protests was widely covered and prompted the *New York Times* to observe on its front page that international politics was, once again, dominated by two superpowers—U.S. military might, on the one hand, and on the other, global public opinion. It led some news organizations to appoint "antiwar correspondents," who did manage to bring to viewers' attention the fact that some people were continuing to oppose plans for the invasion. CNN, in the United States, was one; *Five News*, a service for the United Kingdom's fifth terrestrial television channel provided by the globally renowned Independent Television News (ITN), another.

They too, though, had to work within various constraints and conventions, which limited the extent to which they could interrogate the case for war. Sam Delaney, a freelance reporter who picked up the antiwar brief for *Five News*, took part in the RtW survey, reflecting: "You feel you should be giving a fuller picture but can't when you only get a couple of hours to turn around a story on a complex issue for this evening's program."

Delaney did manage to examine, if only briefly, both the blood-for-oil thesis and the view that the United States was embarking on a neoconservative project for a new American century—at the time, another generally underreported angle. Indeed, most mainstream news outlets fought shy of coming to grips with these issues.

One quantitative study of coverage in U.K. print media found that while oil was mentioned in the buildup to, and debate over, the war, it was almost always in passing and often in the form of readers' letters. Publications that made regular efforts to develop it as a running story "tended to be those like

Lloyd's List or Business A.M., intended to be used as reliable information sources by people with hard-headed commercial decisions to make," the study found. "Mainstream publications, if they rais[ed] the oil agenda at all, usually [did] so only to dismiss it as fanciful." (Lynch 2003).

The alternative response would have been for newspapers and programs to put themselves on the lookout for ways and opportunities to explore this agenda; if the war really was "all about oil," in what sense was it so and with what implications? To do this would have represented a decisive breach with war journalism since it would have entailed an acknowledgement that causes of a conflict can lie outside the conflict arena itself—in this case, the social, political, and economic imperatives summed up in the infamous statement by the first President Bush, at the Rio Earth Summit in 1992: "The American way of life is not up for negotiation."

As for war propositions 4 and 5 in the above list, plenty of alternative means, other than military action, were being discussed for removing Saddam Hussein and improving human rights in Iraq. But because they did not emanate from official sources, they, too, were generally bracketed out by the war-journalism conventions, in this case the firm orientation toward elite agendas.

PRACTICAL PROPOSALS

In the United Kingdom, a dialog based on peace-journalism ideas has taken place under the "brand" name, Reporting the World, or RtW, a think-tank generating discussions, publications, and the website of the same name. By convening gatherings of professionals—many of them editors or senior reporters—and focusing on practical issues in the coverage of specific conflicts, RtW has sought to circumvent the common objection, among journalists, to criticisms from outside their own ranks, namely, that they take too little account of the exigencies of the job.

In RtW papers and discussions about the war on Iraq, several suggestions aired could have formed part of a creative strategy to supplement the war-journalism conventions and thus restore some balance to the coverage. In the spirit of the exercise, each was conceived as a realistic proposed contribution to an evening television news program for a mixed audience, which, polls consistently show, is the source of news most trusted and relied upon by the public at large.

In this, it typifies the way peace journalism has been taken up as a campaign for reform by journalists, activists, journalism educators, and trainers in many countries—as a source of alternative perspectives couched in the form of practical suggestions. So, what were they?

One obviously reportable, but arguably underreported, development came in October 2002, when British Petroleum (BP) chairman Lord Browne, presenting his company's results, said he hoped U.K. oil companies would get a "level playing field" in a postwar Iraq, raising the fear that U.S. majors were poised to clean up. His statement's resonance was all the greater for Lord Browne's reputation as one of Prime Minister Tony Blair's most senior confidantes in the business world.

As a follow-up, the *Business A.M.* website revealed that "Scottish oil and gas executives said the Blair government was failing to back the UK oil industry enough in the international scramble over Iraqi oil developments" (December 10, 2002)—a line backed by two separate sources, albeit quoted anonymously. Outside specialist business media, however, the story failed to catch; the Browne statement was covered in just two national newspapers, in each case some way down one of the inside pages, and subsequently disappeared, virtually without trace, until after the war.

A report by the Center for Oil Depletion Analysis, released in November 2002, illustrated the competitive advantage to be gained by taking control of Iraqi resources, with supplies elsewhere likely to be rapidly exhausted by soaring demand in the coming decades. It was noteworthy because it suggested that Iraqi oil reserves, for various reasons, might be much more strategically important than had hitherto been generally appreciated. The report did form the basis for comment pieces in the *Guardian* (Monbiot 2002) and *Sunday Times* (Humphrys 2002), but, again, was not covered as a news story, which would have given it more impact, especially if it was illustrated in terms of transactions at the gas station!

Then January 2003 saw the launch of the Detroit Group, described on its website as "a grassroots campaign to prod Detroit automakers to build cars that will get Americans to work in the morning without sending us to war in the afternoon—cars that will end our dependence on foreign oil."

It produced a series of three eye-catching TV ads and was fronted by well-known columnist and personality Arianna Huffington. This is, in essence, a peace initiative—a coherent political campaign where previously there had only been an unorganized conversation at the fringes of American political and media discourse and a trickle of violent incidents involving sports utility vehicles' being vandalized or destroyed.

Covering this aspect could have been a way to give vent to not really the same—retain 'ventilate' some alternative explanations as to the true goals of the protagonists, perhaps mentioning some of the key political events in the merging of security and resource issues in U.S. strategic thinking as varied as these:

- The 1981 Joint Chiefs of Staff military posture statement—the first of the Reagan era—which set out a post-Vietnam security concept closely linked to U.S. exposure to foreign resources, chiefly oil
- The abovementioned statement by George Bush the elder at the Rio Earth Summit in 1992 that "the American way of life is not up for negotiation"

- Statements by George W. Bush, in his presidential election campaign and afterward, about the United States facing an "energy crisis"

What about the argument that the only or best way to topple the regime of Saddam Hussein and bring about positive change was by force? Not so, according to Mary Kaldor (2003), who contributed a piece to *Red Pepper* magazine, fruit of her collaboration with an exiled Iraqi sociologist, Faleh Abdel Jabar. In it, she wrote, "We have to develop legal methods of supporting those who resist repressive regimes, and—in some circumstances—this might involve military means to protect people from humanitarian catastrophes such as genocide. But there should be a sharp distinction between humanitarian intervention and war."

Mary Kaldor is professor of global politics at the London School of Economics and Political Science, where she coined an important theory about "new wars," which were likely to bear far more heavily on civilians than on the military themselves. She has also written on democratization in Eastern and Central Europe. In the *Red Pepper* piece, she calls for

- An ad hoc international court to issue indictments for three hundred top regime leaders
- A monitoring system for human rights in Iraq, using UN inspectors
- Handing control of the Oil for Food program over to the United Nations
- A repeat of the Helsinki Process of the 1970s—this time for the Middle East—where the Final Act offered a legal framework for recognizing dissident groups in Eastern Europe, overriding national sovereignty

Kaldor explains how these suggestions were partly based on lessons learned from the most successful example of regime change in modern times, the fall of the Iron Curtain. For a good televisual way to convey these suggestions, the better to test the prowar case against an alternative, countervailing one, why not take Kaldor, who happens to be a fluent speaker and highly telegenic, to Budapest, arguably Europe's most beautiful city, to meet former dissidents now in positions of influence and either opposing or supporting the war on Iraq? Such a piece would be replete with interesting resonances and contradictions. Hungarian prime minister Peter Medgyessy was one signatory to the *Wall Street Journal* letter from the "new Europe" supporting George Bush's policy on Iraq, despite the opposition to war of a large majority of Hungarian citizens. What does a transition to democracy really mean? This would be a useful question to pose, in advance, about grandiose claims being made for the salutary effect of war on a region—the Middle East—dominated by repressive regimes of one stripe or another.

OBSTACLES

To recap, the war-journalism/peace-journalism framework offers an analytical model within which cumulative patterns of omission and distortion in news about the buildup to war on Iraq can be identified. War journalism, it can be established, impedes journalists from performing a public service as prescribed, for instance, by the BBC *Producer Guidelines*.

The aspirations and provisions set out in documents like the *Guidelines* draw heavily on the liberal theory of press freedom, in which news constitutes an essential civic tool in the workings of democracy. It follows that a diet of war journalism is bad for democracy, since it skews and unbalances important public debates about how best to respond to conflicts and crises affecting global security and well-being.

Peace journalism, therefore, can be construed as part of a campaign for democracy, linking reform-minded journalists, activists, educators, and trainers around the world, who have held countless discussions and carried out their own experiments in covering conflicts based on peace-journalism ideas. RtW, in the United Kingdom, is one among many examples.

Drawing on these discussions and experiments, it is possible to say what a peace-journalism approach would look like—to suggest, in practical terms, stories editors could commission and the way reporters would report them, in order to do peace journalism in a particular context. And indeed, while such activity is often confined to the margins, there is some peace journalism going on all the time. So, why do we not see more? What are the obstacles?

This is, broadly speaking, the theme of the ongoing RtW global survey. Respondents are asked to assess the extent to which the media in their own countries are successfully carrying out a public service role as defined by the liberal theory: "speaking truth to power" and "equipping us to assess for ourselves the merits—or otherwise—of the way power is being exercised."

Again, the sample is not scientific (and is inevitably, in any case, biased in favor of those willing to take the time to respond). It was targeted at professional reporters, editors, and producers in mainstream news organizations, rather than activists or commentators on the media. It should be seen as a fund of indicative insights as to how these issues are playing out, here and now, in the everyday working lives of journalists around the world.

By mid-2003, of some 120 respondents from twenty-eight countries, over 60 percent said the media in their own countries were not doing this job well. Those taking part included many senior journalists, eleven of whom held editorial positions. In so far as the media in their own countries were failing, they were asked why? What was the single greatest obstacle out of a choice of four—government restrictions, market conditions, owner interference, or—blamed by more than any other—journalistic conventions.

Perhaps the most interesting responses came in answer to the final question on the survey form, which asked for "general comments about any particular difficulties you have encountered in doing your own job as you think it should be done."

In many cases, these difficulties were experienced in the form of conventions that could be diagnosed as war journalism. For instance, Phil Vine, a correspondent for TV-3 in New Zealand, was sent to cover the Bali bombing in October 2002. From the start, he was under pressure to fit the story into the analytical frame provided by the so-called war on terrorism with its Manichean world picture. "I was encouraged to opt for the accepted view that this was an al Qaeda–planned action as suggested by 'intelligence reports,'" he complained. "A more accurate and complex explanation which cast doubt on these reports would only confuse the viewing public and contravene the KISS principle—'Keep It Simple, Stupid.'"

Supara Janchitfah, a correspondent at the *Bangkok Post*, said that while Thai journalists were notionally free to carry out the task of scrutinizing and interrogating power and its workings, an elite orientation prevailed by default, as the paper was reluctant to adumbrate a clear news agenda of its own: "Our organization has no clear vision of what we want to achieve. Sometimes, to play safe we often sided with the government. Criticizing the government is not our nature. Thus most of the time, we do the self-censorship."

Claire Fox, a writer for *spiked*'s website and commentator on social and ethical issues in the United Kingdom, was concerned about the distortion caused by the familiar bipolar framing of war journalism: "If one's views do not easily fall into convenient categories, e.g., left or right, or black and white positions, particularly broadcast media find it difficult to know how to place you and try and corner you into taking an either/or position."

Binod Bhattarai, a Nepalese journalist who also contributes from Katmandhu to the international media, gave a particularly sophisticated description of how subtly mediated political interests influence the news. These, he wrote, arise from

> the mindset of the classes/cliques which the editors belong to or want to be identified with. Even where there may be no overt government and business interference, the influence of the two is there, which editors often adopt and try to propagate, while pretending to be doing classic journalism. . . . Even reports that appear "impartial" and "objective" are often written in a language that on closer analysis reveals the influences that cause them to be reported in the way they are. It is the same for the "truth"—based as it is on the "facts" that are reported, which can often be manufactured by the parties being written about, which journalists help to convert into "truth" by accepting and propagating them in their media, often because that is the "angle" they are reporting, as they have been guided to.

OBJECTIVITY

Considering why the ideals in the liberal theory seem to be so difficult to live up to, why they tend, instead, to be skewed and compromised by the patterns of omission and distortion we have called war journalism, leads us on a search for contradictions deep into the heart of news: its values, practices, structures, and traditions.

Several writers, in fact, have identified the journalistic concept of objectivity as being at the center of these contradictions. One persuasive account calls objectivity a "knowledge-producing discursive regime" with four main "dimensions" (Hackett and Zhao 1998):

- As a goal or ethic
- As an epistemology
- As sets of practices and methods
- As institutions embedded in concrete social structures

Thinking of objectivity in this way, as a multifaceted whole, certainly resonates with many comments offered by survey respondents who observed, or implied, that the journalistic conventions they experienced in everyday working life were, in fact, imbricated with various aspects of market conditions, government restrictions, or the influence of media owners.

The case we make here is that war journalism is a phenomenon of this objectivity regime. In making it, we highlight the boundaries, ruptures, shifts, and divisions within it—the contradictions, in particular, between practices and methods, on the one hand, and goals and ethics, on the other. The peace-journalism concept, in other words, effectively problematizes objectivity by giving a clear, accessible explanation of how journalistic practice parts company with principle and of how the two could be brought closer together.

Three defining characteristics of war journalism are perhaps most easily traceable to the imperatives of the objectivity regime. One of them, elite orientation, is the most widespread single convention in global journalism. Visit any of the world's capitals, pick up the main local newspaper, and there is a good chance that the front page will feature the words or deeds of that country's main political leaders.

Former *Washington Post* editor Ben Bagdikian (2000) gives perhaps the best concise explanation for this. In the early twentieth century, the growing influence of advertising in a developing consumer economy altered the economics of newspapering, in the United States and elsewhere, to favor products marketable to a mass readership.

There was, therefore, a commercial incentive to devise ways of calibrating a paper's content—or at least part of it, the news columns—as being "all things to all people" and, therefore, as saleable to potential customers of any political view or of none; hence the habit of basing the news agenda on the pronouncements of officialdom, presentable as a noncontroversial basis for taking the most fundamental of decisions—what to include in the news and what to leave out.

For television, usually governed by public service agreements, there was an equivalent political incentive. A recent marketing slogan extols the merits to the U.K. public of having "One BBC," which is a play on words—the corporation's most popular channel is BBC One—but also a statement of fact. And if there is only to be one BBC, funded by the impost of a compulsory tax, the television license fee, then it, too, must be able to present itself as all things to all people.

In these conditions, as Bagdikian comments, "the safest method of reporting news was to reproduce the words of authority figures" (2000, 180). As we have suggested, in the context of reporting the buildup to war in Iraq, in U.K. media, there is a rather obvious problem (one that McChesney has noted with respect to American media): issues that officialdom does not care to discuss tend to drop off the edge of the news agenda, even where this interferes with the public service role the media are supposed to be performing.

Bagdikian puts his finger on another problem: "in the nature of public relations most authority figures issue a high quotient of imprecise and self-serving declarations" (2000, 180). In reporting conflicts, this also means that news reproduces a kind of unexamined realism, which distorts the understanding, conveyed to readers and audiences, of how things change.

Realism as a form of historical and political analysis starts with the proposition that the only authentic and legitimate agents of change are states and governments. Since the Treaty of Westphalia recognized states as having a monopoly on legitimate force in their territories, we tend to overvalue military action as a response to conflicts and crises, even when, as with regime change, the desired outcome has been successfully brought about elsewhere without it.

So, this reflex elite orientation is in fact unhelpful in the job of equipping readers and audiences to form their own views about some of the most important issues facing humanity. It merits the description "war journalism" precisely because it ensures that nonviolent responses are less likely to get a fair hearing, since they would involve pulling levers in the hands of nonstate actors, both in civil society and in supranational structures of global governance, with the United Nations at their apex.

EVENT AND PROCESS

On any given day, the most important fact about a conflict, say, the Israel–Palestine conflict and Israel's ongoing, thirty-six-year (at the time of writing), illegal occupation of Palestinian territory, is that it is an ongoing process, not an isolated event, even on a day when some traumatic event occurs. Or the single most important fact might be the ongoing nature of the international campaign of Islamist terrorism, dedicated to destroying Western-style liberal democracy and targeting Israel as a frontline state.

The former, of course, is the majority view in world opinion and one that is in line with international law, albeit not one that is favored in official Washington or Tel Aviv. The point is, either view would be a controversial lead-in to a report on the conflict. It is altogether less objectionable to concentrate on events—a suicide bombing today, an Israeli military incursion tomorrow.

The trouble is that confining one's reporting to accounts of events—"just the facts"—constitutes its own narrative, a narrative that is, in this case, inherently biased in favor of Israel. Crucially, it supports the claim that Israeli military incursions are purely defensive—carried out to ensure "security" against terrorism—not to sustain an aggressive occupation of someone else's land.

The result is that readers and audiences are being seriously misled. One survey of television viewers in the United Kingdom was carried out in the early months of 2002, when developments in the conflict had been reported almost daily for well over a year.

The proportion of respondents who could correctly identify both "the settlers" as Israeli and "the territories" as Palestinian, was just 9 percent. The proportion who wrongly believed "the settlers" to be Palestinian and "the territories" to be Israeli, was 11 percent (Philo 2002).

The elevation of event over process was particularly noticeable after the attacks of 9/11, which were presented to most U.S. readers and audiences as, in the words of one commentator, "some pure spasm of apocalyptic irrationality" (Lynch 2002).

This is inserted into an underlying narrative, one of the most familiar in global news, that problems considered serious enough to find their way into the headlines demand solutions from political leaders—a consequence of the global news's prevailing elite orientation.

Today, of course, many of those leaders are increasingly attentive to media strategy, not only when presenting policies but also when devising them in the first place. Anyone working in any modern government constantly asks him or herself, how will this be reported?

It follows that the way a problem is diagnosed in media reports will affect what can be presented as an appropriate remedy. Strip violence of its context, report event without process, and it can appear purely irrational, even autistic, justifying more violence as a means of dealing with it; hence, perhaps, the war on terrorism as a plausible media strategy after 9/11.

Draw attention, on the other hand, to political, social, and economic processes constructing the conditions for violence, and it can open the space to urge what EU commissioner Chris Patten called "smart development assistance, rather than smart weapons" as a response to terrorism.

"TWO-ISHNESS"

One of the most familiar reporting frames, particularly in Western journalism, goes something like "on the one hand, on the other," sometimes, according to cliché, leading to the conclusion that "only time will tell," which is right.

This formula gives the impression of balance, one of the key tools permitting journalists, as Robert Hackett and Yuezhi Zhao put it, to "take themselves out of the picture and adopt the stance of an impartial and politically neutral observer, critically examining all sides of an issue and separate from the struggles and events being reported" (1998).

It is also homologous with the way many other questions are framed, at least in occidental cultural and religious and political discourses. Left and Right in politics, the dichotomy of organized work and play, and the superficial presentation of self contrasted with the swirling undercurrents of interiority are all familiar dualities to the modern Western consciousness. There is a deep "two-ishness," meaning that any narrative resting on a duality may strike readers and audiences as common sense, requiring no further explanation or justification (Lynch 1999).

But this is another reason why the label "war journalism" applies. Think of it as a question of geometry. Two points can only be joined by one shape, a line. This means that any change, any movement, must take place along this one axis, resembling nothing so much as a giant tug of war, where any ground can only be gained by one side at the direct expense of the other. It is a classic zero-sum game.

To frame a conflict in this way is to pose only two alternatives to either side—victory or defeat. In the September 2002 *Newsweek* edition mentioned above, the question on the front cover, "Who will win?" arises from the decision to illustrate the conflict with the two counterposed faces of Presidents Bush and Hussein. It could be phrased another way, of course: who will lose?

Defeat being unthinkable, each side steps up its effort for victory. To justify that, propaganda intensifies, until the "other" is seen as the embodiment of evil, which must be overthrown in one last battle. Johan Galtung has called it "DMA syndrome" for dualism-Manicheanism-Armageddon (Lynch 2002). The bipolar, zero-sum conflict model is a recipe for escalation and more violence.

POSTWAR

Some of these issues came into sharper relief after the war. Journalists in many countries—in particular, the main belligerents, the United States,

United Kingdom, and Australia—proved much quicker to engage in critical self-reflection than in the immediate aftermath of other recent conflicts. The RtW survey suggested that U.S. journalists were more likely than anyone else to be dissatisfied with the performance of their own media. A public seminar in New York in August 2003 brought together senior journalists and editors under the aegis of *New York Magazine* for a tough discussion about where the reporting had gone wrong, particularly in the buildup to war on Iraq.

The magazine's media writer, Michael Wolff, chaired the discussion and was keen to draw connections between patterns of omission and distortion in news coverage and the quality of decision making in a democracy—much as we do here. In writing up the highlights, he reflected, "Clearly, the war will be more of a story. It gets bigger every day. Not least of all because the media is now having to rewrite itself. The questions we failed to ask, the stories we declined to pursue, have surely helped to get us into the present mess."

At the equivalent gathering in London, organized by RtW, *Guardian* editor Alan Rusbridger observed that demonizing the "other," an essential element of war propaganda for the reasons outlined above, had become much more difficult because of the unprecedented "calibre and texture" of reporting by correspondents in Baghdad such as the paper's own Suzanne Goldenberg. On several occasions during the war, the *Guardian*, among other papers, suspended an important convention of the objectivity regime by clearing its front page of news, as such, for what were, in essence, feature pieces conveying the hopes and fears of ordinary Iraqis and the reality of daily life.

But the main preoccupation was with the "self-serving declarations" of official sources in London and Washington over Iraq's supposed weapons of mass destruction. The feeling was that before the war, governments had misled the public, and journalists had let them get away with it.

This was, of course, picked over at length in the inquiry, chaired by senior lawyer Lord Hutton, into the death of a government weapons expert, Dr. David Kelly. Kelly killed himself after being unmasked as the anonymous source for an incendiary report broadcast by the BBC suggesting that Britain's intelligence community was unhappy with the way its product was being presented to the public. The specific allegation was that Alastair Campbell, the government's director of communications, had interfered with the compilation of a dossier on Iraq's weapons to "sex it up" before publication in September 2002.

In particular, according to the report by defense correspondent Andrew Gilligan, the dossier included a claim that Iraq could launch chemical or biological weapons "within 45 minutes" even though the government "knew it was wrong." At the inquiry, these allegations proved, indeed, too specific.

Gilligan himself softened his initial line in subsequent broadcasts, claiming merely that the government knew this claim was "questionable."

In many respects, however, evidence at the inquiry vindicated Gilligan, at least in general terms. The forty-five-minute claim, it turned out, referred only to battlefield weapons—tank shells and mortar rounds—not missiles. If such weapons had existed, they would have been a potential threat to any invading army but not to other countries. Many in the intelligence community were indeed unhappy with the dossier; and the language in it was indeed strengthened, to an extent where it became misleading, at Campbell's behest.

Gilligan was, in effect, carrying out a piece of peace journalism, focusing on "our" side's propaganda, not just on that of the "other" side. (During the war, indeed, it was noticeable in the media of many countries, including the United Kingdom, how readily the word itself—"propaganda"—would crop up in discussions of how the war was being presented to the public. One respondent to the RtW survey commented on the much more noticeable "metadiscussion" taking place in media reports.)

After the official end of hostilities, however, and before Gilligan's report, official sources were making a concerted attempt to change the subject, as weeks after the fall of Baghdad, signs of Iraq's supposed weapons of mass destruction rather pointedly failed to turn up. Prime Minister Tony Blair had conjured up images of missiles menacing the outside world, an urgent problem demanding an urgent solution. Now he subtly shifted his rhetoric to a series of predictions that evidence of "weapons programs" would eventually materialize so that a few sheaves of incriminating papers' coming to light would constitute vindication.

Other ministers responded by drawing attention, instead, to the success in ridding the world of an "evil dictator" or tried to tamp down expectations by emphasizing the difficulties of searching a big country ("twice the size of France") for a relatively small item ("after all, 10,000 liters of anthrax would fit into half a petrol tanker").

The point is, the case for war was successfully kept in the public eye, and some of the misinformation and misrepresentations were effectively exposed. Gilligan's piece brought this into the open and was a signal for other reporters to follow up.

CONCLUSION

There is an important balance to be struck here. Putting forward peace journalism as a source of practical alternatives for reporters, editors, and producers does restore a sense of agency and responsibility to discussions about democracy and the media, discussions that can otherwise seem excessively structural-functionalist in tone and content, particularly when further abstractions, like globalization, are added in.

This is helpful for accessibility. Peace journalism is a global campaign, linking activists, educators and trainers, and reform-minded journalists around the world. As an analytical framework, it allows them to articulate clearly what they see as wrong with the dominant discourse of existing news coverage and to call for specific, beneficial changes that could, with a little effort, be carried out straight away.

On the other hand, it is not helpful in pursuing this campaign to adopt the idealist position implicit in some media activism of the Left and Right alike—that the explanation for perceived media biases is to be found in the political prejudices of individual journalists themselves. Indeed, as we have argued here and as responses to the global survey suggest, it is important to recognize how the conventions of war journalism arose out of, and are sustained by, economic and political factors in the development of the modern media industry.

That is what makes Hackett and Zhao's concept of a multifaceted objectivity regime particularly attractive. The regime does, as they suggest, contain an implicit epistemological position that journalists can "stand apart from events without influencing them and transfer the truth or meaning of events to the news audience by means of neutral language," thereby "reflect[ing] or mirror[ing] the world" (Hackett and Zhao 1998).

This notion of detachment seems, to many journalists, untenable, particularly to those in developing or transitional countries where the privilege of being an educated professional, it is widely felt, implies a responsibility to use one's position to improve the outlook for society and the prospects for one's fellow citizens.

Hence, it is in these places—Indonesia, the Caucasus, central Africa, and Colombia, to name but a few—that peace journalism has made the most headway under that or similar names. Initiatives such as RtW, under which much of the discussion summarized here about U.K. media has taken place, represent a bridge for these ideas to places where detachment still sits, albeit perhaps uneasily, alongside the other shibboleths of objectivity.

(How can we tell? The positivist rhetoric in the BBC *Producer Guidelines* calling on journalists to "reflect" public opinion and "mirror" a range of views says as much. This is not a propitious discursive milieu into which to introduce the name "Peace Journalism" as an opening gambit; hence, the survey name "Reporting the World.")

Ultimately, the capacity of news compiled under this regime to serve the cause of democracy may be limited. This is like the old leftist dilemma of reform versus revolution: is it worth along the way exhorting those working the system to make it work better, thus adding to its legitimacy, or is it better that its unacceptable face becomes more clearly seen, the better to hasten its overthrow?

It is clear, in using the peace-journalism concept, that some workable changes in the reporting of conflicts are both possible and, in liberal terms, desirable; they do surface now and again, and if they were carried out on a more widespread and systematic basis, the media would be making more of a contribution to the vitality of whatever democracy we have.

By highlighting the practical consequences of contradictions within the objectivity regime, peace journalism can potentially energize and connect reform agendas across a broad sweep of activism for democratic change. And by offering both a critique of Western journalistic practice, as well as a reform agenda suitable, with some adaptations, for media in rich and poor countries alike, it enables such activism to take place on the basis of global solidarity and mutuality.

REFERENCES

Bagdikian, Ben. 2000. *The Media Monopoly*. 6th ed. Boston: Beacon Press.

Hackett, Robert A., and Yuezhi Zhao. 1998. *Sustaining Democracy? Journalism and the Politics of Objectivity*. Toronto: Garamond Press.

Hargreaves, Ian. 2003. *Journalism—Truth or Dare*. Oxford: Oxford University Press.

Howard, Ross. 2003. *The Media's Role in War and Peacebuilding*. Paper presented to the Geneva Center for Democratic Control of Armed Forces (DCAF) conference, Budapest, February.

Humphrys, John. 2002. "We're Planning a War, but Don't Mention the Oil." *Sunday Times*, December 8, 17.

Kaldor, Mary. 2003. "Regime Change without War." *Red Pepper*, April.

Lynch, Jake. 1998. *The Peace Journalism Option*. Taplow, U.K.: Conflict and Peace Forums, available at www.transcend.org (accessed October 25, 2004).

———. 1999. *What Are Journalists For?* Taplow, U.K.: Conflict and Peace Forums, available at www.conflictandpeace.org (accessed October 25, 2004).

———. 2002. *Reporting the World—A Practical Checklist for the Ethical Reporting of Conflicts in the 21st Century*. Taplow, U.K.: Conflict and Peace Forums.

———. 2003. *Reporting the World—An Ethical Challenge to International News*. Paper presented to the Geneva Center for Democratic Control of Armed Forces (DCAF) conference, Budapest, February.

Monbiot, George. 2002. "Why Blair Is an Appeaser." *Guardian*, November 5, 2002, 17.

Philo, Greg. 2002. "Missing in Action." *Guardian*, April 16, 2002, 10. (Full article in *Developments in Sociology*, May 2002).

14

Finding a Frame: Toward a Transnational Advocacy Campaign to Democratize Communication

Seán Ó Siochrú

Campaigners and activists in media and communication are often surprised and not a little disappointed by a pervasive lack of understanding of and appreciation for the vital matters they believe to be at stake in their domain of activity. They are especially mystified as to why those mobilizing around the environment, human rights, opposition to war, labor rights, and so forth, do not adopt media at least as their second area of concern since "so long as the media are in corporate hands, the task of social change will be vastly more difficult, if not impossible, across the board" (McChesney 1997, 71).

So, how can we get others to listen to us?

This chapter tackles some of the conceptual and strategic issues around framing our concerns about media and communication and relates to the kind of campaign called for in chapter 10. The analysis undertaken here uses the framework developed by Margaret Keck and Kathryn Sikkink (1998a; 1998b). The aim is to test this framework against the reality of the recent history of developments in media advocacy, both to assess its adequacy and to use it as a means to judge the level of development and potential of such advocacy.[1] I conclude with a consideration of the priorities for the emergence of a transnational advocacy movement in media and communication.

Following Keck and Sikkink, I define transnational advocacy networks as networks of actors "working internationally on an issue, who are bound together by shared values, a common discourse, and dense exchanges of information and services" (1998a, 217). They are characterized by "voluntary, reciprocal, and horizontal patterns of communication and exchange" (1998b, 8). Among the major pursuits of networks are campaigns that are by nature focused and impermanent. Campaigns are "sets of strategically linked activities in which members of a diffused principled network develop explicit, visible ties and mutually recognized roles in pursuit of a common goal" (1998b, 6). Advocacy networks organize around campaigns.

Key aspects of Keck and Sikkink's framework are the role of "mobilizing structures" that bring the actors together, the presence or absence of political opportunities to highlight the issues, the need to "frame" concerns effectively so that they resonate with a wide constituency, and a set of tactics to achieve the goals.

To what extent can media advocacy be mapped onto their framework? To what extent and in what ways does the current stage conform to these requirements and exhibit these features? Can Keck and Sikkink help us make sense of where we have to go?

FERTILE OR FALLOW GROUND?

Transnational networks, according to Keck and Sikkink, can most easily mobilize in the presence of a number of organizational and political conditions. These offer opportunities and motives for activists and actors to get together around their common cause. Has this been the case in the incipient advocacy networking identified earlier?

Mobilizing Structures: Picking Up from the Past

Environments conducive to campaigns, for Keck and Sikkink, build on "mobilizing structures" that offer potential network members opportunities to come together to share experiences and build commonalities. Examples include networks that build on previous related struggles and movements, emerge from within professional associations, benefit from supportive individuals in intergovernmental organizations (themselves possibly involved in earlier struggles), or gather around relevant conferences and events.

The reconvening of remnants of previous struggles offers a ready-made platform that can be reactivated in the right combination of circumstances at a national or transnational level. This factor is especially interesting in the case of media and communications.

In the past decades only once has a major global debate on media issues taken place, with the New World Information and Communication Order, the reverberations of which are still felt today, especially in UNESCO (see chapter 1). This was a broad ranging debate culminating with the comprehensive report of the MacBride Commission, which had been asked to study no less than the "totality of communication problems in modern society." Among the most prominent themes were transnational control of global media flows, the Right to Communicate, the rights and responsibilities of journalists, national communication policies, and the so-called New International

Economic Order (Traber and Nordenstreng 1992, 7). This last was an even broader battle within the United Nations as a whole from which New World Information and Communication Order (NWICO) drew its inspiration and in which it was embedded.

For most of NWICO's duration, it was debated exclusively by governments, mainly in UNESCO. And a struggle between governments determined its ultimate fate, symbolically marked by the withdrawal of the United States from UNESCO in December 1984, followed by the United Kingdom shortly afterward. Although some activity continued, the official final end of the NWICO debate was arguably the UNESCO General Conference in 1989 when the new Medium-Term Plan for 1990–1995 was launched. Although a significant number of developing countries continued to call for a NWICO, the plan made only cursory reference to it and dropped all the key issues, while endorsing the industry-friendly free-flow doctrine of the United States and most of Europe.

If the debate was almost exclusively among governments, and it was roundly defeated, how can it be considered to have contributed to the current emergence of concern about media?

Even as UNESCO met in 1989, another meeting was taking place in Harare, Zimbabwe, under the name of the MacBride Round Table on Communication. There were no governments present, only journalists, academics, and media-communication specialists from fourteen countries and eighteen nongovernmental organizations (NGOs). It was organized by the Southern African Journalists Association, the International Organization of Journalists, and the Media Foundation of the Nonaligned Movement. In fact, journalist organizations had played a role, if secondary, throughout the NWICO debate. The most significant NGO involved, the Consultative Club, was a loose coalition of journalist bodies formed under the auspices of UNESCO in 1978, which deliberated quite autonomously from the governmental NWICO protagonists and which met on ten occasions over a twelve-year period (Nordenstreng 1999, 241). Two further UN–UNESCO roundtables were also organized during the early 1980s, bringing together nongovernmental experts from outside the political cauldron.

It was from among these that the MacBride Round Table on Communication picked up the pieces of NWICO in 1989. They recognized that a central weakness of NWICO was that it had never broadened the debate: "To mobilize existing international resources, a network of interested non-governmental organizations is needed to promote dialogue on and advance new initiatives towards 'a new, more just and more efficient world information and communication order'" (MacBride Round Table 1992). The roundtable continued to meet annually, bringing the issues to different countries and widening the circles of debate through many strata of civil society. Many of its members published accounts of NWICO and brought them into contemporary debates. In

1999 in Amman, Jordan, the roundtable, in the light of the emergence of other actors and fora for discussion and action, agreed to throw its resources behind a "growing movement on media and communications . . . spearheaded by innumerable . . . initiatives around the world,"[2] and it disbanded shortly afterward.

Thus, the round table and related activities drew together nongovernment strands of the NWICO debate, maintained a focus on the issues, and broadened it out to other people and organizations. The roundtable bridges the gap between NWICO and present-day advocacy networks and continues to inform and animate several of the strands of discussion within them, in particular around the Right to Communicate.

Equally important was the emergence in the early 1990s of a number of international NGOs involved in media with their feet firmly planted in civil society and in local media activism; among the most important of these were the World Association of Community Radio Broadcasters (AMARC), the Association for Progressive Communications (APC), the now-defunct Videazimut, and the World Association for Christian Communications (WACC). The MacBride Round Table persevered and could draw the historical connections only because the two strands coalesced. These NGOs played, and continue to play, a major role in international-level advocacy in this area. It was they that organized annual or biannual gatherings that went beyond their members' direct interests to enrich understanding and networking. Although representing a defined constituency in themselves, they consciously built bridges to others active in media, recognizing their members' long-term mutual interests. Many of their members were also activists for broader media issues in their localities and nationally. Latin America was particularly very active. During the 1990s, publications such as WACC's *Media Development* and *Zebra* brought a strong grassroots development focus to discussions of media, and a literature began to build up on the notion of democratizing communication. Furthermore, international advocacy initiatives appeared, most notably the People's Communication Charter in the mid-1990s, which achieved wide circulation and endorsement and served to amplify the activities of others.

By the time the MacBride Round Table disbanded, its main members, including the international NGOs, were already involved in the Platform for Democratic Communication, which had been formed in 1996. In a sense, this represented the transition from the "old guard" into the new environment, completing the move to a civil society– and grassroots-driven network. The platform, in turn, launched the Communication Rights in the Information Society (CRIS) campaign in 2001, which is the main focus of its activities today.

Others among Keck and Sikkink's mobilizing structures played a part. At least one professional network had a significant input into linking both to previous struggles and to contemporary academic debates about media. The

International Association for Mass Communication Research[3] for some years championed the Right to Communicate and hosted the MacBride Round Table. It continues to highlight trends in media and communication in seminars and workshops and cross-fertilizes NGOs and academics.

Individuals in UNESCO, the International Telecommunications Union (ITU), and other intergovernmental bodies sometimes took risks to support a broad media-communication debate;[4] as did a number of foundations, such as The Rockefeller Foundation's Communication Initiative and Frederich Ebert Stiftung, as well as donors, such as the International Development Research Center (IDRC), willing to support research, gatherings, and projects covering major strands of the transnational media and communication agenda.

Thus, the evidence suggests that a major catalyst for an emerging transnational advocacy network, with broad media and communication concerns is to be found by reference to the kind of past struggles, fora, and arenas identified by Keck and Sikkink. These are the midwives of such a network, and in their absence, it is highly unlikely that it would have developed to this (albeit still-limited) extent.

Political Opportunity Structure

Political circumstances can sometimes compel national-level activists and networks to look to the international and global levels, described by Keck and Sikkink as "political opportunity structures."

One of the most common, termed the "boomerang effect," involves shifting the arena of struggle from a national to an international level. Transnational activity is used to bring demands to a global institutional authority or framework, which in turn feeds back to put pressure on the national authorities responsible for the issue at home. It begins when a national movement or campaign finds itself blocked from, and unable to influence, state power, or when these avenues are ineffectual for resolving the problems. The only option is to turn to the international arena in search of allies. Usually, initial allies are NGOs and networks in other countries confronting similar problems or those in countries that might be seen as a key link in the "problem chain" or in the solution, hence where the issue might resonate and generate sympathizers and collaborators. An anti-rainforest-logging campaign in Indonesia, for instance, might link to another in Brazil but also with development groups in wealthier countries that consume much of the hardwood produced. These could together bring pressure to bear directly on the relevant international organizations and also lobby or pressure governments into acting within these organizations. The impact in turn boomerangs back to the countries where the problem arose. This strategy was used to good effect in Argentina, where human rights organizations exposed the government's atrocities during the "dirty war" of the 1970s and brought immense pressure to bear from international sources (Keck and Sikkink 1998b, 107–8).

Have communication issues been given an impetus by the need to transcend blockages at the national level, creating the boomerang effect? Here the answer is more complex than it is in Keck and Sikkink's case studies.

For media and communication, the sources of many of the problems have already transcended the national level. First, the engine at the center of the dynamic, a small number of giant multimedia corporations, is truly transnational and largely beyond national control even if there were a will to rein them in. Satellite television, for instance, virtually eludes national regulation or, indeed, international governance structures. The copyright industries are among the most transnational. Second, many issues of concern, such as copyright and surveillance, are already entrenched in World Trade Organization (WTO) agreements, the World Intellectual Property Organization (WIPO) Copyright Treaty, and the Council of Europe's Cybercrime Treaty. It would clearly be futile for NGOs to appeal to the WTO to oblige their governments to create more flexible intellectual property rights (IPR) regimes; rather, NGOs must build a coalition comprising civil society and governments to challenge the WTO agreements.[5] The goal is therefore to reopen these issues at the global level, to put them back on the table. This is the reverse of the boomerang effect: influencing the national level is not an end in itself but rather a means to crack open the international level.

The strategic aim of media advocacy groups here is not so much to bring external pressure on national governments via intergovernmental bodies as it is to exert pressure directly on international bodies, often via numerous national governments. This is more akin to the strategic position of environmental issues, such as global warming, that invoke the common global good and where no government can by itself successfully address the problem.

In other areas, for instance radio-spectrum policy[6] and media regulation, the relevant level of authority remains the national as a matter of policy subsidiarity and sovereignty. Since there is no relevant global authority, such issues are immune to a simple boomerang effect. For instance, community-radio activists faced with a hostile regulatory environment at home need not look to the ITU or other regulatory agencies to rule in their favor or to pressure their government. That is not a current mandate of the ITU or any other agency. Concentration of media ownership is another such area. This remains a matter of national policy, which cannot reach out to influence the effects of global-level concentration. Rather, if the transnational side is to have any impact, it is as part of a longer and more hazardous route—building an international coalition, including governments, that will first empower the ITU or intergovernmental entity to create the frameworks and governance structures that can have a national impact. The boomerang has to be constructed first.

Thus, even if it does not engage the conventional boomerang process, democratic communication advocacy has been forced to move to the transnational level.[7] The difference is that many activists in the first place had their sights set on the global context, there being so few options nationally. But the longer and more circuitous route implied may also discourage some from taking up critical issues outside the national arena. Indeed, this might be a partial explanation for the low level of mobilization around certain issues.

A second Keck and Sikkink idea is "venue shopping" as a means to internationalize the struggle. This relies less on mass mobilization than on careful selection of receptive political venues, temporary and permanent, and tailoring the message and tactics to influence these. Thus, agitational niches may offer unexpected access to policy influence.

Finding an appropriate venue for raising these issues has long been a problem. Since NWICO and the emasculation of UNESCO, media issues have been fragmented among many intergovernmental fora. Furthermore, even where elements have been addressed, it has not been done in a manner conducive to civil society organization. The ITU, for instance, has never facilitated civil society participation at its major events. Since the ambitious Maitland Report published in 1984 (ITU 1984), the ITU had gradually adopted the emerging neoliberal position on telecommunication as its own, fearful of losing its relevance. The Trade-Related Aspects of Intellectual Property (TRIPS) agreement at the WTO met with some opposition, but it was focused on issues such as access to medicines and the patenting of life forms. WIPO has been sidelined by the WTO but has still managed until recently to keep a low profile. None of the summits, including the Social Summit and the Beijing Summit, approached media and communication issues in a comprehensive manner. In the absence of an appropriate venue, various proposals during the 1990s also emanated from civil society to organize its own international event, based on a clear recognition that progressing the campaign depended on reaching out to and drawing together the various strands of civil society to form the beginnings of a network.[8] But these proposals foundered, mainly for lack of resources.

Then came the World Summit on the Information Society (WSIS), first held in December 2003; a second event is scheduled for November 2005. The WSIS is by no means ideal as a venue for a media-and-communication campaign. It is led by the ITU, one of the few UN agencies that has refused to follow UN Economic and Social Council regulations on NGO liaison;[9] also, the ITU tends to be a technical and bureaucratic agency with minimal concern for the social and human implications of what it does (with the limited exception of the ITU development sector). The concept of the information society itself is also highly compromised, having been devised initially by the European Union to give a social gloss to a policy that relentlessly pursued the liberalization and privatization programs of the 1990s, paying, in practice, scant attention to concepts such as universal service (Ó Siochrú 2004). Furthermore, it has tended to limit itself to telecommunication infrastructure and use and to exclude key areas such as mass media and copyright.

Yet, WSIS also has advantages. The origins of the concept of the information society, based on the growing role of information in the economy, culture, and politics, date back several decades and were broadly conceived. Technologies, at that time mainly computing rather than ICTs, were seen as enablers, but the focus was on the growing role of information in society and economy. The WSIS, from the outset, maintained the rhetoric of a broad social, cultural, political, and economic transformation of society. It is only in the small print that we see the narrow focus on technology, infrastructure, and the neoliberal approach—the contraction of many possible information societies to one aspect and one vision.

It is this gap between the huge claims made for the information society and its revolutionary potential and the reality of the narrow focus of the WSIS that civil society can exploit. Obvious questions for the information society, such as who owns information, who controls its dissemination, and who can use it to the best effect, simply cannot be ignored. Even a casual observer can recognize their centrality to building an information society. Indeed, in this respect, the WSIS left itself wide open to the tactic described by Keck and Sikkink as "accountability politics" used to expose the distance between claims and practice.

The Platform for Democratic Communication, which included many of the major international media NGOs, decided in October 2000, shortly after the WSIS was itself announced, to focus its efforts on the WSIS. A conscious and deliberate case of "venue shopping" involving considerable debate was thus the genesis of the CRIS Campaign, the vehicle created by the platform to bring media issues to the WSIS. In deciding this, it was understood early on that success depended only partially on a positive outcome on communication issues at the summit itself; while worth striving for, these were expected to be limited. Rather, success would be judged by the extent to which civil society became mobilized and organized around these issues, in a manner that would spin off from the WSIS into a more general campaign.

In this sense, the CRIS campaign, like many other media activists and NGOs involved in the WSIS, sees itself as part of the larger civil society movement gathering at the World Social Forum and campaigning at various global meetings. Given the limitations of the WSIS, what was purchased through this "venue shopping" was a springboard for the media-and-communication campaign into more mainstream civil society activity. The World Forum on Communication Rights,[10] led by the CRIS campaign and run alongside the WSIS in December 2003, is an expression of this, described by the organizers as going "where the WSIS dares not" (i.e., into issues such as media ownership and concentration, IPRs, and surveillance). It was organized less in opposition to the WSIS than as a means to fill the vacuum generated between its claims and the reality, and more than five hundred people attended during the daylong event.

The CRIS campaign is not the only civil society group to recognize this potential for the WSIS. Others are active in promoting human rights in the information society and to bringing media, IPRs, and other issues onto the agenda. But the explicit goal of the CRIS campaign is to reach out to these other organizations and to build a larger coalition, and a significant degree of success has been achieved.[11]

THE CHALLENGE OF FRAMING MEDIA AND COMMUNICATION

If Keck and Sikkink's ideas are useful for explaining the emergence of a nascent transnational advocacy network in media, they are now called upon to take on a more difficult task—to offer insights into how that network might move forward. While reasonable evidence can be mustered to support the emergence of a loose network of actors, it is clear to most of those involved that core concerns about media have yet to be framed in a manner that appeals to the broad constituencies of a transnational campaign and that can bring coherence to the overall paradigm.

Keck and Sikkink claim that constructing "cognitive frames" is an essential strategic activity for advocacy.[12] It enables other actors to comprehend the issues raised from within their own context, and they can then encourage and guide collaborative actions. "Frame resonance" refers to the extent and manner in which a network's interpretative work can influence broader public understanding, involving both internal coherence and alignment with the broader political culture. The formulation of various frames, including competing frames, is characteristic of the early stages of a campaign or movement, but over time they can become embedded in the campaign's common "reservoir of symbols" from which future and deeper frames can be built.

Framing the issue is difficult in the transnational context since diverse cultural, political, and economic circumstances must be addressed. The gap between wealthy industrial countries and poor rural and traditional countries can be especially difficult to bridge, and concepts that transcend differences or carry compatible, even complementary, interpretations must be devised and articulated. Even where an underlying normative appeal is held in common, for instance to universal human rights, the realization of human rights in different contexts can be very different. Nor is it solely a matter of establishing the logic or rationale of the case—it may require, for instance, an emotive appeal or dramatic presentation. The issue may also demand "reframing," as was achieved in the case of the campaign against female genital mutilation, a renaming of female circumcision and introduction of technical terms like "clitoridectomy" or "infibulation." Linking frames together may also be useful; linking indigenous people's activists and the environmental movement in relation to forestry preservation resulted in the strengthening of both.

Beyond resonating with wider stakeholders, successfully framing an issue can follow a certain logical progression through demonstrating that a problem is not inevitable, that those responsible can be identified, and that credible solutions can be designed, proposed, and implemented. Furthermore, successful framing has often highlighted highly emotive issues or has concerned issues of basic human rights. Little of this comes easily in media issues. Framing may also be achieved most easily where a simple and direct connection between the source or perpetrator of the problem and the victim can be established.

In media and communication, examples of successful framing have focused on specific concerns in certain places. Concentration of media ownership became an issue in the United States in 2003 because of the pending regulatory decision to virtually abolish controls. More trivially, in Ireland, public outrage followed the Irish football association's sale in 2002 to Sky Television of exclusive rights to Ireland's international matches, forcing the government to wake up to the EU legislation that can oblige free-to-air broadcasting of events of national cultural significance. In numerous countries of Asia and Africa, ongoing campaigns are fought against government media censorship,' and there is growing concern regarding the invasion of foreign media; in Latin America, community-radio and media activists have long been building campaigns and networks. But no campaign or network has yet successfully highlighted, at a transnational level, more than one area of concern.

The Platform for Democratization of Communication attempted several times to pose the issues in a coherent, credible, and easily communicated manner. Their efforts vacillated between succinct and straightforward, but overly generalized, statements that failed to seize the imagination, on the one hand, and more complete lists of issues that ended up being long, disconnected, and unfocused, on the other.[13] Others at national (mainly in the United States) and international levels have toyed with various possibilities for a single unifying paradigm or, at least, slogan, such as "a global media justice campaign," "building a global information commons," "creating a global public sphere," "building media democracy," and "reclaiming the media"— each is capable in principal of encompassing a number of key issues but none so far has gained the breadth, coherence, or impetus required to animate a network or campaign around the range of issues.

Thus, perhaps the greatest challenge facing a transnational advocacy network on media right now is to successfully frame the issues in a manner that readily resonates with a variety of noncore actors and in different cultural and economic circumstances. Several specific obstacles must be confronted.

First, the political circumstances of media vary hugely by geography. While a significant portion of the world still suffers direct government control and censorship of media, the dominant trend is toward a problem that emerges only two steps later—countries escaping direct government control, sometimes after a period of media flowering, are often propelled into the welcoming arms of commercially dominated media that bear even more intractable problems. Current copyright regimes have hugely different impacts in Africa as compared to Europe or the United States; and within the South, Brazil and India have significant regional copyright industries. Access to the Internet is now a minor issue in the North, but attempts to bridge the so-called digital divide have run into the sand of failed liberalization policies. At a cultural level, too, there are differences. The notion of the public sphere is not unproblematic. As a concept, it is associated with a liberal European tradition and a relatively narrow intellectual debate. Translating and transporting the underlying universal democratic principles to another cultural context is not easy. Similarly, the propagation of a singular consumerist worldview has very different connotations and effects, good and bad, in a hierarchical, patriarchal, or divided cultural context than it does in countries with long traditions of individualism and individual wealth.

Such challenges await most transnational networks. But another feature adds a further layer of difficulty.

There is very seldom a direct and obvious link between negative communication trends and their victims. There are few smoking guns, no images of children dying from media malnutrition. Only in very exceptional circumstances do media wreak a direct human toll, although it can be devastating. One of the few well-known cases of the direct implication of media in a huge death toll is that of Radio Milles Collines, which during the 1994 Rwanda massacres, broadcast not just hate messages but specific information to abet ongoing genocide. But the prowar positions adopted by most U.S. mainstream print and television media leading up to the invasion of Iraq in 2003, which instilled an environment where invasion was acceptable and even inevitable, can in some respects be seen as equally culpable in the death of innocent people. Apart from the fact that the blood was spilled on foreign soil, a main difference in perception is that the connection between media activities and the killing was not nearly as direct. This distance, the mediation of the messages through U.S. foreign policy, and the fact that the media were acting to maximize revenues, not stir up hatred, effectively allows them to evade responsibility.

Demonstrating the relationship between a war-mongering media and growing commercialization and concentration of media ownership is certainly possible, but it requires several logical steps and an understanding of media dynamics. Similarly, the link between IPRs and the stifling of human creativity is virtually impossible to demonstrate empirically. The most articulate mainstream efforts to expose the dangers of the excesses of intellectual property are not readily grasped, although they are gaining some currency. The same challenge exists in many other areas of concern.

If the emotive frame is unavailable as a means to cut through complex connections and demonstrate agency, then is the other option of a basic human rights frame more feasible?

One might ask how the NWICO debate, much of it conducted in the language of global equity and rights, succeeded in grabbing the attention, if not of civil society, then of governments and their agents? This is instructive but not immediately helpful. Sustained interest in the NWICO debate can largely be credited to its embeddedness in the context of the New International Economic Order, which was itself the result of a unique set of circumstances in which countries of the South found themselves quite suddenly numerically dominant within the United Nations. This suggests that most of the issues of concern in media could be rallied together in the context of a more general challenge to the neoliberal logic espoused by the Bretton Woods institutions and their supporting governments. Yet, such a challenge would have to be powerful and far-reaching to energize major mobilization around media, since so many issues are of more direct concern to that general agenda. The anticorporate globalization movement that comes together at the World Social Forum and its regional and national counterparts might form a useful recruiting ground, an agora of campaigns and movements, but it is a long way from constituting a movement in itself; indeed, it currently does not aspire to.[14] It can also be argued persuasively that until many of the concerns regarding communication are tackled, especially those relating to mass media, then a more general movement will find it extremely difficult to emerge.

Thus, few in the incipient transnational network on media and communication are inclined to wait for a more generally conducive environment. They would rather see themselves as working in parallel with others to create that environment.

One rallying point that resonated somewhat further did emerge from the NWICO debate. This was the idea of a Right to Communicate. Might it offer an adequate frame for a diverse set of issues? The fact that it reemerged in the WSIS suggests that it may potentially gain some traction in wider civil society circles and justifies a more detailed consideration here.

A RIGHT TO COMMUNICATE?

The idea of a Right to Communicate is more politically contentious than the substantive issues it raises merit because of its association with NWICO.

NWICO opponents still claim that attempts to propose a Right to Communicate are merely veiled efforts to revive the NWICO.[15] In some ways, this is true in that many of the issues involved in the NWICO debate have never been resolved. However, it is also entirely inappropriate since the protagonists and antagonists are now very different and the geopolitical landscape that inspired the original opposition has changed utterly.

The Right to Communicate predated NWICO and persists after it, especially in NGO circles. It is generally accepted that it was first articulated by Jean d'Arcy in 1969 when he wrote, "The time will come when the Universal Declaration of Human Rights will have to encompass a more extensive right than man's right to information, first laid down 21 years ago in Article 19. This is the right of man to communicate" (1977). Although suffering a decline in profile in the wake of the NWICO failure, NGOs and academics continued to publish and debate this issue, and some advocacy developed around it. Most recently, the Right to Communicate has been raised at several points during the WSIS process and has gained some prominence. UN Secretary General Kofi Annan recently stated that "millions of people in the poorest countries are still excluded from the 'right to communicate,' increasingly seen as a fundamental human right" (United Nations 2003). And the European Commission noted in the context of the WSIS, "The [WSIS] Summit should reinforce the right to communicate and to access information and knowledge" (2002).

However, a critical ambiguity exists in how the Right to Communicate has sometimes been interpreted, pointing to a political liability that it carries. A central strand in the birth and evolution of the Right to Communicate is the claim that a new human right should be established in international law. This suggests that the objective of any campaign taking it on should be to work toward the amendment of the Universal Declaration of Human Rights or toward the institution of another legal instrument that would establish a Right to Communicate. However, recent debates have highlighted some political risks associated with this approach.

First, the Universal Declaration of Human Rights was agreed to at a unique time in history, in the aftermath of a catastrophic war and buoyed by a determined political will to prevent another such war. The reopening of any aspect of that declaration, especially in the current climate, would most probably see the rolling back of existing rights.

Second, various rights relating to communication are embodied in articles other than Article 19, and indeed, the entire document is an interweaving of various overlapping, interdependent, and hierarchically arranged rights. Some have argued that asserting a strong Right to Communicate might interfere with and vitiate existing rights relating to information, privacy, and other areas. Such a debate also risks heading into arcane territory, understood by few and hence off-putting, around the implications of legally establishing a new right and its relationship to existing legal rights.[16]

Third, and most important, the existing, legally established elements of a Right to Communicate, as identified by protagonists, are not enforceable— the issue is not the absence of rights but the fact that even existing rights are ignored the world over. In this context, focusing on establishing a Right to Communicate would be a waste of time and, indeed, might divert energy from struggling for rights in more concrete ways.

Positing the need for an abstract, legally recognized right as a point of departure appears to some as a top-down imposition, implying that the focus should be on establishing a right in international law as distinct from implementing rights on the ground. Many activists, campaigners, and advocacy groups argue that the priority must be the latter, since rights have only ever been achieved through the struggle of people. A movement around the Right to Communicate cannot be built simply on the perception of a gap in the panoply of international human rights. It must be built on the experiences of people in their everyday lives, which in turn motivate them to reflect on and name the issue, then act on it.

These risks have made the issue divisive within civil society. Some elements in civil society, such as conservative, U.S.-based NGOs associated with the cold war, will always oppose the concept of a Right to Communicate. But in a recent interaction, the Right to Communicate pitted "traditional" free-speech NGOs against those coming from a communication-advocacy perspective.[17] These risks led to rejection by some of the entire concept.

In reality, an exclusive focus on establishing the Right to Communicate in international law has never been advocated. The originators did not base their arguments on a trawl through the Universal Declaration of Human Rights for lacunae around communication. Establishing a Right to Communicate by means of an international legal instrument was seen as one element in a broader strategy, and sometimes as a means to raise awareness of the issue. D'Arcy himself was director of radio and visual services in the Office of Public Information at the United Nations in New York and was specifically motivated by the potential of satellite and telecommunication to revolutionize communication. By the early 1970s, he clearly recognized the dangers of monopoly on information control, as well as its potential in the context of globalization:

Those in power, whether religious leaders, politicians or private individuals, have always known that he who controls communications effectively controls society. But, the time will come, if we so wish it, when living images will be as handy as books and newspapers have been for centuries. This time will come after the monopolies of communications, be they private or public, have had to relinquish control under a two-pronged attack from space and ground technologies.

It is easy to see how the gradual ending of the era in which nations lived turned in upon themselves in closed national communication communities may frighten some people. But for the new generations who have grown up with the communications revolution and who now reach positions of responsibility, the problem will be easier to solve. For them, the problem of the relationship between governments and a mature public opinion will find a solution in a new style of public life. (d'Arcy 1977)

This offers a better starting point for promoting a Right to Communicate and is certainly far seeing. In this article on the implications of direct-broadcast satellites, he argues that technologies will generate a huge variety of means to communicate, rendering national borders meaningless and sooner or later forcing communication monopolies to relinquish their control. He anticipates a maturing public sphere and even a global public sphere.

Of course, the reality has turned out to be more complex. But arguing that a Right to Communicate emerges from objectively evolving circumstances and identifying the potential of emerging technologies are insights that are just as relevant today. And they point to the new common position that is emerging.

Largely as a result of debate around the WSIS, progressive groups in civil society, including the traditional freedom-of-speech NGOs, such as Article 19, and proponents of a Right to Communicate are moving toward a common position that begins by analyzing emerging communication issues as they affect people in their real lives. This may clear the historical decks and enable a less contentious, more multifaceted, and strategically nuanced use of the term *to emerge*.[18]

Expressing this, the phrase "Right to Communicate" is now sometimes used interchangeably with "communication rights," which is a less legalistic term. The CRIS campaign, for instance, has done that, while moving away from a Right to Communicate that focuses on international law. This is not to deny that international law should make reference to the Right to Communicate but rather that it is not a useful demand at this point and, indeed, that its pursuit could be counterproductive. The difference might be seen in switching from arguing that "everyone should have a Right to Communicate, and the right should be codified in international law" to the more colloquial use of rights, as in "everyone has a Right to Communicate, and the right should therefore be protected and enforced."

If the divisive nature can be overcome, then the concept of communication rights and the belief that everyone has a Right to Communicate do have certain advantages. All the issues raised above and in chapter 10 can in principle be encompassed by the idea of a Right to Communicate. All of the trends identified as potentially dangerous to human development can be seen as blocking and limiting people's Right to Communicate. And it appeals directly to universal rights. Furthermore, the idea that communication, not information or knowledge or even free speech and freedom of information, should be at the core of reforming media and communication is appealing.

The interactive nature of communication—that it is not simply a matter of issuing and receiving information but of interacting on matters of substance and thereby setting in motion processes of deepening mutual understanding and of overcoming divisions—is at the heart of the role of media in society.[19]

Yet, even if communication rights can cast off the political baggage, is it capable of carrying the burden of framing a campaign for the democratization of media and communication? Put another way and looking from the ground up, will those people confronted by the negative consequences of the trends identified earlier recognize their problem more clearly and be brought conceptually closer to a resolution by describing it as a denial of their "communication rights" or their "Right to Communicate"? Certainly, it is clear that all such concerns relate to communication in some manner, but appealing to human rights as an explanatory and motivating paradigm is not as clear-cut in the context of communication as it is in some other areas.

For instance, what the concept of the rights of indigenous peoples refers to is clear, bringing to mind a number of accepted core human rights—the right to exist as a people, the right to a territory, and so forth. It resonates strongly with the imperial past (and present) of many powerful countries and can generate moral authority on that basis. The plight of so many indigenous peoples can be depicted in emotive human terms. Most importantly, the right of indigenous peoples is about extending to them rights currently accepted as belonging all people.

In concerns relating to communication, no such direct connection is available. The chasm between such a compressed concept and the issues it attempts to connote is simply too large; there are too many dots to connect, too many uncertainties, choices, and twists for it to resonate in the right direction, indeed in the several directions needed, from so many different starting points. Indeed, whether the overall organizing paradigm be "communications rights" or "global media justice" or any other term, this same challenge awaits it.

How can the process of framing deal with such complexity?

UNIFYING FRAMES AND THEMATIC FRAMES

In chapter 10, I argued that the rationale for grouping these media issues together in the first place is the interconnectedness of target actors and the overlapping nature of their dynamics. The rationale for developing a unifying strategic frame is likewise to activate campaign and networking activities to deal with the same degree of interdependence of causes and overlapping of content. An overarching, unifying frame is needed in order to build the kind of broad movement that alone can be successful. If a campaign can successfully straddle many or all these issues, it thereby builds the critical mass needed to have a realistic chance of succeeding in any one.

However, I now argue that no single term or concept can fully and adequately perform the key functions of "framing" as identified by Keck and Sikkink. These functions might thus need to be separated out and performed at two levels.

The "unifying frame," such as a Right to Communicate, would have strategic functions, the goal of which would be to link and coordinate the various campaigning elements together and to focus their common efforts on the targets of change. Translated operationally into a central or coordinating unit of an overall campaign, it could have several practical dimensions. For instance, it could undertake the research needed to develop and sustain resources for building campaigns on the ground; it could develop the advocacy instruments such as websites and networking tools; it could coordinate fundraising from foundations, members, donors; and so forth. There are clear synergies to be gained and campaign economies of scale and scope.

Although this high-level frame can act as a global rallying point, coordinating and focusing campaign efforts on the most effective targets at any one time and generating common resources, the critical task of establishing the intimate connection to concerns that people and communities can identify with will require a lower and more precise level of framing. Much of the work of framing the issues must be completed at this lower level. The idea proposed here is of "subframes" or "thematic frames" that would divide media and communication issues into several distinct, but interrelated, elements, each of which could be framed individually. Thus, the issues could be conceived of as a set of related campaign components drawn together under a single umbrella.

At this more articulated level, the prospects for developing coherent frames that resonate with wider groups seems far more feasible. The major challenge of the overall complexity and diversity of the symptoms, as well as their mediated relationship to general media structures, is reduced. This is the level at which noncore groups and people can connect, ultimately including the general public. Media and communication issues that impinge on public consciousness can immediately be connected to other related elements through the thematic frame. In turn, the thematic frame is part of a larger unifying frame.

Each of the four themes outlined in chapter 10—erosion of the public sphere, political and cultural diversity, information commons, and civil rights in electronic media—might offer a rough starting point for framing at this lower level, each taking on a unique, but interconnected, set of closely related concerns. Major conceptual work is needed here, and these issues could be reshuffled in various ways. But ideas such as the "building the public sphere," "enclosure and the public commons," "expanding the public domain," "reversing media pollution," "saving the legacy of knowledge diversity," and any number of others could be developed to establish that ground-level link needed to animate and motivate a campaign.

A final point is worth making regarding framing.

So far, we have been discussing the need to frame quite a diverse set of issues that objectively fit together but must be divided into two levels if they are to resonate with people and communities. The idea of vertically linking thematic frames to a unifying frame has been introduced.

However, it is also possible to conceive of linking these thematic frames at the horizontal level, to adjacent issues that are connected together in other ways. An example will clarify this: IPRs are a good case in point and an unusual one in which civil society can take a page from the book of corporate strategists. Susan Sell (2002) demonstrates in a recent article how a group of twelve U.S. transnational corporations, from chemical companies to media companies, set themselves up as the Intellectual Property Committee (IPC) in the mid-1980s and succeeded in instigating the process that led to the TRIPS agreement. A key feature of TRIPS is that it managed, under the umbrella concept of IPRs, to push through the quite disparate ideas of copyright, patents, and trademarks. The IPC succeeded in this in part by framing IPRs as a fusion of property rights (using an analogy with material property rights) and free trade, both of which resonated hugely with the United States and other governments and, indeed, with large parts of the U.S. popular culture in terms of individualism and "rights talk." Terms like "piracy" were then applied to those who, quite legally in their own countries and in historical practice, took another approach to products of the intellect.

Sell claims that the basis of this success was that corporations that do not normally cooperate or, indeed, communicate with each other since they are in such disparate economic sectors decided to act in their common interest and lobby across their own individual spheres for their mutual benefit. Thus, copyright interests lobbied on behalf of patent interests and so forth. She argues that NGOs should take "a page from the IPC playbook." Citing campaigns for fair use, open source, and peer-to-peer interaction, and against copyrights, the Sony Bono Extension Act, genetically modified foods, and biopiracy—and the list could be extended—Sell concludes,

> What all these campaigns have in common is a concern for preserving the public domain, and preventing the over-reach of intellectual property protection. They all seek to retain a public balance in the context of intellectual property rights. One can only imagine what might happen if activists and government agencies working to prevent the over-extension of property rights in agriculture, pharmaceuticals, and copyright got together in a unified protest. It would take hard work to coordinate their substantive positions, but it would have impressive potential as an alternative way of approaching property rights. The TRIPS advocates got as far as they did by banding together; it was not the only ingredient for their success, but it was a necessary one. (2002, 522)

The lesson here is obvious. A thematic frame constructed around, for instance, building a public domain or global media commons could extend horizontally to create strategic alliances with others involved in intellectual-property issues, such as making generic low-cost drugs, patenting life forms, and saving indigenous knowledge. Together these could devise a unifying frame powerful enough to take on the something like the TRIPS agreement, without, however, losing the identity of each component. Such potential, too, should be considered when devising the thematic frames for a media-and-communication campaign.

The notion of framing can thus cut in several ways in such a campaign. On the one hand, vertically linking thematic frames to a unifying frame can build a firmer coherence to a campaign and enable it to take advantage of the economies of scale and scope essential to success. On the other hand, building horizontal linkages between those thematic linkages and other adjacent campaigns, working within a new, shared unifying frame, could greatly strengthen each individual effort and build the critical mass needed to succeed.

Indeed, in the long term this can be seen as an organic means of gradually constructing a larger coalition that can tackle the global neoliberal dynamic that underlies so many of the challenges facing those who wish to build a sustainable and equitable future.

This last perhaps takes Keck and Sikkink beyond where they hoped to bring us, and a different conceptual framework may be more appropriate. Yet, clearly it does help us make sense of the past and immediate future of a transnational campaign to democratize communication. Indeed, considerably more could be added about the tactical level, where they propose information politics, symbolic policy, leverage politics, and accountability politics.[20] The WSIS is an example of the last, but it is not difficult to make the case for information politics. A potential strength of the emerging transnational media campaign is its capacity to identify or generate information and to analyze it. Many of the issues raised in chapter 10 are particularly well documented, although a huge effort is needed to process and disseminate useful material. Symbolic politics and leverage politics can also be deployed in this domain. Developing these is one of the challenges currently facing the emerging campaign.

WHAT ELSE IS NEEDED?

Returning to my introduction, I ask, why are other activists and movements relatively oblivious to the dangers in communications trends?

I have proposed that a major challenge facing those trying to build a transnational campaign in this area is to frame the issues adequately in a manner that will resonate widely and, hence, create the environment for the campaign to grow beyond the converted. We believe that there already exists a sufficient volume of activists and organizations out there, currently working nationally or transnationally on one or a few of the issues identified. But they remain fragmented both geographically and in terms of the scope of their concerns.

The immediate requirement, I believe, is to frame the domain of media and communication in a manner that can allow for regional diversity and for the broad scope of the combined issues. I believe that this will require conceptual action at two levels. At the global level, the idea of a right to communication, or communication rights, may be adequate as a unifying concept, but the major task of framing is to pose the question in a manner that people can identify with and relate to their own concerns. This requires a second level, that of thematic framing, and work here is only just beginning. Such thematic frames must begin from what is there on the ground at the national and local levels. I see this as a critical current requirement.[21]

If these are in place and credible, further steps will quickly become evident. These include the development of campaign tactics and the building of strategic alliances (including, where possible, the construction of horizontal frames). Important also, even at this point, is the articulation of alternatives to the status quo. Better ways to govern media and communication, policies that will yield the kind of results we promise, practical actions, and examples that will back up our claims and initiate change: all of these are needed.

The biggest challenge for a campaign or movement as a whole is to build local-level awareness and mobilization around these issues, a solid base that transnational activity can move in certain fruitful directions. A transnational campaign must not displace these as the driving force and inspiration for change, guiding the direction a campaign or movement must take. Rather, a successful transnational campaign will amplify, augment, and focus concerns that are experienced at the local and national levels and help to provide the mobilization tools and concepts that can unite local concerns and actions into collective forces.

NOTES

1. There have been some interesting critiques of this framework, a discussion of which is beyond the scope of this chapter. See Waterman (1999), who claims that it is a "liberal-democratic pluralist model, in which everything is penetrated or penetrable by enlightened middle-class citizen networking." He argues that it ignores the role of building an alternative to a neoliberal globalization. "Reform from within" needs supplementing with "radicalism from without." I concur.

2. Taken from the minutes of the final roundtable of which the author was the secretary-general.

3. Now called International Association for Media and Communication Research.

4. An indication of how deeply NWICO traumatized UNESCO is the fact that quite a number of people, who then and now strongly support broad action on media and communication as advocated within NWICO, nevertheless disassociate themselves from it, claiming it was a disaster, which, of course, in one sense it was (based on personal communications).

5. This is what happened in the Doha round in relation to the IPRs over antiretroviral drugs, although the final outcome, as agreed upon just before the WTO's Cancun meeting, is unsatisfactory and has been heavily criticized.

6. Obviously, the ITU plays a key role in spectrum allocation at the global level, as the forum in which large tranches are allocated. But with a few exceptions, the key decisions about use within these tranches are made nationally.

7. The emerging media-and-communication activist networks in the United States are a special case as compared to others because of the central role played by the United States in defining current neoliberal trends and because of the power of its industry. Transnational or not, U.S.-owned media corporations still need the power of the U.S. government to underpin their global strategies. However, the extent to which an advocacy campaign confined to the United States will influence the global situation is uncertain, and an area needing more research is the relationship between the United States and transnational advocacy networks. Media activist networks in the United States have, in general, only recently begun to look to the global situation.

8. For instance, proposals were developed and circulated at several meetings during 1997 to hold civil society–led World Congresses on Media and Communication in 1999 and 2000. This was proposed by the People's Communication Charter and the MacBride Round Table.

9. See www.comunica.org/itu_ngo (accessed October 1, 2004) for an account of attempts to open the ITU.

10. See www.communicationrights.org (accessed October 1, 2004).

11. For accounts of the WSIS, see Ó Siochrú 2004, and for general civil society commentary, see www.worldsummit2003.org (accessed October 25, 2004).

12. Keck and Sikkink (1998b) refer to David A. Snow et al., "Frame Alignment Processes, Micromobilization, and Movement Participation," *American Sociological Review* 51 (1986): 464, and David A. Snow and Robert D. Benford, "Ideology, Frame Resonance, and Participants Mobilization, in *From Structure to Action: Comparing Social Movement Research across Cultures,* eds. Bert Klandermans, Hanspeter Kriesi, and Sydney Tarrow, 197–217, Greenwich, CT: JAI Press, 1988.

13. The Platform for Democratic Communication's statement (www.comunica .org/platform/index.htm) is an example of the former, and the Voices 21 statement (www.comunica.org/v21/index.htm, accessed October 25, 2004) of the latter.

14. There are continual debates as to whether the World Social Forum should move beyond a meeting and gathering point toward a more structured form of a movement, but it is unlikely to move decisively in that direction in the foreseeable future.

15. The World Press Freedom Committee, an anti-NWICO industry-supported NGO, explicitly declares this to be the case. See www.wpfc.org/site/docs/pdf/Publications/Working%20Papers-Conf%20Booklet.pdf (accessed October 25, 2004).

16. This is precisely the debate that occurred at PrepCom 2 of the WSIS, which proved to be quite a divisive starting point.

17. The event took place as a workshop on media during the WSIS Second Preparatory Meeting, February 21, 2003.

18. See www.communicationrights.org/statement_en.html for a joint statement from Article 19 and CRIS campaign members (accessed October 25, 2004).

19. The right to communicate thus has a slight advantage over the concept of the democratization of media and communication, another possible "umbrella" frame.

20. Keck and Sikkink have categorized the tactics of transnational advocacy networks and campaigns, pursued to achieve their goal, under a number of headings. Information politics is the critical activity of sourcing, generating, and disseminating to targeted areas information that would not otherwise be available in comprehensible and useful forms for activists and diverse sets of actors and target groups. It often links testimonial information, directly from those affected by the issue, with research and statistical output, aiming both to inform and motivate. Symbolic politics involves the selection or construction of an emblem or representation of the issue that widely reverberates at the symbolic level. It can be an event (the 1973 coup in Chile played this role in relation to human rights in Latin America); it can be an individual (Nelson Mandela for antiapartheid); indeed, anything can be imbued with symbolic value in the right circumstances. Its function is to act as an emotive and easily recognizable shorthand for the issue in question, with the capacity to mustering larger constituencies and become a catalyst for the network or campaign. Leverage politics is a means to gain indirect influence over a more powerful actor or institution by means of inducing a third party to take up the issue in question with the latter. Thus, a very limited potential for direct action can be magnified by the power of the intermediary. Material leverage may be gained, for instance, through boycotts, which can marshal large number of people and organizations into a significant economic weapon. Or human rights might gain leverage by providing policy makers with information that convinces them to cut off aid to countries in flagrant breach of human rights. The final tactic, accountability politics, is not unlike leverage in that it exposes the distance between the claims or discourse of governments, for instance, and the actual practice and impact on the ground. Highlighting this in as many ways as possible can lead to significant pressures being brought to bear.

21. I coordinated a meeting alongside the World Summit on the Information Society in December 2003 on the question of framing communication rights. It brought together several dozen media activists from all continents, and the report illuminates many of the issues to be tackled. Work is continuing on the subject within the CRIS campaign. See www.crisinfo.org/content/view/full/221 (accessed October 25, 2004).

REFERENCES

d'Arcy, Jean. 1977. "Direct Broadcast Satellites and the Right of Man to Communicate." In *Right to Communicate: Collected Papers*, eds. L. S. Harms, J. Richstad, and K. Kie, 1–9. Social Sciences Institute, University Press of Hawaii.

European Commission. 2002. *Position on the WSIS*. May 22. Brussels: International Telecommunications Union (ITU). 1984. "The Missing Link: Report of the Independent Commission for World Wide Telecommunications Development." Geneva, December.

Keck, Margaret, and Kathryn Sikkink. 1998a. "Transnational Advocacy Networks in the Movement Society." In *The Social Movement Society: Contentions Politics for a New Century*, eds. D. Meyer and S. Tarrow, 217–39. Lanham, MD: Rowman & Littlefield.

———. 1998b. *Activists beyond Borders: Advocacy Networks in International Politics*. Ithaca, NY: Cornell University Press.

MacBride Round Table. 1992. "The Harare Statement of the MacBride Round Table on Communication." In *Few Voices, Many Worlds: Towards a Media Reform Movement*, eds. M. Traber and K. Nordenstreng, 24–26. London: World Association for Christian Communication.

McChesney, Robert W. 1997. *Corporate Media and the Threat to Democracy*. New York: Seven Stories Press.

Nordenstreng, Kaarle. 1999. "The Context: Great Media Debate." In *Towards Equity in Global Communication: MacBride Update*, eds. R. Vincent, K. Nordenstreng, and M. Traber, 235–68. Cresskill, NJ: Hampton Press.

Ó Siochrú, Seán. 2004. "Will the Real WSIS Please Stand Up? The Historic Encounter of the 'Information Society' and the 'Communication Society.'" *Gazette—The International Journal for Communication Studies* 66, nos. 3–4: 203–24.

Sell, Susan K. 2002. "TRIPS and the Access to Medicines Campaign." *Wisconsin International Law Journal* (Summer): 481–522.

Traber, Michael, and Kaarle Nordenstreng. 1992. *Few Voices, Many Worlds: Towards a Media Reform Movement*. London: World Association for Christian Communication.

United Nations. 2003. "Statement on World Telecommunication Day." UN Secretary-General, May 17, New York.

Vincent, Richard, Kaarle Nordenstreng, and Michael Traber, eds. 1999. *Towards Equity in Global Communication: MacBride Update*. Cresskill, NJ: Hampton Press.

Waterman, Peter. 1999. "Activists beyond Borders—and Theorists Within." *Transnational Associations* 51, no. 1: 39–40, available at www.uia.org/uiata/kecsik.htm (accessed October 25, 2004).

Index

313

About the Contributors

Arthur-Martins Aginam is a doctoral candidate in communication at Simon Fraser University, Canada. Formerly a public-affairs journalist in Nigeria, his research interests cut across civil society, media and democratization (particularly in sub-Saharan Africa), globalization, social movements and the media, and the political economy of international communication.

Robert A. Hackett is a professor of communication at Simon Fraser University, Canada. His previous publications include *News and Dissent: The Press and the Politics of Peace in Canada* (1991); *Sustaining Democracy? Journalism and the Politics of Objectivity* (with Yuezhi Zhao, 1998); and *The Missing News: Filters and Blind Spots in Canada's Press* (with Richard Gruneau and others, 2000). He codirected NewsWatch Canada, a media-monitoring project, from 1993 to 2003. His current research concerns democratic media reform as a social movement.

Kai Hafez is the chair professor for international and comparative communication studies and the head of the Department of Media and Communication at the University of Erfurt, Germany. He studied political science, history, journalism, and Islamic studies in Hamburg, Germany, and at Georgetown University, Washington, D.C. His research specialization includes the theory of international communication, media coverage and Islamic-Western relations, media development in the Middle East, and political Islam and Western policies in the Middle East. Hafez is an academic advisor to the German government, the editor of several book series and member of the editorial boards of *Political Communication* (APSA and ICA) and *Journal for International Communication* (IAMCR).

Jake Lynch is an experienced international reporter in television and newspapers, currently presenting BBC World News in London. He leads postgraduate courses in peace journalism at the universities of Cardiff, U.K., and Sydney and Queensland, Australia, and online for the TRANSCEND Peace University. He is a director of Reporting the World, the journalism think tank, and the author of numerous articles, papers, reports, and book chapters on the reporting of conflict.

Robert W. McChesney is cofounder and president of Free Press and a professor at the University of Illinois, Urbana-Champaign. He is the author or editor of eight books, including the award-winning *Telecommunications, Mass Media, and Democracy: The Battle for the Control of U.S. Broadcasting, 1928–1935* (1993); *Corporate Media and the Threat to Democracy* (1997); and, with Edward S. Herman, *The Global Media: The New Missionaries of Corporate Capitalism* (1997). McChesney's most recent books include multiple-award-winning *Rich Media, Poor Democracy: Communication Politics in Dubious Times* (1999); *Our Media, Not Theirs: The Democratic Struggle against Corporate Media* (with John Nichols, 2002); and *The Big Picture: Understanding Media through Political Economy* (with John Bellamy Foster, 2003). His work concentrates on the history and political economy of communication, emphasizing the role media play in democratic and capitalist societies.

Annabel McGoldrick is an experienced reporter and producer in radio and television. She made *Against the War*, with Harold Pinter, during the Kosovo crisis of 1999, and *News from the Holy Land*, an educational video with full teaching notes, about the coverage of the Middle East conflict (available from Hawthorn Press, U.K.). She teaches postgraduate courses in peace journalism at several universities. She is a director of Reporting the World, the journalism think tank, and chairs their seminar series in London. She is a trained psychotherapist.

Jan Oberg holds a doctorate in sociology and is a peace researcher, an honorary doctor, and cofounder and director of the Transnational Foundation for Peace and Future Research (TFF) in Lund, Sweden. TFF is an independent, multidisciplinary, team-based organization devoted to theory and field studies in nonviolent conflict resolution, reconciliation, and peace. Cumulatively, he has written about four thousand pages of academic works and delivered more than eleven hundred public lectures. Since 1991, he has acted as head of the TFF conflict-mitigation teams in the former Yugoslavia, Georgia, Iraq, and Burundi.

Seán Ó Siochrú is a writer, activist, and consultant in media and communication. For several years, he was coordinator of the MacBride Round Table on Communication and is now active with the CRIS campaign, which focuses on communication rights. His books include *Global Media Governance, A Beginner's Guide* (with Bruce Girard and Amy Mahan, 2002) and *Communicating in the Information Society* (edited with Bruce Girard, 2003). He works extensively with the United Nations and international organizations as a consultant in more than thirty countries. He is director of NEXUS Research, an independent not-for-profit research organization and chairperson of Dublin Community Television in Ireland, where he lives.

Javier Protzel is a professor at the Graduate School and School of Communications at the University of Lima, Peru. He is currently conducting research on hybridized identities in Latin America and on authoritarianism and social decomposition. His latest books include *La Jaula de Cristal: Televisión y autoritaismo en el Perú* (1999) and *Secularización y fundamentalismo en la escena global* (1999).

Dov Shinar is dean of the School of Communication, College of Management, and professor of communication at Ben Gurion University, both in Israel, as well as professor emeritus at Concordia University, Montreal. He is interested in media and identity, war and peace in the media, peace journalism, and the impact of new media. His many publications include *Internet: Communication, Society and Culture* (2001); "The Mass Media and the Transformation of Collective Identities: Quebec and Israel," in *Media Anthropology* (2004); "Peace Process in Cultural Conflict: The Role of the Media" in *Conflict and Communication Online* (2003); and "Cultural Conflict in the Middle East: The Media as Peacemakers," in *Media and Conflict: Framing Issues, Making Policy, Shaping Opinions* (2002).

Colin Sparks is professor of media studies and director of the Communication and Media Research Institute at the University of Westminster, United Kingdom. He has written widely on various aspects of the media, including the popular press, the impact of the new media, and media in societies undergoing rapid social change. His book *Communism, Capitalism and the Mass Media* (1998) studies the changes to the media during and after the fall of communism in Central and Eastern Europe.

Annabelle Sreberny was educated at Cambridge and Columbia and has held academic posts in Iran and the United States. She was director of the Centre for Mass Communication Research, University of Leicester, United Kingdom, from 1992–1999. She is currently a visiting professor of global media and communication studies in the new Media and Film Studies Programme at SOAS, University of London. Her books include *Media and Political Violence* (forthcoming); *Rethinking International News for the 21st*

Century (2004); *Gender, Politics and Communication* (2000); *Media in a Global Context* (1997); *Globalization, Communication and Transnational Civil Society* (1996); *Questioning the Media* (1995); and *Small Media, Big Revolution: Communications and Culture in the Iranian Revolution* (1985). Sreberny's research interests concern global communication; democratization and gender, particularly in relationship to Iran; the Middle East; and the WSIS as a global political process. She is currently writing a book on media and globalization.

Majid Tehranian is professor of international communication at the University of Hawaii and director of the Toda Institute for Global Peace and Policy Research. A graduate of Dartmouth and Harvard, Tehranian's publications include more than twenty-five books and one hundred articles in a dozen languages. He also edits *Peace & Policy* as well as the Toda Institute Book Series. A global nomad, Tehranian has been banished to paradise where he surfs the Pacific and the Internet.

Pradip Thomas is an associate professor at the School of Journalism and Communication of the University of Queensland. His most recent publication is the coedited volume *Who Owns the Media: Global Trends and Local Resistances* (with Zaharom Nain, 2004).

Yuezhi Zhao is a Canada Research Chair in the political economy of global communication and an associate professor in the School of Communication at Simon Fraser University, Canada. She is the author of *Media, Market, and Democracy in China: Between the Party Line and the Bottom Line* (1998) and coauthor of *Sustaining Democracy? Journalism and the Politics of Objectivity* (1998). She is currently working on a book on communication, power, and contestation in China.

GLOBAL PEACE AND POLICY
Toda Institute Book Series
Series Editor: Majid Tehranian

For more information, please consult the webpage of the Toda Institute for Global Peace and Policy Research at www.toda.org. To purchase, please contact the relevant publisher directly:

- *Worlds Apart: Human Security and Global Governance*, edited by Majid Tehranian. London and New York: I. B. Tauris, 1999.
- *Asian Peace: Security and Governance in the Asia-Pacific Region*, edited by Majid Tehranian. London and New York: I. B. Tauris, 1999.
- *Not By Bread Alone: Food Security and Governance in Africa*, edited by Adelane Ogunrinade, Ruth Oniang'o, and Julian May. Johannesburg: University of Witwatersrand Press, 1999.
- *Nuclear Disarmament: Obstacles to Banishing the Bomb*, edited by Jozef Goldblat. London and New York: I. B. Tauris, 2000.
- *Reimagining the Future: Towards Democratic Governance*, by Joseph A. Camilleri, Kamal Malhotra, Majid Tehranian, et al. Bundoora, Australia: The Department of Politics, La Trobe University, 2000.
- *Managing the Global: Globalization, Employment, and Quality of Life*, edited by Don Lamberton. London and New York: I. B. Tauris, 2001.
- *Dialogue of Civilizations: A New Peace Agenda for a New Millennium*, edited by Majid Tehranian and David W. Chappell. London and New York: I. B. Tauris, 2002.
- *Democratizing Global Governance*, edited by Joseph Camilleri and Esref Aksu. New York: Palgrave Press, 2002.
- *Bridging a Gulf: Peacebuilding in West Asia*, edited by Majid Tehranian. London and New York: I. B. Tauris, 2003.
- *Worlds on the Move: Globalization, Migration, and Cultural Security*, edited by Jonathan Friedman and Shalini Randeria, 2003.
- *Passion for Peace*, by Stuart Rees. Sydney, Australia: New South Wales University Press; Baltimore, MD: Johns Hopkins University Press, 2003.
- *Beyond Reconstruction in Afghanistan: Lessons from Development Experience*, edited by John D. Montgomery and Dennis A. Rondinelli. New York: Palgrave MacMillan, 2004.
- *Democratizing Global Media: One World, Many Struggles*, edited by Robert A. Hackett and Yuezhi Zhao. Lanham, MD: Rowman & Littlefield Publishers, Inc., 2005.
- *Eurasia: A New Peace Agenda*, edited by Michael Intriligator, Alexander Nikitin, and Majid Tehranian. New York: Elsevier, forthcoming.